Empire and enterprise

Series editors
DAVID EDWARDS & MICHEÁL Ó SIOCHRÚ

The study of Early Modern Irish History has experienced something of a renaissance in the last decade. However, studies tend to group around traditional topics in political or military history and significant gaps remain. The idea behind this series is to identify key themes and set the agenda for future research.

Each volume in this series comes from leading scholars from Ireland, Britain, North America and elsewhere, addressing a particular subject. We aim to bring the best of Irish historical research to a wider audience, by engaging with international themes of empire, colonisation, religious change and social transformation.

Already published

The plantation of Ulster: Ideology and practice
Micheál Ó Siochrú and Éamonn Ó Ciardha (eds)

Ireland, 1641: Contexts and reactions
Micheál Ó Siochrú and Jane Ohlmeyer (eds)

The Scots in early Stuart Ireland: Union and separation in two kingdoms
David Edwards and Simon Egan (eds)

Debating Tudor policy in sixteenth-century Ireland: 'Reform' treatises and political discourse
David Heffernan

The Irish parliament, 1613–89: The evolution of a colonial institution
Coleman A. Dennehy

Ireland in crisis: War, politics and religion, 1641–50
Patrick Little (ed.)

Empire and enterprise

Money, power and the Adventurers for
Irish land during the British Civil Wars

DAVID BROWN

Manchester University Press

Copyright © David Brown 2020

The right of David Brown to be identified as the author of this work has been asserted by him in accordance with the Copyright, Designs and Patents Act 1988.

Published by Manchester University Press
Oxford Road, Manchester M13 9PL
www.manchesteruniversitypress.co.uk

British Library Cataloguing-in-Publication Data
A catalogue record for this book is available from the British Library

ISBN 978 1 5261 3199 7 hardback
ISBN 978 15261 6378 3 paperback

First published 2020
Paperback published 2022

The publisher has no responsibility for the persistence or accuracy of URLs for any external or third-party internet websites referred to in this book, and does not guarantee that any content on such websites is, or will remain, accurate or appropriate.

Typeset by Newgen Publishing UK

For Cara

Contents

Series editors' preface	*page* viii
Acknowledgements	ix
Abbreviations	x
Introduction	1
1 Atlantic oligarchy: Ireland in the early English Atlantic world	22
2 The Three Kingdoms	44
3 The Adventure for Irish land	64
4 Grocers' Hall	99
5 Commonwealth	144
6 Republic	167
7 Restoration	193
Conclusion	228
Appendix: the original Adventurers for Irish land	232
Index	288

Series editors' preface

The study of early modern Ireland has experienced a renaissance since the 1990s, with the publication of a number of major monographs examining developments in the country during the sixteenth and seventeenth centuries from a variety of different perspectives. Nonetheless, these works still tend to group around traditional topics in political, military or religious history and significant gaps remain. The idea behind this new series is to identify key themes for exploration and thereby set the agenda for future research. Manchester University Press, a leading academic press with a strong record of publishing Irish related material, is the ideal home for this venture.

This is the third monograph to appear in the series. The term 'groundbreaking' is over-used in reviews but it would be entirely appropriate in this instance. The upheavals of the mid-seventeenth century in the Three Stuart kingdoms have attracted considerable scholarly attention but here David Brown ploughs exciting new ground, exposing how a small group of merchants exploited opportunities in the Atlantic tobacco, sugar and slave trades to become cash rich in the 1620s and 1630s. They returned to London at the outset of the political crisis engulfing Charles I and through a series of shrewd and timely investments, principally in Ireland, gradually assumed control of supplying the English parliamentary war effort. Their financial innovations played a key role in parliament's ultimate victory over the king and helped drive the subsequent conquests of both Ireland and Scotland. The book successfully places all these developments within the context of the emerging English global empire and suggests that the foundations of the English military-fiscal state lie in the mid rather than late seventeenth century. This work will unquestionably become required reading for those interested in the reshaping of the Atlantic world in the early modern period.

David Edwards
Micheál Ó Siochrú

Acknowledgements

In 2012, I worked on the Down Survey of Ireland project at Trinity College Dublin (TCD). The project aimed to create an online edition of the Down Survey maps. These were made by William Petty in the 1650s to facilitate the large-scale seizing of Irish land by the Cromwellian Protectorate and its redistribution to English soldiers and a group of investors, the Adventurers. There was little to explain who these Adventurers were, or why they were being treated with such generosity. Professor Micheál Ó Siochrú, the Principal Investigator of the Down Survey project, suggested that I should take a look at this. So I did.

The availability of the digital edition of State Papers from the National Archives at the TCD library, made possible after a determined campaign by the Department of History, allowed for a thorough immersion in the primary sources for the period. The Commonwealth Records Project, also at TCD and now a module of the Beyond 2022 project, uncovered and reassembled the records of the Commonwealth and Protectorate administration for Ireland. As a researcher on these projects I have had privileged access to the 'lost' archives for the first time since 1922. I was very fortunate to be awarded a Charlemont fellowship in 2018 by the Royal Irish Academy that enabled research at the Barbados Department of Archives. A further fellowship, at the Huntington Library in San Marino, provided the perfect environment to complete this project.

Micheál has been endlessly supportive of this work since it began. The text has been greatly improved with the help of detailed reviews and suggestions from John Adamson, Robert Armstrong, Michael Braddick and Denise Ivory. All have commented on my unwelcome tendency to use long roll calls of names in my text, so I shall stop at this point if only to demonstrate that I have taken note of their suggestions. There is, of course, a long list of colleagues and friends to thank, many of whom fill both roles, but this is a task better done in person. Excepting Cara Lloyd, to whom this book is dedicated.

Abbreviations

A&O	C.H. Firth and R.S. Rait, *Acts and Ordinances of the Interregnum 1642–60*, 2 vols (London, 1911).
BDA	Barbados Department of Archives
BL	British Library
CCAM	Mary Anne Everett (Wood) Greene (ed.), *Calendar of the Proceedings of the Committee for Advance of Money, 1642–1656*, 3 vols (London, 1888).
CCC	Mary Anne Everett (Wood) Greene (ed.), *Calendar of the Committee for Compounding &c, 1643–1659*, 5 vols (London, 1889–92).
CJ	*Journal of the House of Commons*, vols 1–8 (London, 1547–1699).
CSPD	Mary Anne Everett (Wood) Green (ed.), *Calendar of State Papers, Domestic 1652–3* (London, 1878).
CSPI	Robert Pentland Mahaffy (ed.), *Calendar of the State Papers Relating to Ireland, of the Reign of Charles I* (London, 1901).
EEIC	English East India Company
IMA	Irish Military Archives
LJ	*Journal of the House of Lords*, vols 4–8 (London, 1767–1830).
NAI	National Archives of Ireland
NLI	National Library of Ireland
ODNB	*Oxford Dictionary of National Biography*
PRONI	Public Record Office of Northern Ireland
TCD	Trinity College Dublin
TNA	The National Archives, UK

Introduction

This book relates the story of a singular group of English merchants who expected to profit from a massive speculation in the conquest of Ireland. It examines key events in England and Ireland, 1641–60, exploring the role of this small and highly influential oligarchy and demonstrating how its members guided the course of warfare and politics to achieve their desired outcomes in both kingdoms.

By the mid-seventeenth century, the European age of exploration was drawing to a close and its age of colonisation and empire had begun. Success in far-flung shores became a source of status for European monarchs and a focus of pride for the early modern European state as colonial projects were developed. Even the sea that separated home dominions from colonies became a subject for territorial claims. In England's case this was expressed in John Selden's *Mare Clausum*, published in 1635, which established the notion of territorial jurisdiction over the seas adjacent to England and any of its territories.[1] By then, some foreign dominions were of considerable value, for example the Spanish-controlled silver mines at Potosí and the English tobacco plantations of Virginia. Most, however, comprised fragile colonies that would require considerable investment to become viable. Almost all outward development and investment, from Sweden to Spain and in all the maritime states in between, was planned, undertaken and financed not by governments, but by merchants. Merchants from all states operated across colonial borders, and there is a wide gap between the aspirational literature of the period and reality. The contemporary literature would have us believe that colonial development was the work of kings and states, grand strategic minds at the helm of a great endeavour. In reality, colonies were developed initially by merchants from all states, looking for quick profits in any distant theatre and allied to or competing with one another as it suited them. Unlike the world of their political masters, theirs was already a globalised world. Events in one theatre reverberated over considerable distances, sometimes with unexpected consequences. Although some important studies have emerged in recent years, by and large the role of the seventeenth-century English merchant, hidden in plain sight, has managed to elude the attention of contemporary commentators and later historians alike.

THE ADVENTURE FOR IRISH LAND

The Adventure for Irish land of March 1642 was a shared-ownership speculation in the conquest of Ireland. The gentry, merchants and modest artisans who invested in this endeavour intended that their money would finance a private army to crush the Irish rebellion that had broken out in October 1641. The money would be repaid in the form of confiscated land, quickly and at an attractive rate of return. The Adventurers Act of 1642 assumed that the rebellion in Ireland was a general one and that all Catholic-owned land in Ireland would be subject to forfeiture. The speculators thus assumed responsibility for the conquest of Ireland, and they required its unconditional surrender in order to be recompensed. A negotiated surrender might reduce the amount of confiscated land and deny them their spoils. It was this requirement that provided the basis for the Cromwellian land settlement of the 1650s and its subsequent confirmation by Charles II with the Acts of Settlement and Explanation in 1662 and 1665.[2] Denied instant gratification as their army was diverted elsewhere, for twenty-three frustrating years the Adventurers for Irish land engaged in a relentless pursuit of the estates of Catholic Ireland. Their obsession with Irish land provides the central theme of this book and also its central paradox, for although almost all had supported parliament vigorously in its uprising against Charles I, the speculators were eventually awarded this land by his son, Charles II.

There were approximately 1,300 subscribers to the speculation in the conquest of Ireland. They were represented by a much smaller group of around twenty men, hereafter referred to as the 'Adventurers', who led them with remarkable consistency until their claims were discharged. The Adventurers were also the leading financial supporters of parliament in its initial confrontation with Charles I, a confrontation that unfolded as the Adventurers Act was being prepared in the early months of 1642. Consequently, the Irish Adventure and the parliamentary cause became quickly intertwined, with the result that the resources raised to be used against the rebels in Ireland were instead used against the king in England. Rather than focus on the well-documented peers and elected representatives central to this conflict between king and parliament, this book reveals the careers of those merchants who worked behind closed doors in parliamentary committee rooms and financial bureaucracies to divert resources to where they might best serve the

Adventurers' own interests, at times to the benefit of their political leaders, but sometimes against them.

The Adventurers for Irish land were drawn mainly from the burgeoning English Atlantic trade. England's western colonial enterprises were undertaken through individual companies and less formal groups that raised funds to establish plantations. Investors belonged, for example, to the Dorchester Company, created in 1619 to establish a colony in New England and to the London Company of the Somers Isles, created in 1615 to found a colony on Bermuda. The Honourable Irish Society was created in 1609 to develop the plantation of Derry in the north of Ireland and was financed by the Companies of London, who were otherwise primarily responsible for the trade of the capital.[3] The Adventurers also included some notable figures from English chartered trading companies, the Muscovy, Levant and East India companies, together with the Fellowship of Merchant Adventurers. The membership of these groups overlapped to some degree.

The chartered trading companies, officially responsible for England's external trade, were not involved in plantations. These companies exercised commercial monopolies, issued by the king, to trade in specific geographical regions and their investors were drawn from a wealthier and more established class of merchant than those of the smaller western enterprises. In contrast to the Dutch Republic where a West India Company was created to manage all its American trade, English trade in the Atlantic consisted of a proliferation of small, independent colonial ventures. Most participants in the nascent Atlantic trade belonged to a distinct group of merchants with English Puritan or Dutch Calvinist affiliations, religious ties they shared with the peers who backed these enterprises. The largest overseas trade association, the Fellowship of Merchant Adventurers, was a company of merchants specifically concerned with the cloth trade between England and continental Europe, for which the Merchant Adventurers held a royal monopoly. England's external trade was better organised in theory than in practice and the 1630s were characterised by continual attempts of independent merchants to infiltrate business controlled by the monopoly companies, operating usually on a casual basis but sometimes with a seemingly arbitrary commission awarded by the king.[4]

The merchants who organised around the Adventure for Irish land were drawn from these three groups, comprising the rising Atlantic merchants, their established counterparts from the chartered companies and independent traders seeking fortune where they could. They recognised that there were also large profits to be made in military contracting and, in addition, the Atlantic merchants had developed expertise in establishing plantations. They saw the military conquest of Ireland as a step towards the development of another commercially successful colony. All were familiar with the concept of private warfare, through their colonial enterprises or through the development of military contracting in Europe during the course of the Thirty Years War, 1618–48.

Among these merchants, one is central to this narrative. Maurice Thomson's extensive colonial interests and business partnerships were first revealed by Robert Brenner in his study of the rise of what he termed the 'New Merchants' in pre-revolutionary England.[5] Maurice Thomson began his career as a Virginia tobacco planter in the 1620s and he rose to become governor of the English East India Company in 1657, the apex of England's merchant hierarchy. Thomson maintained a continuous engagement with Ireland throughout this period, in trade, finance, military supply and finally with the acquisition of land. He emerged briefly in English affairs, during pivotal episodes, and then receded to concentrate on his business interests. Maurice Thomson is rarely found directly in parliamentary or other official records, yet this study shows that he was never more than one step removed from central political figures and decisions. Of the triumvirate of merchants at the centre of the English parliament's financial arrangements for Ireland, only Thomson had this exclusively colonial background. William Pennoyer, a partner with Thomson in some Atlantic tobacco ventures who also appears throughout this narrative, was a member of the Levant Company. Another of the leading protagonists, Thomas Andrews, was a senior member of the Massachusetts Bay Company and derived his wealth from his association with the Craddock family, leaders of the Eastland Company. Andrews had started out as a linen draper but was Master of the Leather-Sellers Company of London by 1638. It is possible that he spent the winter of 1639–40 in Rotterdam in the company of a radical Puritan preacher, Sidrach Simpson.[6] By late 1642, Thomas Andrews served as the treasurer for the Adventure for Irish land and held a host of other key positions in parliament's financial apparatus.

FINANCE

In its seventeenth-century context, an 'adventure' was a speculation, financial or otherwise. The closest modern equivalent is venture capital, from which the investor hopes to recoup both a share of the profits and the original investment, but risks losing the entire gamble. 'Adventure' was in widespread use among colonial merchants to describe sums of money risked on colonial projects in the hope of a handsome return. An adventure could be in person as well as in money and one could risk oneself as a planter or soldier in the hope of a return in money or property. Financial adventures were typically collaborative. The sharing of risk suited the less wealthy, the merchants of the middling sort who typically participated in colonial schemes. Adventures took many forms and ranged from a small consortium of investors in a single voyage to large projects such as the Second Virginia Company that attracted over 1,000 subscriptions in 1619.⁷ For most large projects a strict class system was observed, with a person of title, who acted as patron and obtained a royal charter for the venture, working with an assortment of lesser peers and well-connected merchants who provided the bulk of the financial and other resources. Most of the colonial schemes launched during the first half of the seventeenth century took this form.

A common opportunity for the less wealthy members of the merchant community to participate in shareholding enterprises was through the shared ownership of merchant vessels.⁸ Although the very wealthy could afford to be sole owners, the risk of owning a ship was normally spread among four to sixteen individuals, who may also have had a share of ownership in her cargo. The number of ships owned by these lesser merchants rose steadily throughout the 1630s, reflecting the increase in trade between London and the Atlantic colonies of New England, Virginia and the Caribbean.⁹ The India trade was the exception as the English East India Company (EEIC) owned its own ships, but each voyage was treated as an individual adventure with its own distinct group of subscribers. The EEIC leased its ships to investors in each voyage and also took a share of the profits. Foreign trade and the shipping required to service it gave rise to a considerable community of merchants familiar with the concepts of shared risk and long-term credit, but who could only afford to participate on a relatively modest scale. The early colonial period was, therefore, characterised by a huge increase in co-operative endeavours. The Adventure for Irish land, in addition to its expected financial rewards, offered an opportunity for social mobility through the acquisition of a landed estate. Consequently, the rising Atlantic merchants and ship-owners featured prominently among its subscribers. In addition to attracting the largest amount of money of any English colonial speculation, the Adventure for Irish land was also the most socially diverse. Although the usual configuration of peers and minor gentry undertook initially to participate, in the end only one peer invested and the leadership of the venture was left in the hands of a few aldermen and an assortment of merchants with no social titles at all.

The body of merchants comprising the Adventurers for Irish land operated on a global scale, realising the colonial and imperial ambitions of their political collaborators, with the lucky few profiting handsomely from their involvement. The interaction of early modern politicians and merchants was characterised by a requirement to keep their political and financial ambitions in reasonable alignment, to allow politics to be financed on one side and a profit to be made on the other. This system permitted an expense on state or military finance to be offset against a subsequent gain in trade or a concession, the normal arrangement between the Adventurers and the series of English governments from 1642 to 1660. Merchants and the polity developed a symbiosis that remains to be fully explored as the historiographical convention is to treat these two topics, politics and money, separately. In political history, the nation state is usually seen as the most appropriate container and most narratives reconstruct a national boundary to describe events within it. This is evident in the histories of most of the geographical regions of the early modern Atlantic world that treat each European state with its nascent empire as a separate entity. The history of commerce is less easily contained within a territory. The concept of 'circum-Atlantic' history attempts to escape territorial boundaries; the idea is that the history of the Atlantic is a transnational one that transcends the European nation states and also draws Asian economies into an expanding Atlantic network.[10] The Adventurers for Irish land belonged to this circum-Atlantic world.

The position of Ireland in the circum-Atlantic has been discussed by Jane Ohlmeyer in her historiographical survey article, 'Seventeenth-Century Ireland and the New British and Atlantic Histories', examining emerging scholarship on the topics of religious, cultural and political commonalities.[11] Ohlmeyer takes issue with the regionalism of Irish historiography and embraces the trend towards including Ireland's history with that of its neighbours. Shared themes in the separate histories of England's Atlantic colonies are also discussed in an edited volume, *The Westward Enterprise*, but this work is essentially a collection of regional histories and emphasises the diversity of the English colonies as opposed to what they had in common.[12] A recent study by Alison Games examines a broad cross-section of English colonial projects, from the Caribbean to the Indian Oceans in the 1630s and 1640s, emphasising migration across colonies and the spread of a conforming worldview.[13] Many of the Adventurers' colonial interests and business partnerships were first revealed by Robert Brenner in his study of the rise of what he termed the 'New Merchants' in pre-revolutionary England.[14] Although Brenner's work is an invaluable guide to English merchant networks, this book demonstrates that his characterisation of these networks as sharply divided between company (old) and colonial (new) merchants is an oversimplification. The majority of colonial merchants was drawn initially from the Levant Company and the Fellowship of Merchant Adventurers and it was their expertise in shipping that drew them into the Atlantic arena. Brenner's narrative ends with the dissolution of the Rump Parliament in 1653; the merchants' actions thereafter disprove his argument that they were revolutionaries.

Aside from their business interests, many of the leading Adventurers were also reforming Puritans and contributed either towards the establishment of the New England colonies or to one of the smaller Puritan ventures in the Caribbean. A number joined campaigns to appoint Calvinist ministers in London and some had Calvinist Dutch connections, both commercial and familial, and maintained regular dealings with the better known Puritan peers, most notably Robert Rich, earl of Warwick. Prior to 1641, they were also deeply involved with an emerging network of New English landlords and merchants in Ireland centred on Richard Boyle, earl of Cork, and provided finance to both Protestant and Catholic landowners in Ireland. These credit facilities, derived from Dutch innovations, marked the progression of the future Adventurers from merchants to financiers. The principal Dutch fiscal innovation of the early seventeenth century was the development of a transparent clearing institution through which instruments of credit could be exchanged.[15] The Adventurers were familiar with the Dutch financial revolution and understood how money worked as a means of exchange.[16] Money also represents a store of value, but the pre-eminent store of value in the early modern world was land. Unless parliament had credit, and early in 1642 this was not the case, it required either money or land to collateralise its military campaigns. Both would be provided by the Adventure for Irish land.

THE HISTORIOGRAPHY OF THE ADVENTURE FOR IRISH LAND

The significance of the Adventurers Act has been interpreted over the years in several ways.[17] John P. Prendergast, writing in 1890, viewed it as a final plantation scheme under which the total conquest of Ireland was envisaged.[18] To Prendergast, the Adventure was a private enterprise over which the king had little control, and it obliged many Catholic landowners, with some reluctance, to take up arms against the crown. Robert Mahaffy (1908) provided an extensive introduction to the initial legislation and the subsequent dealings of the Adventurers with parliament in the preface to his calendar of material relating to the Adventurers in the Public Record Office in England.[19] William Scott's corporatist analysis of the Adventure, published in 1910, includes the observation that although the Adventure was a 'lottery-loan' and not a joint stock company in the technical sense, a successful outcome depended on the Adventurers cooperating in the fitting out of troops and the prosecution of a campaign for the conquest of Ireland.[20] This is an important observation as the Adventurers could not be passive investors if the sharing out of Irish land, their only promised return, was ever to take place.

J.R. MacCormack's analysis of the political loyalties of those Adventurers who were MPs was published in 1956 and it revealed how the Adventure was factional, supported by a far greater proportion of parliamentarians than royalists.[21] Karl S. Bottigheimer observed in 1967 that 'the Adventurers were to play a participating, if never dominant, role in the formulation of Irish policy', a reference to the inclusion of some Adventurers who were not MPs at meetings of the English parliament's Committee for Irish Affairs in 1643.[22] This assertion has become the accepted interpretation of the political role of the Adventurers. Bottigheimer's subsequent monograph, published in 1971, *English Money and Irish Land*, published for the first time, as appendices, lists of the original Adventurers from 1642 to 1643 and their equivalents in 1658, following the initial Cromwellian land settlement.[23] Bottigheimer's work, however, is a study of the Adventure, and not of the Adventurers who subscribed to and managed the investment. This book shows that the significance of the Adventure for Irish land lies not in the capital raised, but in the merchants who provided it, the subsequent use of their money and their relentless campaign to take their profits.

Hugh Hazlett contextualised the fiscal impact of the Adventure in a general study of all of the English fundraising efforts to support the war in Ireland.[24] Hazlett observed that an existing fundraising scheme in 1642, a church gate collection to provide relief to 'the poor Protestants of Ireland', failed due to a general perception that the money raised was being diverted by parliament to be used for its own ends.[25] He provides a useful table showing that the Adventure raised £333,000 out of a total of £2,031,000 raised in England to fund the military conquest of Ireland between 1642 and 1649.[26] These figures demonstrate that although the Adventurers invested a substantial sum, it was hardly one of overwhelming significance in the context of the total amount of English money spent on the conquest of Ireland.[27] There were indeed substantial differences between the purposes for which money was raised during this period and how it was spent. Equally, there were considerable differences between parliament's aspirations to raise funds and the amounts actually collected. Reports of state financing schemes from the early modern period, when taken at face value, have the ability to deceive. Differentiating the intention to raise funds from the amounts actually raised and then from the uses to which these funds were put provides a more accurate picture of parliament's financial arrangements. The most recent study of the Adventurers, published twenty years ago, was by Keith Lindley in his article 'Irish Adventurers and Godly Militants'. Lindley, using Bottigheimer's lists, focuses on the religious motives of some of the Adventurers. He devotes some space to the individuals calendared as members of Adventurers' committees in the 1640s and mentioned in Bottigheimer's text, and highlights the merchants' religious orientation but does not dwell on their commercial activities. The final page of Lindley's article, drawing heavily on the work of Robert Brenner, deals with the colonial connections of some of the Adventurers, although Brenner, as Lindley points out, analysed only the Additional Sea Adventure of July 1642.[28]

All of these works suffer from two distinct weaknesses, both connected to the regionalism prevalent in Irish historiography of the early modern period. Firstly, the analyses are unduly influenced by the consequence of the Adventurers Act, the Cromwellian Land Settlement, and do not focus on the Act itself. The Adventure for Irish land is uniformly portrayed as yet another phase of the English plantation of Ireland, the colonisation of the rest of the country being a logical progression from the regional plantations effected by the Tudors and Stuarts during the preceding century. The framing of the Act itself has attracted little discussion and its text is taken at face value, with no weight given to the circumstances surrounding the framing of the initial legislation. The Adventurers Act was framed in London in a convoluted process that began in January 1642 following the English parliament's initial ousting of Charles I from his capital. Its promoters were central to the faction in the English parliament opposing the king. The process of the framing of the Act must, therefore, be considered in its English context, not solely as a further instrument of plantation.

The second gap in the treatment of the Adventure for Irish land to date is the absence of any meaningful analysis of the 1,300 Adventurers who subscribed to the fund, although they were identified and tabulated by Bottigheimer in 1971. As only a handful were commercially active in Ireland prior to 1642, and hardly any ever visited the country, a cloak of anonymity is maintained and the Adventurers' significant role in England's Civil Wars has eluded Irish and, to a considerable degree, English historians. To the English parliament, it was the Adventurers who were important and not the Adventurers Act. The Adventurers, organised as a corporate body, had a distinct leadership comprising approximately twenty merchants with strong connections among independent MPs and peers, as well as within London's political and military institutions. With their backgrounds in trade and colonial shipping, the Adventurers already possessed, collectively, one of the strongest navies in the early modern world when the 1641 rebellion erupted in Ireland. The Committee of Adventurers, established in March 1642, dispersed into the highest positions in parliamentary finance and occupied leading posts on every important English financial committee by January 1643. The multiplicity of committees created by parliament during this period to finance its militarisation appear disjointed, but there was an Adventurer for Irish land on every one of them and the leading Adventurers met regularly at Grocers' Hall in London throughout the 1640s and 1650s. Understanding the importance of the Adventurers in England is crucial to understanding the paradox of the subsequent Irish land settlement, and in order to make sense of the land settlement it is necessary to appreciate the Adventurers' motives and grasp the scale of their ambitions.

The London merchant polity experienced revolutionary change during the winter of 1641–42, at the same time as the Adventure for Irish land was being developed and negotiated. Respected aldermen on London's representative assemblies were being replaced by merchants from the colonial and shipping trades and an unprecedented struggle for the mayoralty of London underlined a shift in political power away from the existing establishment.[29] The London-based Adventurers were prominent participants in this upheaval. David Cressy offers a more reductionist analysis of this political turmoil than

Brenner, arguing that events were focused almost entirely on London, with an emphasis on religious and cultural disturbances.[30] This interpretation understates the effect of the Irish rebellion of October 1641 on London's merchant community and how Charles's indecisive response to the rebellion gave rise to a further challenge to his authority.[31] Parliament's most significant financial underwriters were the leaders of the Adventure for Irish land, yet despite a vibrant debate that continues today over the political and societal causes of the English Civil War, the role of those who financed its outbreak has not been analysed.[32] This book demonstrates that the raising of money to be used against rebellious Ireland and for rebellious England were components in the same financial machine. Immediately prior to the outbreak of hostilities in England, the English response to the war in Ireland required a fast mobilisation of resources and the creation of an effective coalition to achieve this. This coalition would have a lasting impact, for although the Adventure for Irish land was not a direct cause of the English revolt, it was a facilitator, bringing together Adamson's 'Junta' of peers, central to the confrontation between king and parliament, with Brenner's 'New Merchants' who had the resources to raise both an army and a navy. These peers were already the merchants' best customers and their alliances bypassed the established relationships that existed between parliament and the merchant leadership of the City of London, the normal route through which state finance was raised.

Economic life in England in the first half of the seventeenth century was a slow and unplanned process of commercialisation, a transition from an agrarian to a mercantile economy.[33] It took just twenty years, 1620–40, for the Virginian and Caribbean colonies to achieve the same transition, and to generate a surplus of mercantile wealth, concentrated in the hands of a small number of colonial contractors in London. The historiography of the early English colonies in the Americas tends towards a focus on the social and religious development of the colonies, with less emphasis on the motives and expectations of the promoters of these colonies back in England.[34] The speculators at home wanted to make money and, from their perspective, New England was a failure when compared with the profitable tobacco and cotton plantations to the south. To spread risk, the bigger merchants operated in more than one territory, and colonial Virginia and plantation Ireland had many English investors in common.

English colonial enterprises in Ireland and in the Atlantic colonies of Virginia and Massachusetts Bay were being run along more or less the same lines by 1640. All had local parliaments with local courts and local officers, although only in Ireland were these courts answerable to the Privy Council in England and ultimately to the king.[35] This distinction was important as it allowed the Atlantic colonies to be administered by the peers and companies granted these territorial rights and their agents. Ken Macmillan argues against this theory of 'government by license' and contends that the state took a keen interest in colonial affairs.³⁶ This is true in terms of the conditions written into the various patentees' charters, but practical interventions were rare. Some of the leading Adventurers had lived in Virginia for many years, becoming used to relative independence from absolute rule. Other independently minded colonists, largely from New England and who returned just before the English revolt, took leading political and religious roles on the parliamentary side, having a disproportionate impact when compared to the tiny numbers of returning colonists involved.³⁷ Many of the leading Adventurers feature among the Puritan protagonists in John Donohue's work on the English Revolution.³⁸ With their Dutch links, most of the leading London-based Adventurers were associated with Calvinist churches established in London.³⁹ This provided another opportunity for discourse between like-minded people with many religious, political and commercial interests in common. The Adventurers for Irish land not drawn from the maritime merchant community were often involved in Dutch trade, either through the Fellowship of Merchant Adventurers or independently. Trade links reinforced family connections that made possible Dutch influence over the Adventurers' later innovations in state finance.

Although typically a merchant, the typical Adventurer for Irish land fails to satisfy the classical definition of a mercantilist, who uses trade as a lever to wield power.⁴⁰ Power was not the primary objective of the Adventurers and their leadership rarely sought or accepted political office. Their belligerence in foreign policy in the early 1650s, betraying their Dutch partnerships, was not meant to increase territory. It reflected the widely accepted belief at the time that global trade was fixed in size and the only route to increasing one's share of it was to deprive others.⁴¹ Once battle lines were drawn in England, Ireland and Scotland the Adventurers alternated between the financing of war and the development of their extra-territorial commercial empires. They maintained a particular interest in Ireland where the fate of their Adventure was at stake and eagerly embraced the profits to be made through providing military supplies for Ireland's conquest.⁴² In all of these areas they sought to maximise their share of the spoils to the exclusion of all others.

In examining the events of the Wars of the Three Kingdoms from the perspective of the Adventurers, this book takes a step back from Marxist and revisionist interpretations of the key events of the period but still relies on many of the significant works that have appeared in recent years to provide a political framework to the Adventurers' actions. John Adamson's narrative of the political background to the 1642 rift between the English king and his parliament exposes the organisational framework on which the Adventurers' financial and political structures were first formed.⁴³ To gain insights into the Adventurers' perceptions of the world in which they lived I have relied on Michael Braddick and Sarah Mortimer, while for wider societal impressions of developments at Westminster the work by Jason Peacy on print culture has been invaluable.⁴⁴

For the Irish political context to 1642 this narrative owes much to the work of Robert Armstrong, Eamon Darcy and Jane Ohlmeyer.[45] The area of English parliamentary finance has been the subject of a number of recent studies that deal both with management at the centre and collection at local level.[46]

The Adventurers for Irish land were appointed to leading roles in all of parliament's major financial committees, and also to the later committees that dealt with the sale or letting of royalist, ecclesiastical and crown property.[47] The proliferation of committees appears to be disorganised but each was, in fact, headed by a sub-set of Adventurers who regularly met, in private, at the Adventurers' committee room at Grocers' Hall in London. As a result, the parliamentary financial committees can be considered holistically, as opposed to being treated as separate entities. The Adventurers normally appointed their associates from previous commercial partnerships, or family members, to key and subordinate positions in each committee. To oversee these activities, a Committee of Accounts was appointed by parliament, also mainly comprised of Adventurers for Irish land. Parliament's financial committees were thus far more homogenous than individual studies of the records suggest. As they were controlled, staffed and audited by a small group of unelected merchants, the potential for corruption is all too apparent. It would be a mistake to view these committee-men as prototypes for the high-principled and impartial civil servants of later centuries, as they were nothing of the sort. Their self-regulated state treasury, staffed throughout by family members and business partners, could not have been better designed for widespread corruption and favouritism. Parliamentary sequestrations were, in essence, just another form of plunder and the burden of taxation would always fall more heavily on the Adventurers' competitors than on their partners.

Studies of England's colonies during the Civil War years generally conform to the regional model. There is a convention that describes the Virginia and Caribbean colonies as broadly royalist and New England as supportive of the parliamentary cause, but there is an underlying complication that the economic development of the colonies was primarily in the hands of the Adventurers, parliament's financial managers. There is a noticeable pattern of alignment between economic expansions in the colonies that generated bullion, especially from sugar and the slave trade, and expansions of the parliamentary war effort which consumed it. Throughout the 1640s, colonial profits increased rapidly in importance as a source of funds for the Adventurers to reinvest in the war effort at home. Taken in this monetary context, the colonial uprising in support of Charles II in 1649 and quashed by the parliamentary navy in 1651 was of major significance. Control of the profits from Caribbean sugar plantations played an increasingly important role in England's financial affairs, a point that was probably not lost on the new king. Distant Barbados had become a weak link in the parliamentary financial system forcing the English state, for the first time, to intervene directly in colonial affairs. It is a central argument of this study that far-flung external sources of money were essential to the parliamentary financial system.

Ireland's role in this system, until Cromwell's arrival in the summer of 1649, was frequently as an excuse to raise funds, or a handy source of ready cash to divert to other uses. These patterns were apparent to commentators at the time. Samuel Sheppard's observation in 1647 on a new subsidy of £20,000 per month to be collected for the war in Ireland reflected a popular perception:

> But however posterity may censure their actions, they are agreed to set all their wits a wheeling, to wind up with as much money as may be (before they go) out of the pockets of the people, which they suppose may be best accomplished by the help of the old Engine of Levying money for the relief of Ireland: for which purpose they have passed and published a new ordinance for the raising of £20,000 per mensem. And they have feigned a new victory too (according to their old custom) to usher forward the design, thinking by that means to revive the Old Drooping Purchasers, or at least-wise to encourage some new upstart covetous creatures to a New-Hazard. Yes, and they have (as they used formerly to do) consulted with certain eminent citizens, to make free (but feigned) proffers of lending certain considerable sums for that service, hoping by that means to draw in others whilst (God knows) they intend neither men nor moneys there.[48]

There was little by way of parliamentary opposition to this approach until Cromwell's Irish campaign and his diligence in reliably paying his soldiers. The long war in Ireland was, however, beyond even the financial resources of the Adventurers and the conquering army in Ireland was mired in debt by the mid-1650s.

Consequently, by the time the Irish land settlement was being constructed, the Adventurers' claims competed with those of Cromwell's army whose pay arrears were also to be settled with Irish land. Technical aspects of the land surveys performed in Ireland, and the land settlement itself, have been the subject of extensive academic scrutiny.[49] These studies, however, treat the land settlement within an Irish context, leaving aside the enmity that existed between the two camps, soldiers and Adventurers. Although the land surveys were headquartered in Dublin, where army claims for land were heard, the Adventurers insisted on managing their affairs from London. This book highlights the conflict between Adventurers and army over land that resulted in the Adventurers severing ties with Cromwell and his Protectorate. In his 1962 assessment of the new men appointed by the Protectorate to manage its finances, Maurice Ashley states that 'All of these men must have had a real influence on the determination of policy. They formed a new class of government officials, distinguished alike by their single-mindedness and ability, who were appointed because their special knowledge made them suitable for the work'.⁵⁰ The Protectorate, in fact, was forced to recruit new, inexperienced officials because of the Adventurers' disagreement with Cromwell. The Irish Protectorate was so heavily in debt by 1658 that the Adventurers' claims were tiny by comparison with those of the army, yet the Adventurers maintained that their claims took priority.

The Adventurers, for so long westward-facing, turned east and became preoccupied with developing their Levant and East India trade as a global trade network took shape. As part of this process they absorbed into their circle former royalist merchant grandees who had drifted back to London following the execution of Charles I in 1649. The Adventurers thus acquired a second group of important allies, alongside the Old Protestants in Ireland. As the Cromwellian Protectorate struggled to survive, the Adventurers continued to withhold financial assistance and pressed their claims for land. There was, by 1660, little to distinguish them from the merchant elite they had superseded and their revolution had completed its circle.

SOURCES

As the Adventurers operated both on a global scale and in the most intimate committee rooms at the centre of the government of the Commonwealth, a comparative study from a wide range of primary sources was required to piece their story together. The records of the Adventurers, their partnerships, land transactions and various negotiations with the Protectorate regime in London are found in a discrete set of Irish State Papers at The National Archives in Kew.⁵¹ The majority of Adventurers were drawn from the ranks of investors and merchants active in the colonies, so a detailed inspection of colonial sources, 1620–40, with particular reference to how each Atlantic plantation was financed, was needed in order to unpick their earlier associations.⁵² Some of the colonial entrepreneurs also had dealings with Ireland, archived in Admiralty Court records and in the accounts of individual voyages.

To track the movement of funds from the Adventure to parliament, an inspection of army income receipts and payment warrants was undertaken.⁵³ Army payment warrants confirmed that the Adventurers were both fundraiser for and beneficiary of major army and navy contracts, thus controlling both finance and purchasing from the early stages of the conflict. These activities are even more apparent in the navy records. Parliamentary ordinances provided a vital source to identify the individuals underwriting each financial initiative, particularly with regard to the collection of subsidies and the networks of collectors and assessors in the English provinces. Many of the collectors from coastal towns in the southwest of England were also active in the early colonial plantations.

The Adventurers' involvement in Irish affairs was through their membership of the various iterations of the English parliament's Committee for Irish

Affairs, the only parliamentary committee for the period for which complete minutes survive.⁵⁴ Their key interventions included their opposition to the cessation of hostilities between Charles I and the Irish Confederates in 1643 and their attempts to maintain a monopoly over military supplies sent from England to Ireland. I am very grateful to the History of Parliament Trust in London for sharing their unpublished essays on parliamentary committees, 1640–60, and to Professor John Adamson for pointing me towards this invaluable source. There are separate records in State Papers for some of the larger fundraising efforts, and matching records of repayments by parliamentary finance committees, details of which are referenced in the relevant chapters. These loans were often the subject of popular scrutiny and as men of great wealth often are, the Adventurers found themselves written about in the popular press, especially in royalist news sheets.⁵⁵ The Adventurers were evidently not well liked, as in addition to raising loans, they also collected taxes. Finally, although the Adventurers rarely published petitions of their own, the very few that survive provide significant insights into their motivations.

CHAPTERS

This book is arranged chronologically and relates the development of the Adventurers' activities in various geographical regions within each chapter. It is an approach that demonstrates their involvement across multiple economic and geographical domains and the ways in which these activities were interrelated. Chapter 1 is a survey in an Atlantic context of the English and Irish activities, 1620–41, of those merchants who became leaders of the Adventure for Irish land in 1642. The emergence of Ireland, particularly Munster, as a provisioning stop for traders between Europe and the Americas is examined, as is the network of ship-owners that managed the provisioning and servant trade between the two regions. In chapter 2, these colonial networks emerge as a powerful force in London politics at the outbreak of the city's rebellion against Charles I in January 1642. The central argument of this chapter is that these merchant networks were not operating independently, but were contractors to or under the umbrella of specific peers.

Chapter 3 demonstrates for the first time that the Adventure for Irish land, a suggestion of Richard Boyle, earl of Cork, was instigated and funded by the small circle of radical peers, politicians and merchants at the heart of the rebellion against Charles I. The core purpose of the Adventure was political and the participants' interest in Irish land appears incidental and opportunistic. Much of the money raised was only contributed after it became apparent in July 1642 that the funds would be used to finance parliament's forces in England. Most of the resources raised for the Adventure to Ireland were transferred to the parliamentary cause during the summer of 1642. The key argument in this chapter is that parliament prepared for war in England under the cover of its response to the rebellion in Ireland.

Chapter 4 traces the development of English state finance and policy towards Ireland during the first English Civil War. Following the outbreak of formal hostilities in England, the Adventurers seized control over parliament's financial and military committees, using a network centred on Grocers' Hall. The role of Grocers' Hall is highlighted by demonstrating the process by which the functions of parliament's Committee for Irish Affairs were transferred to it, leaving the Adventurers in command of parliament's policy for Ireland.

The focus of the story widens again in chapter 5 as the Adventurers applied their English war profits to colonial developments, commandeering the chartered foreign trading companies in the process. They retained their grip on parliamentary finances and targeted their colonial profits towards specific loans to finance the parliamentary army, which resulted in further trading concessions. The Adventurers navigated their way through the political upheavals in England, 1647–49, and although quietly opposed to the execution of Charles I, they nevertheless gained control over the Council of State's external trade policy. Chapter 6 commences after the regicide, when the Adventurers appeared to be in an unassailable position. This chapter demonstrates that a core group of merchants dominated the greater part of England's foreign trade, state finance and state expenditure. They had developed an integrated fiscal state and were thus able to project considerable political influence as well as profiting enormously from these activities.

Chapter 7, the final chapter, opens with the Adventurers' breach with Oliver Cromwell over his intention to use most of the confiscated Irish land to settle debts due to the army in Ireland. The disagreement came to a head when Cromwell dissolved parliament in April 1653 and ordered the dismissal of the Adventurers from all state finance committees and other salaried positions. The departure of the Adventurers marked the beginning of a steady decline in the Protectorate's finances and disasters in foreign policy that included the Western Design in the Caribbean and the subsequent naval war with Spain. The chapter concludes with a description of how the Adventurers leveraged an old relationship with General George Monck to help facilitate the restoration of Charles II.

NOTES

1 For the first translation in English see Marchamont Needham, *Mare Clausum* (London, 1652).
2 'An Act for the better Execution of His Majesties gracious Declaration for the Settlement of his kingdom of Ireland, and Satisfaction of the several Interests of Adventures, Soldiers and other his Subjects there' in *Statutes passed in the Parliaments*

held in Ireland, Vol. 1 (Dublin, 1794), pp. 338-364 and 'An Act for the explaining of some Doubts arising upon an Act initiated...' in *Statutes passed in the Parliaments held in Ireland*, Vol. 2 (Dublin, 1794), pp. 1-137.

3   'The Companies of London' describes cooperative ventures organised by the livery companies, for example the Grocers' and Ironmongers' Companies.

4   The most notorious of the royal commissions that concerns the Adventurers for Irish land was one awarded to Sir William Courteen in 1635, permitting him to trade in the East Indies in competition with the English East India Company. See Edward Graves, *A Brief Narrative, and deduction of the several remarkable Cases of Sir William Courten, and Sir Paul Pyndar, Knights; and William Courten late of London Esquire, Deceased: Their Heirs, Executors, Administrators and Assigns, together with their Surviving Partners and Adventurers with them to the East-Indies, China and Japan, and divers other parts of Asia, Europe, Africa and America* (London, 1679), p. 2.

5   Robert Brenner, *Merchants and Revolution* (Princeton, NJ, 1993).

6   David C. Elliot, 'Some Slight Confusion: A Note on Thomas Andrewes and Thomas Andrewes', *Huntington Library Quarterly*, 47:2 (Spring, 1984), pp. 129-132, p. 130.

7   William Waller Hening, *The Statutes at Large; being a Collection of all the Laws of Virginia*, Vol. 1 (Richmond, VA, 1888), pp. 80-98; Samuel M. Bemiss, *The Three Charters of the Virginia Company of London* (Williamsburg, VA, 1957), pp. 76-95.

8   Kenneth R. Andrews, *Ships, Money and Politics* (Cambridge, 1991), pp. 34-61; Ralph Davis, *The Rise of the English Shipping Industry in the Seventeenth and Eighteenth Centuries* (Newton Abbot, 1962).

9   Russell R. Menard, *Sweet Negotiation: Sugar, Slavery and Plantation Agriculture in Early Barbados* (Charlottesville, VA, 2006); Henry A. Gemery, 'Emigration from the British Isles to the New World: 1630-1700: References from Colonial Populations', *Research in Economic History*, 5 (1980), pp. 179-231.

10 David Armitage, 'Three Concepts of Atlantic History' in David Armitage and Michael Braddick (eds), *The British Atlantic World* (Basingstoke, 2009), pp. 18-20.

11 Jane Ohlmeyer, 'Seventeenth Century Ireland and the New British and Atlantic Histories', *American Historical Review*, 104:2 (April, 1999), pp. 446-462.

12 K.R. Andrews, N.P. Canny and P.E.H. Hair (eds), *The Westward Enterprise: English Activities in Ireland, the Atlantic and America, 1480-1650* (Liverpool, 1978).

13 Alison Games, *The Web of Empire* (Oxford, 2008).

14 Brenner, *Merchants and Revolution*, p. 173.

15 For a brief survey article on the development of instruments of credit during the early modern period see Frederick K. Beutel, 'The Development of Negotiable Instruments in Early English Law', *Harvard Law Review*, 51:5 (March, 1938), pp. 813-845. For a detailed description of the methodology for the early form of banking practised by the Adventurers, see Frank T. Melton, *Sir Robert Clayton and the Origins of English Deposit Banking, 1658-1685* (Cambridge, 1986), pp. 16-94.

16 Douglas Fisher, *Monetary Theory and the Demand for Money* (London, 1978), pp. 14-15.

17 John P. Prendergast, *The Cromwellian Conquest of Ireland* (Dublin, 1890), pp. 72-79. For the legislation see Robert Pentland Mahaffy (ed.), *Calendar of State Papers*

Relating to Ireland Preserved in the Public Record Office: Adventurers for Land, 1642–59 (London, 1903). For a corporatist analysis of the Adventure for Irish land see William Robert Scott, *The Constitution and Finance of English, Scottish and Irish Joint Stock Companies to 1720*, 3 vols (Cambridge, 1910), Vol. 2, p. 344. For a treatment of the Adventurers in the context of the ongoing English plantation of Ireland see Karl S. Bottigheimer, *English Money and Irish Land* (Oxford, 1971). For the Adventurers and their association with the Radical faction in the English parliament see J.R. MacCormack, 'The Irish Adventurers and the English Civil War', *Irish Historical Studies*, 10:37 (1956–57), pp. 45–67. See also Keith Lindley, 'Irish Adventurers and Godly Militants in the 1640s', *Irish Historical Studies*, 29:113 (May, 1994), pp. 1–12. The immediate reaction to the Irish rebellion in political circles in London is treated in Michael Perceval-Maxwell, *The Outbreak of the Irish Rebellion of 1641* (Dublin, 1994), pp. 261–284.

18 Prendergast, *Cromwellian Conquest*, pp. 72–79.
19 Mahaffy, *Calendar of State Papers*, pp. i–xlix. On p. v, Mahaffy presents these documents as 'in effect a list of the names and addresses of subscribers, of the places in which the lands were awarded to them or their successors, and of the deeds or transfers by which those who actually received land derived their title from the original subscribers'.
20 Scott, *Constitution and Finance*, Vol. 2, p. 344.
21 MacCormack, 'Irish Adventurers', pp. 45–67.
22 Karl S. Bottigheimer, 'English Money and Irish Land: The "Adventurers" in the Cromwellian Settlement of Ireland', *Journal of British Studies*, 7:1 (November, 1967), pp. 12–27, p. 20.
23 Karl S. Bottigheimer, *English Money and Irish Land* (Oxford, 1971).
24 Hugh Hazlett, 'The Financing of the British Armies in Ireland 1641–9', *Irish Historical Studies*, 1 (1938), pp. 21–41.
25 Hazlett, 'Financing of the British Armies', p. 27.
26 Hazlett, 'Financing of the British Armies', p. 37.
27 According to Hazlett, the Adventure comprised 16% of the total raised in England for the conquest of Ireland. These figures can only be considered as indicatory, and based on intent as most of the money raised prior to 1648, and the Adventure is no exception, was diverted towards military campaigns in England.
28 Brenner, *Merchants and Revolution*, pp. 400–409.
29 Robert Ashton, 'Puritanism and Progress', *Economic History Review*, New Series, 17:3 (1965), pp. 579–587; Robert Ashton, *The City and the Court* (Cambridge, 1979); Alfred B. Beavan *The Aldermen of the City of London* (London, 1913); John Bond, *The Downfall of the old Common-Counsel men…extruded the old out of their corrupted offices, and elected new in their places* (London, 1641); Robert Brenner, 'The Civil War Politics of London's Merchant Community', *Past & Present*, 58 (February, 1973), pp. 53–107; Valerie Pearl, *London and the Outbreak of the Puritan Revolution: City Government and National Politics, 1625–43* (Oxford, 1961).
30 David Cressy, *England on Edge: Crisis and Revolution 1640–1642* (Oxford, 2006).
31 Perceval-Maxwell, *Outbreak of the Irish Rebellion*, pp. 261–284.

32 Conrad Russell, *The Origins of the English Civil War* (London, 1973); Ann Hughes, *The Causes of the English Civil War* (Basingstoke, 1998); Richard Cust, *Charles I and the Aristocracy* (London, 2013); John Adamson, *The Noble Revolt* (London, 2007). The Junta and the Atlantic colonial projectors among the peerage are almost interchangeable.

33 Keith Wrightson, *Earthly Necessities: Economic Lives in Early Modern Britain* (New Haven, CT, 2000).

34 There is a huge body of literature concerning the English colonies in North America. The most valuable works for this study, in addition to the ones already cited are, Susan Myra Kingsbury, *The Records of the Virginia Company of London*, 4 vols (Washington, DC, 1906); James Phinney Baxter, *Sir Fernandino Gorges and the Province of Maine* (Boston, 1890); Carl and Roberta Bridenbaugh, *No Peace Beyond the Line, The English in the Caribbean 1624–1690* (New York, 1972); Frances Rose-Troup, *The Massachusetts Bay Company and its Predecessors* (New York, 1930); Bernard Bailyn, *New England Merchants in the Seventeenth Century* (Cambridge, MA, 1962).

35 Conrad Russell, *Unrevolutionary England 1603–1642* (London, 1990).

36 Ken Macmillan, 'Bound by Regal Office: Empire, Strategy and the American Colonies in the Seventeenth Century' in Stephen Foster (ed.), *British North America in the Seventeenth and Eighteenth Centuries* (Oxford, 2013), pp. 67–89.

37 William L. Sachse, 'The Migration of New Englanders to England, 1640–1660', *American Historical Review*, 55 (January, 1948), pp. 251–278.

38 John Donohue, *Fire Under the Ashes, an Atlantic History of the English Revolution* (Chicago, 2013).

39 Ole Peter Grell, *Dutch Calvinists in Early Stuart London: The Dutch Church at Austin Friars 1603–42* (London, 1989); Grell, *Brethren in Christ, a Calvinist Network in Reformation Europe* (Cambridge, 2011); Ashton, 'Puritanism and Progress'; Christian J. Koot, *Empire at the Periphery: British Colonists, Anglo-Dutch Trade, and the Development of the British Atlantic, 1621–1713* (London, 2011).

40 Jacob Viner, 'Power versus Plenty as Objectives of Foreign Policy in the Seventeenth and Eighteenth Centuries', *World Politics*, 1 (October, 1948), pp. 1–29.

41 Douglas A. Irwin, 'Strategic Trade Policy and Mercantilist Trade Rivalries', *American Economic Review*, 82 (May, 1992), pp. 134–139.

42 Robert Armstrong, 'The Long Parliament Goes to War: The Irish Campaigns, 1641–3', *Historical Research*, 80 (February, 2007), pp. 73–99.

43 Adamson, *The Noble Revolt*; John Adamson, 'The Triumph of Oligarchy' in Chris R. Kyle and Jason Peacy (eds), *Parliament at Work: Parliamentary Committees, Political Power and Public Access in Early Modern England* (Woodbridge, 2002), pp. 101–128.

44 Michael Braddick, *God's Fury, England's Fire, A New History of the English Civil Wars* (London, 2008); Sarah Mortimer, *Reason and Religion in the English Revolution: The Challenge of Socinianism* (Cambridge, 2010); Jason Peacy, *Print and Public Politics in the English Revolution* (Cambridge, 2013).

45 Armstrong, 'The Long Parliament Goes to War'; Robert Armstrong, *Protestant War: The 'British' of Ireland and the Wars of the Three Kingdoms* (Manchester, 2005);

Eamon Darcy, *The Irish Rebellion and the Wars of the Three Kingdoms* (Woodbridge, 2013); Jane Ohlmeyer, *Civil War and Restoration in the Three Stuart Kingdoms: The Career of Randal MacDonnell, Marquis of Antrim, 1609-1683* (Cambridge, 1993).

46 Michael Braddick, *Parliamentary Taxation in Seventeenth Century England: Local Administration and Response* (Woodbridge, 1994); Braddick, *The Nerves of State: Taxation and the Financing of the English State* (Manchester, 1996); D'Maris Coffman, *Excise Taxation and the Origins of Public Debt* (Basingstoke, 2013); Coffman, 'Towards a New Jerusalem: The Committee for Regulating the Excise, 1649-1653', *English Historical Review*, 128 (December, 2013), pp. 1418-1450; Ben Coates, *The Impact of the English Civil War on the Economy of London, 1652-1650* (unpublished PhD Thesis, University of Leicester, 1997).

47 Mary Anne Everett Greene (ed.), *Calendar of the Proceedings of the Committee for Advance of Money, 1642-1656*, 3 vols (London, 1888); Ian Gentles, 'The Sales of Bishops' Lands in the English Revolution, 1646-1660', *English Historical Review*, 95 (July, 1980), pp. 573-596.

48 Samuel Sheppard, *Mercurius Elenticus*, 14 (London, 23 February to 1 March 1648), p. 5.

49 W.H. Hardinge, 'On Manuscript Mapped and Other Townland Surveys in Ireland of a Public Character, Embracing the Gross, Civil, and Down Surveys, from 1640 to 1688', *The Transactions of the Royal Irish Academy: Antiquities*, 24 (1873), pp. 3-118; R.C. Simington (ed.), *Books of Survey and Distribution: Being Abstracts of Various Surveys and Instruments of Title, 1636-1703*, 4 vols (Dublin, 1949-67); Simington, *The Civil Survey*, 10 vols (Dublin, 1931-61); John Andrews, *Plantation Acres: An Historical Study of the Irish Land Surveyor and His Maps* (Belfast, 1985); Andrews, *Shapes of Ireland: Maps and their Makers 1564-1839* (Dublin, 1997). National studies and commentaries relating to the Cromwellian land settlement include: Toby Barnard, *Cromwellian Ireland: English Government and Reform in Ireland 1649-1660* (Oxford, 2000); Barnard, *Improving Ireland? Projectors, Prophets and Profiteers, 1641-1786* (Dublin, 2008); Bottigheimer, *English Money and Irish Land*; Aidan Clarke, *Prelude to Restoration in Ireland: The End of Commonwealth* (Cambridge, 1999); Padraig Lenihan, *Consolidating Conquest: Ireland 1603-1727* (Harlow, 2007); Kevin McKenny, 'The Restoration Land Settlement in Ireland: A Statistical Interpretation', *Irish Historical Studies*, 24 (1994), pp. 14-36; Jane Ohlmeyer, *Making Ireland English: The Irish Aristocracy in the Seventeenth Century* (London, 2012); Prendergast, *Cromwellian Conquest*. Local studies include: L.J. Arnold, *The Restoration Land Settlement in County Dublin 1660-88* (Dublin, 1993); James Barry, *The Cromwellian Settlement of the County of Limerick* (Limerick, 1900); Harold O'Sullivan, 'The Cromwellian and Restoration Settlements in the Civil Parish of Dundalk, 1649-73', *Journal of the Louth Archaeological and Historical Society*, 19 (1977), pp. 24-58.

50 Maurice Ashley, *Financial and Commercial Policy under the Cromwellian Protectorate* (Oxford, 1962), p. 9.

51 TNA SP 63/288-301, *Adventurers for Land*. This is the collection calendared by Mahaffy. There is, however, considerable additional material concerning the Adventurers in further volumes of the Irish State Papers, TNA SP 286-287.

52 Brenner's *Merchants and Revolution* is the most convenient starting point, and almost all of the early American colonies have specific literature devoted to them. *Colonial Papers*, TNA CO 1/5-11, include references to many of the investors and these were used alongside minute books of the Levant Company, TNA SP 110/10 and 55, and East India Company, BL IOR/B/19-26, to establish the pattern of investors migrating from the western colonies to the eastern companies.

53 The data contained in TNA SP 28/1 A-D, the army payment warrants in 1642, with some other records, was treated in this way. The specific dates at which payment warrants were raised, and then paid, were compared with the funds available to the treasurers of each fundraising committee at specific times.

54 The minute books for the Committee for Irish Affairs are dispersed among State Papers in The National Archives and at several other repositories. Taken together, almost a complete series has been preserved. In broadly chronological order they are to be found in National Library of Ireland MS 14,305 (1642-3); TNA SP 16/539/2-3 (1643-4); BL, MS Add 4749A, 4771 (1643-6); TNA SP 63/266 (1647); TNA SP 21/26-29 (1646-9); BL, MS Add 4782 (1647-8).

55 See especially Peacy, *Print and Public Politics*. The majority of the material used in this study has been drawn from the Thomason Collection at the British Library, available through Early English Books Online, http:eebo.cahdwyck.com/. George Thomason, the publisher responsible for the collection, was a member of the Adventurers' committee in London, 1643-45.

1

Atlantic oligarchy: Ireland in the early English Atlantic world

In the minds of early investors, Ireland had a particular role in to play in the English colonial expansion into the western Atlantic at the start of the seventeenth century. Ireland was regarded as a convenient source of labour to be employed in the vast expanses of the New World. As one writer observed in 1607:

> In Ireland there are a certaine kinde of swordmen called Kerne: descended from Horsboyes, idle persons and unlawful propagation. They are base, apt to follow factions, and live always by the spoil, and will never be brought to another conformity there: but if they might be drawn from thence, and imployed to the planting of Virginia the country should be well freed … The number of these people in Ireland, I suppose will not exceed 7 or 8,000.[1]

Unfree Irish labour on a large scale would not be required for a further half century, as the Virginia colony got off to a slow start. Virginia produced its first viable crop, tobacco, in 1617, triggering a surge of planters and labourers hopeful of making their fortunes. At the same time, the government in England was deciding what to do about Ireland in the wake of the pacification of Ulster in 1603. In the early seventeenth century, investors probed for opportunities throughout the Atlantic, although Ireland was seen in the English court as a more respectable endeavour. Sir Arthur Chichester, Lord Deputy of Ireland, opined that he would prefer to 'labor with his hands in the Plantation of Ulster than dance or play in that of Virginia'.[2] For many peers, the nascent colonies of Virginia and Bermuda were little more than expensive kindergartens for young English gentry excited by the prospects of piracy and emulating the fame of Sir Walter Raleigh. For others, the Atlantic offered economic and social advancement or religious freedom. Ireland was by far the most economically developed of these colonial prospects. The key difference between the colonial management of Ireland and England's fledgling dominions further afield was that the English state decided to govern its Irish realm directly, leaving the new colonies in the private hands of entrepreneurial speculators and their patrons, drawn from a cast of ambitious peers.[3]

The rise of tobacco as a cash crop in Virginia and parts of the Caribbean in the 1620s drew the English Atlantic colonies and plantation Ireland closer together. Tobacco, being a highly labour intensive crop, could not be serviced entirely with imported English labour. As some colonial investors owned plantations both in Ireland and in Virginia, and a small group of New English planters resident in Ireland also invested in the Atlantic colonies, it seemed natural to turn to Ireland to fill the gap as the demand for labour intensified in the 1620s.[4] The Virginia colony was nearly wiped out by a massacre of the colonists by the local Powhatan Indians in March 1622, exacerbating the labour shortage. Almost bankrupt, the Virginia Company, the regional patentee, invited new investors and called the opportunity, launched in London on 4 July 1623, 'the Adventure for Necessary Supplies for Virginia'.[5] An obscure London merchant, Maurice Thomson, had subscribed £70 to this fund and he travelled to Virginia to manage the grant of land that this money had purchased on behalf of the consortium of investors. The lead investor was Edward Bennett, a substantial London merchant, the Virginia Company's largest investor and the major shipper of tobacco from the colony.[6] Thomson's role, in addition to managing his own small plantation, was to act as Edward Bennett's agent in Virginia. Representing both a vital new investment to secure the future of the colony, and its largest customer, Maurice Thomson disembarked at Richmond, Virginia early in 1624, complaining of poor rations and a difficult crossing.[7]

Thomson already had excellent connections in the barely viable colony. His sister Mary was married to Captain William Tucker, the Virginia colony's Captain-General.[8] Tucker, like Thomson, had his own estate and was the local agent for another powerful patron, one of the Virginia Company's leading critics, Sir Nathaniel Rich.[9] Between them, while the Virginia Company was fighting for its existence in London, the brothers-in-law Maurice Thomson and William Tucker represented the company's largest investor and its greatest critic, respectively. When the bankrupt company was dissolved in 1624 they were in a unique position to profit from the future development of the colony. Widely regarded in the colony as its saviour during the Powhatan uprising, in June 1623 Tucker had organised a peace conference between the Indians and the colonists in order to avoid another massacre. Having observed that the Powhatans performed a tea ceremony at the start of such a conference, Tucker poisoned their tea, killing 200 Indian delegates.[10] While achieving a short-term military goal, this action ended any hope that the colony, if it survived, would be able to attract labour from the indigenous population. Virginia ceased to expand its territory through trade and reverted to the Elizabethan model of colonial expansion used in Ireland, extending its borders through military conquest. From 1623 until Tucker's final departure for England in 1640, the colony continued under Tucker's style of military rule.

In another role, William Tucker was also the factor in Virginia for Daniel Gookin, the business manager of Richard Boyle, earl of Cork. Gookin migrated to Virginia in 1621 but returned frequently to Ireland and England to oversee other parts of Boyle's business empire.[11] Daniel Gookin was very active as a transporter of servants, cattle and other supplies from Munster to Virginia and he assembled an estate in Virginia of several hundred acres.[12] Gookin's servants suffered a particularly high mortality rate and out of all of those he had shipped to Virginia, there were only seven men alive by June 1623.[13] These deaths do not appear to have harmed Gookin financially, and he made use of Boyle's contacts in Bristol to build ships of his own, specifically to service the colonial trade.[14] Gookin sent out at least one ship each year, delivering, on alternate years, servants and cattle.[15] The three factors, Tucker, Thomson and Gookin, made real the colonial aspirations of their respective patrons, the leading New English earl in Ireland, the London-based peers and the English merchant elite.

Early investments in colonial development were largely financed by the English merchant elite, usually members of major trading companies in London who could afford some additional small and very risky speculations. Lesser merchants such as Maurice Thomson had to personally transplant themselves in order to get a foothold in the colonies. Either through lack of interest or lack of confidence in a financial return, the grand merchants left the further development of the Atlantic colonies to a cohort with more modest means, including Maurice Thomson and his associates, who used their expertise in shipping to assist colonial patentees in the peerage to exploit their newly awarded territories. In parallel, and quite distinct from the men who made their money predominantly from trade and shipping, a separate class of investors known as planters or undertakers emerged. These investors, who specialised in the agricultural development of plantations, entered the Virginia and Irish land markets in large numbers in the 1620s. It was common for British undertakers to have investments in both Ireland and Virginia.[16] One, Sir Edward Blaney of Monaghan, a Welsh planter who settled in Ireland, transported 153 men and 50 'maids and young woemen' from Ireland to Virginia in 1621.[17] The servants were worth 150 pounds of tobacco each upon delivery. In the absence of any regulation, trade of this kind around the peripheries of England's dominions escaped the attention of colonial administrators at the centre, freeing both the patentees and agents to develop the colonies as they saw fit.

On 15 July 1624, the bankrupt Virginia Company was finally dissolved by Charles I and a royal commission was set up, reporting to the Privy Council, to manage the affairs of the struggling Virginia colony.[18] As disappointed investors tried to recoup some of their losses, Maurice Thomson took advantage of the confusion to acquire with William Claiborne, a future key partner in his American activities, a large tract of land known as Blunt Point.[19] Now a major landowner, Thomson returned to England in 1626 leaving his brothers, George and William, who had been transported as children to Virginia as William Tucker's indentured servants, to manage what was now one of Virginia's largest estates. These developments took place under the watchful eyes of the Rich cousins, Sir Nathaniel Rich and Robert Rich, earl of Warwick, the most senior aristocratic family fully engaged in colonial matters. The earl of Warwick had spent the early 1620s mainly at sea, managing his interests in Bermuda and Virginia, while Sir Nathaniel Rich spent much of the year 1622 in Ireland surveying the state of England's plantations. While in Ireland, Sir Nathaniel Rich acquired a deeper understanding of Irish demographics and got to know the New English plantation owners, including the earl of Cork. Sir Nathaniel Rich also dabbled in Irish land investments and loaned £3,000 on the Dublin Staple to Hubert Dillon to enable Dillon to purchase a 350-acre estate in County Longford.[20] With first-hand experience of the Atlantic colonies, the earl of Warwick returned to London in 1624 and was appointed to a royal commission for 'settling the government of Virginia'. Edward Bennett, Thomson's patron, was part of a consortium of merchant grandees competing against a faction led by Sir Nathaniel Rich to gain control of the Virginia Company assets as the company was in the process of being dissolved.[21] Thomson's fortunate connections to both groups – to the Rich cousins through William Tucker and to his own patron, Bennett – left him in an ideal position to broker deals between the factions deciding the future of the colony. One of the first decisions of the Virginia commission was to approve Thomson and Claiborne's land purchase.

Through William Tucker, Maurice Thomson had forged connections with the upper levels of Virginia society and the inner circle of the earl of Warwick's colonial agents. These connections enabled Thomson to explore opportunities in other colonial theatres. Tucker's cousin, Daniel Tucker, was another important figure in the development of England's early colonies. Daniel had started his colonial career as the commercial factor for the Virginia Company's first ever voyage, that of the *Nicholas* in February 1606.[22] He lived in Virginia, on and off, until 1616 when he was promoted to the post of governor of the earl of Warwick's Bermuda colony, the first colony to achieve modest commercial success. In the commercial vacuum created by the implosion of the Virginia Company, and with their high-level connections, all Thomson and Tucker required to expand their colonial trade was capital. When he returned to London, therefore, Thomson set about developing a friendship with Nicholas Corsellis, a London brewer and emerging financier from a wealthy

Anglo-Dutch family. Corsellis was a member of St Augustine's, an outpost of the Dutch reformed church in London.[23] The Corsellis family invested in voyages of the EEIC and through them Thomson was introduced to London's Puritan brethren and their community of ship-owning merchants. Nicholas Corsellis also had Irish interests, and provided loans to Richard Preston, earl of Desmond.[24] A network emerged in the 1620s, connecting the New English planters in Ireland and their counterparts in America with London's emerging colonial merchants and their sources of finance. This network was to grow both in strength and importance over the next decade.

In its early years the Virginia colony was a very small and tightly knit community. The population of the colony during Maurice Thomson's stay was tiny, growing from almost 1,000 people in 1619 to just 1,277 in 1624. This was despite the influx of 5,000 new arrivals during this time: diseases contracted during the crossing and low immunities to pathogens in the New World exacted a heavy toll on the immigrants.[25] The social structure of the small colony was, by necessity, far less stratified than in England, enabling connections to be made that would simply not have been possible at home. A remarkable concentration of future English parliamentarians and their relatives passed through Virginia, or lived there, in the mid-1620s.[26] It was in Virginia, among this cohort, that Maurice Thomson designed the money-making machine that formed the basis of his first fortune: the transport of servants in return for land or tobacco. Following the establishment of tobacco as Virginia's only viable cash crop, the colony began to import indentured servants for farm labour on a large scale. The farm gate price of tobacco in the early 1620s was three shillings per pound, and a labourer could produce 250lb, or £37 worth of tobacco per year. Labourers, who cost just £10 each to ship, would normally be expected to work for no pay for at least four years, with additional years to cover their upkeep. In theory, they were then freed and given a small grant of land on the edge of the colony. On paper, this arrangement was highly profitable for the planter, but the high mortality rate – 50% in the first year and over 70% by the end of the fourth – required a constant supply of new servants. The typical lading for a supply ship to the American colonies comprised a small cargo of manufactured goods and about 100 servants, so even the small migration of 5,000 people to Virginia in the early 1620s required fifty voyages.[27] In addition to the sale price of servants at the quayside, their conveyors received an additional fifty acres of undeveloped land for each delivered person. This system encouraged the shippers to ensure that the servants survived the crossing. In Virginia, however, there was no great incentive for the planters to keep their servants alive until the completion of their service. Once a servant had achieved freedom, there was a risk they would set up in competition with their former master. While the plantation owners were wrestling with these calculations, or perhaps with their consciences, the faster the servants died the more profits were to be made in shipping replacements. The servant transport business did so well that William Tucker's will, written in October 1642 before he left on a diplomatic mission to Ireland, mentioned 9,000 acres of land in Virginia, awarded for importing 180 servants.[28]

In the second half of the 1620s migration into Virginia accelerated and the price of tobacco plummeted, setting off a consumption boom for the addictive and now far cheaper commodity.[29] Tobacco became fashionable and was consumed at all levels of society in England and Ireland by the 1630s. The fall in price did not necessarily mean that the cultivation of tobacco was less profitable. Increases in productivity caused by larger plantations, land clearing, better plant husbandry and reduced shipping costs all contributed to the ability of the planters to produce tobacco more efficiently. The consumption of tobacco in England increased from 100,000lb per year in 1620 to 28,000,000lb per year by 1660.[30] Not all of this tobacco could be grown in Virginia and much was sourced from other English colonies in the Caribbean, and from Dutch and from Spanish merchants when they could offer the commodity at a good price.[31] In Virginia, from 1630 until at least 1636, Maurice Thomson, in partnership with another London merchant, Thomas Stone, held a contract to market the entire crop.[32] To ensure compliance with this arrangement, William Tucker was appointed to 'supervise' the Virginia crop.[33] Tucker also owned the colony's general store, which sold incoming manufactured goods from England. As the principal currency used to purchase goods at the store was tobacco, the Thomson, Tucker and Stone consortium effectively monopolised all of Virginia's import and export trade in the early 1630s. They expanded the trade far beyond the London market and by February 1631 George Thomson, Maurice's brother, had joined a consortium that was also shipping thousands of pounds of tobacco directly to England's western harbours, to the Netherlands and to Ireland.[34]

Maurice Thomson's next venture took him to Southampton where he chartered three ships to purchase sixty slaves in West Africa for transport to St Kitts in the Caribbean.[35] In 1618, James I had granted a patent to a consortium led by the earl of Warwick to trade for gold and other goods on the Guinea coast and at the Bight of Benin.[36] As little gold was forthcoming in the first couple of years, Thomson was tasked with exploiting the patent by bringing slaves to the new Caribbean colonies.[37] St Kitts already had a large population of Catholic Irish indentured labourers who had been forcibly transplanted from Wexford by Sir Arthur Chichester to make way for incoming English settlers in the 1620s.[38] The Irish labourers were removed to the neighbouring island of Nevis. Thomson's commercial partner in the St Kitts venture was Thomas Combes, an experienced planter who had fallen on hard times but who enjoyed a good relationship with James Hay, earl of Carlisle, who was by far the most important patentee in the Caribbean. In 1629, Hay acquired an exclusive patent from Charles I for all of the eastern islands in the Caribbean, from St Kitts to Barbados, for ten years.[39] Hay became as financially troubled as Combes and, unable to develop a colony himself, granted Thomson a patent for 1,000 acres on St Kitts in return for a loan. With Thomson's money, in 1630 James Hay secured the sole right to import goods into Ireland from the Caribbean, and tobacco production began on St Kitts in earnest.[40]

The St Kitts venture brought Maurice Thomson once again into the aristocratic world of Richard Boyle, earl of Cork, and his wide circle of Munster connections. Phane Beecher, for example, had been granted land in Cork by Elizabeth I in 1586 that was inherited by his eldest son, Henry.[41] Henry Beecher built the town of Bandon and sold it on to Richard Boyle in 1618.[42] A second son, Phane Beecher Jnr, left Ireland for St Kitts in 1627, as governor for a plantation financed entirely by New English settlers in Ireland.[43] Overall control of the Caribbean colonies nonetheless remained with the patentee peers in England. The governor-general of the Leeward Islands was Sir Thomas Warner, appointed by the earl of Carlisle in 1629. Warner's personal plantation was financed from London by a key new partnership comprising Maurice Thomson, William Pennoyer and Thomas Povey.[44] Carlisle's many Irish interests included a County Wicklow estate acquired in 1628 in partnership with an established English planter, Sir John Wolverstone.[45] Carlisle used this partnership to send captain Charles Wolverstone, a kinsman of Sir John, to Barbados in 1628. Wolverstone's task was to bring the island under Carlisle's control and oust the Caribbean expedition of Sir William Courteen, a favourite of Charles I, who claimed he had 'discovered' the island first.[46] The end result of these rather fluid arrangements was that the Thomson/Carlisle partnership enjoyed a near-monopoly over the tobacco trade between Ireland and England's American colonies during the early 1630s.

The tobacco trade led to ever closer ties between the Atlantic merchants and their customers in Munster, the Boyle family in particular. Francis Boyle, the son of the earl of Cork and future first Viscount Shannon, was the collector for customs for the port of Cork during these years of development and handled a large proportion of Irish tobacco imports.[47] Nevis, the island close to St Kitts in the Caribbean Antilles, became home to a very large population of indentured Irish labourers in the 1620s, partly as a result of the Warwick/Thomson experiment in slavery on St Kitts. The Nevis plantation was financed by a London-based cousin of the Thomson brothers, Edward Thomson.[48] When Nevis was attacked by a Spanish fleet in 1628, the Irish population was moved again to the nearby island of Montserrat, which boasted an almost entirely Irish population throughout the mid-seventeenth century.[49] This colony was governed by another English planter with Irish roots, Captain Anthony Briskett of Wexford who had moved on in the hope of richer rewards in the Caribbean. Avoiding London's oversight entirely, the Monserrat venture was financed from Virginia by a consortium led by George Thomson giving the Thomsons a major stake in the three islands in the group under English control.[50] From 1631, entire cargoes of Montserrat tobacco were sent by George Thomson to Virginia and these consignments were shipped on by George and Maurice to Cork, avoiding new customs regulations that stated that all Virginia-grown tobacco had to be shipped through London.[51] Given the quantities involved, it is almost impossible that tiny Montserrat produced all the tobacco that the Thomsons claimed to have been grown there. Instead, the arrangement facilitated the widespread smuggling of Virginia tobacco directly to Ireland. This profitable arrangement was not challenged by the earls of Carlisle, Cork or Warwick.

Colonial patentees among the peerage were content to let consortia of merchants manage commercial affairs overseas. With the notable exception of the entrepreneurial earl of Cork, who had risen to the peerage from the merchant community, peers in general were conservative managers of mostly inherited assets. Peers considered their colonial patents to be similar to their landed estates in England or Ireland; they exploited both through the sale of tenancies and the collection of rent. Trade, shipping and commercial finance were outside of their core areas of expertise and best left to specialist subcontractors. Enterprising merchants such as Daniel Gookin, William Tucker and Maurice Thomson, therefore, were left to manage the commercial aspects of the colonial interests of the earls of Cork, Warwick and Carlisle, respectively, in the wider Atlantic arena. As the colonial economies expanded, the contractors were fully aware of the profits to be made, but the peers were content to keep merely collecting their rents. Consequently, it was the merchant contractors who reaped most of the benefits from the first colonial economic boom. As the home markets of England and Ireland became addicted to colonial produce, the planter and servant population of small islands like Barbados exploded, increasing from 1,800 in 1630 to 14,000 in 1640, a similar population to the far larger Virginia and Massachusetts Bay territories. Unexpectedly, Barbados became a magnet for immigration and, with its booming tobacco and cotton plantations, was the intended destination for fully 20% of emigrants from London alone to the colonies.[52] The most widely accepted estimate is that 40,000 people migrated to the British Atlantic colonies between 1630 and 1640, and half of these intended to travel to the Caribbean plantations to take part in the tobacco rush.[53] Suddenly cash rich, the colonial contractors' successes gave them rare access to senior colonial patentees within the peerage, otherwise outside of their social reach. These peers, in turn, would become dependent on the merchants' financial and logistical resources to project their own colonial and political ambitions.

The earl of Warwick's Bermuda Company is a good example of how control of colonial profits passed from the gentry to the shippers to whom the everyday running of the colony was subcontracted. Bermuda was designed as a purely commercial enterprise, without the trappings of a Puritan utopia that characterised some of Warwick's other colonial projects. Warwick's Bermuda was a tobacco plantation that also served as a provisioning stop for transatlantic shipping and as a privateering station. The plantation business was a huge commercial success and Bermuda exported 70,000 pounds of tobacco in 1620, reaping significant profits before increased production in Virginia drove down the price. The initial investors recruited by Warwick in 1618 to develop his Bermuda patent were mainly gentlemen of his acquaintance.[54] By 1642, however, these original investors had been supplanted by a new group of investors almost entirely comprised of the rising colonial tobacco merchants, all of whom also put their money into in the Adventure for Irish land.[55] The Bermuda investors, taken over twenty years, mirror the increasing importance of merchants in Warwick's close circle and his willingness to subcontract his colonial projects to a small, trusted group. The original gentleman investors, entirely dependent on Warwick's contractors to ship their produce at reasonable rates, were ousted.

The earl of Warwick's other Caribbean project was Providence Island, now part of Colombia in the eastern Gulf of Mexico, and this was a very different colonial endeavour. The Providence Island colony existed from 1630 when it was established as a colonial Puritan haven until 19 May 1641 when the Spanish navy destroyed it. It was established under a royal charter by the Providence Island Company, whose members were mainly Puritan peers and their gentleman clients. These shareholders were the very people who made up the leadership of the radical parliamentarian faction that emerged in Westminster in 1642.[56] During the 1630s, the colony was little more than a privateering base from which to attack Spanish shipping in an unofficial war conducted against Spain by the company's promoters. On 25 February 1640 the Providence Island Company contracted with Maurice Thomson to manage the supply of the colony, and authorised him to attack Spanish shipping.[57] The contract was signed by Lord Brooke, viscount Saye-and-Sele, John Pym and Sir Benjamin Rudyard, and it recognised the naval resources then at Thomson's disposal. Maurice Thomson had become a key figure within the world of the Puritan peers, not just as a wealthy merchant but as a projector of naval power. By 1640, Thomson was so confident in his abilities to wreak havoc on Spanish targets that the Providence Island Company was charged only £80 for his services, as he expected to make ample profits from piracy. Providence Island was ideally located between the two main centres of Spanish silver production, Zacatecas in Mexico and the vast motherlode of Potosí in Peru.[58] Famously, a privateer employed by the Dutch West India Company, Piet Heyn, had captured the entire Spanish silver fleet, valued at 11.5 million guilders, in 1628.[59] Maurice Thomson and his partners hoped to repeat this feat and set up a sustained privateering operation on Providence Island. Eventually, these activities irritated the Spanish authorities to the extent that they were forced to extinguish the colony.

Maurice Thomson had spread his interests well beyond Warwick and Warwick's inner circle. Bolstered by his gains from the servant and tobacco trade, Thomson financed his own colonial projects in the 1630s, independently of a noble patron. The first was an unofficial colony, Kent Island in Chesapeake Bay, initiated in 1631.[60] It was a short-lived and contentious affair, but brought together a new group of merchants with interests in Ireland, Virginia, Canada and Scotland that became integrated with the Thomsons' trading network. The Kent Island project was instigated by William Tucker and William Claiborne, both of whom served on the Virginia council. They approached Thomson and William Cloberry, a colonial fur trader in London, with a view to establishing a fur, tobacco and provisioning centre on the island. Cloberry was an old business partner of Richard Boyle and had also financed Sir William Alexander's colonisation project in Nova Scotia in 1628.[61] With the financial backing of Thomson and Cloberry, Claiborne landed on the island in 1631 with a small group of settlers and built a trading post, ignoring the fact that Kent Island was part of a separate colonial patent, Maryland, granted to a Catholic peer, Cecil Calvert, Lord Baltimore, by Charles I.[62] Kent Island became the centre of a protracted dispute between the Virginia and Maryland colonies, including naval engagements in the waters of Chesapeake Bay, until the island was finally confirmed to Calvert's possession in 1638. Although the land grab was unsuccessful, the merchants, who were closely linked to the earls of Cork and Warwick and were probably protected by them, had staged an armed confrontation with a peer of the realm, albeit a Catholic with an Irish peerage. Distance from London was making the social order harder to maintain.

The negotiations over Kent Island brought the end of headright as a means to secure land in both Maryland and Virginia.[63] Using headright, a merchant could claim that because he had transported servants to an unclaimed patch of land, it became his. All Claiborne had to do, therefore, was to land servants on the island. Many of the old headright land parcels patented during the 1620s were completely deserted and Claiborne believed that if he repopulated them, he could claim them. To avoid further conflicts over land, formal letters patent were issued by the Virginia Council from the mid-1630s. This reform brought security of title and precipitated a further rapid expansion of the colony. The largest of these new grants, indeed the largest colonial grant of land awarded prior to the English Revolution, was the Berkeley Hundred, now Charles City County, Virginia, a plantation financed by the city of Gloucester and purchased by a Thomson-led consortium in 1637.[64] This welcome development, the issuing of secure titles for land to Virginian settlers, was mirrored in Ireland by Thomas Wentworth's Commission for Defective Titles. Much reviled at the time, and ever since, as a poorly disguised attempt by the Lord Deputy to raise badly needed cash for Charles I's shaky finances, this Commission created reliable new patents for most Protestant- and Catholic-owned Irish land. These patents, and the surveys commissioned by Wentworth that enabled them, would prove invaluable in facilitating the Irish land confiscations of the 1650s.

The importance of Virginia patentees and settlers to the future Adventure for Irish land during this period of colonial development cannot be overstated. In addition to the merchants mentioned above, thirty Adventurers for Irish land were previous emigrants to Virginia who returned to London prior to 1642.[65] The return of these colonists to England coincided with a renewed interest in Virginian affairs by Charles I and his Privy Council. From July 1624, when the Virginia Company was dissolved, until August 1641, the colony was supervised by the Virginia Commission, comprised mainly of Warwick and a cohort from the Fellowship of Merchant Adventurers who had little direct involvement in colonial trade and who took a rather casual approach to their supervisory duties.[66] On 12 August 1641 the Virginia Commission was recast in order that 'the said colony be regulated as well in ecclesiastical as temporal government'.[67] A new governor loyal to the king, Sir William Berkeley, was appointed and Maurice Thomson's partner, William Claiborne, was replaced as secretary of the colony by another reliable courtier, Richard Kemp.[68] These new arrangements threatened to disrupt the highly profitable business established by the independent tobacco merchants. The Puritan peers and their commercial partners therefore suffered two serious blows in quick succession: the loss of their potentially lucrative privateering operation on Providence Island and their actually lucrative tobacco monopoly in Virginia. There was in addition an outbreak of protests in Barbados, where Carlisle had raised rents to nearly unsustainable levels in 1639, causing many planters to sell up or leave.[69]

A thousand miles to the north, less plantation-orientated English colonies were taking shape on the shores of New England. The charter of New England, then styled North Virginia, was originally granted in 1620 by James I to a consortium led by the Dukes of Lennox and Buckingham, the earls of Pembroke, Southampton and Warwick, and James Hamilton, viscount Clandeboye. The charter was kept by Warwick and the venture was backed by some of London's leading merchants. Shares in the 'Adventurers of the Northern Colony of Virginia' cost £10 each and entitled the holders to land in the new colony, subject to a survey taking place within seven years.[70] There were seventy subscribers to these shares when the first colonists left England in the *Mayflower* on 6 September 1620 to found the Plymouth colony in Massachusetts Bay.[71] The original list of seventy subscribers has not survived, but a later list of the forty-two shareholders remaining in 1626 is extant.[72] In the context of the Adventure for Irish land, the most significant investors in the *Mayflower* mission were the brothers Thomas and Richard Andrews. Thomas Andrews would later act as the treasurer for the Irish Adventure and was a key figure in parliamentary finance. The celebrated 'Mayflower Compact' of 1620, under which the colonists decided to distribute land equally between themselves, was unacceptable to the investors in London and the Northern Colony adventure was dissolved. The Northern Colony's assets were taken over by the newly formed Massachusetts Bay Company with Richard Andrews at its head in London.[73]

A second northern company, the New England Company, was launched in 1628. The earl of Warwick, again, was president of its governing council but avoided recruiting peers to participate in its administration. The subscribers of the New England Company were instead dominated by Puritan merchants led by Richard Saltonstall, Isaac Johnson, Samuel Aldersey and John Venn. The subscribers were wealthy London merchants interested in developing a religious community rather than a plantation with an obvious route to profits. Of the original thirty-six, thirteen investors (or their sons) became Adventurers for Irish land, associated with Warwick rather than as members of colonial trading partnerships.[74] The first governor of the colony was John Winthrop I, who had strong Irish connections. His uncle, also John Winthrop, settled in Kilcolman, County Cork, in 1596 and was a witness to the deed by which Richard Boyle was originally assigned Sir Walter Raleigh's Munster estate in 1602.[75] This transaction established Boyle as a major landowner and enabled his rise to the peerage. In 1622, while Sir Nathaniel Rich was also in residence, Winthrop I visited Dublin to invest in a plantation in Mountrath, County Laois, with Emmanuel Downing, father of the diplomat George Downing, and enrolled his son John Winthrop II at Trinity College Dublin.[76] Emmanuel Downing later became a partner in a fur trading project with Maurice Thomson and William Cloberry.[77]

Warwick next attempted to establish his own Puritan colony without troubling himself to form a company and acquire a charter from the king. Using the Kent Island approach of simply moving onto land, Warwick created the 'Warwick patent' in April 1632, which pretended a claim to most of modernday Connecticut. The 'patent' had no legal basis, but Warwick assumed the right to make direct grants of land to his closest associates.[78] As the investors in Warwick's scheme had much in common with the shareholders in the Providence Island Company, it can be inferred that the contractors used to develop the colony were also drawn from the same stock. The Trinity College Dublin educated John Winthrop II, a preacher who had spent time in the Netherlands, Emmanuel Downing's brother-in-law Hugh Peter, and Sir Henry Vane II travelled together to Massachusetts as employees of Warwick's patentees with instructions to oust any Dutch settlers and to build fortifications.[79] It was an odd move, as Warwick was on perfectly good terms with the promoters of the other New England settlements, but perhaps the pace of development was too slow for the ambitious earl. A more hard-headed approach using Providence Island Company backers and tobacco merchants from further south may have had the potential to develop a viable colony faster than the idealistic Plymouth colonists had managed.

In 1634, John Winthrop II travelled to Ireland and spent Christmas in Ulster with Sir John Clotworthy at his castle in Antrim. Clotworthy was in the process of assembling one of the richest estates in plantation Ulster. They discussed New England at great length and agreed that the future of the colony could best be secured with a 'transmission of yonge children' and an infusion of Clotworthy's sheep and cattle. Winthrop travelled on to London and he next heard from Clotworthy again by way of a coded letter dated 6 March 1635, the cipher of which was kept by a London goldsmith, Francis Allein. Sir John Clotworthy made good on his promise for cattle, sheep and children and asked for a ship to be sent to Ireland to collect them.[80] Secrecy was required as the conspirators were reasonably sure that their transaction was illegal, and Clotworthy signed off with this cryptic message: 'those who are not strong in frinds had neede walk very streightly, for thers nothing falls to the ground'. A final coded communication from Clotworthy was received by Winthrop II in April 1635 advising that, as export of sheep and cattle from Ulster had been banned, he would be unable to provide very many but the partners continued to put plans in place to transport children.[81] Clotworthy attempted to export these children the following year, despatching 140 passengers from Carrickfergus to New England on 9 September 1636 in a locally built vessel, the *Eagle*. The mast broke in heavy seas shortly into the journey and the ship had to turn back, thus ending Sir John Clotworthy's first attempt at people smuggling.[82] Both Sir Henry Vane II and John Winthrop II later became governors of the combined colonies in Massachusetts, while the lands of the Warwick 'patent' were absorbed into the Massachusetts Bay Company in March 1639, having failed to attract any settlers. Although Warwick's plantation failed, he had brought his Caribbean contractors into the New England arena where they promptly set to work. Maurice Thomson had far more expertise in the servant trade than his predecessors and delivered 180 people to New England on a single voyage in May 1638.[83] In May 1639, he set up a small fishing plantation at Cape Ann, Massachusetts, in partnership with John Winthrop II and two additional partners, John Humphrey and William Pierce, Londoners who would become Adventurers in Irish land.[84]

The Massachusetts Bay Company's territory was centred on Boston, south of the New England Company's tract.[85] Once again, the subscriptions came entirely from the merchant class and a £50 investment included an automatic entitlement to a grant of 200 acres of land. This was an important innovation in the context of the Adventure for Irish land as the amount of money invested, not headright, was used as the basis for determining entitlements to land.[86] In economic terms the New England colony proved unsuccessful, yet it continued to attract colonists in search of religious freedom.[87] Colonists were also encouraged by a more familiar climate that resulted in a far lower initial mortality rate than in the southern colonies. Outward migration continued until the late 1630s when the pattern reversed as Puritans, emboldened by events in their home country and the rise of their leaders to positions of influence, began to return home. This process reached a peak in 1641–42 when fourteen of the 114 university-trained men residing in New England left the colonies.[88] The simultaneous migration of both Virginians and New Englanders back to London, in 1641–42, synthesised the commercial and religious groups into one. What both groups had in common was the ambitious colonial peer, Robert Rich the earl of Warwick, and his contractors led by Maurice Thomson.

At the northernmost extremity of the British Atlantic world, the Nova Scotia project attracted English and Scottish planters to develop the region's rich cod fisheries. Many of these investors were already involved in plantation schemes in Connacht and Ulster. Echoing the experience of these investors, early colonial Nova Scotia was structured differently to New England or Virginia and modelled closely on the Ulster plantation of 1609. Each Nova Scotia undertaker was required to send out six skilled men, pay 2,000 marks to the king and 1,000 marks to Sir William Alexander, the principal patentee, in return for the honour of a baronetcy. For Alexander, this was a scheme to make some money quickly. He hoped to repeat the success of James I and VI who sold Ulster baronetcies to 215 English gentlemen for a total of £225,000 in 1613.[89] In 1642, the Adventure for Irish land would offer a similar incentive of a baronetcy in return for a substantial investment. The designers of the Adventure for Irish land incorporated the most successful elements of England's major Atlantic colonies into the Adventurers Act of 1642: the large subscriber base of the Virginia Company, the simple land-for-cash tradition of Massachusetts Bay and the baronetcy honour, borrowed from the Ulster plantation and used successfully in Nova Scotia.

The distinguishing commercial feature of these widely dispersed colonies is that there was no controlling monopoly company, in the mould of the English East India and Levant Companies or the Dutch West Indies Company. This created a space in which unlicensed merchants could operate, building up a huge trade shipping colonists and provisions to the Americas in return for tobacco, timber and other goods sold both in England and throughout Europe. In August 1641 John Pym had been asked by parliament to explore the possibility of establishing such a company, but as the best Pym could suggest was that the colonies should be incorporated into the Providence Island Company, no further progress was made on this issue.[90] With no formally chartered company, an oligopoly had been created under Warwick's supervision and the earl controlled the resources of what was in fact a major enterprise, an English West India Company in all but name.

The commercial network that ran England's colonial enterprises, a small clique of peers, their favoured contractors and the major investors in plantations and plantation companies, comprised a close and interconnected group. Below them on the commercial ladder, but far more numerous, was a fluid contingent of ship-owners, wholesalers and customers for colonial and other imported commodities. Throughout the 1630s most colonial exports were bartered for manufactured goods brought from England. The Atlantic shipping agents became both major suppliers to London and other markets and key customers for finished goods for the return trip. Ralph Davis has estimated that the English merchant fleet comprised 150,000 tons of merchant shipping in 1640, representing £1,950,000 in capital.[91] The merchants were spending £200,000 per year just to maintain the long-distance merchant fleet, far greater than a contemporary estimate of just £30,000 per year to maintain the navy.[92] Despite bitter protests over the raising of larger amounts of ship money, a tax imposed by Charles I to finance his fleet without calling a parliament, the development of the naval resources of the state continued to be outpaced by the merchants' expanding long-distance fleet. This private navy was controlled by colonial, Levant and other long-distance merchants but ownership of the vessels was spread among a much wider group. To manage the risks associated with long distance commerce, most ships were leased or owned by a separate consortium of merchants for each expedition and this obliged them to cooperate on long-term projects.[93] Selling shares in individual voyages spread the risk and discouraged monopolistic behaviour. It was an approach that worked well in any risky but capital-intensive area of commerce, such as military supply. As the 1630s progressed, the colonial merchants ceased to confine their activities to the Atlantic and attacked markets closer to home, using the skills they had developed in pooled finance. As these relationships became firmer, business connections transformed into potent political alliances.

Charles I had built up an impressive network of internal monopolies during the period of personal rule, from 1629 to 1640. The monopolies were trade concessions sold to groups of individuals that were previously held by the London Companies. Although the licensees were normally drawn from London Company members, as they had the necessary expertise to make a success of their new franchises, the effect of the new arrangements was to reduce the commercial and political power of the London Companies. In addition, as licences were normally granted on a national basis, the licensees were no longer restricted to London and could exercise their monopoly throughout the kingdom. This new and less restrictive form of licensing allowed the more entrepreneurial merchants to develop provincial networks, either at the expense of or in partnership with the local incumbent. The king's revenue from internal monopolies proved significant: the wine monopoly brought in £30,000 per annum, tobacco and soap £13,050 and £30,825 respectively. Profits from the more lucrative monopolies enticed Charles to become directly involved in trade and he offered to capitalise the Pin-makers Company with £10,000 when he renewed their charter in 1640 to become a shareholder. This licensing system was governed, overall, by the whims of a capricious monarch and his parlous finances. Solely to raise money, several licences were recalled in 1639, including monopolies for collecting fines levied on the transgressors of the new trade monopolies. These licences were reassigned to court favourites. In 1637, Charles granted the Irish tobacco monopoly to his greatest supporter, Thomas Wentworth, Lord Lieutenant of Ireland, stripping the earls of Carlisle and Cork of the lucrative business they had spent several years developing.[94] Compounding the loss in actual trade, the arbitrariness of the licensing system rendered the trade concessions worthless as they could be recalled at any time. Charles's random interventions were at odds with the structured Atlantic trading system developed by Carlisle, Cork and Warwick although, for a short time, business continued as usual for the Atlantic merchants.

As 1641 drew to a close, and as Warwick and his associates suffered both the loss of Providence Island and the restructuring of the government of Virginia, Charles was also considering rationalising the multiple companies and claims to territory in New England under a single patentee, the royal favourite Sir Fernandino Gorges.[95] This move threatened the entire Atlantic project, targeting the Puritan colonies as well as the commercial plantations. For the colonial merchants in particular, Charles's belated interest in his Atlantic dominions posed a considerable threat. The merchants had comfortable dealings with their aristocratic patrons and had developed a considerable amount of mutual trust, but they had few friends in the court of Charles I. In fact, relations were so poor between the Privy Council and the Atlantic merchants that Maurice Thomson was imprisoned in 1632 for infringing on an Anglo-French treaty that defined the two kingdoms' borders in Canada, refusing to either apologise to the Privy Council or to pay a fine. He was committed to the Marshalsea prison in London for six months.[96] The generally strained relations between the king, an assertive group of peers and their merchant clients would not survive the shock of events closer to home.

NOTES

1 BL, Lansdowne Ms 156, A Volume containing a very large Collection of Treasury Papers (1432–1618), f. 261, 'An advise for Ireland', 19 December 1607.
2 Chichester is quoted by Karl S. Bottigheimer in *English Money and Irish Land* (Oxford, 1971), p. 17.
3 See Bottigheimer, pp. 1–29.

4 Library of Virginia, Colonial Records Project, Survey Report No. 1106/291, No. 291: 'A Note of the shipping, Men and Provisions sent and provided for Virginia, by the Right Honourable, the earl of Southampton, and the Company, this year 1620…Two ships with 100 kine on board to sail from Ireland'.
5 Susan Myra Kingsbury, *The Records of the Virginia Company of London*, 4 vols (Washington, DC, 1906), vol. 1, p. 245. This Adventure raised a total of £1,290. Thomson was only a minor investor but was interested in migrating to Virginia, probably on foot of his family connection. Most of the other investors, Rowland Truelove, William Feldgate, John Godson, etc., were involved in merchant shipping.
6 Library of Virginia, Colonial Records Project, Survey Report No. 1106/291, No. 402: 'Petition of John Bargrave to the Lord Treasurer'. Edward Bennett and his brothers owned 1,500 acres of land in Virginia. Bennett was also deputy governor of the Merchant Adventurers in Delft in the 1620s. His son, Richard Bennett, took over the management of the Virginia Estate in 1625. It is unlikely that Thomson had the capital at this stage of his career to qualify as an investor in The Adventure for Necessary Supplies. He was more likely to have been acting as an agent for the Bennetts who sought to acquire some land outside of the control of the troubled Virginia Company. Lothrop Withington, *Virginia Gleanings in England* (Baltimore, MD, 1980), p. 448); Martha W. MacCartney, *Virginia Immigrants and Adventurers 1607-35: A Biographical Dictionary* (Baltimore, MD, 2007), p. 123.
7 H.R. McIlwaine (ed.), *Minutes of the Colonial and General Court of Colonial Virginia 1622-1632, 1670-1676* (Richmond, 1974), p. 54.
8 Kingsbury, *Records of the Virginia Company*, vol. 1, pp. 441-442.
9 MacCartney, *Virginia Immigrants*, p. 109.
10 MacCartney, *Virginia Immigrants*, pp. 221-222.
11 McIlwaine, *Minutes of the Colonial and General Court*, p. 30.
12 Gookin shipped regularly from Cork to Virginia. In August 1624 he invested £400 in building and fitting out his own vessel, the *Mary Providence of Cork*, to service this trade. See John C. Appleby (ed.), *Calendar of Material Relating to Ireland from the High Court of Admiralty Examinations 1536-1641* (Dublin, 1992), p. 152.
13 Kingsbury, *Records of the Virginia Company*, vol. 1, p. 229.
14 Appleby, *Calendar of Material*, p. 152.
15 Aubrey Gwynn, 'Documents Relating to the Irish in the West Indies', *Analecta Hibernia*, 4 (October, 1932), pp. 162-166.
16 Irish planters Humphrey Allen, Thomas Flowerdew, Sir Henry Pierce and Lt. Charles Pointz invested as did the families of William Barker, Robert Cartwright, Sir Robert Heiborne, Walter Hodges, Sir John Kingsmill, Sir George Mainwaring, Gabriel Throgmorton and Oliver St John. See Victor Treadwell (ed.), *The Irish Commission of 1622: An Investigation of the Irish Administration 1615-22 and its Consequences 1623-24* (Dublin, 2006) and Kingsbury, *Records of the Virginia Company*, vol. 1, both *passim*.
17 Frank E. Grizzard and D. Boyd Smith, *Jamestown Colony, a Political, Social and Cultural History* (Santa Barbara, CA, 2007), p. 31.
18 W. Noel Sainsbury (ed.), *Calendar of State Papers Colonial, America and West Indies*, 1, 1574-1660 (London, 1860), pp. 63-69: America and West Indies: July 1624.

19 Kingsbury, *Records of the Virginia Company*, vol. 1, p. 557. The Blunt Point patentees included Sir Francis Wyatt, governor of the colony.
20 Jane Ohlmeyer and Éammonn Ó Ciarda (eds.), *The Irish Statute Staple Books, 1596-1687* (Dublin, 1998), pp. 139, 208; Treadwell, *Irish Commission of 1622*, pp. 661, 659.
21 Robert Brenner, *Merchants and Revolution* (Princeton, NJ, 1993), p. 102.
22 David B. Quinn and Alison M. Quinn (eds), *The English New England Voyages 1602-1608* (London, 1983), pp. 360-363. The voyage was unsuccessful and Tucker and his ship were arrested by a Spanish fleet and brought, inadvertently, to Bordeaux. The enterprising Daniel Tucker convinced the French authorities to arrest the Spanish vessels and return his ship to him along with some compensation seized from the Spanish.
23 Brenner, *Merchants and Revolution*, p. 176.
24 P.A. Penfold (ed.), *Acts of the Privy Council of England Volume 46, 1630-1631* (London, 1964), pp. 386-387.
25 Christopher Tomlins, *Freedom Bound: Law, Labour, and Civic Identity in Colonizing English America, 1580-1865* (Cambridge, 2010), p. 25.
26 The tiny Virginia colony in 1622 also included a significant number of future investors in the Adventure for Irish land, or their close kinsmen: John Rolfe, John Johnson, John Carter, Thomas Willoughby, Edward Hill and the kinsmen of John Arundel, Matthew Biggs, Thomas Cole, Roger Matthews, Henry Featherstone, Edward Brewster, Thomas Hutchins, William Hobson and Thomas May. It was the home to the kinsmen of many names familiar to students of the Wars of the Three Kingdoms, Fleetwood, Fairfax and Waller to name but a few. See Library of Congress, *Jefferson Papers, Series 8 Virginia Papers 1606-1687*, Volume 7, Virginia Company of London, Court Book 1619-22, Part A, ff. 104-105.
27 Russell R. Menard, 'The Tobacco Industry in the Chesapeake Colonies, 1617-1730: An Interpretation', *Research in Economic History*, 5 (1980), pp. 107-177, p. 157; Henry A. Gemery, 'Emigration from the British Isles to the New World: 1630-1700: References from Colonial Populations', *Research in Economic History*, 5 (1980), pp. 179-231, p. 211; Ralph Davis, *The Rise of the English Shipping Industry in the Seventeenth and Eighteenth Centuries* (Newton Abbot, 1962), p. 198.
28 Norma Tucker, *Colonial Virginians and Their Maryland Relatives* (Baltimore, MD, 1994), p. 17.
29 Menard, 'Tobacco Industry', p. 157.
30 Menard, 'Tobacco Industry', p. 158.
31 Christian J. Koot, *Empire at the Periphery: British Colonists, Anglo-Dutch Trade, and the Development of the British Atlantic, 1621-1713* (London, 2011), pp. 38-40.
32 TNA PC 2/9 1633 May 1 - 1634 May 30, f. 27, 'A warrant as follows directed to Sir John Harvey KT, Governor in Virginia, the rest of the council and to all others whom it may concern'. Opposition to the monopoly was led by William and Thomas Willoughby whose own plantation was forced to sell their crop to Thomson.
33 Tucker, *Colonial Virginians*, p. 13.
34 Appleby, *Calendar of Material*, p. 197.
35 Brenner, *Merchants and Revolution*, p. 127.

36 William Robert Scott, *The Constitution and Finance of English, Scottish and Irish Joint Stock Companies to 1720*, 3 vols (Cambridge, 1910), Vol. 1, p. 19.
37 For the African gold trade see Toby Green, *A Fistful of Shells, West Africa from the Rise of the Slave Trade to the Age of Revolution* (London, 2019), pp. 108–148.
38 Gwynn, 'Documents Relating to the Irish', p. 159. Chichester's distaste for the Americas did not preclude him from selling Irish captives for transportation there.
39 H.T. Barlow (ed.), *Colonising Expeditions to the West Indies and Guana 1623-67* (London, 1925), p. 31.
40 James Morin (ed.), *Calendar of the Patent and Close Rolls of Ireland, Chancery, Charles I, I to VIII* (London, 1863), p. 553.
41 Michael MacCarthy-Morrogh, *The Munster Plantation: English Migration to Southern Ireland, 1583-1641* (Oxford, 1986), p. 253.
42 Vincent Gookin, an uncle of Daniel, was originally a tenant of Beecher before the transfer to Boyle.
43 Barlow, *Colonising Expeditions*, pp. 4–5.
44 Carl and Roberta Bridenbaugh, *The Antilles and the Spanish Main* (New York, 1972), p. 130.
45 Bridenbaugh and Bridenbaugh, *The Antilles*, p. 399.
46 Roy Schrieber, 'The First Carlisle, Sir James Hay, First Earl of Carlisle as Courtier, Diplomat and Entrepreneur, 1580–1636', *Transactions of the American Philosophical Society*, 74:7 (1984), pp. 1–202, p. 172. Courteen turned his attention to breaking into the India trade, setting up in business with Gregory Clement, a regular partner of the Thomsons, John Foulke, a future leader in parliamentary finance, and William Cloberry, a Virginia planter (Brenner, *Merchants and Revolution*, p. 173). For a discussion on Courteen and his pretended proprietorship of Barbados see Gary Puckrein, 'Did Sir William Courteen Really Own Barbados', *Huntington Library Quarterly*, 44:2 (Spring, 1981), pp. 135–149.
47 Morin, *Patent and Close Rolls of Ireland*, p. 541.
48 Brenner, *Merchants and Revolution*, p. 185.
49 Natalie A. Zacek, *Settler Society in the English Leeward Islands 1630-1676* (Cambridge, 2010), p. 1634.
50 Brenner, *Merchants and Revolution*, p. 129.
51 Appleby, *Calendar of Material*, p. 152.
52 Russell R. Menard, *Sweet Negotiations: Sugar, Slavery and Plantation Agriculture in Early Barbados* (Charlottsville, VA, 2006), p. 25.
53 Gemery, 'Emigration', p. 204.
54 Brenner, *Merchants and Revolution*, pp. 369–372. The Adventurers in the Bermuda Company in the 1630s included John Dike, Abraham Chamberlain, Robert Smith, Richard Rogers and Martin Bond, the father of Denis Bond MP. The Company Secretary was William Jessop.
55 TNA CO1/10, f. 10 'A Declaration of the Right Honourable Robert Earl of Warwick… Governour of the Company of London for the Plantation of the Summer Islands'. Adventurers in Bermuda by 1643 included Francis Allein, John Johnson, Sir Gilbert Gerard, Richard Castell, Thomas Alcock, Elias Roberts, Maurice Thomson, Richard Hunt, Gabriel Barber and Richard Castell. Thomas Allen was treasurer of the company.

56 For a comprehensive narrative of the Providence Island colony see Karen Ordahl Kupperman, *Providence Island, 1630–1641: The Other Puritan Colony* (Cambridge, 1993). The company shareholders were: William Ball, Gabriel Barbour, Thomas Barnardiston, Sir Thomas Barrington, Godfrey Bosvile, MP, Sir Thomas Cheeke, MP, Henry Darley, MP, John Dyke, James Fiennes, MP, William Fiennes, viscount Saye-and-Sele, MP, Gregory Gawsell, Sir Gilbert Gerard, MP, John Graunt, Lord Brooke, John Gurdon, MP, Sir Edward Harwood, Richard Knightley, MP, John Michell, Edward Montague (earl of Manchester), Sir Edmond Moundeford, MP, John Pym, MP, Henry Rich, MP, Sir Nathaniel Rich, MP, Robert Rich, earl of Warwick, Lord Robartes, Sir Benjamin Rudyerd, MP, Sir Oliver St. John, MP, Christopher Sherland MP, Thomas Symons, John Upton, MP, Sir William Waller, MP, William Woodcock, William Jessop (Sec.).
57 TNA CO 124/2, Book of Entries of the Governor and Company of Adventurers for the Plantation of the Island of Providence, f. 155 'Articles of Agreement…'.
58 Richard L. Garner, 'Long-Term Silver Mining Trends in Spanish America: A Comparative Analysis of Peru and Mexico', *American Historical Review*, 93:4 (October, 1988), pp. 898–935, pp. 899–901.
59 Claes Janszoon Visscher, *Verovering van de Zilvervloot in de Baai van Matanzas door Admiraal Piet Heyn* (Amsterdam, 1628).
60 J. Herbert Claiborne, 'William Claiborne of Kent Island', *William and Mary Quarterly*, 2nd series, 1 (April, 1921), pp. 73–99.
61 Brenner, *Merchants and Revolution*, p. 185.
62 Claiborne, 'William Claiborne', pp. 73–99; Brenner, *Merchants and Revolution*, pp. 121–124. In 1632 the Catholic Calvert family was granted a charter by Charles I to establish a colony north of the Chesapeake, Maryland. Cecil Calvert, Lord Baltimore, was a major land owner in Ireland whose father had participated in the plantations of counties Longford and Wexford during the reign of James I and VI and lived in Wexford during the final years of his life. He had earlier established, and abandoned, a plantation in Newfoundland.
63 Headrights were the quantity of land awarded to indentured labourers who had completed their service. They were also awarded to the suppliers of those servants, per head. The system allowed for those merchants prominent in the servant trade to acquire substantial landed estates.
64 Eric Gethin-Jones, *George Thorpe and the Berkeley Company: A Gloucestershire Enterprise in Virginia* (Gloucester, 1982), p. 249. The purchasers were William Tucker, Maurice Thomson, George Thomson, William Harris, Thomas Deacon, James Stone, Cornelius Lloyd and Jeremiah Blackman. The main shareholder of the Berkeley Hundred in 1637 was Sir Baynham Throckmorton of Gloucester, a staunch royalist. Indicative of the very small circle in which the colonial merchants operated, in 1645 Throckmorton sold his Gloucestershire estate to Thomas Gookin to avoid paying a parliamentary fine. Thomas Gookin was a cousin both to Daniel Gookin, who owned land adjoining the Berkeley Hundred in Virginia and Vincent Gookin, one of the architects of the eventual settlement of the Adventure for Irish land.
65 Nell Marion Nugent (ed.), *Cavaliers and Pioneers, Abstracts of Virginia Land Patents and Grants 1623–1800*, Vol. 1 (Richmond, VA, 1934); Bottigheimer, *English*

Money and Irish Land; MacCartney, *Virginia Immigrants*, all *passim*. John Baker, John Bancks, George Beck, John Blunt, Edward Brewster, James Campbell, Randolph Carter, Abraham Chamberlain, Thomas Cole, John Culpepper, John Dawes, George Farmer, Richard Farringdon, John Fletcher, John Franklin, Richard Gardiner, Thomas Gouge, William Greenwell, Thomas Hampton, John Harper, John Harrington, John Harris, Hentry Hastings, Thomas Hodges, George Holman, Sir John Meyrick, William Morley, Edmund Peeres, George Preety, Richard Rogers, Richard, John and Edward Smith, Edward Staper and Richard Turner.

66 Sainsbury, *State Papers Colonial*, pp. 72–73.
67 Sainsbury, *State Papers Colonial*, p. 321.
68 MacCartney, *Virginia Immigrants*, p. 439.
69 BDA/3/1, 3–5 Minutes of Barbados Council 1639.
70 Sir Robert Mansell, Sir Dudley Diggs, Sir Thomas Roe, Sir Fernandino Gorges, Sir Francis Popham, Sir John Brooke, Sir Thomas Gates, Sir Richard Hawkins, Sir Nathaniel Rich and Sir Thomas Wroth. The 'Northern Colony' referred to was Massachusetts Bay, north of the New York area settlements already controlled by the Dutch.
71 Abel Ames, *The Mayflower and Her Log* (Boston, 1907), pp. 66–67. In 1619 the ship's captain, Thomas Jones, fulfilled a contract to transport Irish cattle to the Virginia colony and later that year he undertook a privateering mission to the East Indies on Warwick's behalf. He was arrested off the Guinea coast, returned to London and imprisoned until Warwick secured his release.
72 Ames, *The Mayflower and Her Log*, p. 80.
73 Frances Rose-Troup, *The Massachusetts Bay Company and its Predecessors* (New York, 1930), p. 8. Andrews evidently found the Puritan colonists rather difficult to deal with, accusing them of conduct 'unbecoming fairdealing men'. It evidently took seventeen years to recover the money from the Plymouth colonists.
74 Bottighemer, *English Money and Irish Land*, pp. 175–195; Rose-Troup, *Massachusetts Bay Company*, p. 20. These investors were: Thomas Adams, Andrew Arnold, Richard Davis, Edward Foorde, John Humfrey, Thomas Hutchins, Joseph Oldfield, Richard Perrie, Francis Webb, Simon Whetcomb and Richard Young.
75 Francis J. Bremer, *John Winthrop, America's Forgotten Founding Father* (Oxford, 2003), p. 98.
76 Bremer, *John Winthrop*, pp. 139–140.
77 Roger Downing and Gijs Rommelse, *A Fearful Gentleman: Sir George Downing in The Hague, 1658–1672* (Hilversum, 2011), p. 32.
78 Charles Hoadly, *The Warwick Patent* (Hartford, 1902). 'Warwick' patentees included several Adventurers for Irish land. The patentees were viscount Saye-and-Sele, Lord Brooke, Robert Rich, earl of Warwick, Charles Fiennes, Sir Nathaniel Rich, Sir Richard Saltonstall, Richard Knightly, John Pym, John Hampden, John Humphrey, Herbert Pelham, Henry Laurence, Henry Darley, Sir Arthur Hesilrige, Sir Matthew Boynton, Robert Barrington, Philip Nye and George Fenwick. Each patentee was awarded a grant of land along the Massachusetts River.
79 Sir Henry Vane II was the son of Sir Henry Vane, a Privy Councillor and later parliamentarian.

80 John Winthrop, *Winthrop Papers: Vol. III, 1631–1937* (Boston, 1943), p. 193.
81 Winthrop, *Winthrop Papers*, p. 196.
82 W.D. Killeen (ed.), *A True Narrative of the Rise and Progress of the Presbyterian Church in Ireland by the Reverend Patrick Adair* (Belfast, 1866), pp. 41–44.
83 Nathaniel Shurtleff, *Records of the Governor and Company of the Massachusetts Bay in New England*, 5 vols (Boston, 1853), vol. 1, p. 274.
84 Shurtleff, *Records of the Governor*, pp. 256–258.
85 The Massachusetts Bay Company investors who also invested in the Adventure for Irish land were Thomas Andrews, Richard Andrews, William Arnold, John and William Ballard, Sir Nathaniel Barnardiston, Sir William Brereton, John and Thomas Bright, John Browne, Edward Cooke, Samuel Crowther, John Goodwin, William Hubbard, Thomas Hutchins, John Oldfield, Henry Rosewell, William Spurstowe, Charles Witchcote and John and Thomas Young.
86 Rose-Troup, *Massachusetts Bay Company*, p. 63.
87 New England was the destination for one half of registered travellers from London in 1635. See Alison Games, 'The English Atlantic World: A View from London', *Pennsylvania History: A Journal of Mid-Atlantic Studies*, 64 (Summer, 1997), pp. 46–72.
88 William L. Sachse, 'The Migration of New Englanders to England, 1640–1660', *American Historical Review*, 55 (January, 1948), pp. 251–278, p. 260.
89 This account of the foundation of Nova Scotia and its comparison with Ulster is based on Alexander Fraser, *Nova Scotia, The Royal Charter of 1621 to William Alexander* (Toronto, 1912), pp. 12–16. William Alexander relied on finance from William Cloberry, Maurice Thomson's partner in the Kent Island project.
90 John Adamson, *The Noble Revolt* (London, 2007), p. 363.
91 It cost £2,000 to build a typical West Indian trader of 180 tons and £3,500 to build a tobacco ship of 240 tons, an average cost of construction of £13 per ton. See Davis, *Shipping Industry*, pp. 140–156.
92 For naval expenditure in the 1630s see Andrew Thrush, 'Naval Expenditure and the Development of Ship Money' in Mark Charles Fissell (ed.), *War and Government in Britain, 1598–1650* (Manchester, 1991), pp. 193–224.
93 Davis, *Shipping Industry*, p. 17.
94 J.P. Cooper, 'The Fortune of Thomas Wentworth, Earl of Strafford', *Economic History Review*, New Series, 11:2 (1958), pp. 227–248, p. 244.
95 Carla Gardina Pestana, *The English Atlantic in the Age of Revolution, 1640–1661* (London, 2007), p. 17.
96 TNA PC 2/42 Privy Council Registers, f. 75: 'Touching on interlopers to Canada'.

2

The Three Kingdoms

SCOTLAND

In addition to their own poor personal relationships with the crown, the merchants were also caught up in the worsening political crisis in London as relations between Charles and the Providence Island peers deteriorated. Charles's increasing interest in commerce and his Atlantic dominions was driven in part by the worsening financial crisis at court triggered by the Bishops' Wars, the two engagements between English and Scottish armies in 1639 and 1640. To vehement opposition both in Scotland and among the Providence Island Company peers, Charles imposed religious reforms across his kingdoms and caused a new prayer book to be read aloud in Edinburgh on 23 July 1637.[1] The Scottish responses were a summary rejection of the new prayer book and the signing of the National Covenant in February 1638, which promised to defend the Reformation by force. The king responded by taking an army north to confront the Scots. The English and Scots faced each other at Berwick-on-Tweed in June 1639 and the sides decided not to fight. Charles, in a move which further tarnished his reputation as an upholder of the Protestant religion, secretly recruited a Catholic Irish army under Randal MacDonnell, the earl of Antrim, to invade western Scotland.[2] To pacify his subjects in Scotland, Charles realised that he would need a far larger army. He could not pay for one without raising taxes and he had very few options short of summoning a parliament at Westminster. The Short Parliament met on 13 April 1640 but was flooded with grievances against the king's recent conduct. Parliament stalled over the hated ship money tax and failed to create legislation to raise money for a campaign in Scotland. By 27 April, Charles had agreed to suspend the ship money collections, the only tax he could raise without parliament's endorsement, but he required a supply of £100,000 per month for his war in Scotland before he would address any further grievances.[3] The

Short Parliament buried itself in procedural business and Charles delivered a sharp message on 2 May, reminding the members that 'a Delay of his Supply is as destructive as a Denial'.[4] The exasperated King Charles dissolved parliament on 5 May and turned instead to Thomas Wentworth, now the earl of Strafford, to organise his campaign.

In tandem with the financial pressures that encouraged Charles to take a deeper interest in his colonial dominions, the Bishops' Wars threatened the Atlantic merchants with conflict closer to home. The Scottish Covenanters had earned the sympathy of backers in the Dutch provinces of Holland and Zeeland, who were happy to supply Scotland with weapons.[5] Sweden contemplated more direct involvement, and prefaced this with the release of Scottish officers in Sweden's service to take up arms at home. Charles, for his part, seriously contemplated assisting Spain against the Dutch using an Irish army and an English navy. Both scenarios, a Scottish army supported by Dutch sympathisers fighting the English or an English naval war with the Dutch, risked pitting the English Atlantic merchant fleet against their Dutch competitors with potentially ruinous consequences. Luckily for the merchants, the catastrophic defeat suffered by the Spanish navy at the hands of the Dutch fleet in the Battle of the Downs off the coast of Kent in October 1639 put an end to these machinations. With the return of their experienced soldiers from Europe, and egged on by the sympathetic group of peers from the Providence Island Company in London, a Scottish army invaded England in August 1640 and advanced to near Newcastle-upon-Tyne. Charles set up court at York and summoned a 'Great Council of Peers' on 5 September 1640 to meet at York three weeks later.[6] Not only did the king unexpectedly draw the earl of Warwick and his friends to York, he also received a visit from Maurice Thomson.

A peers' petition of grievances, organised by the Providence Island Company grandees that included the earls of Essex and Warwick, and Lords Brooke, Mandeville and viscount Saye-and-Sele, was delivered to Charles I at York on 9 September 1640.[7] Written by two Providence Island Company officers who had been prominent in the Short Parliament, John Pym and Oliver St John, earl of Bolingbrooke, the petition touched on religion and the difficulties of the Scottish war, and was specific in its criticism of the king's management of monopolies and patents. The peers also demanded the recall of parliament. In London, a strikingly similar petition circulated within the merchant community and was seen by the Privy Council, which ordered the Court of Aldermen to suppress it.[8] Despite this opposition, Thomas Alford, Maurice Thomson and Richard Shute brought the petition from the merchants of London to Charles I at York, where they could be sure of the protection of their noble patrons.[9] It was hardly a coincidence that the two proposals with similar demands circulated simultaneously. Maurice Thomson was after all the Providence Island Company's principal contractor and Shute was Thomson's commercial factor in London, while members of the Alford family were significant Boston planters and involved with both Brooke and Warwick during the 1630s.[10] Both peers and merchants presented the king with the now familiar set of grievances that had been aired during the brief sitting of the Short Parliament.[11] They were able to negotiate using classic carrot-and-stick tactics. The peers threatened Charles with the possibility of an armed uprising, the arrest of his favoured courtiers and a reversal of recent reforms of the church of which the king was the titular head. The merchants offered Charles a loan of £50,000 to maintain his army. Negotiations with both groups were conditional on the king's recall of parliament.

London's main organs of local government, the Court of Aldermen and the Common Council, had no hand in the circulation of the merchants' petition, nor knowledge of the loan, and they condemned what looked like an initiative taken by private citizens.[12] The merchants' petition is evidence of the emergence of a new political group, centred on Warwick House and involving the Providence Island Company partners and their wide circle of maritime contractors. The earl of Warwick and Lord Brooke, in particular, were able to persuade merchants like Maurice Thomson and his associates to risk their capital, ships and lives to their mutual benefit. If recalled, merchant assets could be channelled through parliament to support closely aligned MPs such as John Pym and Sir Thomas Barrington. This was the new political structure that circumvented the established political order and would shortly enable the Adventure for Irish land. As Charles still had his Irish army to call upon, on 17 September the king was visited by Lewis Boyle, Lord Kinalmeaky and Roger Boyle, Lord Broghill bearing a gift of £1,000 from their father, the earl of Cork.[13] The persuasive Boyles helped Charles to see that he could only expect to receive money in dribs and drabs from even the wealthiest of his peers. Charles desperately needed the support of the Boyles to maintain his authority in Ireland. Unable to resist sustained pressure from English and Irish peers and the representatives of a great mass of London's merchants, the king succumbed and parliament was duly summoned for 3 November. Stripped of his authority, Charles was to receive the small consolation from Maurice Thomson's group of merchants of £50,000 to maintain his army, but this army was also soon abandoned. Charles signed the Treaty of Ripon with the Scottish Covenanters on 26 October 1640 and was forced to leave two English counties and the city of Newcastle in Scottish hands as hostages until England paid financial reparations to the Scots.

ENGLAND

At York and on behalf of the merchants who had signed the mass petition, Maurice Thomson had demanded the recall of parliament to address specific grievances relating to royal policy: ship money, patents and monopolies. The petitioners also called for the release of persons imprisoned for their opposition to these policies.[14] As one of its first actions, on 9 November 1640, parliament expelled 'all projectors, monopolisers, promoters or advisers of them'.[15] London elected four partners of Pennoyer and Cloberry from the Levant Company to represent the city's interests in parliament: Sir Thomas Soames, Isaac Pennington, Samuel Vassall and Matthew Craddock.[16] Three of these Levant Company merchants also had close ties with the Atlantic merchant leadership. Samuel Vassall was Maurice Thomson's most important trading partner in Virginia and the West Indies, as well as an investor in the Massachusetts Bay Company.[17] Matthew Craddock jointly owned the merchant ship *Rebecca* with Maurice Thomson and was the first governor of the Massachusetts Bay colony.[18] Craddock's daughter, Damaris, was married to Thomas Andrews.[19] Isaac Pennington also was related to Craddock through his kinsman Robert Mainwaring, who was, in turn, a leading member of London's Common Council and a partner of Thomas Andrews in the Virginia provisioning trade.[20] In 1640, Craddock died and was replaced by a senior Merchant Adventurer, John Venn, an organiser of the merchants' petition that was brought to York in 1640 and also a member of the Massachusetts Bay Company.[21] The families and businesses of the dominant parliamentary faction in London comprised a tightly bound network with many links in common.

Important though the national parliament was, London was governed on a day to day basis by its local representative institutions. The City of London was divided into twenty-six wards, each of which elected an alderman. An alderman had to be a member of one of the Livery Companies and these companies exercised control over most aspects of the city's economic life. The aldermen and the Livery Companies were broadly royalist and in January 1642 were opposed to the radical faction in parliament which was supported by the London MPs. The longest serving alderman was normally elected mayor and the Court of Aldermen was supposed to implement the policies laid down by the Common Council, which had a much wider constituency. The Common Council included the members of the Court of Aldermen, in addition to some 220 common councilmen elected by the freemen of each ward from candidates who were usually selected at parish meetings. Although any common councillor could attend a meeting of the Council, it was governed on a day-to-day basis by a committee comprised of one councillor selected from each ward. The weakness in the system was that the Court of Aldermen could veto the decisions of the Common Council, and as the aldermen were elected by the Court of Common Hall, the Livery Companies' representative body, these Companies had an effective veto over the decisions of the Common Council. In December 1641, the Common Council attempted to replace as candidate for mayor the longest serving alderman, Richard Gurney, who was a key supporter of recent increases in customs duties, with the radical London MP, Sir Isaac Pennington. The royalist London sheriff, George Clarke, simply ignored the vote and brought Gurney's name to the Court of Aldermen for approval.[22]

Robert Brenner has estimated that only 40% of common councillors can be termed parliamentarian in 1641.[23] In contrast, the freemen of the City had elected some of the House of Commons' most vocal opponents to Charles's policies, members of a group known as the 'fiery spirits', to be their MPs, a difference explained by geography.[24] The numerically superior maritime merchants were concentrated in the wards closest to the river Thames, the wards of Billingsgate, Candlewick, Dowgate, Tower and Portsoken.[25] Even with the addition of the Puritan-dominated wards of Coleman Street and Broad Street, the supporters of the radical group of MPs were still unable to achieve a majority on a council whose representation was drawn evenly from all wards. The 'fiery spirits' who were able to dominate elections to parliament could not muster enough support in every ward to nominate their members to the Common Council or to dominate the Court of Aldermen. The Court of Aldermen, especially, survived as the preserve of the loyal merchant elite. During the long years of absolute rule, the elite had become used to having things its own way, and it was unprepared for the political reconfiguration that came with the election results for the Long Parliament.

Of all the colonial merchants, only Maurice Thomson ranked among the merchant elite in 1641, equivalent to his fellow merchant grandees in terms of wealth, but, through a combination of truculence and the protection of the earl of Warwick, he avoided the expense of lending to the king to gain favour.[26] The rising Atlantic merchants, who were still under-represented in London's political institutions in September 1640, dominated instead the new, alternative source of political power, parliament. By December 1641, guided by their noble patrons, the Atlantic merchants simply bypassed the City of London's established political institutions. Instead of needing to ask the Common Council or an alderman to petition parliament with their grievances, they could instead go directly to their MP to have their concern raised in the House of Commons, or to the peer with whom they were already doing business to take the matter up in the House of Lords. The Providence Island Company peers and MPs could now also tap parliament to extend their influence, as they could draw on the financial clout and naval power of their merchant subcontractors. The Bishops' Wars with Scotland had been a disaster and the king seemed intent on pocketing at least part of the profits coming from New England, Virginia and the Caribbean. When confronted in force, the king had complied with their demands, but this was not a sustainable way for the merchants to do business over the long term. When the king felt stronger, both peers and merchants would need protection against any backlash. The rebellion that broke out in Ireland on 23 October 1641 and a rash action on the part of Charles I on 4 January 1642 presented, together, an opportunity for the combined 'fiery spirits' to take military control of the capital.

IRELAND

Charles I was in Scotland dealing with the aftermath of his English-Scottish war when he was informed about the rebellion in Ireland, which had erupted on 23 October 1641. The king, hoping that parliament could manage a response, 'recommended the care of those affairs' to parliament on 2 November 1641.[27] In so doing, he transferred his royal prerogative to deal with Ireland to parliament and, thereafter, policy for Ireland and the money loaned to implement these policies were under parliamentary authority. A joint parliamentary committee was established, comprised of twenty-eight peers and fifty-six MPs, to 'consider the state of the Irish affairs', and this committee became known as the Committee for Irish Affairs.[28] Parliament delegated much of the day-to-day management of the affairs of Ireland to it. The four London MPs joined this committee, and much of its work was managed by John Pym, the Providence Island Company member. Pym also reported between the Committee for Irish Affairs and the House of Commons, giving him considerable personal influence over policy for Ireland.

Parliament attempted to quickly raise a loan in London for £50,000 to reinforce and supply Protestant forces in Ireland, in the hope of crushing the rebellion before it spread. On 2 November Sir Thomas Barrington, another Providence Island Company man, was sent to the City of London to convince aldermen and other wealthy merchants to lend, while John Pym formed a small subgroup of MPs, including Sir John Clotworthy and Denzil Holles, a Leinster landowner, to manage this initial effort at Westminster.[29] The London aldermen resisted, requiring security from parliament for a new loan as well as security for the existing loan of £50,000 made to the king in September 1640. When money was loaned to the king in return for the calling of parliament, the aldermen had expected that their candidates would be elected to it, not the candidates promoted by the colonial merchants. The colonial merchants refused to lend also, grumbling that if the loan was administered by the mayor and aldermen, they would not contribute to it.[30] The impasse was resolved by a group of peers, led by the earl of Pembroke and including the Providence Island Company's leadership, who agreed to guarantee the loans with bonds drawn on their personal estates. Taking this action as an instruction from the peers to proceed, the colonial merchants responded promptly and delivered £20,000 in Spanish coin to Sir Nicholas Loftus, not only vice treasurer for wars in Ireland but also a neighbour of Warwick in Holborn.[31] Sheriff Gurney never saw the money, as it was administered by two of Warwick's merchant associates, George Henley and William Hawkridge.[32] Henley was a major importer of tobacco while Hawkridge was an experienced captain who was formerly employed transporting currency for the earl of Warwick and as master of one of Maurice Thomson's ships, the *Truelove*.[33] On 23 November, Hawkridge departed for Carrickfergus carrying £20,000 in silver bullion for the garrison there, in a ship chartered from Maurice Thomson.[34] This vessel was one of four armed merchantmen chartered from Thomson to supply English and Scottish forces intended for Ireland and to guard the Irish Sea.[35] Maurice Thomson was a key figure in England's response to the Irish revolt from its earliest phase.

Almost two months before the Irish rebellion, on 6 September 1641, the earl of Warwick, John Pym and Sir Henry Mildmay had been given responsibility for managing the finances of the navy. This small committee met at Warwick House, where the Providence Island Company peers also had their meetings, and contracted Maurice Thomson to manage the security of the Irish Sea. As the colonial merchant fleet was in the Thames getting ready for spring voyages, Warwick and Thomson were fortunate to have a large supply of suitable vessels at their disposal.[36] A further large source of funds, the 'Brotherly Assistance' collected to pay the Scottish army still camped in the occupied counties in the north of England, was also administered from Warwick House.[37] Part of this money could be used to send the Scottish army to Ulster to support Protestant forces sympathetic to parliament. These resources allowed the Puritan MPs and colonial merchants to ignore the established city structures for raising state loans and to insert themselves at the centre of Irish affairs, using the alternative arrangement of parliament and Warwick House. For Maurice Thomson and his partners this meant not only lucrative state contracts, but also the opportunity to protect some business in Ireland. In 1638, Randall MacDonnell, the Catholic earl of Antrim, had borrowed £80,000 from a consortium of London merchants that included the Thomsons and their close circle of financiers.[38]

Shamed to some degree by the ability of the Warwick House circle to despatch supplies to Ireland, the Court of Common Hall, the London Companies' representative body, approved a £100,000 loan for the relief of Ireland in December 1641.[39] The initiative was not entirely altruistic, as the London Companies were responsible for the security of their own plantation, Londonderry. The ship sent by parliament using contractors from Warwick House was bound for Carrickfergus to provide assistance to Sir John Clotworthy, the MP charged with organising the relief effort. The London Companies pooled loans from wealthy merchants including £1,000 each from Sir Robert Bateman and Dame Rebecca Rumney. Valuable as these efforts were, they fell far short of the resources and leadership required. Parliament was unable to either commit funds directly to the Irish campaign or to raise taxation to combat the rebellion, although it guaranteed to repay suppliers who provided goods on credit. The merchant community had little confidence in parliament's creditworthiness as parliament already had repayment obligations for £500,000, outstanding since the Scottish wars.[40] By December 1641, the Irish campaign had run up £50,000 in debt to its suppliers and parliament was forced, on 14 December, to raise £400,000 in new taxes, termed subsidies. Although intended to pay for parliament's response to the Irish rebellion, the new tax was only sufficient to pay down most of the old debt.[41] Charles's disaster in Scotland had ensured that the English state could not hope to combat what was a widespread rebellion in Ireland by the end of December 1641.

New money could be raised for a decisive Irish campaign only with loans secured on the future proceeds of the subsidy, or through a new initiative. Fractious London was by no means the ideal place in which to try anything new and only the initial loan of £20,000 out of the £50,000 originally asked for and guaranteed by the Warwick House peers had been sent to Ireland. The fundraising was so fragmented that Warwick had to personally convince Sir Robert Bateman to loan a further £2,000 to meet the cost of hiring Maurice Thomson's four ships.[42] As a condition of the loan, perhaps anticipating what was to come, Bateman stipulated that his money could not be used for any other purpose. As a last resort, on 24 December parliament turned to the Fellowship of Merchant Adventurers to see if they would advance the balance.[43] Parliament was not making an appeal to their altruism as the Merchant Adventurers held a monopoly over the cloth trade and would profit greatly from the raising of an army that required clothing in the middle of winter. The central committee of the Fellowship of Merchant Adventurers included Laurence Halstead, who was to become the fourth treasurer for the Adventure for Irish land, along with Thomas Andrews, John Towse and John Warner.

The Westminster parliament received a constant barrage of petitions from groups with a vested interest in Ireland, all expressing frustration with the delays in organising relief supplies. Eighteen New English landowners resident in London petitioned the House of Commons on 21 December and blamed the spread of the rebellion on parliament's indecision and lack of resources.[44] A second petition, signed by 110 London merchants and sent to the king but referred back to the House of Lords, claimed that 'a million of money' due to them from landowners and merchants in Ireland was at risk of being lost, and that this financial disaster would have serious consequences for England's trade as a whole.[45] Half of these petitioners subscribed to the Adventure for Irish land in March 1642, an indication that for many the Adventure was a necessity to protect their business interests in Ireland.[46] The petition was organised by John Towse and Samuel Warner, also an Atlantic trader and a brother of John Warner.[47] The petition provides evidence of how closely these merchants had integrated Ireland into the wider Atlantic colonial trading network. Of the 110 merchants claiming to be trading into or supplying credit in Ireland, thirty-nine had close personal or familial links with the Atlantic colonies, including planters and officials in senior positions. Thomas Allen, for example, was treasurer of the earl of Warwick's Bermuda Company and William Davenport was the brother of the New England Puritan luminary, John Davenport.[48]

ENGLAND

While the aldermen of London were treating Charles to a lavish banquet upon his return to London on 25 November 1641, a number of Puritan merchants active both at home and in the wider Atlantic were taking steps to seize control of the Common Council, targeting the elections due to take place on 21 December.[49] A sub-committee of the Common Council, the Committee for Safety, was responsible for nominating and arming the foot soldiers of the Trained Bands, London's militia. Victorious at the ballot box, the men central to the Adventure for Irish land coalesced for the first time in the newly elected Common Council. As is always the case with elected bodies, the important members are the ones who attend the meetings, vote and lay down policy. Foremost among these were the future treasurers for the Adventure for Irish land, John Towse and John Warner, together with James Bunce and Stephen Estwick, who managed a subsequent Adventure for Ireland in 1643.[50] Bunce was, like Thomas Andrews, a leatherseller. He held a number of important financial positions until 1647, when he led the London militia in an assault on parliament to force negotiations with the king. Bunce was subsequently convicted of high treason but escaped to continue his campaigning.[51] Stephen Estwick joined the Company of Silkmen in 1636, and was immediately drawn into an argument over the company's debts and the protests over ship money.[52] In 1642, he emerged as a major supplier of clothing to parliament's armies. The Estwicks operated major plantations in Barbados and Stephen Estwick had probably made the acquaintance of the Adventurers for Irish land through this activity.[53] Of the twenty-eight Common Councilmen elected, twenty-six subsequently supported the Adventure for Irish land and twenty-four of the twenty-eight were also involved in the collection of money for parliament by the end of 1642.[54] The Adventure for Irish land and the raising of money for the parliamentary cause which closely followed it can both be considered to be part of the same process. Both collections were primarily Common Council undertakings and were instigated by the same people.

By the start of 1642, Parliament had discovered that it could bypass the usual sources of state finance (subsidies, the City of London and unpopular special taxes), albeit on the condition that money raised be used to suppress the rebellion in Ireland. Furthermore, as parliament held the authority to suppress the Irish rebellion, it had sweeping powers to decide how that money was spent. Parliament was, in fact, empowered to take whatever steps it felt necessary to protect Protestant Ireland. These powers took on a new significance when, on 2 January 1642, Charles issued an arrest warrant against five MPs – John Pym, John Hampden, William Strode, Sir Arthur Hesilrige and Denzil Holles – and charged them with plotting against the queen. All five were involved in Puritan colonial projects. Pym was a member of the Providence Island Company and a partner in the 'Warwick Patent', the earl of Warwick's Puritan colonial project in New England.[55] Hampden and Hesilrige were partners in the 'Warwick Patent' scheme, while William Strode had inherited his father's share in the Dorchester Company, an English West Country-based Puritan venture that also attempted to establish a plantation in New England.[56] Holles was another shareholder in the Dorchester Company. An arrest warrant was also issued against a member of the House of Lords, the Providence Island Company peer, Lord Mandeville.

The five MPs and Lord Mandeville refused to surrender themselves and on the morning of 4 January Charles visited the Common Council in person at the Guild Hall and demanded that the Council see to the arrest of the MPs. The Common Council would not agree to this demand and Charles went to parliament in person with an entourage of soldiers to arrest the MPs, but they had by then disappeared.[57] Threatened by the king's soldiers, parliament went into recess but the Committee for Irish Affairs continued to meet safely inside the walls of the city, at Grocers' Hall, in order to continue organising the suppression of the Irish rebellion. Another group of MPs formed an emergency Committee of Safety, which also met at Grocers' Hall, although this was not established under any legislative authority.[58] From 4 January until the recall of parliament on 10 January, the Committee of Safety and the Committee for Irish Affairs were the only branches of parliament functioning and they assumed the authority of the parent body. The constitutional position of the Committee for Irish Affairs was crucial in that Charles had delegated his royal authority to parliament to manage England's response to the Irish rebellion, and this authority was in turn delegated to the parliamentary committee. In effect, the Committee for Irish Affairs at Grocers' Hall was fully responsible for Ireland while parliament was in recess.

As soon as Charles left the Guildhall on 4 January, the Common Council voted to mobilise the city militia in order to secure the safety of the city. Tensions in the city were running high and mob violence was an ever-present danger. For additional security, the Common Council petitioned the king to release arms from the Tower for the militias, but received no response.[59] Parliament, in the form of the Committee for Irish Affairs, then requested the Common Council to elect a Committee of Safety for London, responsible for deploying the City's militias and selecting its officers. The Common Council's newly formed Committee of Safety was comprised of the same colonial and Puritan merchants who would become the political leaders of the Adventure for Irish land.⁶⁰ Using its power to suppress the rebellion in Ireland, on 5 January the Committee for Irish Affairs authorised the release of 1,000 muskets and 1,500 swords from the royal armoury in the Tower of London. These arms were supposed to be provided to the troops assembling in London for transport to Ireland but once out of the Tower, the weapons found their way into the hands of the London militias.⁶¹ The troops in London destined for Ireland were placed under the command of Edward Viscount Conway, who had been nominated for the Commons seat of Yarmouth by Lord Brooke, and Sir John Clotworthy, nominated for the seat of Malden by the earl of Warwick. Both men, Conway and Clotworthy, were very much intertwined with the colonial circle centred on Warwick House. The fathers of Conway and Clotworthy had both invested heavily in the first Virginia Company of 1609 and both men were neighbouring landowners in County Antrim. Viscount Conway's estates in Warwickshire were leased to Lord Brooke on a long-term basis and, although Conway held the post of Lord Marshall of Ireland, his poor military performance against the Scots in 1640 left him dependent on the support of the Providence Island peers for a command.⁶²

On 8 January, parliament's Committee of Safety asked the Committee for Irish Affairs to make the necessary preparations for raising London's Trained Bands for its protection, using the emergency in Ireland as its justification.

> For as much as the necessitie of providinge money and other supplies for the present releife of Ireland require the consideracon of both Houses of Parliament, and for as much as they cannot sit in safetie without strong and sufficient guard from the Citty of London and the adjacent partes. It is therefore ordered that it be referred to the consideracon of the Committee for Irish Affaires to consider of a way for securing of both houses by guard as aforesaid.⁶³

The Common Council quickly agreed to the request and confirmed that the Committee for Irish Affairs was entitled to request its military protection. To ensure that its instructions were carried out, the Common Council also declared that the custom under which the Trained Bands were commanded by the Lord Mayor was illegal and that the Council would put in place a new command structure. The Committee for Irish Affairs drew its authority from the assumption that, if left unchecked, the rebellion in Ireland would quickly engulf England as well. Using the pretext that Ireland would fall were parliament unprotected and unable to send military supplies, the Common Council's Committee of Safety announced that eight companies of the Trained Bands would be drawn together without further ado, under the command of major-general Philip Skippon.⁶⁴ These forces could protect parliament from a theoretical unruly mob, but would also protect it from the very real presence of the king. Skippon's instructions included a provision that his orders would come only from the Committee for Irish Affairs and he would not be subject to any counter command from another authority. The Trained Bands were armed with the weapons released from the Tower of London, which were supposed to be despatched to Ireland. To ensure that nothing illegal could be seen to have taken place, the House of Lords' Committee for Irish Affairs, comprised almost exclusively of Providence Island peers, assented to these measures on 10 January on behalf of the entire parliament, still in recess. For procedural purposes, the Common Council appointed independent arbitrators and a specific militia committee to nominate the officers. The arbitrators chosen were three merchants who had been imprisoned alongside Samuel Vassall for refusing to pay the Forced Loan of 1626 and who were hostile to the king: Sir Nicholas Rainton, Sir John Gayre and Thomas Atkins.[65] A newly elected militia committee, that undertook to meet the cost of the Trained Bands, was comprised entirely of colonial merchants who were associates of the earl of Warwick's primary contractor, Maurice Thomson.[66]

Of the thirty officers of the Trained Bands ranked as captain or colonel, twenty-two became Adventurers for Irish land in March 1642.[67] The Trained Bands were organised into six regiments, the most strategically important of which, the red regiment, had responsibility for the area around the Tower of London and the docks, including the armoury in the Tower and the armed merchant fleet on the Thames.[68] Two of the captains in the red regiment were William Tucker and William Thomson, placing the Tower's arsenal, the Custom House and the headquarters of the Artillery Company firmly within the grasp of Warwick's closest agents.[69] Tucker and Thomson were well suited to their new roles, as both had acquired significant military experience in Virginia. Tucker had risen to Captain-General of the Virginia militia in 1635, the most senior military rank.[70] The white regiment, responsible for the area around the main guild halls and the area to the north of the city that included Warwick House and Brooke House, was commanded entirely by future leading Adventurers for Irish land.[71] Robert Thomson, another brother of Maurice, who acted as his financial manager in London, was an ensign in the white regiment and had previously served in the New England militia.[72] These returned emigrants from Virginia and New England took roles in the initial military mobilisation against the authority of the king. Two further regiments were also under the complete control of future Adventurers for Irish land: the blue regiment was stationed along the Thames and provided access to armed merchant shipping and the orange regiment controlled poorer areas of the city around the Puritan parish of St Dunstan in the East, the home parish of John Foulke and Maurice Thomson.[73]

The distribution of so many future Adventurers among the officer ranks of the trained bands indicates that they were already leaders within London's emerging military hierarchy. The military ties that bound London's merchant community were based around the Honourable Artillery Company, established in 1507, which rebuilt itself from 1620 after a period of decline and purchased the Artillery Gardens to the north of the city in 1641 to perform its exercises.[74] These exercises comprised regular training, an annual parade and various meetings and sermons. They appeared to be, above all, social gatherings. The meeting house was near the Tower, close to the Thames-side strongholds of the Atlantic merchants. The individual Adventurers for Irish land who were also members of the Artillery Company are noted in the appendix, and include almost all of the Adventurers' leadership. This leadership included most of the senior officers in the trained bands and among the most senior of these was Maurice Thomson, who 'borrowed' some of the Company's artillery and stationed it near the Guildhall.[75] Prior to January 1642, the militias trained at the Artillery Company's exercise grounds, led by the company's captain-general, Phillip Skippon.

Although the Committee for Irish Affairs that convened in London and requested the Common Council to mobilise its forces was comprised of fifty-six members, the quorum for committee meetings was just fourteen.[76] Parliamentary committees often had a wide membership but the work of the committee was normally performed by a much smaller group with a direct interest in the outcome of the work of that committee. It is not known exactly which MPs attended on 8 January 1642, but as an indication fourteen MPs were nominated to a subsequent parliamentary group on 19 February 1642, the 'Commissioners for the Speeding and Dispatching of the Businesses for Ireland'.[77] This small committee, intended to advance negotiations for the Adventure for Irish land, temporarily assumed the responsibilities originally assigned to the Committee for Irish Affairs in November 1641. Although there may have been others, these fourteen MPs, dealing actively with the emergency in Ireland, are most likely the group that convened at Grocers' Hall on 4 January 1642. These MPs were Sir Richard Cave, Sir Robert Cooke, Oliver Cromwell, Sir Walter Erle, Sir John Evelyn, Sir Robert Harley, Denzil Holles, Nicholas Martin, Sir John Meyrick, Sir Robert Parkhurst, John Pym, Sir Robert Reynolds, Robert Wallop and Sir Henry Vane II. Of this group only one member, Sir Richard Cave, was a royalist. The remainder emerged as supporters of parliament in the weeks that followed and were, for the most part, involved in many of the same colonial projects as the Providence Island peers and their subcontractors who had taken control of the Common Council in London. It is probable that the four London MPs were also present, as they had a right to attend meetings of the Committee for Irish Affairs, further increasing the dominance of the committee by the Warwick House circle.

In addition to the London MPs who had direct connections with the Atlantic merchant community, the Committee for Irish Affairs was further dominated by men with colonial Atlantic connections. Sir Walter Erle, the MP for Poole with a long history of opposition to Charles, was also an investor in the Dorchester Company. This company's main achievement was to establish a colony at Cape Ann, Massachusetts in 1623, subsequently taken over by Maurice Thomson and John Winthrop II in 1639. Sir John Meyrick, Sir Robert Harley, Sir Robert Cooke and Sir John Evelyn all served on the board of the Virginia Company.[78] Although there is no direct evidence that Oliver Cromwell invested in any colonial schemes, he did attempt to migrate to New England in 1634 while Warwick and Lord Brooke were developing the 'Warwick Patent'.[79] Nicholas Martin, the Exeter MP declared a traitor by the king, had sold his Virginia plantation, Martin's Hundred Parish, to a consortium of London merchants in 1637.[80] Sir Robert Parkhurst held a small estate in County Roscommon and also advanced credit on the Dublin Staple.[81] The reason he was on the Committee for Irish Affairs was that his largest creditor in Ireland was Sir Phelim O'Neill, the leader of the Irish rebellion in Ulster.[82] Parkhust held the mortgage to the entire O'Neill estate and would be able to take possession of it as soon as O'Neill was arrested. The remaining two members of the committee, Robert Wallop and Denzil Holles, had large plantation estates in County Wexford. The committee was an overwhelmingly Puritan group with many links to both Irish and Atlantic colonial projects. Their commercial interests had brought them into close contact with the merchants who now dominated the Common Council and the London militia.

Parliament had stretched to the limit the rights granted when the king had 'recommended the care of those affairs' in Ireland to it.[83] Both houses of parliament had in turn delegated powers to the Committee for Irish Affairs while parliament was in recess. This tiny Committee for Irish Affairs, meeting in Grocers' Hall under the protection of the Trained Bands, had assumed the royal prerogative. It had ordered the release of weapons for Ireland, transferred these to the Trained Bands, and then provided the Common Council with legal cover to stage an armed confrontation with the king. The Providence Island peers had succeeded therefore, through the Committee for Irish Affairs, the Common Council and the Trained Bands, in effecting a revolution at arm's length, using their client MPs and merchant contractors as proxies. Faced with an army commanded by experienced officers such as Captain William Tucker, one of Warwick's oldest associates, Charles left London on 10 January 1642 and did not return until his trial and execution. The ousting of Charles had been achieved largely at the expense of a Protestant Ireland that was, it was widely believed in London, suffering a wholesale slaughter at the hands of Irish Catholic rebels. A faction within parliament had discovered that popular opinion would support any measure to rescue Protestant Ireland. Furthermore, Charles would find it very difficult to obstruct any initiative, financial, military or otherwise, that could plausibly claim to be intended to crush the Irish rebellion. In these circumstances, the opposition to the king continued unchecked.

There were limits to the control which the Providence Island, or wider Warwick House circle of peers and MPs, could assert over the merchants. The merchants had not staged a revolt of their own but were acting in concert with the peers as their interests were in alignment. The hated ship money tax was replaced with a general subsidy spread across the country and parliament prioritised the work of dismantling Charles's network of monopolies. The London MPs, familiars but not central to Warwick House, fully exercised their right to sit on the Committee for Irish Affairs. Very shortly after news of the Irish rebellion reached London, Maurice Thomson and William Pennoyer took a leading role in reinforcing the Irish coastal cities that remained under Protestant control. They were indeed doing what the earl of Warwick and the Committee for Irish Affairs wanted, but these men and their own very wide circle of commercial partners had a habit of probing for opportunities at the margins of territorial domains or in zones of conflict. Ireland had suddenly presented itself, not just as an opportunity to further serve their political masters and defend the Protestant reformation, but as an unexpected and rather fortuitous windfall.

NOTES

1 Jonathan Scott, *England's Troubles: Seventeenth-Century English Political Instability in European Context* (Cambridge, 2000), p. 138.
2 Mark Fissell, *The Bishops' Wars: Charles I's Campaigns against Scotland, 1638–1640* (Cambridge, 1994), pp. 268–280.
3 CJ, 2, p. 12: 27 April 1640: Lords Interference in Matters of Supply.
4 CJ, 2, p. 19: 2 May 1640: Message from the king for Supply.
5 For this wider dimension in more detail see Allan I. Macinnes, 'The Scottish Moment' in John Adamson (ed.), *The English Civil War, Conflict and Contexts, 1640–49* (Basingstoke, 2009), pp. 127–131.
6 John Adamson, *The Noble Revolt* (London, 2007), p. 77.
7 John Rushworth, *Historical Collections of Private Passages of State*, Vol. 3, 1639–40 (London, 1721), p. 1236: 'The Petition of the Earl of Essex, Hertford, &c. to the king to call a Parliament'.
8 Rushworth, *Historical Collections of Private Passages of State*, Vol. 3, p. 1248: Sept. 11. 1640. 'To stop the Londoners Petition to his Majesty'.
9 TNA SP16/467, Letters and Papers, 1640, Sept 10–23, f.225 Sept. 19 1640: Note of a report that 'Alford, a linen draper, of Cheapside, Shewte, a merchant, and Maurice Thomson, merchant, went last Wednesday afternoon with the petition from the citizens of London'.
10 Robert Brenner, *Merchants and Revolution* (Princeton, NJ, 1993), p. 313; Bernard Bailyn, *New England Merchants in the Seventeenth Century* (Cambridge, MA, 1962), p. 36.
11 Adamson, *Noble Revolt*, p. 58.

12 Brenner, *Merchants and Revolution*, p. 314.
13 Charlotte Fell Smith, *Mary Rich, Countess of Warwick (1625–1678), Her Family and Friends* (London, 1901), p. 87. According to Lewis Boyle, Charles spent much of his time playing chess with William Fielding, earl of Denbigh.
14 Rushworth, 'Historical Collections: 1640, August-September', in *Historical Collections of Private Passages of State*, Vol. 3, pp. 1281–1286, 'A Petition of the Londoners to the king to call a Parliament'.
15 Robert Ashton, *The City and the Court 1603–1643* (Cambridge, 1979), p. 152.
16 Brenner, *Merchants and Revolution*, p. 81.
17 Brenner, *Merchants and Revolution*, pp. 135–137.
18 Frances Rose-Troup, *The Massachusetts Bay Company and its Predecessors* (New York, 1930), pp. 60–62; Brenner, *Merchants and Revolution*, p. 139. The Craddocks were also leading members of the Eastland Company, so it was probably the potential timber trade that drew them into New England.
19 Brenner, *Merchants and Revolution*, p. 139; Rose-Troup, *Massachusetts Bay Company*, p. 133.
20 Martha W. MacCartney, *Virginia Immigrants and Adventurers 1607–35: A Biographical Dictionary* (Baltimore, MD, 2007), p. 473; Brenner, *Merchants and Revolution*, p. 483. A branch of the Mainwaring family was established in Stillorgan, County Dublin.
21 Brenner, *Merchants and Revolution*, p. 313; Rose-Troup, *Massachusetts Bay Company*, pp. 60–62.
22 Melvin C. Wren, 'The Disputed Elections in London 1641', *English Historical Review* (1949), pp. 34–52; Brenner, *Merchants and Revolution*, pp. 319–321; Valerie Pearl, *London and the Outbreak of the Puritan Revolution: City Government and National Politics, 1625–43* (Oxford, 1961), pp. 50–65.
23 Brenner, *Merchants and Revolution*, p. 388.
24 Parliament's factions are identified and explained in Jason Peacy, 'Perceptions of Parliament: Factions and "The Public"' in John Adamson (ed.), *The English Civil War, Conflict and Contexts, 1640–49* (Basingstoke, 2009), pp. 82–105.
25 TNA SP16/453, ff. 116–165, May 1640, 'The names of persons who are conceived able to lend his Majesty money…'. The survey is organised by London ward and classifies potential lenders according to their wealth; the first class, the second class and so on. See also Adrian Johns, 'Coleman Street', *Huntington Library Quarterly*, 71:1 (March, 2008), pp. 33–54.
26 TNA SP16/453, f. 152. Maurice Thomson is the only merchant of the first class who was not a senior member of one of the chartered companies or involved in state finance. Many of his business partners, however, are to be found in the second and third classes.
27 Patrick Little, 'The English Parliament and the Irish Constitution' in Micheál Ó Siochrú (ed.), *Kingdoms in Crisis: Ireland in the 1640s* (Dublin, 2001), pp. 108–109.
28 For the formation of this committee see Robert Armstrong, 'Ireland at Westminster' in Chris R. Kyle and Jason Peacy (eds), *Parliament at Work: Parliamentary Committees, Political Power and Public Access in Early Modern England* (Woodbridge, 2002), pp. 80–81.

29 CJ, 2, pp. 301-303.
30 CJ, 2, p. 304.
31 CJ, 2, pp. 308-309.
32 CJ, 2, pp. 311-312.
33 Brenner, *Merchants and Revolution*, p. 183n; MacCartney *Virginia Immigrants*, p. 379; Elaine Murphy, *Ireland and the War at Sea* (Woodbridge, 2012), p. 89. Henley was a brother of Sir Robert Henley, master of the king's bench, who entered into a bond to guarantee the safe delivery of the money (CJ, 2, p. 322).
34 TNA SP16/1, Letters and Papers, 1625 Mar 27-Apr, f. 135: The king to the Commissioners of Customs; SP 71/26, f. 5 Secretaries of State: State Papers Foreign, Barbary States, Tunis, 1622–1662: 'Petition of Capt. William Hawkridge for letters of marque against pirates of Algiers and Salé'. In 1626 Hawkridge transported coin for the earl of Warwick on an expedition to discover the Northwest Passage. The investors in this voyage included Warwick, the Duke of Buckingham, Sir Thomas Smith and Sir John Wolstenhome. See also: Parliamentary Archives, HL/PO/JO/10/1/73, 23 November 1641, Order for the payment of £5,000 by the chamberlain of London to the merchants who undertook to transport £20,000 into Ireland.
35 Parliamentary Archives, HL/PO/JO/10/1/73, 20 November 1641, Draft order of the Lords and Commons for the Lord High Admiral to prepare four ships for the service of Ireland.
36 Adamson, *Noble Revolt*, p 363.
37 The Brotherly Assistance loans were transacted through Warwick House to secure the disbandment of the Scots army deployed in England in accordance with the Treaty of London signed in August 1641.
38 Parliamentary Archives, HL/PO/JO/10/1/115, 4 February 1642: 'Petition of Alexander MacDonnell'. Antrim's loans were guaranteed by Archibald Stewart. I am grateful to Professor Jane Ohlmeyer for drawing my attention to the MacDonnell loan.
39 TNA SP16/493, ff. 65–78 'Book containing a general account of money paid in to the Chamber of London from Nov. 1641 to Dec. 1642 as loans, in accordance with orders of Parliament'; CJ, 2, p. 330. The 'Warwick House circle' is a term coined by John Adamson to describe the group of associates of the earl of Warwick that met at the earl's home in Holborn. It is somewhat wider than the Providence Island Company membership identified by Kupperman.
40 CJ, 2, p. 337. The treasury contained £18,000 out of which a short-term loan had been made for £12,000 to send Henley and Hawkridge on their way pending the collection of the £50,000.
41 CJ, 2, p. 343.
42 TNA SP26/139 part 15, 'The accounts of Sir John Heyden', f. 150.
43 CJ, 2, pp. 355-357. For a fuller account of parliament's efforts to establish a military force for Ireland see Robert Armstrong, 'The Long Parliament Goes to War: The Irish Campaigns, 1641-3', *Historical Research*, 80 (February, 2007), pp. 73-99, pp. 74-80.
44 Parliamentary Archives, HL/PO/JO/10/1/74, 'Petition of divers Lords and gentlemen of Ireland, now in London, that steps may speedily be taken for the suppression of the rebellion'. The petitioners included Sir Arthur Annesley, Sir John Clotworthy,

Thomas Cromwell viscount Lecale, Lord Henry Blaney, Sir Francis Mounteney, Sir Adam and Nicholas Loftus and Sir Robert Parkhurst.

45 Parliamentary Archives, HL/PO/JO/10/1/75, *Petiton of divers citizens, merchants and others of London, trading into the realm of Ireland, pray for the speedy relief of Ireland*.

46 As noted by Lindley, the Adventure for Irish land was factional.

47 William Thomson, who had returned from Virginia in 1640 with George Thomson and William Tucker, married the daughter of Samuel Warner.

48 MacCartney, *Virginia Immigrants*, p. 165; Rose-Troup, *Massachusetts Bay Company*, p. 62. Other examples include Herriot Washbourne, the brother of the secretary of the Massachusetts Bay Company (Brenner, *Merchants and Revolution*, p. 155; Rose-Troup, *Massachusetts Bay Company*, p. 64); William Drinkwater, who supplied Irish beef directly to Barbados in January 1641, one of several involved in colonial provisioning (Peter Wilson Coldham, *English Adventurers and Emigrants, 1609–1660* (Baltimore, MD, 1984), p. 217) and Edward Waterhouse, son of a former chancellor of the Irish exchequer, was secretary of the Virginia Company and had witnessed the massacre of 1622. Waterhouse was an old friend of Captain William Tucker, who had arrived in London to defend his tobacco monopoly. Returning from America, Edward Waterhouse established the Castlewaterhouse estate in County Fermanagh and married Elizabeth, the daughter of Richard Bateman, a brother of Robert and also a leading member of the Levant and East India Companies.

49 See Wren, 'Disputed Elections'; Brenner, *Merchants and Revolution*, pp. 373–374.

50 The attendances and members are compiled from London Metropolitan Archives, COL/CC/01/01/4 Minutes of the Common Council 1642–7, ff. 8v-18.

51 See Thomas Bayly Howell, *A complete collection of state trials and proceedings for high treason and other crimes and misdemeanors: from the earliest period to the year 1783: with notes and other illustrations* (London, 1820) for a full account of the 1647 incident.

52 TNA SP 16/314, f. 189. Feb. 26, 1636, Petition of Stephen Estwick and others, haberdashers of small wares on behalf of themselves.

53 BDA RB6/14, p. 32. 28 January 1661, Will of Christopher Estwick, gentleman.

54 The members of the Common Council identified from the minutes and correlated against Wren's list of petitioners were: Thomas Atkins, William Barkley, Nicholas Baynton, Edward Bromfield, James Bunce, George Clarke, Stephen Estwick, John Foulke, Thomas Foote, John Gage, Thomas Gardiner, George Garrett, John Gayre, William Gibbs, Jacob Gerard, Edward Hill, Randall Mainwaring, Alexander Normington, Francis Peck, Thomas Perkins, Abraham Reynardson, Owen Rowe, James Russell, John Towse, John Warner, Sir John Wollaston and Nathaniel Wright. An EEIC grandee, Abraham Reynardson, and the tobacco importer Randall Mainwaring were the only petitioners who did not join the Adventure for Irish land.

55 The shareholders in the Warwick Patent were: Robert Rich, earl of Warwick, viscount Saye-and-Sele, Lord Brooke, Charles Fiennes, Sir Nathaniel Rich, Sir Richard Saltonstall, Richard Knightly, John Pym, John Hampden, John Humphrey,

Herbert Pelham, Henry Laurence, Henry Darley, Sir Arthur Hesilrige, Sir Matthew Boynton, Robert Barrington, Philip Nye and George Fenwick.

56 Hesilrige was married to the daughter of Lord Brooke, principal of the Providence Island Company and Saybrook colony.
57 *Diurnal Occurences*, 3-10 January 1642.
58 Parliamentary Archives HL/PO/JO/10/1/114, 11 January 1642: Resolutions of the Lords and Commons for Irish Affairs. Annexed, 8 January 1642, 'Report from the sub-committee appointed to treat with the Committee of the Common Council'.
59 TNA SP16/488, f. 33, 5 January 1642. Minutes of proceedings at a Common Council of the City of London held this day before Sir Richd. Gurney, Lord Mayor, Sir Thos. Gardiner, Recorder, &c.
60 Pearl, *Puritan Revolution*, pp. 140-143. The Common Councillors appointed to manage the militia were Thomas Atkins, John Towse, John Warner, Sir John Wollaston, Randal Mainwaring, John Foulke, Stephen Estwicke, Owen Rowe, James Russell, Nathaniel Wright and William Berkley.
61 Adamson, *Noble Revolt*, pp. 488-498.
62 Daniel Starza Smith, *John Donne and the Conway Papers: Patronage and Manuscript Circulation in the Seventeenth Century* (Oxford, 2014), pp. 99-102. Smith quotes a contemporary rhyme: 'Here is no room for Conaway/ nor many more that run away'.
63 Parliamentary Archives, HL/PO/JO/10/1/114, 11 January 1642; 'Resolutions of the Lords and Commons for Irish Affairs', annexed, 8 January 1642, Report from the sub-committee appointed to treat with the Committee of the Common Council.
64 In 1642, Skippon was captain-general of the Artillery Company and Maurice Thomson an officer.
65 London Metropolitan Archives, COL/CC/01/01/4, Minutes of the Common Council 1642-7, f. 10v. Gayre was the father-in-law of George Henley, the merchant carrying supplies to Carrickfergus.
66 COL/CC/01/01/4, William Berkley, James Bunce, Thomas Foote, William Gibbs, Randall Mainwaring, Alexander Normington, Thomas Perkins, James Russell and Nathaniel Wright.
67 G.E. Cokayne, *The Complete Baronetage*, Vol. III, 1649-1664 (Exeter, 1903), p. 24.
68 Richard Thrale, *The Names, Dignities and Places of all the Collonells...and ensigns of the City of London* (London, 1642); Lawson Chase Nagel, *The Militia of London* (PhD Thesis, University of London, 1982), p. 51.
69 Nagel, *The Militia of London*, p. 98. Tower Hamlets was also home to the greatest concentration of gunsmiths and this regiment was trained on a daily basis from April 1642.
70 Norma Tucker, *Colonial Virginians and Their Maryland Relatives* (Baltimore, MD, 1994), p. 12.
71 Isaac Pennington, Thomas Chamberlain, Thomas Player, Edmund Harvey and Christopher Whichcote.
72 Anon, *Roll of Members of the Military Company of Massachusetts: Now Called the Ancient and Honorable Artillery Company of Massachusetts, with a Roster of the Commissioned Officers and Preachers, 1638-1894* (Cambridge, MA, 1895),

p. 4. Robert Thomson served in New England with Francis Willoughby, William Rainsborough, Robert Long and Richard Davenport, among others.
73 Nagel, *The Militia of London*, p. 55; Tai Liu, *Puritan London: A Study of Religion and Society in the City Parishes* (London, 1986), p. 86.
74 John Rees, *Leveller Organisation and the Dynamic of the English Revolution* (PhD Thesis, Goldsmiths, University of London, 2014), pp. 60–62.
75 Members of the Artillery Company, organised by the date in which they joined, can be found in G.A. Raikes (ed.), *The Ancient Vellum Book of the Honourable Artillery Company, being the Roll of Members from 1611 to 1682* (London, 1890), pp. 35–70.
76 CJ, 2, pp. 301–303.
77 CJ, 2, pp. 450.
78 William Waller Hening, *The Statutes at Large; being a Collection of all the Laws of Virginia*, Vol. 1 (Richmond, VA, 1888), pp. 80–98. Sir John Evelyn was the MP for Bletchingly, Surrey.
79 Anon 'The Acorn Club', *The Warwick Patent* (Hartford, 1902), pp. 7–13. Warwick recruited investors for this scheme between 1632 and 1635 including John Pym, John Hamden, Sir Arthur Hesilrige, Charles Fiennes and Robert Barrington. Hugh Peter, Sir Henry Vane II and Winthrop travelled to the plantation in 1635 sponsored by Rotterdam merchants.
80 Brenner, *Merchants and Revolution*, p. 146; H.R. McIlwaine (ed.), *Minutes of the Colonial and General Court of Colonial Virginia 1622–1632, 1670–1676* (Richmond, 1974), p. 114. The Martins were in business with the Stone brothers, partners of Thomson and Tucker, while they had their plantation. It was sold to Richard Quiney, John Sadler and Simon Turgis.
81 Robert C. Simington (ed.), *Books of Survey and Distribution, Roscommon* (Dublin, 1949), pp. 89–92; Jane Ohlmeyer and Éammonn Ó Ciarda (eds.), *The Irish Statute Staple Books, 1596–1687* (Dublin, 1998), p. 132.
82 TNA SP 63/286, 1 Feb 1655, Copy of the Decree of the Court in the case of Parkhurst and Stowell, complainants, and William Basill, Esq., Attorney General, defendant.
83 Patrick Little, 'The English Parliament and the Irish Constitution' in Micheal Ó Siochrú (ed.), *Kingdoms in Crisis: Ireland in the 1640s* (Dublin, 2001), pp. 108–109.

3

The Adventure for Irish land

THE ADVENTURERS ACT

The Adventure for Irish land was initially suggested to the earl of Warwick by the earl of Cork in January 1642. Cork proposed the complete removal of Irish Catholics from Ireland, and recommended total conquest with a subsequent plantation by English settlers. In Cork's words, 'if it would please his Majesty, with assent of Parliament, to cause an act to be passed there, to attaint them all of high treason, and to confiscate their lands and estates to the crown, it would utterly dishearten them, and encourage the English to serve courageously against them in hope to be settled in the lands of them they shall kill or otherwise destroy'.[1] The earls of Cork and Warwick had become closer during the campaign to oust the king's favourite courtier, Thomas Wentworth, earl of Strafford. The friendship was cemented in 1641 when their children, Mary Boyle and Charles Rich, were married. They also had a common association with the Thomson brothers, George and Maurice. In Warwick's case this was a direct association and in Cork's case it was through his agent, Daniel Gookin.

One element in particular of Cork's plan had an attraction for the men of the Warwick House circle. As the king had left London and the rift between king and parliament had widened, it was unclear what authority parliament had to raise an army or taxes without the king's consent. The exception was the raising of money and arms to suppress the rebellion in Ireland. The money previously raised for Ireland in November 1641, however, was secured on the peers' estates and their credit was not inexhaustible. The problem was not a lack of cash, of which there was plenty at hand in London for such a worthy a cause as rescuing Protestant Ireland. The difficulty that lenders had, particularly the wealthiest ones, almost all of whom were royalists, was with the 'public faith'. This was parliament's guarantee that lenders would get their money back, a promise that was less secure while king and parliament were at odds. Irish land offered a real source of security that would not disappear if parliament were dissolved. As both royalist grandees and many of the colonial merchants and planters in Warwick's circle had investment interests at risk in Ireland, the Adventure was attractive to a relatively wide base.

Two unrelated events had combined to leave large stocks of cash in the hands of merchants throughout London. The first was a raid by Charles on the Royal Mint in July 1641 when he helped himself to £120,000 in silver bullion that was held there by merchants for their own security. Although Charles promised that the money would be repaid with interest, he presented no plans to do so and imposed a total ban on the withdrawal of gold from the mint the following December. For all practical purposes the king had stolen both the silver of the lesser colonial merchants and the gold of the wealthier goldsmiths and others who acted as their bankers. London's international merchants, who transacted some of their banking in Amsterdam and Middelburg, suffered a simultaneous crisis of confidence in the Amsterdam mint as a flood of debased currency from the Spanish Netherlands into these banking centres caused a temporary suspension of the minting of Dutch silver coins.[2] With both mints in disrepute, the merchants had little alternative but to store their money in their own homes. Distrust of both the king and of Spanish silver of dubious quality resulted in an unquantifiable and uncontrollable store of bullion deposited around London.

At first glance, there was nothing particularly new in Cork's proposal to Warwick. It was established practice for English victors to seize the lands of Irish rebels after each incursion and partial conquest. Indeed, it was the offspring of the most recent plantation generation, the sons of the New English planters from the 1620s, who were now clamouring at Westminster for funds. Previous plantations were undertaken subsequent to state-sponsored military conquest, and the lands were distributed to military officers and British investors after a successful campaign. The proposed Adventure for Irish land departed from this convention in that instead of the Irish plantation model, the methodology of England's Atlantic expansion was adopted that relied on private enterprise to conquer and exploit each new colony. The most crucial point of difference between colonial Ireland and the wider English empire up to this point was the treatment of the indigenous population. In Ireland, the native population was frequently accommodated on British plantation estates where they provided rent and labour, whereas in the wider Atlantic world the native population was usually displaced. Although London was rife with newspapers and pamphlets filled with lurid stories of the Irish and the atrocities committed by them, it is unclear how much of this was tavern talk and how much was taken seriously at Warwick House. Nonetheless, the formulation of the Adventurers Act, that envisioned the removal of the Irish population, marked the point at which plantation Ireland became colonial Ireland and its people were in mortal danger.

As the Adventure for Irish land emanated from the circle of Puritan peers and their contractors at Warwick House, not from parliament, it consisted primarily of elements learned from colonial conquest and governance as opposed to the precedents of earlier campaigns in plantation Ireland. Gone was the sanctimony of its immediate predecessor, 'An Act for a speedie contribucon and loan towards the releife of his Majesties distressed subjects of the kingdome of Irelande', intended as a charitable fund for newly destitute settlers.[3] The preamble of this earlier fundraising effort had drawn heavily from the popular press and claimed that the 'divers cruell murthers and massacres of the Protestants there have beene and are daily committed by Popish Rebells ... great multitudes of godly and religious people have been enforced to forsake their habitations'. The contribution or loan of money was requested for the 'honour of Almightie God and the preservation of the true Protestant Religion and Professors thereof'. In stark contrast, the Adventure for Irish land was all business and laid out the financial rewards that would surely accrue to those who contributed, with scant reference to the obligations of the godly.

Structurally, the Adventurers Act was a compilation of the most successful elements of its colonial predecessors. The land was remarkably undervalued, reflective of the prices current in New England land patents rather than the valuations which prevailed in Ireland. Although detailed instructions were given as to the amount of land to be allocated from each county and how it should be surveyed, the act assumed a simple form of ownership without the baggage of mortgages, leaseholds and other debts. The legislation granted the right to those who invested enough to receive more than 1,000 acres to create manors and hold court barons.[4] This idea was borrowed from a similar scheme used to attract investment to the Nova Scotia fisheries, which created new Nova Scotia baronets in Scotland and Ireland and offered easy ascent into the ranks of the minor gentry. Towns and other bodies corporate could invest on the same basis as a person, a rare privilege in early modern England, borrowed from the plantation schemes of Plymouth and other West Country ports of decades earlier. Of utmost importance was the statement that forfeiture would be applied, not only to those who were actively taking part in the rebellion, but to all who 'willingly assist or countenance' it.[5] This description could be applied to most of Catholic Ireland and it was this that made the Irish rebellion of October 1641 a war without end. Ultimately, the legislation was a legal fig leaf for the earl of Cork's original recommendation, that the Irish should be indiscriminately killed or otherwise destroyed. Once they had paid in their money, the investors, or Adventurers, were obliged to continue their campaign until the Irish had surrendered and their lands had been seized, otherwise they would not be able to recoup their investments. For the Irish, an unconditional surrender or even an overture for peace was simply not an option: it would mean total ruin.

Richard Boyle, earl of Cork, had suggested that his plan for conquest be presented to parliament by John Hampden, John Pym and William Strode, three of the five MPs that Charles had attempted to arrest on 4 January 1642. Warwick decided instead to use the channel that had successfully called out the Trained Bands and forced the king from London. On 12 January, only two days after the king had fled, Sir Thomas Barrington, MP and officer of the Providence Island Company was duly despatched once again from Warwick House to appear before the court of London's Common Council. Barrington advised the Common Council that merchants from London would provide a loan of £100,000, to be repaid with land forfeited by the defeated rebels in Ireland. This money would specifically be used to pay the forces then mustering in London for an Irish expedition under a royal warrant.[6] The intention of this proposal was to bring the only other large military force then in London under the control of the Warwick House circle. As the proposal had a military component, the Court of Common Council agreed to refer the proposal to its Committee of Safety, responsible for all military forces in the city and completely under the control of the colonial subcontractors. To prevent any opposition to the proposal from the Court of Aldermen, Barrington also arranged that the matter be referred to the London Companies to work out how it could fit with a strategy of supporting the London Companies' interest in their Londonderry plantation. Charles had restored the Londonderry plantation to the Companies' Irish Society in November 1641, with an amended charter that made the Companies responsible for the defence of their plantation. What Barrington achieved was to make it very difficult for the royalist Court of Aldermen to oppose the Adventure, as it offered the Irish Society a chance to escape the expense of defending the Londonderry plantation. The partly royalist Court of Common Council was in no position to oppose a serious proposal to deal with the Irish rebellion, and allowed it to progress without comment. By these multiple defaults, London's Committee of Safety came to be responsible for a proposal that would place the army for Ireland in the hands of the king's enemies.

While Barrington was doing the rounds in London, two further men were despatched from Warwick House to Westminster, John Pym and Nathaniel Fiennes. Their first task was a procedural matter, to raise an ordinance which enabled the reconvened parliament to meet officially with the Common Council's Committee of Safety to discuss these new preparations for the defence of Ireland. Once this was passed, the Adventure for Irish land ceased to be instigated by emissaries from Warwick House and became a series of bilateral discussions between groups representing London's Common Council and the Westminster parliament. The result was that a general warrant for the release of arms from the Tower of London for use in Ireland was issued, facilitated by the sudden arrest of Sir John Byron, the royalist lieutenant of the Tower. Parliament replaced Byron with Phillip Skippon, the commander of the Trained Bands.[7] Skippon now had ready access to the Tower's armoury, albeit with the caveat that warrants would need to be passed by parliament before each tranche of weapons for Ireland could be released.

As Sir Thomas Barrington negotiated with the Common Council on 12 January, Charles published his accusations against Pym and the other indicted MPs. Parliament countered with news that both the French and Spanish fleets had arrived in Ireland with arms and reinforcements, indicating that it had more pressing problems to deal with than the king's quarrel with five of its members.[8] Charles also issued a warrant on 12 January that authorised the removal of thousands of muskets, swords and other weapons from the armouries at the Tower of London and the city of Hull for his own forces.[9] As the capital was no longer under military control, he had no way to enforce the warrant or to take possession of the armoury before the Common Council made its own move. A further loan of £20,000 was provided by the Merchant Adventurers to parliament on 15 January 1642. This loan enabled the purchase and transport of arms as well as providing payment for an additional small expeditionary force to Ireland, and removed for the time being the appearance that despite much posturing and proposals, nothing was being done.[10] The drafting of an additional act for another loan from the City of London gave the impression that parliament could ensure the constant supply of new funds, albeit in a piecemeal way.

The Common Council duly reported on its deliberations to Westminster on 25 January.[11] The City refused to participate in the new loan for £100,000, principally on the grounds that £50,000 had already been loaned in December 1641 but little progress had been made in sending over troops or supplies.[12] The Common Council complained in their presentation that as their members were owed hundreds of thousands of pounds by creditors in Ireland, they too would have difficulty raising any further funds. Furthermore, the Common Council was convinced that any new funds could be spirited away by the king or his agents and then used against them. As evidence for this, the Common Council delegation drew attention to the perceived facts that no Catholics in England had been disarmed, that the navy was making no effort to prevent the flow of arms and men from Catholic Europe into Ireland and that London's suburbs contained 'many thousands of unknown persons' ready to take up arms against parliament. In parliament, Pym presented two petitions from the counties of Essex and Hertfordshire calling for the removal of Catholic peers from the House of Lords, and concluded with a fine speech concerning an international conspiracy of Catholic powers on the verge of conquering Ireland, and then turning on England. According to Pym, England had been betrayed by a king who obstructed efforts both to raise forces in England to send over to Ireland and to restrict the movement of Irish subjects between the two kingdoms. Moreover, the king had been betrayed by his own counsellors who were clearly mad.[13] Charles, exiled from the capital, could do little to stem the torrent of abuse from Westminster. The king became increasingly frustrated by the slow pace of deliberations in London, which undermined his own efforts to alleviate the suffering of his subjects in Ireland.[14]

To develop a sense of urgency, Sir John Clotworthy informed the House of Commons on 4 February that the Irish rebels had raised £180,000 and were in the process of using that money to purchase arms in Dunkirk.[15] John Pym recognised that the fifty-six-member Committee for Irish Affairs was far too unwieldy to meet regularly and manage an emergency. He requested that parliament appoint a smaller parliamentary commission to manage day-to-day affairs, the sixteen-member 'Commission for Managing the Affairs of Ireland', mandated to 'establish true peace and religion in that country'.[16] This commission was approved following Clotworthy's speech and its members were to be drawn from the Committee for Irish Affairs.[17] Despite yet another initiative, parliament continued in its failure to raise any money. Consequently, while the membership of the Commission for Managing the Affairs of Ireland was being considered, an alternative method for raising funds for Ireland, the Warwick House proposal under discussion at the Common Council, was being mulled over by yet another small group of MPs.

Recognising that smaller parliamentary commissions were a more efficient way of expediting resources for Ireland, Denzil Holles chaired his own small group, 'the commission for raising and levying money for the defence of Ireland'. Ignoring the Common Council, Holles met directly with the colonial merchants and on 11 February 1642 he delivered a petition to the House of Commons from 'certain Londoners offering to send forces to Ireland at their own expense', the proposal that became the Adventure for Irish land. The original sum offered by the 'Londoners', as reported by Holles, was £100,000, to be repaid in Irish land, and the Adventurers of this money would nominate their own officers. As the offer was identical to the scheme proposed by the earl of Cork to the earl of Warwick, it is clear that the 'certain Londoners' involved had been recruited by Warwick, as the original plan was not public knowledge. The naming of officers was essential if the Adventurers were to retain control of their army, and a further demand, that the state would allow the Adventurers access to arms, was also agreed to by parliament.[18]

Pym held a meeting with the merchants on 14 February at the Inner Court of Wards, where the Adventurers, represented by William Withers, a linen-draper, councillor for Cheapside and Warwick's provisioning agent for Virginia and New England, provided further details of the proposal.[19] The

£100,000 offered was for the provision of 1,000 horse and 10,000 infantry and in return the Adventurers expected to receive 800,000 acres of land in Ireland. The Adventurers offered to double the existing crown rent, in order to make the scheme more attractive to Charles.[20] This initial proposal for the conquest of Ireland valued the land at 2s 6d per acre, half of the typical value of land in New England at the time.[21] In the ensuing negotiations a further £250,000 was offered to maintain the army for each year that it was required. It was calculated that a total investment of £500,000 would be required to send and maintain a force of 20,000 cavalry and foot soldiers for the entire campaign. Parliament offered 1,320,000 Irish acres to repay the total sum, if needed, driving up the price of land to approximately 7s 12d per acre. The negotiations stand as a testament to the skills of Pym and Holles, for they had secured the promise of a huge sum, far more than what had been offered in the original proposal, and which valued Irish land at three times the Adventurers' initial offer.

On 15 February 1642 the earl of Warwick communicated the following summary of the proceedings to the earl of Cork:

> Here is a brave proposition made by some in the city of London, 1,000 people for £5,000 each to pay the 15,000 foot and 2,000 horse (English) and 10,000 foot and 700 horse (Scots), and 10,000 more troops for 1,000 acres for every £200 in Ulster, and 1,000 acres for every £400 in Munster out of the rebels land, and will plant it with Protestant tenants. Men have written £10,000 each and tomorrow it will be presented to both houses. Ordinance passed in Parliament for £35,000 victuals to be paid by the Lord Mayor of London, £5,000 for Londonderry, £5,000 for Youghal, £10,000 for Dublin and £15,000 for Carrickfergus. Lord Conway on his way tomorrow and John Clotworthy and Lord Lieutenant soon after.[22]

Denzil Holles and John Pym had managed both to arrange funds from the Fellowship of Merchant Adventurers, available forthwith, and to secure a far larger promise of funds from an unnamed group of London merchants, the emerging Adventurers for Irish land, without needing to resort to begging the king to raise a tax to finance the suppression of the rebellion in Ireland. It was a remarkable fundraising effort, achieved in the face of opposition from the usual financial backers of king and parliament. At this point, Warwick envisioned that the Adventure would be financed by the merchant elite, those who could speculate the very substantial sum of £5,000 each, and not the multitude of lesser colonial and Puritan merchants who would be the eventual investors. Parliament had agreed alternative proposals on 7 February 1642 for persons of modest means to contribute to the cause of Irish Protestantism, the 'Contribution for the Relief of the poor distressed subjects of Ireland', a national church gate collection.[23] On 7 February parliament also approved the despatch of a 20,000 strong Scottish army to Ireland, financed with the 'Brotherly

Assistance' loan managed from Warwick House.[24] Brotherly Assistance was raised in large amounts from financiers and peers, and Warwick assumed that the Adventure for Irish land, with far better rates of return for investors, could attract interest from similar sources. It was the management of Brotherly Assistance that enabled the Warwick House peers to seek money from outside their own circle. A major tranche of this money, £50,000, was raised and sent to the Scottish army in November 1641, lent by the same peers and MPs struggling to design a response to the rebellion in Ireland.[25]

The merchants who framed early drafts of the Adventure significantly undervalued Irish land in order to make their investment as profitable as possible. In 1635, for example, Arthur Hill had recruited English tenants from Cheshire and Lancashire for his Ulster estate and charged an annual rent of six shillings per acre for good ploughing land. In general terms, land in Ireland at this time was valued as a multiple of between ten and twenty times the annual rent, meaning Hill's land was worth a minimum of three pounds per acre.[26] The Adventure for Irish land valued land in Ulster at a mere four shillings an acre for a freehold, a pittance. Adventurers could recoup their investment within one year. Investors stood to make huge financial gains, and several reports emphasised the quality of Catholic Irish land and how it could support many thousands of 'true hearted English'.[27]

The Committee for the Speeding and Despatching of the Business for Ireland, the core of the Committee for Irish Affairs, presented a draft of their agreement with the Adventurers to the House of Commons on 16 February 1642, confirming the low price for land but doubling the amount of money to be raised to £1,000,000, a vast sum which entitled the investors to a total of 2.5 million acres. This figure represented over one-quarter of the Catholic-owned land in Ireland.[28] Even if parliament intended to follow a normal course of justice in the aftermath of the victory they expected, the combined estates of the leaders of the rebellion in Ireland represented only the smallest fraction of this total. This point did not go unnoticed by Charles I. The king observed in his reply to parliament on 22 February that he did not have the time to 'examine whether this course may not retard the Reducing of that kingdom, by exasperating the Rebels, and rendering them desperate of being received into Grace, if they shall return to their Obedience'.[29] The king was clearly aware that the Adventure risked prolonging the war in Ireland rather than bringing it to a swift end. The members of parliament's Committee for Irish Affairs should also have been aware of this risk but, if they were, they chose to ignore it. The £1,000,000 budget, well in excess of any prior calculation of the cost of crushing the rebellion, was attractive security for a more general raising of funds. If parliament could use the Irish rebellion as justification to raise arms and eject the king from his capital, it could also use Ireland for both security and repayment of all of parliament's financial needs.

Parliament was in the process of passing an ordinance confirming the temporary Committee of Safety, formed in London on 8 January, as the Adventurers' proposals were being discussed and modified. The intention of the MPs was to place town and county militias across England under parliament's authority. The 24 February 1642 Militia Ordinance confirmed the arrangements made on 8 January between the Committee for Irish Affairs and London's Common Council. A Committee for Safety was established for London that included representatives from both parliament and the Common Council. All of the Common Council's nominees were deeply involved in the negotiations for the Adventure for Irish land and of the ten MPs nominated by parliament to the Committee of Safety, six were Adventurers.[30] The composition of the committee was approved behind closed doors at a meeting of the Common Council when its chair, the royalist Lord Mayor, Richard Gurney, was too ill to attend.[31] The parliamentary ordinance to establish Committees of Safety for the remainder of England and Wales was finally published on 5 March 1642 and identified the rebellion in Ireland as a likely cause of further disturbances in England.[32] The same reasoning would later be invoked to divert money subscribed to the Adventure for Irish land to the parliamentary militias.

Parliament, therefore, had already established that Ireland would be used as a pretext should it become necessary to divert Adventurer subscriptions to its own forces, while Charles was still deciding whether or not he would approve the Adventurers Act. To avoid confronting the king with oppositionist peers or MPs, parliament sent Francis, Lord Willoughby of Parham, Sir Anthony Irby and Richard Boyle, Lord Dungarvan, to Windsor to secure Charles's signature on the Adventurers Act.[33] Lord Dungarvan, the son of the earl of Cork, was critically important to the process of persuading Charles to sign the Adventurers Act, as the support of the Boyles could determine the success or failure of any policy for Ireland that the king was considering. He was already a trusted intermediary between the king and Warwick's circle, as was demonstrated by his calming presence at York eighteen months earlier. Pym maintained pressure on the king to sign by informing parliament on 28 February that the Adventurers had already raised £100,000 and were wondering who was to receive the money.[34] Charles resisted, and attempted to tie his assenting to the Adventurers Act to parliament's militia proposals, passed without his consent on 5 March.[35] The passing of the militia ordinance made Charles realise that parliament no longer required his consent to pass the Adventurers Act. It could proceed without him and had raised a substantial amount of money in any case. The best he could hope for, by approving the act under the royal signature, was to assert his control over it at a later stage. By opposing it he would be seen as appeasing Catholic Ireland and forgiving the atrocities against Protestants, widely reported in the popular press. The final version of the Adventurers Act, the last act to be passed by both king and parliament until 1660, was published without any further modifications on 19 March 1642.[36] In the meantime, on 28 February, parliament had passed an additional ordinance that allowed debts incurred by soldiers performing military duties in Ireland to be repaid, if the soldiers wished, with Irish land confiscated from the rebels.[37] This minor addition removed the upper limit of 2.5 million acres that could be confiscated before the Adventurers Act had even passed into law, and from this point Ireland faced unlimited liability for the actions of the rebels. Together, the act and the ordinance spelled the end, in landowning terms, of Catholic Ireland.

THE INVESTORS IN THE ADVENTURE FOR IRISH LAND

The Adventure for Irish land attracted some 1,300 investors between March 1642, when the act was passed, and July when the Adventure was closed. All of the original investors are listed in the appendix. The investors elected a committee to represent their interests, which met in Grocers' Hall in London alongside the Committee for Irish Affairs and, for the remainder of 1642, the Committee of Safety. Many of the investors were, and remained, minor merchants or artisans drawn from England's cities and market towns. Despite the political gymnastics being performed in London, many of the smaller investors had a genuine interest in helping their Protestant brethren in Ireland in their hour of need, as evidenced by the widespread church gate collections that were organised successfully across England at the same time. Some of this original cohort perhaps aspired to a new life as landowners in Ireland, a nearer point of migration than the Atlantic colonies. The larger investors, and the committee that was chosen to represent all participants, had quite different motivation to those who adventured smaller sums. Most of the Adventurers' leaders were already involved in encouraging the king's departure from London.

The collection of the Adventurers' money was placed in the hands of four treasurers who met at the Guildhall as guests of the Common Council. Thomas Andrews was a rising London merchant and alderman who had invested in the Massachusetts Bay Company.[38] John Towse had travelled to Virginia in the 1630s and was involved in the tobacco trade as a close business associate of the Thomsons.[39] As one of the Common Councillors who had supported Sir Thomas Barrington's original proposal for the Adventure for Irish land on 12 January, Towse had supported the scheme from its inception. John Warner was active in the Virginia colonial trade as an importer of tobacco and exporter of manufactured goods.[40] He was the brother of Sir Thomas Warner, the governor of the Leeward Islands, who managed the Thomsons' interests there, and also of Samuel Warner, another tobacco merchant and William Thomson's father-in-law.[41] The fourth treasurer was Laurence Halstead, the Merchant

Adventurer. Halstead's presence would, it was hoped, widen the circle of potential investors to the wealthier, royalist, merchant grandees. Thomas Andrews and John Warner were not, in fact, the original choices for treasurer. The two men that had been suggested were Robert Bateman and a royalist merchant, John Garrett.[42] This configuration, most likely agreed between Charles and Lord Dungarvan, would have left an even 50:50 split between parliamentarian and royalist treasurers but it was subsequently rejected by the Court of Common Hall, which had been asked by the Lord Mayor to approve the project on behalf of the merchant establishment. The appointment of Andrews and Warner left Halstead as something of an outsider, a royalist Merchant Adventurer with few connections within the colonial group. While it was well paid, the post of treasurer was an onerous undertaking and the treasurers were obliged to be present at the Guildhall for eight hours per day to receive the subscriptions.[43]

John Pym had been somewhat disingenuous concerning the Adventurers' readiness to pay in their money, as only £35,500 was received in March 1642 and a further £67,250 in April.[44] According to Bottigheimer's calculations, there were over 1,000 subscribers to the original Adventure for Irish land, with the remainder investing in its much smaller successors over the next two years. Subscriptions were dominated by just thirty-seven individuals who subscribed one-fifth of the money.[45] Not all of these larger investments are as they appear in the surviving lists of subscribers. The largest sum adventured for Irish land in 1642 – £10,000 by the Corporation of London – was actually a charitable investment contributed to benefit Christ's Hospital School at Newgate in London.[46] The Corporation of London investment was not even new money but was the transfer of a previous loan made to parliament by the Corporation for mustering soldiers for Ireland on 20 December 1641.[47] The trustees had decided that after the events of early January, a potential Irish estate was a more secure investment for the school than money loaned to parliament. The second largest investment was also corporate in nature, contributed by the Corporation of Dartmouth on behalf of Dartmouth's merchants, many of whom were previously involved in the Dorchester Company and were closely tied to the Committee for Irish Affairs and those MPs accused by Charles. The largest individual investor was the former cashier of the Virginia Company, Sir David Watkins, with £6,000, who became the secretary for the Adventurers' committee at Grocers' Hall.[48] To create the widest possible pool of investors, the Adventurers were careful to attract speculators with interests in all of the colonial theatres.

There are two investors of £2,000 in the lists: the Custom House of London and Denis Bond, the MP for Dorchester. There are no supporting records for the Custom House, indicating that it may also have been a transferred debt similar to the arrangement made by the Corporation of London. Denis Bond was formerly the president of the Dorchester Company and had lent his name to a pooled investment in Irish land, similar to that of the nearby town of Dartmouth. The investment later fell under suspicion when Bond could not produce any receipts, suggesting that the money collected was not remitted to the treasurers. Bond had raised the £2,000 for the fortification of Dorchester at the outbreak of the English Civil War, but pretended that the money had been raised for Ireland.[49] Bond's case is an example of a running pattern with the subscription list – debts were assigned to the Adventure for Irish land but the money was used for other purposes or not paid in the first place. Three men apparently invested £1,500 or more. William Heveningham, MP, a Virginia planter who supposedly invested £1,600 and was present at the trial of Charles I in 1649, could only produce receipts for £600. Humphrey Mackworth, who invested £1,706, was MP for Shropshire and brother-in-law of Sir William Waller, the parliamentary general. Other than Mackworth's own testimony, there is no supporting evidence that he invested any money in the Adventure for Irish land.[50] Charles Vaughan, who invested £1,630, was a nephew of Sir John Hawkins, the famous English privateer who inspired the original development of the Bahamas, St Kitts and Leeward Island plantations. Vaughan would be appointed county treasurer for the parliamentary army in Devon in the summer of 1642. Vaughan claimed that his receipts were lost during the siege of Exeter.[51]

The next two investments, taken in descending order of the amounts apparently invested, continue the pattern. The cities of Taunton (£1,360) and Gloucester (£1,350) both became important parliamentary enclaves in 1642, and there are no receipts for either, again apparently lost.[52] Gilbert Millington (£1,275) was investing on behalf of somebody else: Samuel Burroughs, a business partner of the earl of Warwick.[53] Millington was a partner in Maurice Thomson's cotton plantation on St Kitts where his son, Rowland Millington, was plantation manager.[54] Gilbert Millington would later sign Charles I's death warrant. After Sir David Watkins, the second largest individual investor for whom there is reliable evidence, was another brother-in-law of Maurice Thomson, William Hawkins. Hawkins' (£1,250) investment is understated in Bottigheimer's list. A separate list of 'Those Adventurers who paid in their subscriptions in full' states that Hawkins invested £3,675.[55] Hawkins' career as a manager of merchants' affairs began in 1626 when he was sent to France as deputy to the ambassadors extraordinary, Henry Rich, earl of Holland and Sir Dudley Carleton.[56] In 1642 Hawkins served both as the secretary to parliament's Committee for Irish Affairs and as a business manager for Robert Sidney, the earl of Leicester, appointed by Charles as Lord Lieutenant of Ireland. Hawkins was uniquely placed to inform the Adventurers' committee at Grocers' Hall of everything that was under discussion concerning Ireland within both parliamentary and royalist circles. The largest individual adventures that can be verified were, therefore, those of Sir David Watkins and William Hawkins, respectively the secretaries of the Adventurers' committee and parliament's Committee for Irish Affairs in 1642.

The difficulty with Bottigheimer's composite list of investors in *English Money and Irish Land* is that it does not consist solely of the money invested in the Adventure for Irish land in the spring of 1642, but includes all of the debts subsequently assigned against Irish land, regardless of their original purpose. Only the major subscribers for whom there are receipts preserved in the Adventurers' collection in State Papers at the National Archives can be considered to be genuine Adventurers for Irish land. This cohort and the individuals prominent at Westminster and London's Common Council during the upheavals of January 1642 are almost identical. From these receipts it is clear that the Adventure for Irish land was primarily supported by a group of merchants and MPs with close connections to Warwick House and the Atlantic plantations. These investors subsequently took leading roles both in parliamentary finance and in the direction of parliament's Irish policy. The leading verified investors, with subscriptions of £1,000 or more, are a Who's Who of parliamentary activism and include Thomas Andrews, Sir Thomas Barrington, Sir John Clotworthy, William Hawkins and Maurice Thomson.[57] After the leaders, the lists of investors in Bottigheimer and the State Papers tally more closely for smaller sums. The appendix of this book is a composite of these lists: Adventurers who paid in their full subscriptions, a separate list of Adventurers who only paid in part of their instalments, and the remainder, investors drawn from Bottigheimer's list and Mahaffy's Calendar of the Adventurers' collection in State Papers. The appendix differentiates the subscribers who paid in money from those who were awarded 'certificates' or other instruments of entitlement.[58]

The middling class of merchants that trusted their money to the treasurers was drawn mainly from the Atlantic tobacco and fish trades.[59] A smaller cohort with businesses based in London had gained some political experience complaining about trade policy after the recall of parliament.[60] For the most part, the smallest adventures were invested by ship-owners, reflecting their existing relationships and their habit of sharing risk that was the norm within the colonial merchant community. The Trinity House Certificates provide a certain amount of information as to the identity of these networks of ship-owners and their preferred partners.[61] Trinity House was established by royal charter in 1514, initially to provide pilotage on the River Thames, but its responsibilities were extended to include the sale of ballast and the registration of new English vessels and their armaments. The certificates identify the first registration and initial armament of each vessel, and provide the name of the leading partner behind the ship's construction, some additional partners and, usually, the name of the shipbuilder and intended master for her first voyage.

The limitations of the Trinity House Certificates are that they do not list all of the subsequent partners, as the ships frequently had different owners for each voyage. Furthermore, Trinity House only kept records for London and not for any other port. It is not possible to trace the owners of the ship if it was subsequently sold. Even with these limitations, the certificates provide the names of 291 promoters and shareholders in merchant shipping between 1630 and 1638 and, of these, eighty-four became investors in the Adventure for Irish land in 1642.[62]

In Bottigheimer's analysis, out of 1,533 Adventurers, the home town of 1,331 could be determined, and out of these 750 were from London and they provided approximately half of the money.[63] More specifically, ship-owners and their siblings, according to the Trinity House Certificates, contributed approximately £40,000. Although the certificates list only the lead partners in each vessel, if the contributions of their known business associates are included the proportion of money subscribed by the shipping group to the Adventure for Irish land rises to almost one-third of the total sum subscribed in the capital.[64] Of all the subgroups who participated in the Adventure for Irish land, the ship-owners were the most integrated. As each ship had up to sixteen fractional owners, and the total number of long distance ships numbered in the low hundreds, the merchant ship-owners had very strong commercial ties, often reinforced by marriage. Merchant ships normally travelled in convoys, further expanding the number of individual merchants involved in each voyage, and trade patterns were well established. The tobacco fleets were normally scheduled to arrive in the colonies in April/May, at the end of the Caribbean dry season, and returned to England in July or August.[65] The ships would then be chartered by new consortia for a shorter voyage to a European destination. A shipment of wine from the Canary Islands, for example, was usually required to arrive in London before Christmas so the ship was ready for the next Atlantic season.[66] These fleet movements are significant as the normal pattern of Atlantic trade meant that the combined fleet of armed merchant ships was concentrated on the Thames in January and February. A survey from 1627, before the great increase of ships that came with the boom in tobacco exports from the colonies, shows seventy-eight armed merchantmen on the Thames or in the Thames Estuary, carrying almost 1,800 pieces of ordnance between them.[67] Most merchants were specialists with a developed network of contacts and factors, but all were used to the concept of investing together in specific voyages and projects, and to acting in concert when their interests were threatened.

Given the strong representation of maritime merchants and investors among the London-based Adventurers, it is unsurprising that in the second strongest area of support for the Adventure, the ports of the English West Country, the investors followed a similar pattern, even if their money never made it to the treasurers. Adventurers from Dorset, principally the port of Dartmouth, were drawn almost entirely from merchants involved in colonial provisioning or who owned plantations in the colonies. Dartmouth was the port from which the Virginia Company's pioneering mission set sail in 1606.[68] But despite a long tradition of involvement in the servant and tobacco trade, the Dorset Adventurers were drawn almost entirely from investors in the Puritan-backed Dorchester Company, the failed colonial experiment in New England of the 1620s, established to 'provide religious instruction for the fishermen and others of our nation'.[69] Original Dorchester Company shareholders or their sons, who included most of the investors in the Corporation of Dartmouth's corporate subscription, invested over £5,000 in Irish land in 1642.[70] The enthusiastic response of Dorset to the Munster plantation in the 1580s and the family links between Dorset and Munster that ensued until 1641 helps to explain this solidarity. Family connections between the southwest of England and southern Ireland indicate that these contributions, usually very small sums, were made more in the spirit of charity than for profit.

The eighty Adventurers who invested between £500 and £1,000 comprise a further 20% of the total value of subscriptions and follow a similar pattern to the larger purported investors. This group consisted overwhelmingly of parliamentarians or Puritan merchants who were active in the Americas and Europe. Warwick's colonial partners are present in large numbers, although there are some notable royalist merchants listed as well.[71] The most senior of these was Sir Nicholas Crispe (£900), a Commissioner for Customs and key financier of the royalist navy. There was a branch of the Crisp family living in County Carlow at the outbreak of the rebellion, which could explain how Crispe felt able to support an overtly parliamentarian undertaking.[72] Crispe, a business partner of long standing with William Cloberry and the earl of Cork, was very well known among the senior Atlantic merchants. Were it not for his status in the merchant community, his contribution to the Adventure for Irish land might have been refused. Charles subsequently complained that three of the treasurers – Andrews, Towse and Warner – had screened subscribers and only accepted subscriptions from men whom they considered to be reliable supporters of the parliamentary cause.[73] It was then normal practice for the treasurers of loans and benefices to draw up their own lists of likely subscribers and the leaders of the Adventurers for Irish land were doing nothing out of the ordinary in excluding the royalist merchant elite and reserving the spoils for their friends.[74] When Warwick first circulated the idea of the Adventure for Irish land around London, however, his intent was that a small number of wealthy merchants would provide £5,000 each. Excluding London's richest men caused the Adventure to raise far less money than originally envisioned, and far too little to mount a lengthy campaign in a hostile kingdom. This policy, completely at odds with the Adventure's aim of ensuring a rapid and decisive end to the rebellion in Ireland, raises the suspicion that the treasurers were not being completely frank as to their intentions.

The Adventure was not well received in royalist circles. Giorgio Giustinian, the ambassador of the Doge of Venice in England, observed succinctly in his weekly report of 28 February: 'The City of London has offered to undertake the task of reducing the (Irish) rebels and recover the kingdom completely on condition that all captures shall be possessed and enjoyed by the citizens. But the offer has not been accepted, as it did not seem desirable to increase the advantage of this great city.'[75] At some point in March or April 1642 it had become clear within the upper echelons of London's merchant community that the Adventure for Irish land was not what it seemed and Andrews, Towse and Warner were not the most reliable of people to entrust money to. The royalist MPs were slower to react, still believing in March 1642 that the purpose of the Adventure for Irish land was to alleviate the sufferings of Protestant Ireland. When they became aware that the money would not be used for this purpose, the subscriptions stopped. Royalist MPs who had paid their first quarter of subscription money by the 1 April 1642 deadline declined to pay the remainder of their instalments.[76] One of the four treasurers, the royalist Merchant Adventurer Laurence Halstead, also made no further payment after his initial contribution. Halstead continued to sign receipts for contributions until July 1642, for which he received his commission, but took no further part in parliamentary fundraising. He was not involved as treasurer in any of the fundraising bodies established by parliament following the Adventure and fled to Amsterdam in 1643. Despite all of these suspicions, opponents of the Adventure were in no position to resist it as this would mean they were preventing the only realistic response to the rebellion in Ireland that had emerged so far. As the money continued to pour in, the men who controlled it began to assert themselves.

GROCERS' HALL

Although the Westminster parliament resumed business as usual, its two key committees, the Committee for Irish Affairs and the Committee for Safety, continued to meet at Grocers' Hall and not at Westminster. Parliament had been managing its response to the Irish rebellion with the unwieldy structure of fifty-six MPs and twenty-eight peers nominated to the Committee for Irish Affairs, and a proliferation of smaller commissions that dealt with individual financing initiatives. These were consolidated into the more manageable, and permanent, 'Commissioners and Council for the Government and Defence of Ireland', established under the Great Seal on 4 April 1642 with Pym as chairman.[77] This body adopted the name of the original Committee for Irish Affairs and installed the MPs of an earlier committee, those who were appointed on 19 February as 'Commissioners for the Speeding and Dispatching of the Businesses for Ireland', as a permanent secretariat. The number of peers was reduced to seven: Algernon Percy, earl of Northumberland, Robert Devereux, earl of Essex, Philip Herbert, earl of Pembroke, Henry Rich, earl of Holland, William Fiennes, viscount Saye-and-Sele, Edward Montague, Lord Kimbolton and John Lord Robartes.[78] When William Hawkins was appointed as secretary to the Committee for Irish Affairs, the Adventurers' committee, which also met at Grocers' Hall, granted a loan of £10,000 to deal with its most pressing business.[79] William Hawkins would keep Maurice Thomson and the rest of the Adventurers' committee apprised of any discussions at meetings of parliament's Committee for Irish Affairs, and Hawkins remained in this post until 1649, when he left for Ireland with one of its more vocal MPs, Oliver Cromwell. As a foretaste of the relationship the Adventurers' leadership would have with parliament, on the day that the Committee for Irish Affairs first met, parliament also discussed a reduction of the 'excessive rates' of customs levied on tobacco imports from the Caribbean.[80] This petition was delivered to parliament by Samuel Warner, one of the leading Adventurers. Everything the Adventurers did from this point would come at a price, and the price for a loan of £10,000 was a large reduction in their tax bill.

The ink was barely dry on the Adventurers' Act when raising money for Ireland became less urgent. On 26 March, parliament and the king together approved a subsidy of £400,000 to be collected throughout England and Wales.[81] Although much of this money had already been promised to creditors, parliament used the subsidy as security for a new loan of £100,000 for Ireland, negotiated with the City of London.[82] A published list of MPs who had undertaken to subscribe money to the Adventure for Irish land included a pledge from the County of Buckinghamshire for £6,000, arranged by John Hampden and John Goodwin.[83] Instead of paying their money into the Adventure, Buckinghamshire opted instead for the loan to parliament secured against the proceeds of the new subsidy.[84] The point of difference was that money loaned against the subsidy was under the control of parliament and disbursed via the Committee of Irish Affairs, while money paid in to the Adventurers was to be used, as it saw fit, by a group of private merchants assembling their own army. With access to cash from the king's supporters, subscriptions for the City loan rapidly overtook subscriptions for the Adventure and Parliament took the leading role in supporting a military response to the Irish rebellion.

The Adventurers had established their own committee, the Committee of Adventurers for Ireland, that included neither peers nor MPs and only two aldermen.[85] This committee met at Grocers' Hall from March 1642 until the restoration of Charles II in June 1660. Its membership, after allowing for changes in financial circumstances and mortality, was remarkably consistent, especially in its early years. From the Committee of Adventurers came many of the treasurers and leading administrators of the parliamentary financial and taxation committees that followed it. Parliament's financial arrangements from 1642 to 1653 appear fragmented, but were far more undivided than at first sight. The leaders of all of the financial committees met at Grocers' Hall, at the regular meetings of the Adventurers for Irish land. The men who made up the Committee of Adventurers controlled most of parliament's finances. The influence of the Adventurers on parliament's Irish policy was not the result of their investment in a speculative scheme of conquest – this conquest did not actually take place. It came instead from their total control over parliament's finances.

In the close confines of Grocers' Hall, the colonial traders who had become Adventurers in Irish land were conspicuously successful in obtaining contracts to supply British forces already in Ireland. William Pennoyer, a privateering partner of Maurice Thomson in the Caribbean in the 1630s, undertook to ship gunpowder and shot from Holland to Ireland in ships owned by Samuel Vassall, an MP and founder of the Massachusetts Bay Company.[86] Maurice Thomson's ship, the *Charity*, was commissioned to carry munitions to Carrickfergus Castle.[87] Another of Thomson's armed merchant ships, the *Ruth*, was hired on behalf of the earl of Cork to deliver £6,000 in money to Boyle's forces in Munster.[88] Benjamin Whetcomb, a New England trader whose family had invested in the Massachusetts Bay Company with Hugh Peter and Samuel Vassall, and whose brother was mayor of Dungarvan, undertook to provide biscuits, peas and cheese to the Munster forces to the value of £150. Vassall's brother was based in Limerick when the rebellion broke out. All of these goods were ordered on foot of the loan of £30,000 provided by the Merchant Adventurers to parliament for the Irish campaign.[89]

Richard Turner, a tobacco importer and Bermuda Company member who had contributed £200 to the Adventure for Irish land, was contracted by the Committee for Irish Affairs to supply 10,000 coats and pairs of cotton stockings on 9 May 1642, to a total value of £4,500.[90] There were considerable profits to be made in supplying the army, with the guarantee of payment from parliament offsetting the uncertainty of ever recouping any land from the Irish Adventure. It was well worth the merchants' while to invest a small sum in the Adventure to win favour at Grocers' Hall when it came to bidding for contracts. John Browne, gun-founder of London, adventured £106 for Ireland and was rewarded with a contract for £1,041 worth of arms and ammunition.[91] On 31 May 1642, Maurice Thomson was awarded a contract to supply £5,000 worth of wheat to the army in Ulster. Thomas Alcock and Sir John Wollaston adventured £300 and £900 respectively and were awarded a contract to supply £1,375 worth of cloth to the army in Ireland.[92] It is important to note that these army contractors undertook the risk of ensuring that their goods were delivered safely, and would not normally expect to get paid until at least six months after delivery. It was a trade well suited to the long-distance Atlantic merchants and not one for new entrants who were unused to the uncertainty of trading in hostile territory.

AN ARMY FOR IRELAND

On 16 June the Committee for Irish Affairs provided £34,000 to parliament's Commissioners for the Scots army in the north of England, to enable the Scots army to transport itself to Ulster.[93] There were already 8,000 Scots soldiers in Ulster under the pay of parliament, paid using money raised from the Merchant Adventurers and secured on the £400,000 assessment.[94] The deal was brokered by Sir William Armyne, Nathaniel Fiennes, Sir Philip Stapilton and John Hampden. The money was to be paid out of the final instalment of £110,000 from the 'Brotherly Assistance' finance managed through Warwick House to end the Bishops' Wars, and failing that, guaranteed with proceeds from the £400,000 assessment.[95] This money was subscribed promptly by the peers who had retreated from investing in the Adventure, and by senior parliamentarian and royalist merchants.[96] This cohort was identical to the one that Warwick had originally envisioned for the Adventure for Irish land, and proved willing to lend through an acceptable channel. London's establishment was reluctant to place its money into the hands of suspect commoners at Grocers' Hall, but was warily agreeable for it to pass through Warwick House.

Two armies for Ireland were thus developed in parallel at Grocers' Hall. Once the Scottish initiative was in progress, parliament approved a list of officers for the Adventurers' army on 17 June.[97] By June, however, contributions to the Adventure for Irish land had almost dried up and less than £9,000 was collected in the entire month. On 22 June, parliament made the surprising announcement that land was to be denominated in Irish rather than English acres, which meant an increase of 60% in the amount of land to be awarded.[98] This concession persuaded the London Companies to convert their £10,000 into an Adventure for Irish land, but little new money was forthcoming.[99] Instead, the London Companies announced an additional loan of £100,000 on 1 June 1642, to be disposed of by the Committee for Irish Affairs but not to fall into the hands of the Adventurers.[100] This money was raised from individual livery company members, according to their capacity. The loan, specifically for the relief of Ireland, was intended to be repaid within one year, with a proviso that the loan could be of indefinite duration bearing an interest rate of 8% per annum.[101] Each company was allocated a proportion to collect from its members and the largest contributions were expected from the companies most likely to benefit from the mass purchase of food and clothing. Consequently, although the Glazers' Company was only obliged to contribute £80, the Grocers contributed £9,000, the Haberdashers £5,500 and the Drapers

£7,500. In effect, the London Companies were financing their own relief effort, selling their goods on credit into Ireland on the basis of an indefinite loan secured by an ordinance of parliament, and military supplies began to flow from London to the Londonderry plantation as a result. The London loan was also used to pay the earl of Leicester, the Lord Lieutenant of Ireland, while he waited to leave for Ireland and take command of the king's army.[102]

This work towards financing a military intervention in Ireland was undertaken in conjunction with parliament's financial preparations for an increasingly likely military engagement with the king. Charles had arranged finance both from his own loyalists and by pawning the Crown Jewels in Amsterdam. He had purchased a large quantity of military material in the Netherlands which was transported to York, replacing the arsenals lost at Hull and in the Tower of London to parliament. Parliament had responded to Charles' initiative with the 9 June ordinance for bringing in plate, money and horses.[103] This measure was a straightforward loan, to be supplied by citizens at an interest rate of 8%. Although contributions from London were to be paid directly to the London Committee of Safety for the use of the Trained Bands, contributions from the rest of England were vested with the treasurers appointed for this loan, three of whom were the same treasurers appointed to deal with the Adventure for Irish land: Thomas Andrews, John Towse and John Warner. The fourth treasurer, the leading Adventurer Sir John Wollaston, was formerly Deputy Governor of the Irish Society and became both colonel of the Gold Trained Band and member of the London Committee of Safety by 1642.[104]

On 11 June, the Adventurers published the muster for their army, under the command of Philip Lord Wharton.[105] The mustering of this force took place at the same time as the deal with the Scots was being brokered. Had the Adventurers' army been deployed to Munster, as intended, a larger and possibly decisive British force would have taken to the field in Ireland in the summer of 1642. As it was, although parliament mustered considerable force, and over 10,000 English troops arrived in Ireland during the winter and spring of 1641–42, the Adventurers' army and the forces nominally under the command of the Lord Lieutenant were unable to effectively pool their resources. The Adventurers' army remained in England. The Committee for Irish Affairs took four regiments into its pay on 12 April, commanded by William St. Leger, Viscount Cromwell, Michael Earnley and Sir Foulke Hunks.[106] Half of the cost of raising these forces was met with a loan of £4,000 provided by the Adventurers, to be repaid by parliament, and the soldiers were mustered around London before some were despatched to Dublin.[107] A frustrated earl of Leicester wrote to his sister-in-law, the Countess of Carlisle, in August 1642:

> The Parliament bids me to go presently, the king commands me to stay till he despatch me. The supplies of one, and the authority of the other, are equally necessary.

I know not how to obtain them both, and am more likely to have neither; for now they are at such extremes … The one says, why should we give money and arms which may be employed against us and the other says why should I give power and authority which may be turned against me?[108]

Neither king nor parliament wished to see another army formed on English soil without being certain who it would be used against. The Scottish army was being shipped from the north of England to Ulster, and would only pose a threat to English forces if shipping could be arranged to bring it back. Moreover, Leicester could not expect any practical support from the Adventurers, who were insisting on retaining control over the appointment of their own officers. With the departure of the Scots, the largest trained army in England was in the pay of the Committee of Adventurers at Grocers' Hall. The king's opportunity to muster an army for Ireland and appoint its officers had passed. Charles had announced on 14 April that he would lead the expeditionary force to Ireland, an idea swiftly rebuffed in the House of Commons.[109] This may have been his intention since 19 March, when he signed the Adventurers Act. If successful, he would have taken command of a substantial army and emptied the purses of his enemies, but the king's plan failed when he did not immediately act upon it. The Adventurers' army continued its training exercises at the grounds of the Artillery Company in London, in plain sight of the king's supporters, but untouchable.[110]

AN ARMY FOR ENGLAND

On 26 July, the House of Commons instructed the Adventurers to loan £32,000 to the earl of Leicester, ostensibly to settle the arrears of Leicester's soldiers still in England, but in effect to bring them into the pay of the Adventurers.[111] Parliament's remaining strategy for Ireland was to use a recent treaty between the English and Scottish parliaments that brought all of the Protestant forces in Ulster under the command of the Scottish army, on condition that the Westminster parliament bring the soldiers' pay up to date.[112] The Committee for Irish Affairs began winding down its activities and paid off its major commissaries: Gualter Frost for supplies sent to Dublin and William Dobbins of Bristol for supplies sent to Munster and Galway.[113] An order was signed for the release of a small amount of arms, £1,700 worth of artillery, from the Tower of London for despatch to Dublin.[114] The remainder of the arsenal, although purchased for Ireland, was hoarded in London for the Adventurers. Finally realising what was going on in London, Charles wrote to parliament on 23 July and stressed that he would not permit any of the money raised under his authority to be diverted and used against him.[115] Parliament's response, on 28 July, was for its Committee of Safety, still at Grocers' Hall, to request £100,000 from the Committee of the Adventurers for Irish land.[116] The request was signed by earls Bedford, Essex and Holland, viscount Saye-and-Sele, Denzel Holles, John Hampden, Sir Philip Stapilton and Sir William Waller.[117] Parliament's Committee for Irish Affairs also met on the same day at Grocers' Hall, but did not discuss the arrangement between the Committee for Safety and the Adventurers. It is a very surprising omission, not least because Saye-and-Sele, Denzel Holles and Sir William Waller attended both meetings.[118] Instead, the Committee for Irish Affairs discussed the departure from London of both Nicholas Loftus, who managed all payments for English forces in Ireland, and the earl of Leicester, the Lord Lieutenant of Ireland.[119] Loftus was travelling to Ireland on urgent personal business and Leicester had also left London to take up his post. These apparently coincidental departures of key personnel, the overall military commander and the paymaster for British forces in Ireland, removed the most powerful potential critics of parliament's new financial arrangements from the capital and concentrated power in Grocers' Hall.

On 30 July 1642 parliament ordered that £100,000 be taken from the Adventure for Irish land and transferred to the Committee of Safety, responsible for the military affairs of London and also for parliament's military affairs.[120] Ever careful, Maurice Thomson had transferred £4,000 owed to him by the Adventure to a bond drawn on customs on 23 July.[121] Thomson's action indicates that the decision to transfer the Adventure from Ireland to parliament had already been taken before Charles wrote to parliament to complain about it. On 16 August, the Committee for Irish Affairs lost the authority to take payment decisions without having them first approved by a parliamentary sub-committee at Westminster, an attempt by MPs to have some oversight over the goings-on at Grocers' Hall.[122] The committee was to meet just twice per month, and attendance also contracted as its members were drawn into the parliamentary war effort. The implication is that a faction of MPs at Westminster was deeply unhappy with the extra-parliamentary activities at Grocers' Hall. Even though parliament had passed a Declaration on 28 July, prepared by the Committee of Safety and delivered by Denzel Holles from Grocers' Hall, that expressed the 'reasons and grounds for parliament to raise arms', parliament was not a party to the financial arrangements that suddenly enabled it to raise arms on such a huge scale. These arrangements were made between the three committees at Grocers' Hall: Safety, Ireland and Adventurers. Debating the merits and demerits of raising arms was a very different proposition from actually doing so. Even as Grocers' Hall was ready to go to war, parliament as a whole was not, and the declaration to raise arms that was passed by the Commons was delayed by the House of Lords pending a conference to discuss the matter.[123]

There was nothing the Lords could do, as it happened, to delay the transfer of the money. All that needed to happen for it to take place was for Thomas

Andrews, John Towse and John Warner to write a payment warrant and present it to the Committee for Safety. At a stroke, the Adventurers for Irish land became parliament's largest and most important creditor. This action also profoundly changed the nature of the Adventure, transforming it from a speculation in the conquest of Ireland to a state loan, secured on the real estate of Catholic Ireland. Although the loan was not intended to be a long-term arrangement it became so and parliament, not the Grocers' Hall committee, eventually became responsible for the conquest of Ireland. For the creditors, the 1,000 merchants who had contributed to this first Adventure, the transfer of their money marked a profound shift in the type of investment they had signed up to. The vast majority had no experience in long-term state finance, mostly because they lacked the financial resources but also due to their social status. Led by the Grocers' Hall committee, they now found themselves committed to a financial arrangement they had hitherto avoided with little prospect of seeing their money again. The despatch of the Adventurers' army to Ireland was also postponed indefinitely as this army followed their money into the hands of the Committee of Safety.

The Committee of Safety's reason for the transfer of funds was that much of the Adventure had been remitted in plate, precious metal in various forms which needed to be minted into coin before it could be used for military wages. The idea was that the plate could be used as collateral for cash borrowings on the public faith, and the cash then used to purchase military supplies. The collateral would be returned to the Adventurers in time for an expeditionary force to depart for Ireland.[124] In the event, the money was spent and not even notionally repaid by June 1649, when twice the original amount was allocated from the expected proceeds of the sale of Dean and Chapter lands in a further effort to delay repayment.[125] This was long into the future, and the £100,000 ordered by parliament was quickly transferred from the treasurers of the Adventure for Irish land to Richard Shute, treasurer of the Committee of Safety, the merchant who had originally co-delivered, along with Maurice Thomson, the Citizens of London's petition to Charles I at York in September 1640.[126] The Committee of Safety began construction of a highly visible munitions works and the assembling of a train of artillery at the Artillery Grounds, where the Adventurers' army was already mustered. Under the direction of the Providence Island Company peer, Lord Brooke, £6,000 was spent in August 1642 constructing buildings and assembling and manufacturing the materials, tools and transport for a campaign.[127] These materials were supplied by London artisans who had, in most cases, subscribed small sums to the Adventure for Irish land or were related to its leaders. John Browne of London, for example, who contributed £100 to the Adventure for Irish land, supplied food.[128] Browne was an associate of the Rosewell Patentees, a small Massachusetts plantation established in 1629.[129] Thomas Bateman, a member of the Massachusetts Bay Company, and Edward Thomson, a cousin of Maurice, supplied artillery wagons.[130] John Shuttleworth, whose brother Richard subscribed £300, supplied £216 worth of wagons; Richard Mitchell subscribed £25 and delivered £425 worth of pontoons.[131] Stephen Estwick, a Barbados planter who had subscribed £100 and was a member of the Adventurers' committee, was entrusted with £500 to purchase supplies and horses to fortify the town of Watford.[132] Although many Adventurers had been slow to come forward and supply material for the war in Ireland, they acted swiftly to support parliament's preparations in England.

As rumours circulated in London that the Adventure was to be placed in parliament's hands, the month of July saw a remarkable surge in subscriptions, with almost £110,000 paid in. In all, roughly one-third of the entire sum raised by the Adventure for Irish land was remitted to the treasurers just before the £100,000 loan to the Committee of Safety was announced. The Adventure for Irish land eventually provided almost all of the money for parliament's initial mobilisation in August 1642.[133] As half of the 215 collectors for plate, money and horses in London and its adjacent boroughs were also Adventurers, support for the transfer of the Adventure to the Committee of Safety had support among the leading investors.[134] For many subscribers, the Adventure contained an element of deniability should their opposition to the king end in defeat. They had lent in good faith to support Protestant Ireland and the diversion of their funds was the responsibility of the Adventurers' committee, not theirs. Their money was distributed among officers appointed to muster troops for parliament, including Arthur Goodwin, Oliver St John, William Fairfax, Sir Henry Vane II, George Thomson, Francis Thomson, Oliver Cromwell and the Warwick House circle of peers.[135] The largest payment during these early weeks, however, was not to military officers but to a merchant, the Adventurer Stephen Estwick, who provided uniforms for the soldiers to the value of £1,500.[136]

The parliamentary ordinance for bringing in money, plate and horses relied heavily on individual leading Adventurers for horses, a relatively scarce resource of considerable value.[137] Lord Wharton, George Thomson and William Pennoyer all contributed £150 worth of horses by the end of the first week of June 1642.[138] Maurice Thomson provided not only horses, but the cavalrymen as well. Smaller contributions, provided mainly by Adventurers, continued through the month of June but the process accelerated rapidly from 1 July. The Providence Island Company peers finally came forward, as their strategy of using the subcontractors as their proxies had run its course. There was no longer any point in pretending that they were in some way removed from the proceedings. Henry Rich, earl of Holland, delivered thirty-six horses and riders worth £1,200 on 1 July; Lord Mandeville, twelve horses and riders worth £380; and the earl of Essex a further twenty horses and riders worth £560 – all on the same day.[139] The sudden appearance of the peers at the

Artillery Grounds galvanised both financial contributions to the Adventure for Irish land and the donation of horses for use by the Trained Bands. Some leading Adventurers continued to avoid risking their own fortunes. Sir David Watkins, for example, the secretary of the Adventurer's committee, used £250 he held in trust for the Court of Wards.[140]

By September 1642, its money diverted to the parliamentary cause, the first Adventure for Irish land had been expended. Its treasury was empty and its army, intended for Munster, had been sent to join the main parliamentary force at Edgehill, where it took part in the first major engagement of the English Civil War.[141] Some merchants were left with their bills unpaid when the adventure ran out of money, most notably two London aldermen who were not Adventurers, Maurice Gethin and Tempest Milner.[142] Gethin and Milner were both cloth merchants and their consortium was owed £42,051.[143] Although the bulk of this debt was for clothes ordered for the Adventurers' army, the Adventurers took little interest in debts owed to merchants outside of their own inner circle. On 26 July 1642, parliament instructed the Adventurers to transfer £10,000 to Adam Loftus for the payment of these contractors, but this payment instruction was ignored.[144] These actions undermined parliament's further efforts to attract finance for Ireland from sources other than the Adventurers. Far from helping the English war effort in Ireland in a coordinated way, individual Adventurers avoided the formal route of parliament and Loftus, limiting themselves to small loans and supplies of weapons sent directly to the Boyles in Munster. William Pennoyer bought up most of the remaining weapons and gunpowder in London, and shipped these in small consignments to Dungarvan, County Waterford, and Bandonbridge, County Cork, dealing with Lord Dungarvan directly.[145] Although he was supposed to travel with Leicester's army, Dungarvan remained in London and negotiated the transfer of arms from the Adventurers' stores to the Committee for Irish Affairs, but the contributions were small and not likely to have a decisive impact in the progress of the war in the south of Ireland.[146] The only large scale English military interventions in Ireland were supplies paid for with loans from the London Companies and destined for Londonderry and Dublin. These supplies supported the redeployment of the Scots army to Ulster, financed by the earl of Warwick-controlled Brotherly Assistance fund.[147] The only additional significant English military intervention in Ireland in 1642, funded entirely by private subscriptions under similar terms to the Adventure for Irish land, was the Additional Sea Adventure, promoted by the Providence Island Company peers and contracted entirely to Maurice Thomson.

Although, during the summer of 1642, king and parliament were still holding back from a full military confrontation, the Adventurers had assembled a large army around London and provided parliament with the financial resources to launch a major military campaign on English soil. Away from Westminster, in

Grocers' Hall, the three committees, Safety, Irish Affairs and Adventurers, had conspired to create an army that could challenge the king. The Adventurers were the most belligerent of these three groups and they used the parliamentary committees to push their own agenda at Westminster. In effect, the old Providence Island Company had moved from Warwick House to Grocers' Hall, where it joined forces with Maurice Thomson and the rest of its former subcontractors. Were it not for the Adventurers, parliament would have been unable to train and equip an army in London without being challenged by the king's allies. As to the Adventurers' agenda, their principal concern before the outbreak of the Civil War in England was Charles's concerted attempts to reform the government of the Atlantic colonies. They grasped the opportunity presented by the Irish revolt for a once-in-a-generation financial windfall in the form of Irish land. Although they were entirely complicit in the transfer of both their army and their money to parliament, with considerable sums contributed to the Adventure after these decisions were taken, the Adventurers had placed their Irish project in doubt. The Adventurers may have sincerely believed that their loan to parliament would be a temporary arrangement, but the transfers of men and money became permanent.

After an inconclusive engagement at Edgehill in October, it became clear to the parliamentarian side that a far more ambitious financial programme would be required if it was to sustain its military challenge to the king. The original Adventure for Irish land had evaporated, all of the proceeds of the £400,000 subsidy were either spent or spoken for and the proceeds from the ordinance for plate, money and horses were relatively modest. In order to raise sufficient funds to proceed with its confrontation with the king, parliament required a new system of state finance that was organised and centralised. To achieve this, England's rebellious peers and MPs once again beat a path to Grocers' Hall.

NOTES

1 Charlotte Fell Smith, *Mary Rich, Countess of Warwick (1625–1678), Her Family and Friends* (London, 1901), p. 100.
2 Stephen Quinn and William Roberds, 'An Economic Explanation of the Early Bank of Amsterdam, Debasement, Bills of Exchange and the Emergence of the First Central Bank' in Jeremy Atack and Larry Neal (eds), *The Origins and Development of Financial Markets and Institutions from the Seventeenth Century to the Present* (Cambridge, 2009), p. 51.
3 John Raithby (ed.), *Statutes of the Realm*, Vol. 5 (London, 1819), p. 141.
4 Raithby, *Statutes of the Realm*, p. 170.
5 Raithby, *Statutes of the Realm*, p. 168.
6 London Metropolitan Archive, COL/CC/01/01/4, *Minutes of the Common Council*, Vol. 41, f.17.
7 CJ, 2, pp. 371–375, 12 January 1642.

8 Anon, *Articles Against the Lord Mandeville, Mr John Pym*, etc. (London, 1642).
9 CJ, 2, pp. 381–383, 15 January 1642.
10 CJ, 2, p. 384, 17 January 1642.
11 Anon, *The Humble Petition and Answer of the Mayor, Alderman and the rest of the Common Council of the City of London* (London, 1642).
12 TNA SP28/1/B, ff. 319–375; 425–438. Payment warrants show that loans from the City of London totalling £30,000 had been paid in two tranches of which £22,000 had been spent by 25 January. A further £2,000 was loaned directly from the Chamber of London to Lord Dungarvan. These funds were primarily used to pay and supply the regiments of Clotworthy and Conway in Ulster and to garrison and provision Duncannon fort.
13 Anon, *The Humble Petition and Answer of the Mayor, Alderman and the rest of the Common Council*, p. 20.
14 Robert Armstrong, *Protestant War: The 'British' of Ireland and the Wars of the Three Kingdoms* (Manchester, 2005), pp. 51–57.
15 Wilson H. Courtney, Anne Steele and Vernon Snow (eds), *The Private Journals of the Long Parliament, Vol. 1* (New Haven, 1982), p. 274.
16 Courtney et al., *Journals of the Long Parliament*, p. 266.
17 Courtney et al., *Journals of the Long Parliament*, p. 275.
18 Courtney et al., *Journals of the Long Parliament*, p. 353.
19 Peter Wilson Coldham, *English Adventurers and Emigrants, 1609–1660* (Baltimore, MD, 1984), p. 12.
20 Courtney et al., *Journals of the Long Parliament*, p. 369.
21 Frances Rose-Troup, *The Massachusetts Bay Company and its Predecessors* (New York, 1930), p. 87.
22 Alexander Balloch Grosart and Richard Boyle (eds), *The Lismore Papers*, Vol. 2, part 3 (London, 1886), p. 288.
23 CJ, 2, p. 416, 7 February 1642.
24 CJ, 2, p. 416. Gualter Frost, Lord Brooke's business manager, was despatched from Brooke House in London to Chester, and took up the post of Commissary for the Scottish force. Frost's appointment ensured that the delivery of supplies for Ireland was kept within the Adventurers' close circle.
25 For this loan see SP 28/1C, ff. 10–63. The peers who lent £500 included earls Bedford, Essex, Salisbury, Warwick, Bristol and Holland with Lords Wharton, Paget, Brooke, Montague and Paulet. The MPs who lent £500 were John Pym, Sir Charles Wray, Sir John Hotham, William Cage, Henry Marten, Sir Walter Erle, Sir Gilbert Gerard, Harbottell Grimston and Edward Hales.
26 Peter Roebuck, 'The Making of an Ulster Great Estate: The Chichesters, Barons of Belfast and Viscounts of Carrickfergus, 1599–1648', *Proceedings of the Royal Irish Academy*, 79 (1979), pp. 1–25.
27 Anon, *A True Diurnal or a continued Relation of Irish Occurrences, from the 12th of February to the 8th of March* (London, 1642).
28 For the latest research on mid-seventeenth century Irish land owning statistics see, Micheál Ó Siochrú and David Brown, 'The Down Survey and the Cromwellian Land Settlement' in Jane Ohlmeyer (ed.), *The Cambridge History of Ireland, vol.2, 1550–1730* (Cambridge, 2018), pp. 584–607.

29 CJ, 2, p. 451, 24 February 1642.
30 The Common Council nominees were Sir John Wollaston, John Towse, John Warner, Philip Skippon, Stephen Estwick and Samuel Warner and the MPs were Nathaniel Fiennes, John Hampden, Henry Marten, Sir John Meyrick, John Pym and Sir William Waller.
31 Valerie Pearl, *London and the Outbreak of the Puritan Revolution: City Government and National Politics, 1625–43* (Oxford, 1961), pp. 147–155. The Common Council nominees were Randolph Mainwaring, William Gibbs, John Fouke, James Bunce, Francis Peck, Samuel Warner, James Russell, Nathaniel Wright, William Berkley, Alexander Normington, Stephen Estwick and Owen Rowe.
32 A&O, Vol. 1, pp. 1–5. 'March 1642: An Ordinance of the Lords and Commons in Parliament, for the Safety and Defence of the kingdom of England, and Dominion of Wales'.
33 Vernon R. Snow and Anne Steele Young (eds), *The Private Journals of the Long Parliament 7 March to 1 June 1642* (New Haven, CT, 1987), p. 73.
34 *Perfect Diurnal*, 28 February to 7 March (London, 1642), p. 3.
35 CJ, 2, p. 460, 28 February 1642.
36 Raithby, *Statutes of the Realm*, pp. 168–172.
37 *Perfect Diurnal*, 28 February to 7 March (London, 1642), p. 3; TNA SP 28/1D, Army Warrants, ff. 350, 360, 428, 428, 431.
38 Rose-Troup, *Massachusetts Bay Company*, p. 133.
39 John Bennett Bodie (ed.), *The Seventeenth Century Records of Isle of Wight County, Virginia* (Chicago, 1938), p. 153.
40 Robert Brenner, *Merchants and Revolution* (Princeton, NJ, 1993), p. 183.
41 Lucien C. Warner and Josephine Nichols, *The Descendants of Andrew Warner* (New Haven, CT, 1919), p. 8.
42 CJ, 2, pp. 463–466, 2 March 1642.
43 Parliamentary Archives, HL/PO/JO/1/113, ff. 146–147.
44 These figures are derived by adding up the receipts calendared in Robert Pentland Mahaffy (ed.), *Calendar of State Papers Relating to Ireland Preserved in the Public Record Office: Adventurers for Land, 1642–59* (London, 1903), *passim*.
45 The most convenient source for the total number of investors is Karl S. Bottigheimer, *English Money and Irish Land* (Oxford, 1971), pp. 175–195. There is evidence of further Adventurers who are not recorded by Bottigheimer, in Mahaffy's Calendar or the manuscript State Papers. For example, on 2 October 1642 George Fenwick, a London merchant who settled in New England in that year, wrote to Sir Thomas Barrington recalling his Adventure for Irish land that was entirely in Maurice Thomson's hands. Maurice Thomson was provisioning Warwick's Saybrook colony on credit and holding Adventures as security. This is presumably the source of Thomson's £350 Adventure. See *The New England Historical and Genealogical Register*, Vol. 46 (Boston, 1892), p. 358.
46 William Trollope, *A History of the Royal Foundation of Christ's Hospital* (London, 1834). The London Companies' trust was taken over by the merchant Erasmus Smith in 1662.
47 TNA SP 28/1D, f. 425.

48 Nell Marion Nugent (ed.), *Cavaliers and Pioneers, Abstracts of Virginia Land Patents and Grants 1623–1800*, Vol. I (Richmond, VA, 1934), p. 46.
49 Mahaffy, *Adventurers*, p. 234.
50 Mahaffy, *Adventurers*, p. 286.
51 Mahaffy, *Adventurers*, p. 116.
52 Mahaffy, *Adventurers*, p. 136.
53 Mahaffy, *Adventurers*, p. 136; Brenner, *Merchants and Revolution*, p. 407.
54 Thomson's cotton plantation was yet another source of friction between the colonial and EEIC merchants. Caribbean cotton was shipped directly to England for processing and weaving while finished Indian cotton was the most important part of the EEIC's trade by volume. See Sven Beckert, *Empire of Cotton: A New History of Global Capitalism* (New York, 2014), pp. 37–40.
55 TNA SP 63/302, *An Index to the Irish Adventurers*.
56 C.H. Firth and S.C. Lomas, *Notes on the Diplomatic Relations of England and France, 1603–1688* (Oxford, 1906), p. 9. My thanks to Dr Bríd McGrath for this reference.
57 The full list of investors of £1,000 or more is: Thomas Andrews, Samuel Avery, Sir Thomas Barrington, Stephen Beale, John Brett, Gregory Clement, Sir John Clotworthy, Thomas Giles, John Gunning, Sir Edward Hales, Robert Hales, William Hawkins, Rowland Hill, Edmund Lewin, William Methold, Isaac Pennington, Thomas Pury, Sir Robert Pye, Sir John Reynolds, Samuel Rolle, Thomas Soame, Maurice Thomson, William Thomson, Richard Waring, Samuel Warner, Sir David Watkins and Sir John Wollaston.
58 This composite list of the original Adventurers for Irish land is drawn from four sources: TNA SP 63/302, a list of all Adventures paid in full (full); TNA SP 63/301, ff. 197–200, a list of all Adventures not paid in full (part); Mahaffy, *Adventurers* and the remainder from Bottigheimer, *English Money and Irish Land*, Appendix A. The names in Bottigheimer's list were derived from state papers and from a list drawn up by John Prendergast, the source of which was lost in the Public Record Office of Ireland fire in 1922. The term 'cert' indicates that these additional names were given certificates as a substitute for their missing receipts.
59 Robert Brenner has identified sixty merchants who imported 10,000 lbs or more into London in a single year from 1627 to 1640 (Brenner, *Merchants and Revolution*, p. 183n.). Out of these, the Adventurers included Thomas and William Allen, Margaret Barker, Edward Barton, John Bradley, Henry Brooke, Nicholas Corsellis, Edward and John Davies, Edward Harris, George Henley, James Jenkins, Samuel Matthews, Richard Perry, William Pierce, Elias Roberts, Israel Scarlet, George Smith, Thomas Stone, Robert Swinnerton, George, Maurice and William Thomson, Robert Tucker, John Turner, William Underwood, William Webb, John White and Robert Wilding.
60 Thomas Andrews, Thomas Frere, Thomas Chamberlain, William Lane, Henry Spurstowe and other Adventurers feature in a petition of over eighty merchants to the House of Lords. See Maurice F. Bond (ed.), *Manuscripts of the House of Lords*, Vol. 11 (New Series), *Addenda 1514–1714* (London, 1962), pp. 299–300.
61 TNA SP 16/17, Trinity House Certificates, 1630–1638, *passim*. The proportion of Trinity House registrants is actually higher than the 39% that these figures suggest

◆ THE ADVENTURE FOR IRISH LAND ◆

as in some cases the certificates list all of the sibling partners. Alexander, Squire and Robert Bence are all listed as the owner of one ship in the certificates, but only Alexander's name is given in Bottigheimer's list, although the brothers subscribed jointly to their Adventure (Mahaffy, *Adventurers*, p. 231).

62 Samuel Aldersey, James Allen, Francis Ashe, William Ashwell, Thomas Babb, John Baker, Thomas Bannister, Matthew Barrett, William Bateman, Thomas Beale, Alexander Bence, William Blackwell, Thomas Browne, Humphrey Browne, John Browne, Robert Clement, Thomas Collins, Nicholas Crispe, Henry Croane, John Daniel, Thomas Davis, Joseph Day, John Dike, Jeremy Drury, John Ellis, George Farmer, William Farringdon, John Fletcher, John Floyd, Thomas Foote, Robert Folliot, John Fowler, Thomas Freeman, William Goddard, Adam Graves, George Henley, John Harpur, James Harrington, Thomas Hawkins, John Hayward, George Henley, Richard Hill, James Hubland, James Humphrey, William Hunt, Thomas Hutchins, John Johnson, William Johns, John Juxon, William Knight, Edward Knightly, Richard Lambert, John Langham, William Lee, Richard Leigh, John Lucas, Thomas Mann, Thomas Masham, John Morrice, Robert Moyer, David Otger, Robert Page, Edmund Partridge, James Pickering, William Rainborrow, Edward Read, Sir John Reynolds, Nicholas Roberts, Burow Saunders, John Severne, Thomas Skinner, Robert Smith, John Smith, Thomas Soame, Maurice Thomson, John Thomson, Edward Waller, William Waring, Edward Webb, William Webster, Robert Wheatley, William White, William Willoughby.

63 Bottigheimer, *English Money and Irish Land*, p. 64; Mahaffy, *Adventurers*, pp. 234–235. Bottigheimer's aggregates for the total number of Adventurers are highly problematic as they are simplified in the cases of Adventurers, mainly MPs, who were subscribing as the head of consortia. The most extreme case is Denis Bond, the Dorchester MP who is listed by Bottigheimer as having subscribed £2,000. This investment was on behalf of fifty-one individual subscribers who do not feature in Bottigheimer's list. It is more accurate, therefore, to compare proportions of money subscribed, as opposed to numbers of subscribers, in order to compare the relative importance of one group over another. The Dorchester list includes a strong representation of West Country merchants with family and trade connections in Virginia, the Bushrods, Goulds, Coles and Mahers.

64 The additional merchants are drawn mainly from Brenner's partnership tables, *Merchants and Revolution*, pp. 184–193, excluding merchant MPs who are dealt with as a separate group in this text. Many of the leading Adventurers feature in these partnership tables, including Thomas Andrews, John Dethwick, Stephen Estwick, Martin Noel, William Pennoyer and the Thomsons. For a list of merchants involved in financing the English servant trade up to 1640 see *Virginia County Records*, Vol. VI (New Jersey, 1909). William Barker, John Parrott, William Pierce, William Shippey, Thomas Willoughby and the Stones all feature.

65 Ralph Davis, *The Rise of the English Shipping Industry in the Seventeenth and Eighteenth Centuries* (Newton Abbot, 1962), p. 143.

66 G.F. Steckley, 'The Wine Economy of Tenerife in the Seventeenth Century', *Economic Historical Review*, 2nd Series, Vol. 33 (1980), pp. 335–350.

67 TNA SP 16/137, *Survey of Shipping on the River Thames*, ff. 2–8.

68 Philip L. Barbour (ed.), *The Jamestown Voyages under the First Charter*, Vol. 1 (Cambridge, 1969), p. 322. The pioneers sailed into Cork harbour and stole the contents of two vessels at anchor to provision their journey.
69 Rose-Troup, *Massachusetts Bay Company*, p. 13.
70 Thomas Crossing, Dartmouth Corporation, James Gould, John Guy, Thomas Hussey, John Long, Richard Mallock, John Pitts, John Poole, Henry Smith and William and John Underwood.
71 Examples of the cohort of investors in Irish land drawn from Warwick's projects include: Sir Gilbert Gerard, Richard Hunt, Cornelius Burges, Cornelius Holland and Sir William Masham (all Bermuda Company); John Pym and Sir Gilbert Gerald (Providence Island); William Brereton, Nathaniel Barnadiston, Thomas Andrews, Edward Cooke, Thomas Adams, Richard Crispe (Massachusetts Bay Company); John Pym (Warwick Patent); John Parker, John Brett, Peter Langley, George Butler, Richard Crispe, William Glanville, Thomas Gouge, Thomas Hampton, Thomas Hodges, Charles Lloyd, James Martin, Sir William Masham and William Wade (all Virginia Patentees). Out of this group of Adventurers, Sir John Wollaston, John Towse, James Bunce and John Foulke were captains in the London Militia in January 1642.
72 TCD MS 812, ff. 046r–047v, Deposition of Ruth Crispe.
73 BL, MS Add 4782, p. 352.
74 Michael Braddick, *The Nerves of State: Taxation and the Financing of the English State, 1558–1714* (Manchester, 1996), pp. 84–89.
75 'Venice: February 1642', in *Calendar of State Papers Relating To English Affairs in the Archives of Venice*, Vol. 25, 1640–1642, ed. Allen B Hinds (London, 1924), pp. 286–298. www.british-history.ac.uk/cal-state-papers/venice/vol25/pp286-298 [accessed 2 December 2015], 28 February 1642.
76 TNA SP 63/301, f. 197, 'A particular of all those person's names who did not pay in their original subscriptions'. The majority of MPs who only made this initial payment were royalists: Sir John Culpeper, Sir Anthony Ashley-Cooper, Sir William Morley, Edward, Lord Littleton, John Browne, William Harrison and William Morley.
77 Vernon Snow, Wilson H. Coates and Anne Steele Young (eds), *The Private Journals of the Long Parliament, 3 January to 5 March 1642* (New Haven, CT, 1997), pp. 403–468. See also Robert Armstrong, 'Ireland at Westminster: The Long Parliament's Irish Committees, 1641–1647' in Chris R. Kyle and Jason Peacy (eds), *Parliament at Work: Parliamentary Committees, Political Power and Public Access in Early Modern England* (Woodbridge, 2002), pp. 80–81.
78 NLI, MS 14305, f. 1, 'A Commission for Establishing a Councell for the Irish Affairs'. Lord Robartes was married to Lucy Rich, daughter of the earl of Warwick.
79 CJ, 2, p. 509, 4 April 1642.
80 Parliamentary Archives, HL//PO/JO/1/113, ff. 150–152. Robert Chambers, the last appointee to the Committee for Irish Affairs, was an auditor charged with ensuring that the money raised for Ireland was discharged as intended. Chambers had received employment for life from Charles I in January 1640 as auditor for the rents of the Londonderry plantation and had some experience with the management of an Irish plantation (CSPI 1633–1647, p. 232, 'Docquet of the king's grant to

Robert Chambers, Esq., for life of an office of Auditor of the Revenues of the late Co. Londonderry in Ireland').

81 Raithby, *Statutes of the Realm*, pp. 145–167, 'An act for the raising and levying of Moneys for the necessary defence and great affaires of the kingdomes of England and Ireland and for the payment of debts undertaken by the Parliament'.

82 NLI, MS 14305, p. 61.

83 Anon, *The Names of Such members of the Commons House of Parliament, as have already subscribed in pursuance of the Act of Parliament, for the Speedy Reducing of the Rebels...9 April* (London, 1642).

84 TNA SP 28/1D, f. 503, Buckinghamshire's loan was diverted by Parliament on 3 May 1642 to pay Sir John Hotham's garrison at Hull.

85 CJ, 2, pp. 510, 4 April 1642; BL, MS Add 4771, f3v.

86 Snow et al., *Journals of the Long Parliament*, p. 423.

87 Snow et al., *Journals of the Long Parliament*, p. 422.

88 Snow et al., *Journals of the Long Parliament*, p. 425.

89 TNA SP 28/1B, f. 438, 27 April 1642. The loan was negotiated by Sir Thomas Barrington, Isaac Pennington, William Spurstowe and Humphrey Beddingfeld.

90 Snow et al., *Journals of the Long Parliament*, p. 443.

91 TNA SP 28/1B, p. 452.

92 TNA SP 28/1B, p. 462.

93 TNA SP 28/1B, f 559. Receivers of Brotherly Assistance loans included the earls of Essex and Bedford, John Pym and Sir Walter Erle.

94 *Perfect Diurnal*, 13–20 June 1642.

95 The payment was due by midsummer 1642. The treasurers for the Brotherly Assistance were the earls of Bedford, Essex, Warwick, Holland, Stanford, Lord Wharton, Lord Mandeville, Lord Brooke, Henry Martin, Sir Thomas Barrington, Mr Capel, Sir Arthur Ingram, Sir Gilbert Gerard, Sir Robert Pye, Mr Henry Belasis, Sir Walter Erle, Sir William Litton, Sir Henry Mildmay, Sir Thomas Cheek, Sir John Strangways, Arthur Goodwin, John Hampden, Thomas Soame and Thomas Pennington. See Raithby, *Statutes of the Realm*, pp. 120–128.

96 TNA SP 28 Vol. 1C, f. 56. The subscribers were peers Bedford, Hertford, Essex, Salisbury, Warwick, Bristol, Holland, Berkshire, Wharton, Paget, Brooke, Montague, Paulet, Howard, Savill and Dunsman, with Denzille Holles, John Pym, Sir Charles Wray, Sir John Hotham, William Cage, Humphrey Martin, Sir Dudley North, Sir Edward Aiscough, Sir John Culpepper, Sir Robert Crane, John Hamden, Sir Walter Erle, Sir Gilbert Gerard, Sir Thomas Withrington, Harbottell Grimston, Henry Lord Gray of Ruthven, Sir Philip Stapilton, Sir Edward Hale and Robert Crane.

97 CJ, 2, p. 629, 17 June 1642.

98 Anon, *Some Special Passages from Westminster, London, York, and other parts... 20-28 June* (London, 1642).

99 Mahaffy, *Adventurers*, p. 309; TNA SP 63/285, f. 16, 'Power from the Committee appointed by the several companies of London for managing the affairs of Ireland'. The £10,000 loan was managed by Francis Kirby, Maurice Thomson's partner in the Cape Ann, Massachusetts, fishing project.

100 NLI, MS 14305, p. 61.
101 TNA SP 46/443, ff. 79–82.
102 Snow et al., *Journals of the Long Parliament*, p. 463; SP 28, vol. 1B, ff. 546–601.
103 A&O, Vol. 1, pp. 6–9, 'June 1642: Ordinance of both Houses, for bringing in Plate, Money, and Horses'.
104 Sir John Wollaston shared his militia post with John Venn, MP and Captain-General of the Artillery Company.
105 Anon, *A List of the Field-Officers chosen and appointed for the Irish Expedition, by the Committee at Guildhall...* (London, 1642).
106 TNA SP 28/1B, ff. 443–447.
107 *Perfect Diurnal*, p. 151.
108 R.W. Blencowe (ed.), *Sidney Papers, consisting of A Journal of the Earl of Leicester and Original Letters of Algernon Sidney* (London, 1825), p. xxi.
109 Bottigheimer, *English Money and Irish Land*, p. 81.
110 All of the leading Adventurers were members of the Artillery Company. Maurice Thomson was an elder and Phillip Skippon the Captain-General.
111 NLI, MS 14305, p. 123.
112 NLI, MS 14305, pp. 125–127. The money was raised by combining the loans secured on the £400,000 subsidy with the City of London's loan.
113 TNA SP 28/1B, ff. 674, 687.
114 TNA SP 28/1C, f. 156.
115 Parliamentary Archives, HL/PO/JO/10/1/130, 23 July 1642, The king's answer to the petition of parliament.
116 John Benjamin Heath, *Some Account of the Worshipful Company of Grocers of the City of London* (London, 1829), p. 14; CJ, 2, p. 386, 17 June 1642, 'and Irish Affairs continued to meet at Grocers Hall'; Anon, *The Parliamentary and Constitutional History of England...*, Vol. 10 (London, 1758), pp. 217–218.
117 Parliamentary Archives, HL/PO/JO/10/1/130, 28 July 1642, Letter from the Committee for the defence of the kingdom, to the Committee for the Irish adventurers.
118 NLI, MS 14305, p. 124.
119 NLI, MS 14305, pp 125–126.
120 Anon, *The Answer of The House of Commons to His Majesties Message* (London, 1642), p. 4.
121 Parliamentary Archives, HL/PO/JO/10/1/130, 23 July 1642, Order for payment of £4,000 to Maurice Thomson.
122 NLI, MS 14305, p. 123.
123 CJ, 2, p. 696.
124 *Answer of The House of Commons*, p. 5.
125 A&O, Vol. 1, pp. 140–142, 'June 1649: An Act for Instructions for the Trustees Treasurer and Register-Accountant for the Sale of the Deans and Chapter Lands, for the admitting such as have moneys owing them by the Parliament, to double the same upon the Credit of the Lands of the Deans and Chapters' ... '100000 l. of the money, advanced for the Purchase of Lands in Ireland'. The June 1649 Ordinance allowed an Adventurer to transfer their claim to English ecclesiastical

Robert Chambers, Esq., for life of an office of Auditor of the Revenues of the late Co. Londonderry in Ireland').
81 Raithby, *Statutes of the Realm*, pp. 145–167, 'An act for the raising and levying of Moneys for the necessary defence and great affaires of the kingdomes of England and Ireland and for the payment of debts undertaken by the Parliament'.
82 NLI, MS 14305, p. 61.
83 Anon, *The Names of Such members of the Commons House of Parliament, as have already subscribed in pursuance of the Act of Parliament, for the Speedy Reducing of the Rebels…9 April* (London, 1642).
84 TNA SP 28/1D, f. 503, Buckinghamshire's loan was diverted by Parliament on 3 May 1642 to pay Sir John Hotham's garrison at Hull.
85 CJ, 2, pp. 510, 4 April 1642; BL, MS Add 4771, f3v.
86 Snow et al., *Journals of the Long Parliament*, p. 423.
87 Snow et al., *Journals of the Long Parliament*, p. 422.
88 Snow et al., *Journals of the Long Parliament*, p. 425.
89 TNA SP 28/1B, f. 438, 27 April 1642. The loan was negotiated by Sir Thomas Barrington, Isaac Pennington, William Spurstowe and Humphrey Beddingfeld.
90 Snow et al., *Journals of the Long Parliament*, p. 443.
91 TNA SP 28/1B, p. 452.
92 TNA SP 28/1B, p. 462.
93 TNA SP 28/1B, f 559. Receivers of Brotherly Assistance loans included the earls of Essex and Bedford, John Pym and Sir Walter Erle.
94 *Perfect Diurnal*, 13–20 June 1642.
95 The payment was due by midsummer 1642. The treasurers for the Brotherly Assistance were the earls of Bedford, Essex, Warwick, Holland, Stanford, Lord Wharton, Lord Mandeville, Lord Brooke, Henry Martin, Sir Thomas Barrington, Mr Capel, Sir Arthur Ingram, Sir Gilbert Gerard, Sir Robert Pye, Mr Henry Belasis, Sir Walter Erle, Sir William Litton, Sir Henry Mildmay, Sir Thomas Cheek, Sir John Strangways, Arthur Goodwin, John Hampden, Thomas Soame and Thomas Pennington. See Raithby, *Statutes of the Realm*, pp. 120–128.
96 TNA SP 28 Vol. 1C, f. 56. The subscribers were peers Bedford, Hertford, Essex, Salisbury, Warwick, Bristol, Holland, Berkshire, Wharton, Paget, Brooke, Montague, Paulet, Howard, Savill and Dunsman, with Denzille Holles, John Pym, Sir Charles Wray, Sir John Hotham, William Cage, Humphrey Martin, Sir Dudley North, Sir Edward Aiscough, Sir John Culpepper, Sir Robert Crane, John Hamden, Sir Walter Erle, Sir Gilbert Gerard, Sir Thomas Withrington, Harbottell Grimston, Henry Lord Gray of Ruthven, Sir Philip Stapilton, Sir Edward Hale and Robert Crane.
97 CJ, 2, p. 629, 17 June 1642.
98 Anon, *Some Special Passages from Westminster, London, York, and other parts… 20–28 June* (London, 1642).
99 Mahaffy, *Adventurers*, p. 309; TNA SP 63/285, f. 16, 'Power from the Committee appointed by the several companies of London for managing the affairs of Ireland'. The £10,000 loan was managed by Francis Kirby, Maurice Thomson's partner in the Cape Ann, Massachusetts, fishing project.

100 NLI, MS 14305, p. 61.
101 TNA SP 46/443, ff. 79–82.
102 Snow *et al.*, *Journals of the Long Parliament*, p. 463; SP 28, vol. 1B, ff. 546–601.
103 A&O, Vol. 1, pp. 6–9, 'June 1642: Ordinance of both Houses, for bringing in Plate, Money, and Horses'.
104 Sir John Wollaston shared his militia post with John Venn, MP and Captain-General of the Artillery Company.
105 Anon, *A List of the Field-Officers chosen and appointed for the Irish Expedition, by the Committee at Guildhall…* (London, 1642).
106 TNA SP 28/1B, ff. 443–447.
107 *Perfect Diurnal*, p. 151.
108 R.W. Blencowe (ed.), *Sidney Papers, consisting of A Journal of the Earl of Leicester and Original Letters of Algernon Sidney* (London, 1825), p. xxi.
109 Bottigheimer, *English Money and Irish Land*, p. 81.
110 All of the leading Adventurers were members of the Artillery Company. Maurice Thomson was an elder and Phillip Skippon the Captain-General.
111 NLI, MS 14305, p. 123.
112 NLI, MS 14305, pp. 125–127. The money was raised by combining the loans secured on the £400,000 subsidy with the City of London's loan.
113 TNA SP 28/1B, ff. 674, 687.
114 TNA SP 28/1C, f. 156.
115 Parliamentary Archives, HL/PO/JO/10/1/130, 23 July 1642, The king's answer to the petition of parliament.
116 John Benjamin Heath, *Some Account of the Worshipful Company of Grocers of the City of London* (London, 1829), p. 14; CJ, 2, p. 386, 17 June 1642, 'and Irish Affairs continued to meet at Grocers Hall'; Anon, *The Parliamentary and Constitutional History of England…*, Vol. 10 (London, 1758), pp. 217–218.
117 Parliamentary Archives, HL/PO/JO/10/1/130, 28 July 1642, Letter from the Committee for the defence of the kingdom, to the Committee for the Irish adventurers.
118 NLI, MS 14305, p. 124.
119 NLI, MS 14305, pp 125–126.
120 Anon, *The Answer of The House of Commons to His Majesties Message* (London, 1642), p. 4.
121 Parliamentary Archives, HL/PO/JO/10/1/130, 23 July 1642, Order for payment of £4,000 to Maurice Thomson.
122 NLI, MS 14305, p. 123.
123 CJ, 2, p. 696.
124 *Answer of The House of Commons*, p. 5.
125 A&O, Vol. 1, pp. 140–142, 'June 1649: An Act for Instructions for the Trustees Treasurer and Register-Accountant for the Sale of the Deans and Chapter Lands, for the admitting such as have moneys owing them by the Parliament, to double the same upon the Credit of the Lands of the Deans and Chapters' … '100000 l. of the money, advanced for the Purchase of Lands in Ireland'. The June 1649 Ordinance allowed an Adventurer to transfer their claim to English ecclesiastical

land. How many did so is unknown, but this could explain the purchase of some ecclesiastical land by Adventurers.
126 CCAM, Vol. 1, p. 2. Maurice Thomson was treasurer for the Additional Sea Adventure and this money was kept separately. For Shute's role on the Committee of Safety see Pearl, *Puritan Revolution*, pp. 252–253.
127 TNA SP 28/13/2, 'August Anno: 1642, In London. An account of divers necessary provisions, materials and Instruments of war bought of several persons for the train of artillery under the command of his excellency the earl of Essex Lord General of the army employed for the defence of Protestant religion, the safety of His Majesty's person etc.'.
128 TNA SP 28/13/2, f. 4.
129 Rose-Troup, *Massachusetts Bay Company*, p. 35. Browne was an ardent Puritan who went as far as objecting to the use of the Book of Common Prayer during the course of his voyage to New England.
130 TNA SP 28/131/2, ff. 8, 54.
131 TNA SP 28/131/2, 53, 55. There are numerous other examples in this volume.
132 TNA SP 16/539/2, f. 180.
133 TNA SP 26/143/6, 'August 1642, received…by order of the Committee for Defence of the kingdom'.
134 Parliamentary Archives, HL/PO/JO/10/1/131, 29 August 1642: List of collectors appointed in the several wards and parishes under the ordinance for raising money and plate in London.
135 TNA SP 26/143/6, unfol., 'August 1642, received…by order of the Committee for Defence of the kingdom', pp. 12–18.
136 TNA SP 26/143/6, unfol., 'August 1642, received…by order of the Committee for Defence of the kingdom', pp. 12–16.
137 A&O, Vol. 1, pp. 6–9, 'June 1642: Ordinance of both Houses, for bringing in Plate, Money, and Horses'. The names and amounts with subscribers in London under this Ordinance are all drawn from SP 28/131/3.
138 TNA SP 28/131/3, ff. 2–3.
139 TNA SP 28/131/3, f. 8.
140 LJ, Vol. 6, p. 148, 'The order for Sir David Watkins' Indemnity, 5 July 1643.
141 Anon, *Reasons Delivered by the Committee of Citizens, Adventurers in London for Lands in Ireland, to the Committee appointed by the Right Honourable the Lord Mayor, Aldermen and Common Council of the said City… of their refusal to lend monies…* (London, 1645).
142 Gethin and Milner were regular business partners and Gethin was a business partner of an Adventurer, Samuel Turner, Richard's brother (Mahaffy, *Adventurers*, p. 240). He was married to Elizabeth, the elder sister of Thomas Juxon MP. He was also related to Samuel Langham, a member of the Committee of Adventurers. Tempest Milner was the brother-in-law of Richard Turner. Milner was married to Anne, the daughter of Richard Turner. All were in the cloth trade, but the Turners were also importers of Virginia tobacco in the 1630s. Keith Lindley and David Scott (eds), *The Journal of Thomas Juxon, 1644–1647* (Cambridge, 1999), p. 2; Martha W. MacCartney, *Virginia Immigrants and Adventurers 1607–35: A*

Biographical Dictionary (Baltimore, MD, 2007), p. 705. The loan was, in effect, a joint Hawkins/Turner undertaking.
143 LJ, Vol. 6, pp. 274–282.
144 TNA SP 28/1D, f. 726.
145 TNA SP 28/1B, ff. 477, 543.
146 NLI, MS 14305, p. 33.
147 CJ, 2, p. 143, 12 May 1641. This Scots army was financed by Providence Island Company members Nathaniel Fiennes and John Hampden to be repaid as soon as the funds came in from the £400,000 subsidy.

4

Grocers' Hall

THE SEA ADVENTURE

The Additional Sea Adventure to Ireland of 1642, dismissed by Karl Bottigheimer as a 'floating mockery of the conquering expedition the adventurers had desired', was the direct response of the Adventurers in London to King Charles I's declaration, on 14 April 1642, that he would travel to Ireland and take command of his forces.[1] The Sea Adventure was the first large military force raised by supporters of parliament that was deployed against a garrison flying the king's colours, uniting what had been separate conflicts into the Wars of the Three Kingdoms. Moreover, it was a strikingly brutal campaign, using ships and men originally recruited to conduct raids against Barbary pirates and in the Caribbean, conducted around the southern and western coasts of Ireland during the summer of 1642. In many ways, the Sea Adventure was a harbinger of the civil war that was to engulf England in the coming months: a coming together of vague strategy, military necessity, business opportunism and private vendettas. The introduction of a mercenary army to the shores of Munster and Connaught in the summer of 1642 brought with it the most brutal aspects of the Thirty Years War still raging in Europe, the conduct of war for annihilation and plunder. As David Parrott put it: 'The officers' aim was to increase their profits from paying little or nothing to their disposable soldiers, while making still larger gains from systematic plunder and looting.'[2] It was also the first real demonstration that the Adventurers were able to unleash indiscriminate destructive force in Ireland, as the Sea Adventure was not a state enterprise, but a private amphibious task force.

Taking the king's announcement as a threat to take over their army, the Adventurers responded with a petition to parliament on 14 April, offering to 'relieve their brethren who are in distresse' and stating readiness to 'further supply by Sea for coming thither and to spoyle and waste those Rebells by

Land, doe propose to this Hon. Assembly to sett out at their own charge 5, 6, or 7 shippes & pinnaces with 500 soldyers as an Additional Supply to their former subscription'. The Adventurers' initiative coincided with the circulation of rumours in London that there may be more to the original Adventure for Irish land than it appeared, and contributions had slowed. The new proposal stipulated that the subscribers would have 'freedom to choose all officers employed in this service'.[3] A clearly piratical venture, all spoils and prizes were to be divided among the crew and the Sea Adventure's financial backers who, furthermore, were to receive Irish land at the same rate as the original Adventure for the full amount of their subscriptions. There were no restrictions imposed on who could be attacked and the vessels were exempted from being forced under the command of the English navy. *An Additional Declaration of the Lords and Commons*, of April 1642, legitimised the Adventurers' position, stating that 'the king's going to Ireland ... will cause men to believe that it is out of design to discourage the Undertakers and hinder the other propositions for raising money for the defence of Ireland'.[4] Having engineered an opportunity to acquire Irish estates on very attractive terms, what the Adventurers feared most in April 1642 was a negotiated peace. If the king had travelled to Ireland and was successful in negotiating a truce, the Adventurers would be excluded from this settlement.

The event in Ireland that directly triggered the Sea Adventure involved one of the five merchant vessels hired from Maurice Thomson to deliver supplies to Ireland. On 9 March 1642, a group of Galway merchants seized a merchant ship commanded by Captain Robert Clarke and took away a consignment of arms intended for St Augustine's fort outside the town.[5] A stand-off ensued between the Catholic townsmen and the Protestant garrison of the fort, under the command of Captain Anthony Willoughby. As the town prepared to besiege the fort, Captain Willoughby set fire to its outer suburbs and fired shots over its walls. As far as the authorities in Dublin were concerned, based on intelligence communicated to them by Ulick Burke, earl Clanricarde, the town was in open rebellion and had 'joyned in an Oath of Confederacy'.[6] On 23 April a second supply ship, the *Employment*, this one owned by Maurice Thomson and under the command of Captain Ashley, was diverted from Dublin with supplies and munitions for the fort.[7] Ashley successfully petitioned Ulick Burke, earl of Clanricarde, to intervene with the Galway townsmen, and the situation was stabilised. In their submission to Clanricarde on 6 May, the townsmen declared their allegiance to Charles, prompted by the king's announcement that he was to come over to Ireland. Their fear was that the arming of the fort by parliamentarians represented a threat to overwhelmingly Catholic Galway and they requested that their town be put under royal protection.[8] Through Clanricarde's efforts, peace was restored between the fort and the town on 11 May, although tensions remained high.[9] Ashley continued to provoke the town, remaining in Galway Bay, refusing to respond to Clanricarde's orders to leave and encouraging Willoughby to maintain a posture of defiance. Clanricarde petitioned Sir Henry Stradling, the vice-admiral of the Irish coasts, who issued a direct order to Ashley to withdraw, but to no effect.[10]

Details of Clanricarde's arrangements reached the Committee for Irish Affairs on 21 June. This committee, meeting in Grocers' Hall rather than Westminster, was attended by earls Warwick, Essex, Pembroke and Holland, Lord Brooke, viscount Saye-and-Sele and John Pym. William Hawkins, Maurice Thomson's brother-in-law, was appointed secretary.[11] The committee decided that the town of Galway should be included in the forfeited lands to be made available to the Adventurers for Irish land. John Pym was sent to parliament the following day to secure an ordinance. Pym produced a letter written by the earl of Clanricarde at Portumna dated 18 May that detailed the terms for the pacification of Galway Town.[12] Under the terms of the agreement, Catholic worship would continue to be allowed in the town, and Pym moved that the agreement between Galway and Clanricarde be annulled. 'That this form of protection, as it is granted to that Citty [Galway] is against the Act of Parliament lately made, against the declaration of Parliament touching the Advancement of Protestant Religion in that kingdom, against the peace and settlement intended to be had there, and the satisfaction which the inhabitants of that City ought to make to those of his Majestys subjects that have received losses and injuries by them.'[13] Oliver Cromwell moved that the matter be delegated to his colleagues on the Committee for Irish Affairs, enabling the committees at Grocers' Hall to make any arrangements they thought fit.

The Committee for Irish Affairs quickly passed the Galway question on to the Committee for Adventurers. On 22 June, James Harvey, an ensign under Willoughby's command, arrived in London and invited the Adventurers to mount an expedition against the town of Galway.[14] The *Employment* remained in Galway Bay throughout, heavily armed and with munitions for 1,000 men, originally intended for Dublin, while another vessel part-owned by Thomson, the enormous *Ruth*, lurked in the Shannon Estuary.[15] Despite Galway being under royal protection, a plot was hatched for a private army to seize the town: the Additional Sea Adventure. In preparation for their arrival, Ashley blockaded the town, preventing Clanricarde from leaving for Dublin by sea to protest against a letter he had received from the Lords Justices, disowning his agreement with the Galway townsmen.[16]

Although the political backing for the Sea Adventure emanated once again from Warwick House, most of its material backing came from entrepreneurs involved in the Barbary Company.[17] The Sea Adventure was thus an alliance between England's two most belligerent naval organisations, the Providence Island Company and the Barbary Company, who joined forces to launch a privately funded attack on Ireland. As it happened, the resources for this venture were readily available, as two naval crusades were already planned by the earls of Essex and Warwick for the spring of 1642.[18] The first was intended for the Caribbean, with the goal of retaking Providence Island from the Spanish. This project was delegated to John Pym, and the expected profits were to be divided between the Electoral Palatinate, the crucible of the Thirty Years War, and the Providence Island Company. The second mission, contracted to the powerful Rainsborough merchant family, was designed to attack Barbary pirates at their base in Algiers. The Algiers mission had most recently been discussed by parliament on 9 February 1642 and the three ships for Algiers were made available for service in Irish waters.[19]

Maurice Thomson, who would have managed the Providence Island expedition, instead convened a committee to manage the Sea Adventure. This committee included his brothers, George and William, and his closest trading partner, William Pennoyer. Sir Nicholas Crispe and Abraham Chamberlain, both of the Guinea Company and former business partners of the earl of Cork, were prominent members of the Sea Adventurers' committee, but declared as royalists in the aftermath of the mission.[20] Two further committee members, John Wood and Humphrey Slany, were members of both the Barbary Company and the Guinea Company. Another committee member, Thomas Rainsborough, was the son of William Rainsborough, a Levant Company grandee and veteran of the Sallee raid against Barbary pirates in 1637.[21] Gregory Clement was a veteran of the East India Company until he was dismissed in 1630 for illegal trading. Clement was another long-time partner of Maurice Thomson, both in the tobacco trade and in privateering, as were the remaining members of the committee.[22] Additional merchants, who were not members of the organising committee, also contributed huge sums.[23] John Dyke, the largest investor by far in the Sea Adventure with £5,200, was one of the earl of Warwick's longest standing business partners, and the first deputy governor of the Providence Island Company.[24] Dyke was also a warden of the Fishmongers Company, along with Isaac Pennington, who became Lord Mayor of London in 1643.[25] Stephen Beale, who advanced £1,200 to the Sea Adventure, was one of three members of the same family who had made smaller investments in the Adventure for Irish land. Beale's father, William, was an investor in the 1609 Virginia Company, and his brother, Thomas, was an East India Company merchant. After the Sea Adventure, Stephen Beale fought briefly on the royalist side before moving to Virginia in 1645.[26] John Bigg contributed £1,500. He was a cousin of Stephen Beale, who had lived for a short time in New England and whose family had a tobacco plantation near Charles City, Virginia.[27] Thomas Cunningham, who adventured £1,800, was involved in Scottish trade to the Indies and was an important supplier of provisions to the army in Scotland.[28]

Maurice Thomson and William Pennoyer had taken the lead in getting provisions to Protestant forces in Ireland following the outbreak of the 1641 rebellion. Robert Brenner has noted the close associations between Maurice Thomson and the other Sea Adventurers, but not the importance of the Barbary and Levant Company merchants who contributed most of the resources. This was not a colonial endeavour but a piratical onslaught. The Additional Sea Adventure raised £42,906, mainly in goods and services for its mission, from 180 subscribers. Of these, thirty-three were associates of the Thomsons and contributed 30% of the money.[29] The entire Sea Adventure fund was paid directly to Thomson, who managed the campaign.[30] Its leadership was connected to the Providence Island Company, which does not mean that it was a colonial endeavour but does locate its planning within the walls of Warwick House.[31] Robert Greville, Lord Brooke, was the intended commander of the mission. Brooke became associated with Hugh Peter, the Sea Adventurers' chaplain, in his teenage years at The Hague during a Grand Tour in 1629.[32] Hugh Peter used his influence to ensure that his brother, Benjamin, was appointed Admiral for the naval component of the Sea Adventure.[33] The land forces, under the notional command of Lord Brooke, who did not travel, were placed under the direct command of Alexander 10th Lord Forbes. Forbes was a kinsman of John Forbes, who was also an old associate of Hugh Peter from his days in Holland.[34] Lord Forbes also held a patent by inheritance to Castleforbes in County Longford, attacked during the course of the 1641 rebellion.[35] Forbes was one of the experienced officers who had returned from Sweden to fight for the Scottish Covenanters in the Bishops' Wars and had offered his services to parliament as a mercenary soldier in August 1641.[36] He had already, therefore, been involved in a war against Charles I and seemed keen to instigate another one.

There was no recent precedent for launching a naval attack on Ireland without a royal commission, but the vague legal basis for issuing parliamentary letters of marque for this privateering mission was provided by a vote in parliament of 14 March 1642, declaring that if the king was unwilling to give his permission 'due to ill counsel', parliament could provide such assent.[37] Charles was horrified, and flatly refused to sanction the Sea Adventure with a royal commission.[38] The Sea Adventure thus marked a further significant escalation in the powers which parliament assumed to defeat the Irish rebellion. It authorised a private navy to attack a dominion of Charles I and allowed that navy to bear the king's colours, despite royal opposition.

The Sea Adventurers had their own reasons to mount a campaign around the coasts of Ireland. The security of the harbours along the south coast of Ireland was vital to the continuing transatlantic trade of the Sea Adventure investors, due to Ireland's roles as a provisioning station for the colonies and as a large market for colonial produce. As the Irish ports were vulnerable from both land and sea, it made sense to reinforce them as soon as possible. Another attraction for Maurice Thomson and his partners was that Wentworth had acquired the hugely profitable tobacco monopoly for Ireland.[39] The licence for this monopoly was originally wrested from the earl of Carlisle by Wentworth in 1633, in partnership with Sir Arthur Ingram and Sir Francis Annesley, Lord Mountnorris, for £7,000 per annum. Wentworth then bought or forced his partners out of the consortium, and replaced them with his close friend and deputy, Christopher Wandesford. The deaths of both Wandesford in 1640 and Wentworth in 1641 created an opportunity for the colonial merchants to retake the Irish tobacco market, a return to the Carlisle/Thomson monopoly. Wentworth, using money secretly borrowed from the Irish exchequer, had built up a store of tobacco worth £46,000 before he died.[40] At the time of his execution he owed £107,000 to various creditors, including his suppliers of tobacco.[41] The tobacco store was in Kinsale and this is where the Sea Adventure made its first rendezvous in Ireland on 11 July 1642. Strategically, the Irish Confederates' privateering base at Wexford was the more obvious military target, but Wentworth's tobacco store was a far more enticing prize.

There were also perfectly valid strategic reasons for the Kinsale stop. William Pennoyer had organised a small network of sutlers that operated along the coast from Kinsale and for a short distance inland.[42] The principal distributors were the Gookins, Sir Vincent and his son, who distributed supplies in a corridor from Kinsale to Bandon. A second sutler, Thomas Payne, who handled merchandise in Castletown, was another of Maurice Thomson's Virginia connections. Phane Beecher, the sutler in Abbeymahon parish, had recently returned from the Caribbean. A fourth, Sir William Hull of Clonakilty, was closely associated with the earl of Cork.[43] Hull managed military supplies for Drimoleague and Clonakilty while his son, also called William, joined the Sea Adventurers' land force as a captain.[44] The distribution of military supplies was, therefore, conducted through a network of trusted agents. At Kinsale, Forbes conferred with Lewis Boyle, Lord Kilnalmeaky, and it was agreed that the land forces would march eight miles inland to relieve Bandon, commanded by Sir William Hull, who was supplied with gunpowder by Pennoyer.[45] The march began on 15 July, one force sent to Bandon and a second to Clonakilty, slaughtering eighty Irish as they progressed and stealing all of their livestock. After making contact with Hull and agreeing to engage a company of Irish soldiers under MacCarthyreagh in the area, the entire force converged on Clonakilty, driving the Irish into the sea and watching 600 men drown. Forbes lost 100 of his own men during this engagement and occupied the town, taking up lodging in Sir William Hull's home. On 17 July, Forbes' army returned to Bandon with 1,000 stolen sheep and hundreds of cattle and horses, sold for a good price to starving Protestant refugees who had sought sanctuary there.[46] The Thirty Years' War had reached Munster.

The next phase of the campaign was to relieve Drimoleague, Hull's second supply station, but on the way the campaign diverted to attack Timoleague, the home of Sir Roger O'Shaughnessy, a liegeman of the earl of Clanricarde and a party to Clanricarde's hated peace deal with Galway town. On a pretext of requiring lodging, Forbes' men arrived on 21 July and demanded that Lady O'Shaugnessy, in residence, yield the castle to them. O'Shaugnessy refused in the absence of a command from Lewis Boyle whereupon the Sea Adventurers burnt the town and carried away all of the livestock.[47] It must be stressed that the O'Shaugnessys were not in rebellion and that the attack was certainly revenge for the events in Galway. The mission to take the fight to the Irish rebels, therefore, only lasted for the week that the Sea Adventurers assisted Hull's forces around Bandon. After Clonakilty, Forbes and his men made no distinction between rebels and Catholic royalists and, in fact, preferred royalist targets.

The naval squadron and some of the men left Kinsale on 24 July, and their next stop was Castlehaven where they destroyed O'Donovan's Castle, the town and all the ships in the harbour. Although Castlehaven had a large garrison, it held back from engaging the Sea Adventure, taunting them from a distance as Parliament- or Puritan-dogs.[48] Castlehaven's men simply did not know what to do. Although not in rebellion, Castlehaven had gone to Dublin to offer his support to the Lords Justices but was imprisoned. His garrison in Castlehaven harbour was stranded without instructions when Forbes and his men turned up and they had no orders to engage an English expeditionary force. Without organised opposition, the fleet moved on to Baltimore, arriving on 27 July, and, while waiting to regroup, staged a revenge attack on O'Driscoll's castle in the town, burning it and many of the houses. The O'Driscolls were widely blamed for facilitating an attack on the town by Barbary pirates in June, 1631, that resulted in the capture and enslavement of Baltimore's English inhabitants.[49] It was simple vendetta destruction. Hugh Peter's recollection of the campaign in Ireland, printed and sent to 'a leading London merchant', claimed that 'If we had men and money here, I verily believe this Summer would be an end of this Rebellion'.[50] In Baltimore, the Sea Adventure was faced with a choice between suppressing the rebellion and prosecuting its own agenda. Two letters were received, one from the earl of Cork requesting that the fleet turn around and assist Duncannon, then under a sustained Irish attack. The second was from Captain Ashley at Galway Bay, inviting the fleet to join him to subdue the town. The Sea Adventurers opted for Galway.

The Sea Adventure sailed into Galway Bay on 9 August and Forbes announced himself as 'lieutenant-general of the additional forces by sea and land, sent by his majesty, our dread sovereign lord Charles, by the grace of God, king of Great Britain, France and Ireland, and the parliament of England, for reducing of Ireland'.[51] Forbes had, of course, no commission of this kind. Forbes demanded the surrender of the town and threatened that there would be no pardon or mercy for its inhabitants. The terms of surrender, that the town was to place itself under Forbes's protection until such a time as the king persuaded the Westminster parliament to order him to withdraw, were impossible. In effect, the Sea Adventurers wanted to take possession of the town and have Clanricarde's authority taken away. Clanricarde's strategy was to contact Willoughby and demand that the fort not be made available to the Sea Adventurers. He also wrote to Sir Charles Coote, Lord President of Connaught, imploring him to travel to Galway and present a united front.[52]

As no instant response from Galway was forthcoming, Forbes adopted a scare tactic of landing men on the Clare side of the bay and burning a village within sight of the town.[53] The following day he landed men on the west side of the town, occupying St Mary's church while under fire from the local residents. Now well within range of the town walls, Forbes brought ashore siege artillery and began a bombardment.[54] In a report sent the following day to the Lords Justices in Dublin, Clanricarde made it explicit that Galway was the Sea Adventurers' target and they were not interested in combing the countryside to suppress the Irish rebellion. Dublin was quick to disown the mission, having received multiple reports of the Sea Adventurers' indiscriminate attacks on supposed rebels and random targets in Munster. To demonstrate his anti-rebellion credentials, Forbes sent a party of 500 men along the coast of west Galway to burn what they could, but this was a distraction. The following day, 11 August, the townspeople awoke to find their abbey destroyed and its timbers used as a platform for thirty-six of the Sea Adventurers' cannon.[55] In response, the townsmen raised batteries along the walls of the town, trained them on the Sea Adventurers and sent out a raiding party to seize the land forces' horses.[56] Artillery fire was exchanged between both sides.[57]

This was standard siege warfare, but fought between a town flying the king's colours and an armada commissioned by the parliament of England. Although Charles did not raise his standard at Nottingham until 22 August, formally signalling the start of the first English Civil War, the siege of Galway was far more than a skirmish. This was a full scale siege battle orchestrated by an amphibious navy with 1,200 men. Galway then, on 11 August 1642, is the place and day on which the civil war between king and parliament began. Forbes had hoped that Coote would provide him with reinforcements, but was disappointed. Coote saw no reason to escalate the conflict or besiege the town, pointing out that the inhabitants had little choice but to defend themselves, as the alternative was total annihilation.[58] In addition, Coote had deep reservations about Forbes's plan to reinforce his expected prize with some of the Scottish forces then pouring into Ulster, opining that 'the cure is worse than the disease'.[59] Rumours had spread throughout the town that Forbes intended to remove the inhabitants and garrison it with 800 of his men, reinforced by the presence in the town of 700 families from the surrounding countryside, chased inside the walls by Forbes's men. These soldiers, however, were beginning to become restless. The Adventurers' cannon had proved ineffective against the town's fortifications, the houses within the town 'being like Castles, and the walls strong and hard to mine'.[60] Soldiers began to succumb to the 'country disease', probably smallpox, the scourge of soldiers confined for long periods aboard ship. The gloomy mood was lifted temporarily when one of the ships broke away from the squadron and captured an incoming Barbados tobacco ship with a cargo worth £5,000, but with it intelligence that a French fleet had been despatched to Ireland with naval reinforcements for the Irish. Panicking, the Sea Adventurers resolved to burn both Galway and Limerick before these imaginary troops arrived.[61] Forbes stated that he would rather die in Galway before abandon it, and let it be known that his forces would assault the town on 15 August.[62]

Clanricarde's arrival near the town put a stop to this assault, and the ensuing lengthy negotiations left Forbes in no doubt that his actions would cause a general war to break out, with Catholic rebels and Catholic forces loyal to the king united against him.[63] Throughout the assault on Galway, Forbes had been spurred on by Hugh Peter but, faced with the courteous and diplomatic Clanricarde, he decided to finally confer with his captains, who had already decided that the Sea Adventure was over and had prepared to re-embark. An offer of £400 in gold from Clanricarde, in return for a share in the tobacco ship, encouraged Forbes to draw a line under his adventure.[64] Forbes, now accepting Clanricarde's authority, agreed to leave one pinnace behind under the command of Thomas Rainsborough, to wait and convey Clanricarde's letters to England. In parting, he plundered the western part of Clare for cattle, and presented his haul to the town of Galway as compensation for their own losses suffered a few weeks earlier.[65]

At this point, the Sea Adventure more or less fizzled out. Forbes offered his mercenary soldiers to Barnaby O'Brien, earl of Thomond, who warily and politely declined. As soldiers continued to succumb to smallpox, the vessels converted from troop carriers to refugee ships and evacuated hundreds of displaced Protestant settlers from the Shannon estuary, for a reasonable profit.[66] In mid-September, the fleet dispersed, some to remain in the area as parliament's Irish guard. This small squadron retained from the Sea Adventure was the only significant force deployed in Ireland using the funds of the original Adventure. It remained under the command of Lord Forbes, anchored in the Shannon estuary during the autumn of 1642 and selling the remainder of the tobacco stolen from the French ship to Protestants and Catholics alike.[67] Hugh Peter returned to London to write his now well-known account, while the Adventurers' land army continued to train at the Artillery Ground. Some small-scale alternative arrangements were attempted, for example an ordinance of 5 July for the raising of 5,000 men and 500 horses under the command of Philip Lord Wharton.[68] A budget of £40,000 was approved for this project, which was also entrusted to Maurice Thomson and William Pennoyer, although nothing came of it.[69] The Adventurers kept up the appearance of concern for Protestant Ireland but took no further practical measures as a group. Thomson and Pennoyer, between 1642 and 1644, provided five additional ships to patrol the Irish sea, but financed the £6,000 cost themselves.[70]

Most of the Adventurers' treasury had been diverted to the parliamentary war effort, which was bolstered by the recruitment of several Adventurers and their associates to positions of command in the parliamentary army. On 25 July 1642, George Thomson was commissioned as a captain of horse in the earl of Essex's army, and joined the earl's life-guard. Thomson appointed John Coish as his lieutenant, and William Coish as quartermaster.[71] The Coish brothers were the sons of Richard Coish who had adventured £200 in Irish land.[72] Fellow Adventurer captains in Essex's army included Oliver Cromwell, John Allured, Thomas Hammond, Sir Arthur Hesilrige, Sir Walter Erle, George Austin, Walter Long, Sir Robert Pye and John Sanders. They served alongside Edwin Sandys, formerly of the Virginia Council. An officer of the Providence Island Company, Sir Gilbert Gerard, was appointed treasurer of the army and Sir Henry Vane II was retained as treasurer of the navy. Parliament's initial mobilisation was, therefore, also heavily influenced by the committees at Grocers' Hall.

THE ADVENTURERS AND THE IRISH PARLIAMENT

Although the Adventurers were no longer in the business of sending an army to Ireland at their own expense, they sought to establish control over the supplies of materials for war. The six months from January to June 1642 saw them gradually tighten their grip. Initially, orders for supplies and weapons were signed by the earl of Leicester, and passed to Nicholas Loftus, the Deputy Treasurer of Wars for Ireland, based in London, for payment.[73] Although Loftus was in overall charge of parliament's Irish expenditure, starting in February 1642 he delegated the day-to-day accounting to the two subcontractors initially recruited by Warwick and Maurice Thomson to send money to Ulster: George Henley and John Hawkridge.[74] From February until April 1642, as ultimate responsibility for Ireland shifted from the earl of Leicester to parliament, the payment orders were increasingly signed by Henry Elsinge, Clerk of the House of Commons, as the orders were emanating from the Committee for Irish Affairs, and not from the Lord Lieutenancy.[75] From April 1642, as parliament ceded its authority to Grocers' Hall, the orders were simply signed by Sir David Watkins, the secretary of the Adventurers' committee, supplanting Westminster.[76] These changes reflect how the English response to the Irish rebellion passed from the king to parliament, from the main body of the Lords and Commons to the Committee for Irish Affairs, and finally to the Committee for Adventurers at Grocers' Hall.

The Adventurers had not given up on Ireland altogether, and began to explore further methods of raising finance from within their own circle for its conquest. On 22 August 1642 a House of Commons order authorised the raising of a loan, at 8% interest for a term of one year, from 'mariners of the river Thames' to supply forces in Ireland.[77] This initiative raised only the modest sum of £2,340 from forty-three contributors, all of whom were connected with Trinity House or the wider circle of acquaintances of Rainsborough and Maurice Thomson, who had become master of that institution. William Batten, who had a prosperous trade in indentured servants for Virginia, was the most prominent member of this group of lenders.[78] Batten was appointed Surveyor General of the Navy by Charles I in 1638 and a Commissioner for Navy and Customs by the earl of Warwick in July 1642.[79] His £100 contribution for Ireland probably helped with this appointment. A second lender, a former EEIC captain called Richard Swanly, was appointed admiral of the Irish Guard by Warwick in the spring of 1643, charged with preventing Irish soldiers from crossing the sea to England and joining the king's army.[80] The limitation of the Mariners' loan was that there were no prizes on offer or Irish land, just 8% interest from a fractious parliament. Despite this, the Adventurers were reluctant to open out the Adventure to new subscribers.

Instead, the Adventurers at Grocers' Hall latched onto a diplomatic mission sent by the English parliament to the Irish parliament in Dublin, led by the MPs Sir Robert Reynolds and John Goodwin. This expedition was originally planned by Sir Henry Mildmay, a treasurer for the church gate collection for distressed Irish Protestants, but he was commanded by Charles not to go.[81] Sir Robert Reynolds was the Adventurers' principal liaison with both parliament and the army, while Goodwin, formerly a principal master of the navy, was their liaison with parliament's navy committee.[82] Sir Adam Loftus, the vice-treasurer for Ireland, was the closest connection the Adventurers had with the government in Dublin, as his London-based kinsman, Nicholas Loftus, managed the funds disbursed towards the English parliament's military efforts in Ireland. As this was not an especially close connection, it left the Adventurers at a serious political disadvantage. They had not seen to the election of men from their own circle to the Irish parliament as they had done in London. The Adventurers' committee added Captain William Tucker to the parliamentary delegation, initially to act as their observer, but on 8 October, the Committee for Irish Affairs raised his status to that of full participant.[83] Tucker was an unusual choice for a diplomat so it is most likely that, with his renewed Sea Adventure fleet in Irish waters and further ships patrolling the Irish Sea, Maurice Thomson wanted his brother-in-law to collect intelligence as to how the Adventure for Irish land could be progressed. The delegation arrived in Dublin on 2 November 1642 carrying £20,000 in cash, with the aim of exploring how the Adventurers' money could be put to best use.[84] On 3 November, however, the conference between representatives of the English and Irish parliaments broke up after only one day, when news of the battle of Edgehill reached Dublin.[85]

Edgehill occurred on 23 October and it is highly unlikely that the English delegation was unaware of what had occurred. The parliamentary forces at Edgehill were comprised primarily of Lord Wharton's regiment, raised and paid for by the Adventurers for service in Ireland, and also Essex's regiment, funded by the £100,000 loaned to the Committee of Saftey by the Adventurers. The delegation to Dublin had been approved on 10 September, but there had been no particular urgency regarding its departure until a military confrontation with the king seemed inevitable.[86] As the civil war in England entered its military phase, it suddenly became urgent to figure out a way of depriving the king of Irish reinforcements, which meant continuing the war there. In principle, the more benign objective of the delegation, as it claimed, was to disburse some of the Adventurers' funds and to convince Protestant Ireland to accept payment for their military service in Catholic Irish land under the same terms as the Adventurers, but neither side trusted the other. Although there were some initial discussions between the Westminster delegation and a group representing the Irish parliament concerning a campaign to besiege Wexford, the earl of Ormond insisted on a recess to assess the situation.[87] During this recess Tucker attempted to ingratiate himself with Dublin's merchant community by issuing £2,000 worth of bills of exchange for goods supplied to Protestant forces in Ireland, which could be redeemed for cash with Samuel Warner in London.[88]

The representatives of the two parliaments met again on 28 November, by which time the differences between the two bodies had crystallised. The English delegation insisted that their support for forces in Ireland was conditional on those same forces taking the Protestation Oath, to defend the 'true reformed Protestant religion as expressed in the doctrine of the Church of England, against all Popery and popish innovations'.[89] They made a clear distinction between merely suppressing the rebellion and launching a religious war, irrespective of the allegiance of individual Catholic leaders. On 10 December 1642 a small group of army officers came forward and undertook to exchange their pay for land, but this initiative was only partially successful.[90] Unknown to William Tucker and the Westminster MPs in Dublin, Charles was already making overtures of peace to the Irish rebels.[91] On 11 January 1643, the Lords Justices in Dublin – the king's representatives – were instructed to receive overtures from the leaders of the Irish Confederacy in Kilkenny. This was anathema to the Adventurers. Negotiations between the king's advisers and the Confederate leadership were evidently at an advanced stage before this instruction, as Charles included detailed notes as to his negotiating positions.

In private, Ireland's leaders began to talk about the fragmentation of the war in Ireland, and the extremes of cruelty committed by Scottish and English forces in Ireland, forces of parliament and not of the king.[92]

On 2 February 1643, the Lords Justices formally invited the Irish Confederates to send a negotiating team to Dublin, while the language used by the respective parties when referring to one another became markedly sharper. This was the culmination of a series of setbacks for Adventurer diplomacy. From the beginning of January, the English parliament, its soldiers and political representatives began to be termed 'rebels', and Irish lords began to refer to them thus with impunity. Sir Robert Reynolds was of the opinion that if the wars in England continued in the king's favour, he would instruct the authorities in Dublin to arrest them, and that these instructions would be swiftly carried out. On 21 January 1643 the Lords Justices of Ireland ruled that the English parliament's promise to secure the pay of soldiers on forfeited land was illegal and they voided the arrangements made the previous December.[93] On 27 January, the campaign that the two parliaments had planned against Wexford was cancelled, on the pretext that a major military campaign was the responsibility of the Lord Lieutenant, and not for under-officers in Dublin. This decision was taken by Ormond, who was not going to allow the Adventurers to assemble another army in Dublin, given what had occurred in England. Ormond was in continual correspondence with the king, and over dinner with the Westminster delegation he suggested that they should seriously consider leaving. This was flatly refused by Tucker, who replied that he only took his instructions from London.

Tucker received his instructions from Maurice Thomson, who was directing negotiations by courier from London.[94] Reynolds, Goodwin and Tucker began to worry that they would be arrested in Dublin on the king's order, and prepared to abandon their mission. Fearing that Charles I would bring the war in Ireland to an end without the surrender of the Irish and, in consequence, with no Irish land to be distributed, the Adventurers switched their political campaign from Dublin to London. Sir David Watkins and Richard Shute, purporting to be 'designers and managers of the public affairs of the city', delivered a large-scale merchants' petition to parliament in December, opposing any cessation of hostilities with the king in England and voicing their fears that a peace of sorts would quickly follow in Ireland.[95] With this logic, the Committee of Adventurers in Grocers' Hall tied the military defeat of Charles in England to their Irish prize. There was little support for the Adventurers' stance. Their petition had been thrown out by the Common Council and was presented at Westminster in a personal capacity by Watkins, Shute and Hugh Peter on behalf of ninety merchants. The Common Council organised a counter petition, in favour of opening peace negotiations, which attracted 5,000 signatures.

Although the Lords Justices in Dublin had been holding preliminary negotiations with the Confederates at their base in Kilkenny for some weeks, these negotiations were not finally revealed to Tucker until 30 January 1643, when he was informed that the most senior Protestant and Catholic figures in the king's administration in Ireland, including Ormond and Clanricarde, were about to agree a truce. William Tucker addressed a meeting of the Privy Council in Dublin the following day, recounting all of the cruelties committed against English settlers by the native Irish since the outbreak of the rebellion in October. It was Tucker's last opportunity, for on 3 February, the day after the Confederates were invited to Dublin, a letter arrived in Dublin from Charles ordering the Irish parliament to have no further dealings with the London delegation.[96] An additional letter from the king to Ormond on 12 February revoked the delegation's observer status, and it was barred from the chamber of the Irish Council of State.[97] Tucker, for his part, refused to hand over any of the Adventurers' money if there was a risk it would end up in Kilkenny. The port of Dublin was blockaded with royalist ships, trapping the Westminster diplomats.

On 16 February 1643 the Lords Justices demanded the book of contracts with army officers in Ireland who had agreed to take their pay in Catholic land, which William Tucker had assembled with much effort. This was surrendered by Sir Robert Reynolds when Tucker was absent from the delegation's chambers. The Lords Justices now had the list of officers in Ireland who were prepared to serve under parliament's banner but, without the contracts, officers would not be able to make their claims. One of these officers was Lord Lisle, the son of the earl of Leicester, Lord Lieutenant, and Ormond abruptly took over his command.[98] Parliament finally managed to slip an armed merchant ship into Bullock Harbour near Dublin, enabling Tucker, Reynolds and Goodwin to escape Ireland.[99] Just as the Sea Adventure marked the opening of serious military hostilities between king and parliament, the failure of Westminster's effort to gain allies in Ireland divided Protestant Ireland into factions. It was no longer just about the Irish rebellion of 23 October 1641.[100]

In Grocers' Hall, a new petition was drafted and sent via Westminster to the king on 24 February 1643, begging him to order the Irish parliament to accept the Adventurers' money and military assistance, but this overture was also rejected. Much of this was bluster, however, as the Adventure for Irish land had run out of cash. This became apparent when, on 23 February 1643, the Adventurers' regular meeting in London was attended by Sir John Franklin to collect a payment due to Tobias Norris, a Dublin merchant who was owed £3,336.[101] Norris had been told he could collect his money by William Tucker. In order to avoid a default, it was agreed with Westminster that Franklin would claim Norris's debt from money raised on English delinquent estates, the property seized by parliament from supporters of the king. As Dublin did not take the Adventurers' money when it was offered to them, Dublin's merchants would have to wait to be paid through the sale of the assets of English royalists.

FINANCING PARLIAMENT

As previously detailed, in July 1642 almost half of the collectors of plate, money and horses were Adventurers for Irish land. During the autumn of 1642, parliament sought to formalise its sources of finance by establishing financial committees and the Adventurers' committee was at the forefront of this effort. The Committee for Advance of Money was created on 26 November 1642, to receive loans secured on the 'public faith', meaning future taxes, to finance the parliamentary cause. This committee was formed on the instigation of the earls of Essex and Warwick and its affairs were controlled by Adventurers.[102] Money could be advanced on a voluntary or involuntary basis, and the expected contribution was 5% of real estate, or 20% of personal estate; a tax on either assets or income.[103] Those who refused to lend would be compelled to pay but would never get their money back. The physical collection of the money was contracted to London's Lord Mayor and two sheriffs, respectively the Adventurers Isaac Pennington, Thomas Andrews and John Langham. The sheriffs, in turn, selected under-sheriffs for each ward who saw to the actual collection of the money, a cohort also dominated by Adventurers.[104] The Committee for Advance of Money exempted those who had already contributed to the parliamentary cause through such funds as the Adventure for Irish land, recognising that the Adventure was really a parliamentary fundraising effort. The work of assessment and the power to enforce payment was devolved by parliament to a committee of citizens: the closely connected John Foulkes, Maurice Thomson, Sir Thomas Soame, Samuel Vassall, John Venn and Richard Waring. The treasurers were Sir John Wollaston and, once again, the treasurers for the Adventure for Irish land: Thomas Andrews, John Towse and John Warner.[105] Despite all of these detailed preparations, the Committee for Advance of Money failed to quickly bring in the expected amounts.

A small number of royalist Adventurers and Levant Company merchants was prominent in financing the Additional Sea Adventure, but the leaders of both the EEIC and Fellowship of Merchant Adventurers had kept a low profile. On the night of 29 October 1642, fifty-one leading royalist merchants from London were arrested, taken from their homes and disarmed.[106] These merchants included Sir Henry Garraway, the governor of the Levant Company, who was replaced by Isaac Pennington in 1643.[107] Sir George Whitmore, Lord Mayor in 1632 and William Acton, whose election as Lord Mayor was successfully opposed by the colonial merchants in 1640, were also held. Arrested members of the General Court of the EEIC included Sir William Middleton,

John Cordwell, receiver of fines for the Chamber of London, William Garway, a former EEIC factor, and Robert Abdy, the company's Deputy Governor.[108] Maurice Thomson's former partners in the Virginia tobacco monopoly, the Stone brothers, were also rounded up.[109] The suspected royalist merchants were not held for long or injured, but were certainly intimidated and the Adventurers gained access to their commercial documents. Their combined assessments amounted to £318,000.[110] Sir David Watkins, the Adventurers' secretary, was appointed as the arbiter for claims, with powers to decide if an assessment was fair and to imprison those who refused to pay.[111]

Although Maurice Thomson and the citizens' committee made assessments totalling £1.4 million from June 1643 to June 1644, the amount actually collected was only £260,000.[112] A lot of the money was forgiven, reduced in return for a bribe or simply stolen. The subscriptions were managed entirely by the Adventurers, and their friends received special treatment. For example, when Richard Boyle, 2nd earl of Cork, was assessed to pay £5,000 in 1644, with a further £5,000 noted in unpaid arrears, the entire amount was set aside due to his misfortunes.[113] As subscriptions to the Adventure for Irish land were offset against the assessment, the assessment of William Hawkins, for example, was reduced to zero while Abraham Corsellis, who bankrolled the original Thomson/Tucker tobacco business, found his reduced from £400 to just £28.[114] In London, the collection of assessments at local level was undertaken by common councillors, leading to still wider scope for favours and arbitrary penalties to increase the collectors' bounties.[115] In February 1645, Lord Forbes, the returned Sea Adventurer, was appointed 'Discoverer of Delinquents' in the English provinces, a lucrative post with commissions of up to 50% for the more difficult to extract assessments.[116] By October 1645, Forbes's commissions were so great that his payment was the entire estate of Dr John Warner, the Bishop of Rochester.[117]

With the royalist EEIC leaders terrified, the Adventurers infiltrated the company's planned General Voyage of 1643. The Company had already experienced some problems with Charles, particularly the king's approval of an independent voyage by Sir William Courteen to the Indies in the 1630s, in breach of the company's monopoly. The EEIC petitioned parliament for a firm reinstatement of their monopoly in February 1642, which was granted in return for a loan.[118] After the arrests of October 1642, Sir Nicholas Crispe and Sir Thomas Abdy were forced to sell their shares in the voyage to pay their assessments and a host of Adventurers scooped up these shares in a business from which they had until this point been barred.[119] The infiltration of the EEIC's General Voyage was the Adventurers' first major success in breaking the monopolies of the merchant grandees. Maurice Thomson did not invest in the General Voyage as he, with William Pennoyer, had taken over the India business of a bankrupted William Courteen, who fled to the Continent.[120] The leadership of the Adventure for Irish land had taken over the entire Indies trade by the start of the 1643 season of voyages.

A NEW ADVENTURE FOR IRISH LAND

In January 1643 the treasurers of the Adventure for Irish land – Andrews, Halstead, Towse and Warner – were replaced by Thomas Foote, John Kendrick, James Bunce and Samuel Avery, partly to check the belligerence of the Committee of Adventurers at Grocers' Hall, but also because three of the treasurers now had other duties.[121] Kendrick's uncle, also called John Kendrick, had been a close business partner of Halstead.[122] Kendrick and Avery were both Merchant Adventurers and all four emerged as political Presbyterians, 1646–47, seeking the disbandment of the army and a negotiated peace.[123] These treasurers were left with the unenviable task of securing the return of £100,000 from parliament. The Committee of Adventurers that lobbied for the original investors continued to be dominated by the merchants who had emerged to take the lead in parliamentary finance: Maurice Thomson, Sir David Watkins, John Dethwick, Richard Hill, Samuel Moyer and the stationer, George Thomason.[124] The Adventurers' committee met with the Committee for Irish Affairs to assess how things stood, and calculated that the Adventure for Irish land had received £215,000, out of which £143,000 had either been spent on Ireland or promised to creditors.[125] The treasurers had paid out £78,000 but owed £37,000 to the Maurice Gethin consortium. The Gethin debt was still in the hands of the treasurers, but the balance owed to creditors was no longer there. £100,000 was loaned to parliament, although much of the resources that had been purchased with the £78,000 were also consumed in England. While the team in Grocers' Hall was deciding what to do, Maurice Thomson and William Pennoyer met the cost of maintaining the flow of supplies to Ulster and Munster, and both men financed a supply ship to Carrickfergus. Pennoyer took on the sole cost of replenishing the arsenals of Youghal, the city of Cork, Frekes Castle and Bandon.[126] In a separate arrangement, the Committee for Irish Affairs negotiated a loan of £1,500 from Maurice Thomson and George Henley to bring munitions to Athlone.[127]

Although Thomson and Pennoyer had kept the supply lines to Ireland open, it was only on the basis of thirty days' credit. The decision of a meeting in January 1643 between the Adventurers and the Committee for Irish Affairs was that a new Adventure would be required.[128] In addition to meeting ongoing demands for funds to pay suppliers in London, the leading Adventurers were also under pressure from its Irish diplomatic mission to provide credible proof as to how it could meet the costs of an army in Dublin.[129] Important merchants, such as Pennoyer with his stocks of gunpowder, were able to have themselves moved up the preferment order for payment. Other merchants, for example

Michael Casteel, an important regional broker for military supplies, began to withdraw from supplying goods to Ireland.[130]

Bulstrode Whitelocke, who had opposed the raising of parliament's army for Edgehill, was assigned the task of drafting an ordinance for a new Adventure, which was published on 30 January 1643.[131] The selection of Whitelocke would, it was hoped, reduce the fears of new investors that this money would, once again, be transferred to other uses. The replacement of the original treasurers helped to reinforce this impression. Whitelocke decided to offer investors a choice between repayment in Irish land or capital with interest, reflecting the diminishing chances of an imminent distribution of Irish land and testing the appetite of merchants for parliament's credit. Whitelocke also proposed that the national network of collection agents created for the £400,000 subsidy in 1640 should be used to collect the contributions for Ireland.[132] On 7 February the Committee for Irish Affairs authorised the publication of 4,000 copies of a new ordinance for a loan or contribution for Ireland to be read out in churches, so that the public might be 'stirred up to lend and contribute to so good a work'.[133] Bills of exchange for the goods sent to Ireland continued to pile up in London, and the credit of parliament began, for the first time, to be questioned.

A new group of treasurers was named for what was a new Adventure for Irish land, comprising Sir Paul Pindar, Michael Casteel, Benjamin Goodwin, John Kendrick, William Pennoyer and Maurice Thomson. Three of the treasurers, Casteel, Pennoyer and Thomson, were deeply involved in the provisioning trade to the English and Scottish armies in Ireland, and were also among the leading creditors of the Adventurers. Casteel was chiefly involved in provisioning Dublin through his intermediaries in Chester. Pennoyer maintained supplies to the Boyle-related theatres of war in Munster and Thomson provided armed merchant shipping to cover the entire Irish coastline.[134] All three needed to control the money coming in to ensure they were at the forefront of the payment queue. Benjamin Goodwin was on the Committee for Irish Affairs supporting his brother, Robert, who was at the time still in Dublin as part of the parliamentary delegation. Sir Paul Pindar was one of the wealthiest men in London – a customs farmer, Levant Company grandee and formerly a leading financier of Charles I.[135] He was owed vast sums by the king, including £18,000 for a precious stone – the 'Pindar Diamond'. Before Charles pawned the diamond in Holland, he had mortgaged it against the farm for customs on sugar, which brought him into the orbit of the new customs commissioners, including Maurice Thomson. Pindar was no strict monopolist, and had been as active as any of the Adventurers in trying to break into the licensed trade of others. For example, William Courteen's vessels for his Indies voyage, the *Bona Esperanza* and *Bona Adventura*, had been leased from Pindar. Early in 1643, these ships were seized in India by the Dutch East India Company at a cost to Pindar of £75,000.¹³⁶ As Thomson and Pennoyer had also invested in Courteen's doomed voyage, Pindar had little option but to remain friends with his new partners by joining the latest Irish Adventure.

Whitelocke's collection structure had several weaknesses. The original Adventurers comprised a small circle of closely connected merchants who were able to leverage their London associates, but the loan and contribution for Ireland had to be collected by county committees with which Thomson, Pennoyer and Casteel had no existing relationship apart from some of their contacts in the western ports. As a result, subscriptions for the new loan were slow to come in. Although the Adventurers were given what was left of the cash from the Relief for Poor Protestants in Ireland from 1642, requests for the payment for goods sent to Ireland, and for soldiers' pay, continued to be bounced between the Committee for Adventurers and parliament.¹³⁷ Relations between the Adventurers and the commissaries for Ireland worsened, as William Pennoyer was moved to the front of the payment queue and secured the small amount of money that came in. In protest, Michael Casteel and Anthony Kirle withheld further supplies until some payments were made to them also.¹³⁸

Five thousand printed copies of the ordinance for the contribution for Ireland were finally distributed to the counties in March 1643, but the agents sent from London were not associated with any of the leading Adventurers.¹³⁹ The distribution of the ordinance did create enough confidence, in the short term, for merchants to resume military supplies to Ireland on foot of letters of credit drawn against the forthcoming contributions. Although £14,000 was collected in London, no money came in at all from the provinces.¹⁴⁰ This was hardly surprising, as by the middle of 1643 parliament controlled only the southeastern counties of England, with a narrow swathe of territory through the midlands, and some western ports. The king's assent to the new bill was not forthcoming, and parliament's agents were subject to arrest for attempting to bring copies of the printed ordinance into royalist areas.¹⁴¹ As the ordinance was to be distributed by the church, but the money collected by a committee, further complications arose as some churchmen, for example the Dean of Winchester, refused to publicise the ordinance on the assumption that more money would simply end up in the hands of the parliamentary army, as had been the case with the original Adventure. The mayor of Newport in south Wales collected the money but then refused to send it to Westminster.¹⁴² Benjamin Goodwin, who had financed £500 worth of supplies from his own pocket, took it upon himself to travel to Canterbury to collect the contribution money as his payment.¹⁴³ In mid-May 1643 Charles sent a letter to Westminster from Oxford, outlining his objections to the new Adventure. The king wanted guarantees that no further funds would be diverted to parliament's forces in England, and that parliament would return the £100,000, which it had already spent, to the original Adventure. He raised a particular objection to the continuation of Andrews, Towse and Warner as treasurers, seemingly unaware that these individuals had been replaced.[144] Had he known that the treasurers for the new ordinance were Thomson and Pennoyer, he may not have troubled himself to reply at all. As it was, parliament did not dignify the king with a response, but the Committee for Irish Affairs claimed that parliament was owed £50,000 in arrears from the Irish campaigns so far, not the other way around, raising the prospect that any new collections for Ireland would indeed be diverted. The January 1643 Loan and Contribution for Ireland duly collapsed, with little to show for it other than the continued shipping activities of Maurice Thomson and William Pennoyer, who could expect payment from any contributions from London, where the collector was George Thomson.

As the Thomson/Pennoyer partnership had proved itself unable to raise funds outside of its close circle of colonial merchants and ship-owners, parliament turned for help to the new treasurers of the first Adventure for Irish land, Samuel Avery, James Bunce, Thomas Foote and John Kendrick.[145] A fourth Adventure was launched, with accompanying declarations which made the terms on offer to potential investors even more generous.[146] Parliament was becoming increasingly desperate for funds for its Irish campaign, as MPs became creditors by honouring the payment warrants from merchants, which could not otherwise be paid and averting, for the time being, a crisis of trust in the credit of parliament.[147] The terms of the new Adventure amounted to a giveaway of land. Existing Adventurers could opt to pay in an additional 25% on top of the value of their initial Adventure of 1642, and receive twice their initial allocation of land. Pre-empting any peace agreement between the king and the Irish rebels, the ordinance also laid claim to the land of anyone involved in rebellion, regardless of whether or not they had been pardoned by the king. The towns and liberties of Galway, Limerick, Waterford and Wexford were included in a separate arrangement, with a fixed price assigned to each city, for purchase by an individual Adventurer or a consortium.[148] Finally, the new Adventurers could select the province in which they wished their land to be drawn, and not have to subject themselves to the vagaries of a lottery. Despite all of this, the amount raised proved disappointing, to say the least. Gregory Clement contributed £600; Maurice, George and William Thomson contributed £600, but this was a joint contribution. There was little additional interest as a quick return, the prerequisite for an adventure of any kind, appeared unlikely.

THE FISCAL REVOLUTION

Although their plans for the conquest of Ireland were unravelling, the Adventurers tightened their grip on parliamentary finance. The Committee for Advance of Money comprised, in effect, a tax on the assets of merchants who were not part of their network. The purpose of this tax was to collect any money stored in London that had not been loaned voluntarily, either to the Adventure for Irish land or during the subsequent collection for plate, money and horses. The next step was to seize control of the remaining major source of state revenue and, on 12 January 1643, the Adventurers John Foulke, Thomas Andrews, Stephen Estwick, Maurice Thomson, William Allen and John Russell formed a consortium with Richard Berkeley and John Chambers to become the Commissioners for Customs.[149] As customs commissioners, and not farmers, the new consortium would receive 3% of all future customs collected in London. They did not have to make an up-front payment based on expected customs receipts, but instead granted a loan to parliament of £20,000 in return for the franchise. The first act of the new commissioners was to halve the customs on tobacco, greatly increasing their profits as importers but reducing the amount of taxation available for the war effort. Control of customs also afforded the Adventurers an opportunity to reward their friends with lucrative posts as collectors. For example, Edward Watkins, a brother of Sir David Watkins, became Searcher for the Port of London. The job involved searching ships and seizing any undeclared merchandise and the Searcher retained 50% of the value of any goods seized.[150] The Adventurers had a deep, vested interest in the control of customs as it was they who were England's leading importers. Any reduction in customs, as had already been achieved for Virginia tobacco, would yield larger profits for the importers, assuming the wholesale price at the port remained the same. This would, of course, reduce the amount of revenue for parliament and require further invention to cover the shortfall.

In order to raise the large amounts of money necessary to field an army that could hold the king at bay, the Adventurers' next step was to import into England the primary Dutch system of indirect taxation, the excise. This was a tax on retail sales to be collected locally, and was applied to home-produced as well as imported goods.[151] The excise was intended to pay the army, while customs revenue was reserved for the navy.[152] It was a neat division of influence that allowed the merchants and ship-owning groups within the Adventurers' inner circle to concentrate on their own areas of dominance. Excise was charged on domestic commodities, greatly reducing parliament's reliance on taxation based on commodities imported by the colonial merchants. The excise commissioners were John Towse (an original treasurer for the Adventure), Thomas Foote and John Kendrick (the new treasurers for the Adventure), John Langham (the brother of Adventurer Samuel Langham and Sheriff of London in 1643) and the Adventurer John Lamott, along with merchants Edward Claxton, Thomas Culme and Symon Edmonds.[153] The excise commissioners kept 2.5% of any money they brought in. Although radical in appearance, the excise had a similar function to the replacement of the customs farmers with commissioners. A tax on the retail price of goods has an inflationary effect, increasing the price of the taxed commodity to the consumer to allow a portion of the retail price to be remitted to the government by the retailer. In the case of the excise of 1643, however, the new tax was replacing the monopoly system of the Stuarts, which, by restricting competition, had inflated retail prices in a similar way.[154] The excise, therefore, probably had a neutral effect on prices as the monopoly system broke down, but centralised yet more power into the hands of the financial committees. Conversely, by attacking monopolies, parliament had reduced its own powers of patronage and transferred these to the committees. A sub-commission for one of the new taxes was a juicier plum than an old trade concession. It required little capital, just some willing manpower to collect the new taxes. The excise was levied on as many commodities as feasible, although the most important early sources of revenue were imported cloth, groceries and domestic beer. The Excise Commissioners had wide powers to enforce collection, including imprisonment for noncompliance, but the money could only be spent on foot of an order of both Houses of Parliament. The exception to this rule was Ireland, where orders continued to be issued from Grocers' Hall.

In November 1643, parliament moved away from the summary approach operated by the Committee for Advance of Money and established the Committee for Compounding that offered those assessed an opportunity to negotiate a settlement with this committee in return for prompt payment. This committee sat at Goldsmiths' Hall and became the most important instrument of military finance during the English Civil Wars. The treasurers were two members of the Adventurers' committee at Grocers' Hall, Michael Herring and Richard Waring. Herring was a member of the Committee of Adventurers for Irish land while Waring was a member of the Sea Adventurers' committee, maintaining the army/navy division of interests. The Committee for Compounding was supervised by a parliamentary committee, again dominated by Adventurers: John Ashe, Denis Bond, John Browne, Sir John Clotworthy, William Ellis, William Gerard, Robert Goodwin, John Gurdon, Sir Arthur Hesilrige, Sir John Holland, Sir Robert Reynolds, Oliver St John and William Spurstowe. The only member of the Committee for Compounding who was not an Adventurer for Irish land was Sir Henry Vane II, nominated to this committee to ensure that the navy received a reasonable share of the proceeds, and hardly a stranger to the Grocers' Hall committee men.[155] The idea underpinning the compounding arrangement was that once an assessment had been agreed and paid, the payee would be safe from any further assessment by the Committee for Advance of Money. The assessments were made by Sir David Watkins, Jerome Alexander, Richard Shute, William Thomson and Samuel Moyer. William Thomson was also assigned to a 'Citizens Committee for Scottish Affairs' at Goldsmiths' Hall, a point of contact to ensure the Scottish army in Ireland was not forgotten amid all these changes.[156]

Any person who compounded but did not then pay was considered to be a delinquent, and their property could be sold at public auction unless the amount due from their assessment had been raised before the sale started. The critical difference between making a payment through Advance of Money, as opposed to through Compounding, was that contributions to the former were interest-bearing loans to parliament, albeit with only a vague promise of repayment. Compounders, in contrast, although they could negotiate to pay less, would certainly never see their money again. Compounders and delinquents could hold out hope of redress when Charles returned to London, whereas loans made to parliament, however involuntarily they were offered, were unlikely to ever be repaid. The Adventure for Irish land was the only exception as a source of parliamentary finance, as repayment in land was also guaranteed by the king's signature.

The various parliamentary funding schemes had so many senior personnel in common, almost all of whom were regular attendees at Grocers' Hall, that debts could be moved from one fund to another. A debt could also be converted into an annuity for life.[157] The Adventurers, with their colonial experience, were well used to alternative forms of currency, especially bills of exchange which had most of the characteristics of paper money. Commercial paper and government paper have much in common, the most important attribute of both being trust that the paper will hold its purchasing power. The innovative use of paper by the Adventurers gave the parliamentarians the purchasing power necessary to create a fiscal state, which could then challenge the real wealth of the king. The regular meetings of the Adventurers for Irish land at Grocers' Hall was the point of contact between the treasurers of all of these financial committees, as at least one treasurer from each committee also sat on the Adventurers' committee. The treasurers of Customs, Excise, Advance of Money and Compounding all issued paper credit vouchers in return for real money loaned to parliament. This paper, which normally bore a rate of interest, was intended to be redeemed with taxes collected by the various committees at some point in the future.

As parliament could move this paper around at will, and as long as its creditors believed that one day they would be repaid (or they had little choice in the matter), the ability of this paper to multiply, and to guarantee far more than the currency currently available, created a purchasing power which greatly exceeded the resources of the individual Adventurers. Maurice Thomson and his friends may have become rich with their tobacco and servant business, along with occasional raids on the Guinea coast, but they had nowhere near the real wealth of either the royalist merchants or the landowning peers.[158] The use of paper as a substitute for real wealth placed parliament's financiers on more equal terms with their royalist counterparts, as parliament could purchase supplies with paper promissory notes. This innovative use of paper is normally credited to eighteenth-century American revolutionary armies, but by 1643 the Adventurers were demonstrably operating a similar paper system, which had quickly evolved from merchants' bills of exchange.[159] The idea of the bill of exchange was not a new one, and the instrument was widely used by Italian merchants in the fourteenth century. A further Dutch innovation, the Exchange Bank of Amsterdam, founded in 1609, added much needed liquidity to the Dutch financial system, and created a general market for bills of exchange which was enthusiastically embraced by merchants. The English colonial merchants, with their very close commercial and familial ties to the Dutch financial markets, had a good working knowledge of the Amsterdam Exchange. Taken together, the financial committees comprised an exchange in all but name, using the credit of the English parliament, the 'public faith', vigorously defended by MPs as a notional substitute for a treasury. Perhaps without realising it, the committee at Grocers' Hall had created a rudimentary form of central bank.

The Adventurers had long sought to bring Dutch money into their schemes for military conquest, and Dutch merchants were initially invited to subscribe to the original Adventure for Irish land, although no subscriptions were forthcoming.[160] The 30 January 1643 ordinance also included an invitation for the Dutch to invest but, again, to no avail. Parliament returned to the issue of obtaining supplies in the Dutch Republic for use in Ireland with the publication on 29 July 1643 of an ordinance appointing Maurice Thomson, Nicholas Corsellis, Derrick Hoast and Adam Laurence to travel to the Netherlands and raise funds for Ireland. Nicholas Corsellis's son was married to Thomson's daughter, and Hoast and Laurence were both Dutch merchants living in London.[161] The Dutch Adventure for Irish land was accompanied by an admission by parliament that they had 'not been able to afford to the Protestants in Ireland such supplies as was necessary for them', and, by appealing to religious solidarity, successfully raised £31,000 which was spent on supplies for Ireland.[162] This Adventure also created a substantial and sudden Dutch interest in the colonisation of Ireland, as the amount invested represented roughly 10% of the total Adventure for Irish land.

The Dutch collection agents, appointed by Maurice Thomson and his partners to receive the money on their behalf, provide further insight into the international world of the Adventurers, and the many ways in which they were linked across national borders. Of the four named agents, two, Bouden Courteen and Jeronimo Asheman, were in Middelburg, in Zeeland province. Asheman had invested with the Adventurers for Lewis, a Dutch fishing colony established on the Isle of Lewis in the Hebrides in the 1620s. Paradoxically, he was also associated with the Dunkirk privateers, a scourge of the English merchant navy and a crucial supply source for the Irish Confederates. Bouden Courteen had inherited part of the shipping empire of his English family following the death of Sir William Courteen in 1636. He had become a director of the Dutch West India Company, with colonial interests in the Dutch Leeward Islands adjacent to the English colonies dominated by the Thomsons and their associates.[163] Maurice Thomson, Nicholas Corsellis, Hoast and Laurence were all involved in Sir William Courteen's East Indian projects, financed by Sir Paul Pindar.[164] Thomson and the Anglo-Dutch merchants, with their feet firmly under the Courteen table, had not joined with the other leading Adventurers in their assault on the English East India Company in 1643, preferring their own, independent enterprise.

The original Dutch coloniser of both St Eustatius and Tobago was Pieter van Corsellis, from a branch of the Corsellis family which was also based in Middelburg. Corsellis arrived in Tobago in 1635 and established a colony on the island, before moving it to St Eustatius a few months later. This colony was a success commercially, and St Eustatius began shipping tobacco to Flushing before making the shift to sugar production in the 1640s. Both islands were included in Carlisle's general grant of the Leeward Islands, a grant ignored by the Dutch in the same manner that the English ignored Spanish claims to the region. Despite these conflicting claims, the trade of all of the Leeward Islands was, for a time, dominated by the combined Corsellis/Thomson families, who operated with a considerable degree of independence from the colonial patentees.[165] Pieter van Corsellis was also involved in the Dutch West India Company that, like the Providence Island Company, derived most of its revenues from privateering.[166] The two remaining Dutch collectors, William Watson and Jonas Abbells, resided in Amsterdam and were associated with the English Reformed Church, and with Hugh Peter.[167] Abbells had lived in London during the 1610s, and pioneered the trade in Spanish tobacco from Trinidad to London, before viable crops were produced in the English colonies.[168]

The Dutch Adventure for Protestant Ireland was grounded in a plea for religious solidarity. The General Assembly of Divines at Westminster delivered a special sermon to both houses of parliament on 4 August 1643, praying for the success of the mission, stating that 'In the past four months the papists have killed 154,000 Irishmen. Imagine what they did in the previous seventeen months'.[169] A further ordinance of 5 October allowed the four English treasurers of the Dutch Adventure to negotiate for funds individually, and Maurice Thomson left the three Anglo-Dutch commissioners to arrange the supplies of aid for Ireland while he conducted some business of his own.[170] The supplies were collected in Amsterdam by Watson and Abbells, and arrived at Duncannon, County Wexford, in January 1644.[171] The work of the commissioners was not helped by the simultaneous presence of Hugh Peter in Amsterdam, who was attempting to purchase arms for the English parliament, despite the embargo of the Dutch States General.[172] To many Dutch administrators, the collection for Ireland was just another attempt to raise arms for England, using the Irish rebellion as the excuse.

Maurice Thomson's business in Amsterdam concerned the purchase of a sugar mill, as he and his partners had decided to establish a sugar plantation on Barbados.[173] The Dutch, led by the West India Company, had, in 1630, taken control of the Portuguese sugar-producing colony of Pernambuco in Brazil and, with it, the technology which enabled the establishment of integrated plantations. These plantations both grew and refined the crops. The most direct access to this technology was through the expertise of Dutch colonial investors who had returned to the Netherlands from the Caribbean, most notably Pieter van Corsellis.[174] As with so many of the Adventurers' activities, the prospect of cheap Irish land was a good way to open the doors of Dutch merchants, who may have been otherwise reluctant to allow English merchants access to their technology and trade.[175]

One notable characteristic of the Adventure for Irish land was that it was a distinctly Puritan undertaking with close links to Calvinist circles in London. In June 1643, parliament summoned an Assembly of Divines that became the Assembly of Westminster and sat until April 1653. It had responsibility for the reformation of the Protestant church and all of the Puritan peers of the Providence Island Company were represented there, along with Edward Lord Conway, who led the parliamentary expedition to Ulster, and Philip Lord Wharton, the intended commander of the Adventurers' army. A significant number of divines from London and the Home Counties, two-thirds of the total, were Adventurers for Irish land.[176] These associations had deep roots: Maurice Thomson in 1632 had sent money to Calvinist exiles in Germany via St Augustine's, the Dutch reformed church in London.[177] For its time, this was a highly dangerous gesture to make in public, considering his recent imprisonment by the Privy Council over his illegal incursion into Canada. Nicholas Corsellis was then Deacon of St Augustine's, becoming Elder in 1647, and Nathaniel Shute, the brother of Richard, its pastor.[178] These close religious links helped the Adventurers to secure permission to seek funds in the Netherlands. Parliament listened to the assembly and it was common for assemblymen to preach before a sitting. There were always sound financial reasons to attract Dutch finance to help resource parliament's allies in Ireland, but until the assembly's intervention on the Adventurers' behalf, parliament had not exploited this option.

To control the flow of resources to and from Ireland, on 12 September 1643 parliament passed an ordinance prohibiting the transport of any person from Ireland to England, with the exception of merchants carrying a licence to travel recorded in the Committee of Adventurers' 'Private Book'.[179] The royalist armies were already bolstered by an influx of troops from Ireland, and parliament needed to match these numbers by attracting troops from Scotland.

The strategy chosen to increase their forces was an alliance with the Scottish Covenanters, and the signing, on 25 September 1643, of the Solemn League and Covenant, the purpose of which was to provide parliament with access to Scottish troops for deployment in the north of England.[180] To pay this Scottish army, parliament formed a special committee which summoned the leading Adventurers to discuss a loan of £100,000.[181] These Adventurers, now central to parliament's hopes for a military victory, included Maurice Thomson, John Oldfield, Richard Shute, Christopher Pack, Michael Herring, Richard Waring, John Bateman and Sir David Watkins. They agreed to provide £50,000 within six days, securing a commitment by the Scots to march south into England by the middle of November.[182] The only merchant on the committee to fund the Scottish army who was not an Adventurer for Irish land was Sir William Alexander, although he was previously involved in Maurice Thomson's Kent Island project and his father was caught up in the same border dispute with France concerning Canada that had resulted in Thomson's imprisonment.[183] Short of cash, parliament suggested that the Scottish forces would be paid, in part, with Irish land at the same rates as the Adventurers, although no accounts of any subsequent distribution survive.[184] The financial cost of the Scottish incursions into England dwarfed the money spent on sending Scots to Ireland, which amounted to less than £35,000 between 1639 and 1651, compared to the £600,000 bill for the Bishops' Wars (1639–40). In total, the English parliament sent £1.25 million to Scotland (1639–51), a figure which comprised half of all Scottish government income.[185]

THE ADVENTURERS AND POLICY FOR IRELAND

The next crisis for the Adventurers in Ireland emerged on 30 September 1643, when parliament published what were alleged to be Charles I's terms for a peace treaty with the Irish rebels, foreshadowing serious financial losses for the Adventurers if the king abandoned the goal of an unconditional surrender.[186] Opposition to a cessation in Ireland was largely managed from Grocers' Hall, where a special sub-committee was appointed to lobby against it, using Sir Robert Reynolds as its spokesman in parliament.[187] Parliament's decision to bring the Scottish army in Ulster under its direct pay, and the potential for Scottish military service to be repaid in Irish land, resulted in the merging of the Adventurers' committee and the Committee for Irish Affairs.[188] In addition to giving the Adventurers a direct role in parliament's Scottish alliance, albeit only for Ireland, this arrangement also enabled the Adventurers to raise further funds for the conquest of Ireland on the public faith. The Committee of Adventurers now spoke for parliament. Given that this committee also included the treasurers for all of the important sources of parliamentary funding, and the Adventurers were also represented on all of the committees which decided how any money raised could be spent, the men at Grocers' Hall could protect their investment and ensure that no further funds need be secured against Irish land. From their perspective, it was better for the Scots to be paid with cash and for no further loans to be guaranteed with Irish land, as this could dilute their investment. From this point on, the conquest of Ireland would be paid for with money secured on English assets, or with English taxes.

As 1643 drew to a close and the chances of an early conquest of Ireland receded, the Adventurers returned to their colonial interests and sought to bring the Atlantic colonies under parliamentary control. Following a lobbying campaign by the Adventurers, on 2 November 1643 parliament confirmed the earl of Warwick as Governor in Chief and Lord High Admiral over all of the American colonies.[189] A Commission for the Colonies was established, which was almost identical in composition to the Committee for Irish Affairs of January 1642. It comprised the MPs Sir Gilbert Gerrard, Sir Arthur Hesilrige, Benjamin Rudyard, John Pym, Oliver Cromwell, Denis Bond, Miles Corbett, Cornelius Holland, William Spurstowe, Samuel Vassal, John Rolle and Sir Henry Vane II. In addition to Warwick, the peers on the commission included the earls of Pembroke and Manchester, viscount Saye-and-Sele and Lord Robartes, all of whom had been connected with the Providence Island Company, together with Lord Wharton who had been in command of the Adventurers' army. The commissioners had the power to appoint each colonial governor, although this power would be exercised with some difficulty.

Central to the Adventurers' financial concerns at the end of 1643 was the rise to pre-eminence of Barbados as the main engine of their profits in the Atlantic world. A small number of Adventurers had been quietly developing their plantations on the island, and they were ready to switch production from the established crops of cotton, indigo and tobacco to the far more profitable and labour-intensive sugar. This change in production generated ongoing supply and policy challenges for both planters and policymakers. It would also, crucially, provide the supplies of bullion necessary to sustain both the parliamentary and colonial projects. On 20 October 1643 the Commons was read a petition from 'divers merchants trading to … Barbados, and of divers inhabitants there' claiming that the earl of Carlisle and the Catholic Lord Baltimore intended to seize the island and 'may join [it] to the popish party'.[190] There is no further evidence for this plot although, as the Adventurers were well aware, there remained a significant number of Irish planters on the island. Parliament formed a new Committee for Foreign Plantations, headed by Warwick and including Denis Bond, Oliver Cromwell, Cornelius Holland, John Pym, Sir Henry Vane II and Samuel Vassall. The Committee for Foreign Plantations of late 1643 bore a striking resemblance to the Committee for Irish Affairs from early in 1642. Both relied on the same group of merchants to project their policies and in order to preserve this tight circle, William Jessop, the secretary of the Providence Island Company, became secretary to the Committee for Foreign Plantations.[191]

The financial returns from the Virginian tobacco monopoly in the 1630s were impressive, but the returns from Barbados sugar in the 1640s would be spectacular. The substantially Adventurer-managed colonies of Montserrat and St Kitts had placed themselves under the protection of James Ley, earl of Marlborough, who was appointed Admiral of the royalist fleet at Dartmouth.[192] The earl of Carlisle's overall patent to the Caribbean was, due to his support for the king, in the process of being sequestered by parliament, and additional proceedings were underway in the Court of Chancery for the collection of the first earl's debts, owing since his death in 1636. The governorship of Barbados had been assumed by Phillip Bell, formerly a governor of Providence Island. Despite the apparent neutrality of the island in terms of the English Civil War, Barbados was firmly under the control of Warwick and his agents and the initial project to convert the islands from cotton and tobacco to sugar started there, led by Thomas Andrews, Martin Noel, William Pennoyer and Maurice Thomson. The development of the sugar industry required the introduction of technology adopted in Dutch Brazil, and researched by Thomson during the Dutch Adventure mission.

The Adventurers, with healthy profits from customs and excise and encouraged by the prospect of further Dutch finance, decided to strike out on their own in pursuit of the conquest of Ireland. In December 1643 the Adventurers circulated leaflets among the Protestant armies in Ulster, opposing the cessation, and encouraging soldiers to take the Solemn League and Covenant.[193] On 4 January 1644 the Adventurers' committee in Grocers' Hall published their new policy for Ireland, rejecting the cessation, and undertaking to meet the pay of any soldier who took the oath. New shoes and clothing were promised, at the Adventurers' expense, as a reward to any soldier who opposed the cessation. These supplies were to be provided by their new Dutch allies.[194] This critical decision, to maintain the war in Ireland despite a cessation agreed by the king, was taken by the Committee for Irish Affairs, following its merger with the Committee of Adventurers on 27 November 1643.[195] Although the merged committee included the twenty-four MPs nominated to the Committee of Irish Affairs, alongside an additional twenty merchants on the Committee of Adventurers, the decisions were taken by a core group of twelve members who attended at Grocers' Hall: John Goodwin, Sir John Clotworthy, John Reynolds, John Vaughan, Maurice Thomson, George Thomson, William Hawkins, Gregory Clement, Thomas Ayers, Henry Featherstone, Richard Floyd and Richard Leader.[196] The remainder of the MPs only attended sporadically.[197] To oppose the cessation the Adventurers began, in the late autumn of 1643, to channel money into Ulster, even though there had been no new subscriptions to the Adventure since the previous July.[198] The money came from the reserve for the large debt outstanding to Maurice Gethin's clothing consortium, transferred to the Committee for Sequestrations on 26 October, with a long repayment schedule of £1,000 per month.[199] The Adventure for Irish land transformed into an adventure for English land, as repayment of its outstanding debts depended on the sequestration of the estates of Catholics and royalists in England to finance both arrears and forthcoming expenditure for parliament's campaigns in Ireland.

Now with some control over parliament's policy for Ireland, the Adventurers next proposed, by way of a petition presented to the Commons on 9 January 1644, a new plantation of Ulster, intended to 'support the forces there that oppose the cessation'.[200] Commissioners were to be sent to the nine counties of Ulster and to County Louth to identify all landowners who had been in rebellion, or had committed treason against the parliament of England. The forfeited lands would be surveyed and divided between the Adventurers and the parliament of Scotland, with the Adventurers' committee responsible for the allocations. The Ulster Adventure would be opened for new subscribers, and existing Adventurers could increase their subscriptions, to ensure they received large estates. Finally, all church land in Ulster would be seized, and clergy replaced by nominees of the Adventurers and Committee for Scottish Affairs in London, with the approval of the Westminster Assembly. To placate the Irish Society, owner of the Londonderry Plantation on behalf of the London Companies, an additional fund was proposed, managed by the Company of Salters, which would allow the London Companies to extend their plantation lands in Derry at the Adventurers' rates.[201]

It was an ambitious plan, but attacked the military supplies business of Sir John Clotworthy and his agent, the commissary general for Ulster, John Davies. Clotworthy had recommended Davies for the post of commissary for Carrickfergus and made him responsible for the purchase of all supplies for the Scots and Protestant Irish armies in Ulster, with the exception of those in Derry.[202] Davies was highly competent and had worked both with the Adventurers and with Nicholas Loftus in London to supply English forces, and also with Scottish merchants to supply the Scots forces in Ulster.[203] The Adventurers decided to undermine him. According to them, Davies had brought in supplies worth £160,000 between December 1642 and October 1644 and had made excess profits, at the army's expense, of at least £15,000 plus a commission of £9,600.[204] Clotworthy and Davies were also making money at the delivery side, charging soldiers for food at local rates, and accepting payment in vouchers for putative land allocations. The Adventurers would later claim that Davies's profiteering was the reason why the forces in Ulster never advanced beyond their own territories.[205] They cut off Davies's supplies and to separate the two sides, parliament ordered that money owed by Davies to Maurice Thomson and William Pennoyer be transferred to the Adventurers' treasury for payment, rather than leaving it to Davies to settle the bill.[206] For the time being, Thomson's Dutch contributors were keeping Carrickfergus adequately supplied, and in May 1644 the Dutch delivered £1,000 in silver, with substantial quantities of food and clothing, to the garrison.[207] The well-timed Dutch intervention allowed some breathing space for parliament to deal with the Adventurers' colonial ambitions in Ulster.

The Adventurers had over-reached themselves and had begun to irritate their friends in parliament. Prolonging the war and colonising Ulster was one thing, but cutting off Davies's military supplies with the potential to starve the armies in Ulster was another. Parliament's and the Adventurers' interests were in reasonable alignment until January 1644. These interests began to diverge when the Scottish Covenanters intervened in the English Civil War on parliament's side, culminating in their joint victory against the king's forces at Marston Moor on 2 July.[208] The parliamentary army in Ulster was mainly Scottish, supporting a large civilian population of recent Scottish descent. On 16 February 1644, parliament inaugurated a new committee, the Committee of Both Kingdoms, to develop a coordinated response from Derby House, away from the Adventurers at Grocers' Hall.[209] Although this committee was also led by the earl of Warwick, and the earls of Essex, Manchester and Northumberland were frequently present at its sittings, the London merchant MPs were not nominated to it and the Adventurers were not invited to attend. In response, and while the Committee of Both Kingdoms was being established, the Adventurers continued with their own meetings at Grocers' Hall and excluded the peers and MPs.[210] The Adventurers' activities included intercepting letters sent from the Scottish forces in Ulster and withholding them from the Committee for Irish Affairs.[211] John Dethwick, William Fetherstone and Samuel Moyer continued to attend meetings of the Committee for Irish Affairs but its meetings became sporadic as powers were transferred to the Committee for Both Kingdoms. When this committee finally convened, it included only five Adventurers, John Crewe, Oliver Cromwell, Sir Gilbert Gerard, Oliver St John and Sir William Waller.[212] The committee then split along 'war' and 'peace' lines and Irish affairs were moved down the agenda.[213]

Excising the Adventurers from the committee rooms of parliament was a minor matter compared with loosening their grip on parliament's finances. The Committee for Both Kingdoms relied on funds from the Committee for Compounding to be effective, and that remained under the Adventurers' control.[214] Sir Thomas Barrington and William Heveningham were recalled from Essex and Norfolk respectively, where they had been collecting money raised for Ireland from the loan of January 1643, and tasked with disciplining the Adventurers.[215] It was not difficult to find infractions. Stephen Estwick, for example, had been paid £4,000 by the army treasurer, Sir Gilbert Gerard, for clothes supplied to the Essex regiment on its formation in 1642. These had simply been removed by Estwick from the Adventurers' stores in London, so he had been paid for the same goods twice, by Gerard and by the Adventurers.[216] Most of the money collected for the January 1643 contribution for Ireland, problematic as the collection was, had not been disbursed by the treasurers.[217] The treasurers had projects of their own and Sir Paul Pindar was caught smuggling gold up the river Thames to Charles at Oxford.[218] Although not at all disloyal to their Irish cause, Maurice Thomson and William Pennoyer were distracted with a project to gather an £80,000 fund for a project in India, and were less interested in developments in Ireland.[219] In punishment, a stay was put on the payment of £3,000 to Thomson and Pennoyer for ships chartered from them to patrol the Irish Sea.[220] A committee of enquiry was ordered, chaired by Edward Montagu, earl of Manchester, and including, somewhat pointlessly, Maurice Thomson who conducted the investigations.[221] Thomson's swift investigation found that four under-collectors, William Hale, John Broughton, William Jennings and Thomas Fossan, with no links to the central group of Adventurers, had been diverting funds for their own use and they were imprisoned. The money due to Maurice Thomson was duly cleared for instant payment out of the Adventurers' funds, and Davies was placed behind him in the payment queue.[222] In return, the Adventurers agreed to stop meddling in state business. Although Thomson remained on the joint Committee for Irish Affairs, he was frequently the only non-MP in attendance. Irish affairs were taken up again by MPs, mainly Sir Robert Reynolds, Benjamin Goodwin, Sir John Clotworthy, Sir Thomas Barrington and William Massam.[223] John Goodwin took over responsibility for communicating with the Dutch Adventurers on parliament's behalf, but they were unhappy with the new arrangements and withdrew from providing finance for Ireland.[224] The Dutch military supplies specialists were happy to play both sides of the conflict, and continued to send large consignments of supplies to parliament's allies in Ireland after the cessation of arms in Ireland became known, while also continuing to supply the king's forces with weapons.

The earl of Manchester's enquiry rumbled on, and agents were despatched to the county collectors in search of missing contributions supposedly made under the January 1643 ordinance. Meanwhile, it became apparent that the military supplies purchased by the Adventurers had been sold from their stores to all comers and that it was not only Stephen Estwick who had supplied the same goods twice.[225] The Adventurers' stores were kept by Sir David Watkins, who ignored repeated summons to appear before the Committee for Irish Affairs, until a warrant for his arrest was issued by parliament.[226] Parliament seized the stores, but all that remained were a few bags of old clothes, which were distributed to Irish Protestant refugees in London.[227] The enquiry found that the January 1643 collection for Ireland had failed because the money had been stolen by collection agents in the provinces. The accounts of John Davies, the original cause of the Adventurers' complaints, were inspected by Sir Thomas Trevor, chief baron of the Exchequer, and found to be perfectly in order. The money due to Davies, however, was secured against the next contributions for Ireland 'which may become available', a small consolation.[228] Although the committee men all escaped unscathed, there were to be no further Adventures for Irish land and the Committee of Adventurers in Grocers' Hall withdrew, for the time being, from playing an active role in the formation of policy for Ireland.[229]

The Adventurers had learned that parliament would not tolerate excessive meddling in its business and that their complete control over an important parliamentary committee, the Committee for Irish Affairs, had become unwelcome. The cessation in Ireland of 1643 dealt a crushing blow to their hopes of a quick return on their original investment, and their attempt to instigate their own plantation of Ireland, even though the war had not ended, was quickly forgotten. In London, however, among the parliamentary finance committees, their control strengthened to a remarkable degree. This guaranteed their sustained influence at the heart of government which would eventually lead to the reassertion of their claims for Irish land. Rebuffed by Sir John Clotworthy and the political Presbyterians, the Adventurers decided to throw in their lot with the rising military commanders they had supported in the summer of 1642. In so doing, they were consistent with their assessment that the military defeat of the king in England was an essential prerequisite for an unconditional surrender in Ireland. Their position on Ireland was unchanged and a negotiated settlement with the Irish Confederates at Kilkenny would not be contemplated. Consequently, the Adventurers and the war party in parliament had common cause, if different goals. The Adventurers realigned their support to suit their interests, towards the army and the Committee for Foreign Plantations that included many of their friends.

NOTES

1 Karl S. Bottigheimer, *English Money and Irish Land* (Oxford, 1971), p. 81.
2 David Parrott, *The Business of War: Military Enterprise and Military Revolution in Early Modern Europe* (Cambridge, 2012), p. 150.
3 Library of Kings Inns, Prendergast Ms, 6, pp. 33–35.
4 *The Manuscripts of his grace The Duke of Portland, preserved at Welbeck Abbey,* I (London, 1891), p. 35.
5 For an earlier account of this incident see James Hardiman, *History of the Town and County of the Town of Galway* (Galway, edition of 1975), pp. 109–118.
6 TNA PRO 31/1/3, p. 48, Lords Justices and Council to Leicester, 23 April 1642.
7 Elaine Murphy, *Ireland and the War at Sea* (Woodbridge, 2012), p. 25; TNA PRO 31/1/3, p. 48.
8 TNA PRO 31/1/3, pp. 68–71, Submission of the Town of Galway.

9 Ulick Bourke, *The Memoirs and Letters of Ulick, Marquiss of Clanricarde* (hereafter *Clanricarde*) (London, 1857), p. 135, The Submission of the Town of Galway, and their adherents.
10 *Clanricarde*, p. 158.
11 NLI, MS 14035, unfol., p. 89.
12 Vernon F. Snow and Anne Steele Young (eds), *The Private Journals of the Long Parliament 2 June to 17 September 1642* (London, 1992), pp. 119–120. For the details of these negotiations see *Clanricarde*, pp. 119–135.
13 NLI, MS 14035, unfol., p. 90.
14 NLI, MS 14035, p. 94; *Clanricarde*, p. 239.
15 TNA PRO 31/1/3, p. 116; David Edwards and Thomas Powell, 'The Ship's Journal of Captain Thomas Powell, 1642', *Analecta Hibernica*, 37 (1998), pp. 251–284. See p. 274.
16 *Clanricarde*, p. 164.
17 Kenneth. R. Andrews, *Ships, Money and Politics: Seafaring and Naval Enterprise in the Reign of Charles I* (Cambridge, 1991), pp. 183–184.
18 John Adamson, *The Noble Revolt* (London, 2007), p. 363.
19 Anon, *The Diurnal Occurences or The Heads of the proceedings in Parliament from the Seventh of February to the Fourteenth* (London, 1642), p. 3. For the reduced Caribbean mission that left in July 1642 see Vincent Harlow, The *Voyage of Captain William Jackson*, Camden Miscellany, 13 (II) (London, 1923).
20 Peter Wilson Coldham, *English Adventurers and Emigrants, 1609–1660* (Baltimore, MD, 1984), p. 100; Alexander Grosart, *Lismore Papers*, 2 (London, c. 1886–88), p. 300; Hugh Kearney, 'Richard Boyle, Ironmaster: A Footnote to Irish Economic History', *The Journal of the Royal Society of Antiquaries of Ireland*, 83:2 (1953), pp. 157–161.
21 Andrews, *Ships, Money and Politics*, p. 160.
22 TNA SP 16/343 f.120; TNA SP 16/130 f. 34. William Willoughby was part owner of the *Elizabeth of London* with Maurice Thomson, a vessel attacked by Barbary pirates in the bay of Penzance, Cornwall, in the spring of 1640 (Adrian Tinniswood, *The Rainborowes* (London: Vintage Books, 2013), p. 102); Richard Waring campaigned for the Providence Island Company to be awarded letters of marque in the Caribbean (Robert Brenner, *Merchants and Revolution* (Princeton, NJ, 1993), p. 373); Richard Shute was joint-owner of an armed merchantman, the *America*, with Gregory Clement (Coldham, *English Adventurers*, p. 106); Richard Hill also had an interest in the Newfoundland fishing stations (Brenner, *Merchants and Revolution*, 165n); Samuel Moyer's interests included trade with the Levant as well as Massachusetts (*Publications of the Colonial Society of Massachusetts*, vol. 42 (Boston, 1964), p. 46; John Rowland Powell, *The Navy in the Civil War* (Hamden, CT, 1962), p. 200).
23 The merchants' names can be found in Bottigheimer, *English Money and Irish Land*, pp. 179–195, Appendix A, Column 2.
24 Arthur Percival Newton, *The Colonising Activities of the English Puritans* (New Haven, CT, 1914), p. 60. Dyke transferred his share in the Providence Island Company to John Pym in 1636, drawing Pym further into the Warwick House circle.

25 William Herbert, *The History of the Twelve Great Livery Companies of London*, Vol. II (London, 1836), p. 4.
26 H.R. McIlwaine (ed.), *Minutes of the Colonial and General Court of Colonial Virginia 1622–1632, 1670–1676* (Richmond, 1974), p. 207; Henry Stevens, *The Dawn of British Trade to the East Indies* (London, 1967), p. 60.
27 Anon, *The New England Historical and Genealogical Register*, Vol. 29 (Boston, 1875), p. 253.
28 Thomas Cunningham, *The Journal of Thomas Cunningham of Campvere, 1640–1654: With his Thrissels-banner and Explication Thereof* (Edinburgh, 1928).
29 Brenner, *Merchants and Revolution*, pp. 405–407.
30 CSPI 1660-[1670], p. 558, Documents relating to the case of William Barker and others. Copy of Petition of William Barker to the king.
31 Karen Ordahl Kupperman, *Providence Island, 1630–1641: The Other Puritan Colony* (Cambridge, 1993), pp. 181–187.
32 Francis J. Bremer and Tom Webster (eds), *Puritans and Puritanism in Europe and America* (Santa Barbara, CA, 2006), p. 387. Peter returned to England from New England in 1640 was employed as an agent of the Council of Massachusetts Bay.
33 TNA SP 63/488, f. 164. Benjamin Peter was captain of the *Speedwell* and a Levant Company captain. Thomas Rainsborough, also a Levant Company captain, was vice-admiral and captain of the *Zant Merchant*, one of two committee men to sail with the fleet; the other was William Thomson, captain of the *Goodhope* and Maurice Thomson's brother. The owners of the remaining eight ships, the *George Bonaventure*, *Mary Bonaventure*, *Achilles*, *Hopewell*, *Pennington*, *Dolphin*, *Lily* and *Leghorne* demonstrate that the backers of the Sea Adventure were drawn from a very small circle. The *Lily* and the *Zant Merchant* were both owned by Thomas Rainsborough. The *Leghorne* was also a Levant ship. The *Goodhope* and *Hopewell* belonged to Maurice Thomson. The *Mary Bonaventure* was owned by Richard Swanly, an East India company captain and already hired for the Royal Navy, as was the *Lily*. The *Pennington* was owned by Isaac Pennington, also a Levant Company trader.
34 Brenner, *Merchants and Revolution*, p. 405.
35 John Burke, *General Peerage…*, Vol. 1 (London, 1833), p. 485; Victor Treadwell (ed.), *The Irish Commission of 1622: An Investigation of the Irish Administration 1615–22 and its Consequences 1623–24* (Dublin, 2006), p. 657.
36 HMC, *Fourth report*, I (London, 1874), p. 114, 'Petition of Alexander Lord Forbes'.
37 John Bruce (ed.), *Notes of Proceedings in Long Parliament Temp Charles I by Sir Ralph Verney* (London, 1884), p. 162.
38 Anon, *His Majesties Message to the House of Commons concerning an Order made by them for the borrowing of one hundred thousand pounds of the Adventurers Money for Ireland, together with the Answer of the House of Commons in Ireland Thereunto*' (London, 1642), p. 4.
39 J.P. Cooper, 'The Fortune of Thomas Wentworth, Earl of Strafford', *Economic History Review*, New Series, 11:2 (1958), pp. 227–248, p. 231
40 Cooper, 'Fortune of Thomas Wentworth', p. 245.
41 *Historical Manuscripts Commission, Fourth Report*, Vol. 1, p. 79.

42 BL, Add Ms 46926, Perceval Papers, f. 63, memorandum relating to pilchard fishing off the coast of Munster.
43 George Thomson, a member of the committee of Sea Adventurers, organised the shipping of tobacco from St Kitts to Cork during Beecher's tenure.
44 Add Ms 46926, f. 64; Hugh Peter, *A True Relation of the present state of Ireland* (London, May 1642), p. 4.
45 Peter, *True Relation*, p. 4; TCD, Ms 840 The 1641 Depositions, ff. 47r–48v: Account of the rising in Munster by James Cleland.
46 Peter, *True Relation*, p. 9; Cleland, f. 48r.
47 Cleland, 48v; Peter, *True Relation*, p. 9.
48 Peter, *True Relation*, p. 10.
49 Theresa Murray, 'From Baltimore to Barbary, the 1631 Sack of Baltimore', *History Ireland*, Features, Issue 4, July–August 2006, Vol. 14.
50 Peter, *True Relation*, p. 6.
51 *Clanricarde*, p. 205.
52 *Clanricarde*, pp. 206–207.
53 Hugh Peter, *A True Relation of the Passages of God's Providence in a Voyage for Ireland* … (London, 1642), p. 12.
54 *Clanricarde*, p. 207.
55 Peter, *God's Providence*, p. 13.
56 *Clanricarde*, p. 213.
57 Peter, *God's Providence*, p. 13.
58 *Clanricarde*, p. 216.
59 *Clanricarde*, p. 224.
60 Peter, *God's Providence*, p. 15.
61 David Edwards and Thomas Powell, 'The Ship's Journal of Captain Thomas Powell, 1642', *Analecta Hibernica*, 37 (1998), pp. 251–284, see p. 272.
62 *Clanricarde*, p. 222.
63 TNA PRO 31/1/3, p. 123.
64 *Clanricarde*, pp. 256, 274.
65 *Clanricarde*, p. 243.
66 Peter, *God's Providence*, p. 19.
67 TCD, Ms 829, *The 1641 Depositions*, fols. 103r–104v.
68 A&O, I, pp. 12–13, 'July 1642: Ordinance for raising 5000 Foot and 500 Horse for Ireland'.
69 TNA SP 16/539/1, f. 309.
70 TNA SP 16/539/2, f. 214.
71 TNA SP 28/1/D, f. 142r.
72 Bottigheimer, *English Money and Irish Land*, p. 179.
73 TNA SP 28/1A, f. 23.
74 TNA SP 28/1D, f. 19.
75 The payment orders were technically parliamentary ordinances. These had to be validated by Henry Elsinge as secretary of the House of Commons.
76 Sir David Watkins was married to Honora Fleetwood and was the brother-in-law of Charles Fleetwood. He was well known in Adventurer circles as former treasurer of the Virginia Company, 1622–24. In this role, Watkins was responsible for issuing patents for land on behalf of the company.

77 TNA SP 46/443, ff. 83–87 'Money received from diverse mariners upon the River Thames, which they lent for the service of the realm of Ireland for one year at the rate of 8% per annum – according to the order of the commons house of parliament'.
78 www.virtualjamestown.org/indentures [accessed 1 November 2019].
79 Rif Winfield, *British Warships in the Age of Sail, 1603–1714: Design, Construction, Careers and Fate* (Barnsley, 2009), p. xii.
80 Adrian Tinniswood, *The Rainborowes* (London, 2013), p. 140.
81 Anon, *A perfect relation or summarie of all the declarations, messages, and answers, passages and proceedings between the kings Majesty and both Houses of Parliament* (London, 1642), p. 8. Mildmay married Anne Halliday in 1619, the daughter of William Halliday, governor of the East India Company. Mildmay was also a member of the New England Company and, in 1624, managed the Virginia Colony on behalf of the Privy Council when Maurice Thomson and his partners made their initial investment in a Virginia plantation.
82 BL, Add Ms 4771, f. 6; TNA SP 16/210, f. 257, *Petition of Principal Masters of the Navy*.
83 C.L. Falkiner, *Calendar of the Manuscripts of the Marquis of Ormond preserved at Kilkenny Castle* (London, 1903), p. 236; BL, Add Ms 4771, f. 11.
84 John Gilbert, *History of the Irish Confederation and the War in Ireland, Vol II 1641–43* (Dublin, 1882), p. 171n; BL, Add Ms 4771, f. 47. Gilbert records that the delegation arrived in Dublin on 9 October 1642, but this is not possible as all three men were, on this date, engaged in London on Committee of Irish Affairs business. The most likely date of departure is 28 October, when Goodwin withdrew £10,000 in plate from the Tower, ostensibly to be brought to the army in Munster.
85 Gilbert, *History of the Irish Confederation*, p. 171.
86 Robert Pentland Mahaffy (ed.), *Calendar of State Papers Relating to Ireland Preserved in the Public Record Office: Adventurers for Land, 1642–59* (London, 1903), p. xii.
87 Gilbert, *History of the Irish Confederation*, p. 175.
88 BL, Add Ms 4771, f. 178. With this arrangement, bills of exchange were issued by Maurice Thomson's brother-in-law to be redeemed by William Thomson's father-in-law.
89 For an analysis of the Protestation Oath see Julie Spraggon, *Puritan Iconoclasm in England 1640–1660* (PhD Thesis, University of London, 2000), pp. 40–47.
90 BL, Add Ms 4771, f. 91.
91 Gilbert, *History of the Irish Confederation*, p. 158.
92 Bodleian Library, Carte Ms, IV, p. 313: Thomas Preston to the Earl of Clanricarde.
93 Bodleian Library, Carte Ms, IV, p. 176: Warrant of the Lords Justices and Council.
94 Gilbert, *History of the Irish Confederation*, p. 176: '*Diary of Captain William Tucker*'. Tucker writes that he sought instructions from 'M.T.'.
95 Sir David Watkins, *A true copie of the remonstrance and petition, presented to the Honourable the House of Commons assembled in Parliament* (London, 1642); (Mr. Shute, *The true and original copy of the first petition which was delivered by Sir David Watkins* (London, 1642), pp. 7–8).
96 C.L. Falkiner, *Calendar of the Manuscripts of the Marquis of Ormond preserved at Kilkenny Castle*, Vol. II (London, 1903), p. 287.

97 Gilbert, *History of the Irish Confederation*, p. 196.
98 Vernon Snow, Wilson H. Coates and Anne Steele Young (eds), *The Private Journals of the Long Parliament, 3 January to 5 March 1642* (New Haven, CT, 1997), p. 357.
99 Sir Robert Reynolds and Robert Goodwyn, *The True State and Condition of the kingdom of Ireland, Sent to the House of Commons from Their Committee There, Whose Names are Signed Thereto* (London, 1642).
100 This was William Tucker's last involvement in Irish Affairs. He returned to London and was promoted to the rank of Colonel of the Trained Bands. He was killed at the first battle of Newbury on 20 September 1643 – shot in the head with a cannonball. See John Barratt, *The First Battle of Newbury* (Stroud, 2005), p. 108.
101 BL, Add Ms 4771, p. 195.
102 CCAM, I, p. 1; *Journal of the House of Lords*, Vol. 6, p. 269. The members of this committee included lords Brooke and Wharton, Walter Long, John Pym, William Spurstowe, William Strode and Samuel Vassall. The ever-present Sir Henry Vane II was also a member and the committee was completed by William Purefoy, a brother of Captain Thomas Purefoy, a neighbour of the Thomsons in Elizabeth City during the 1620s. The collectors at London's Guildhall were the Adventurers Richard Willett, Henry Coles, Thomas Stock and John Brett. Thomas Vincent, who was not an original Adventurer but became the largest owner of Adventures by 1653, also served as a treasurer on this committee.
103 CCAM, I, p. 7.
104 CCAM, I, pp. 1–2: Robert Sweet, Richard Willett, Hoogan Hovel, Christopher Nicholson, Thomas Leigh, Thomas Lenthall, Thomas Hutchins, Richard Smith, Robert Meade, William Farringdon, Mark Hildesley, John Dethwick, John Kendrick, Thomas Foote and Edward Vaughan.
105 A&O, I, pp. 38–40, 'November 1642: An Ordinance for the assessing of all such as have not contributed upon the Propositions of both Houses of Parliament, for the raising of Money, Plate, Horse, Horsemen, and Armes, for defence of the king, kingdom and Parliament, or have not contributed proportionably to their Estates'.
106 *Manuscripts of The House of Lords*, Vol. 11 (New Series), p. 357.
107 Alfred C. Wood, *A History of the Levant Company* (Oxford, 1935), p. 52.
108 For Cordell see Lynn Boothman and Sir Richard Hyde Parker (eds), *Savage Fortune: An Aristocratic Family in the Early Seventeenth Century* (Woodbridge, 2006), p. 79.
109 Thomas Stone invested £300 in the Adventure for Irish land and £200 in the Additional Sea Adventure. In 1638, Maurice Thomson imported 38,000 pounds of tobacco from St Kitts, compared with 32,000 for Thomas Stone. They retreated to the Americas and William Stone became governor of Maryland in 1648, remaining in that post until the restoration.
110 TNA SP 19/79 (unfol.), No. 26 'Persons returned to the Committee of Examinations in whose houses no distresses could be found to satisfy the sums on them assessed by the ordinance of 29 November 1642'.
111 CCAM, I, p. 365.

112 CCAM, p. vii.
113 CCAM, p. 423.
114 CCAM, pp. 17, 351.
115 TNA SP 19/79 (unfol.), No. 29, 'Subscriptions of Common Council'.
116 CCAM, I, p. 40.
117 CCAM, p. 264.
118 Ben Coates, *The Impact of the English Civil War on the Economy of London, 1652–1650* (unpublished PhD Thesis, University of Leicester, 1997), p. 111.
119 Thomas Andrews, William Allen, Gregory Clement, Thomas Chamberlain, Richard Hunt, Thomas Hutchins, John Langham, William Methold, John Oldfield, John Towse and William Vincent. Of this group, only William Methold was an established East India Company member. See TNA SP 19/79 (unfol.), No. 113 'List of Adventurers in the General Voyage'.
120 Brenner, *Merchants and Revolution*, p. 175.
121 BL, Add Ms 4782, ff. 322. Laurence Halstead, the Merchant Adventurer, absconded with £1,000 from the treasury and travelled to Holland, ostensibly to purchase supplies, but did not return.
122 Christine Jackson, 'Kendrick, John 1574–1624', ODNB.
123 Brenner, *Merchants and Revolution*, p. 482n.
124 BL, Add Ms 4669A, f. 1r.
125 BL, Add Ms 4771, ff. 125–126.
126 BL, Add Ms 4771, ff. 131–135.
127 NLI, MS 14305, p. 193.
128 BL, Add Ms 4782, f. 136.
129 NLI, Ms 14305, p. 197.
130 BL, Add Ms 4782, ff. 184, 190.
131 A&O, I, pp. 70–73, 'January 1643: An Ordinance for New Loans and Contributions as well from the United Provinces, as from England and Wales, for the speedy relief of the miserable and distressed estate of the Protestants in the kingdom of Ireland'; Ruth Spalding, 'Bulstrode Whitelocke', ODNB.
132 BL, Add Ms 4782, f. 200. For the list of agents see Raithby, *Statutes of the Realm*, Vol. 5, pp. 148–158.
133 BL, Add Ms, f. 162.
134 For examples see TNA SP/28/1B, ff. 397, 214, 477, 481, 599, 603 and 605.
135 Robert Ashton, 'Pindar, Sir Paul (1565/6–1650)', ODNB.
136 Thomas Lister, *Life and Administration of Edward, First earl of Clarendon*, 3 vols (London, 1837–88), Vol. ii, p. 237.
137 BL, Add Ms 4782, ff. 197–217.
138 BL, Add MS 4782, ff. 184, 232, 227. The army in Ireland was supplied by an assortment of commissaries who managed the supply of food, clothing and armaments on a regional basis. Some commissaries were based in England, for example Gualter Frost in Chester, and they purchased and consolidated supplies for shipment to Ireland. Some, for example John Davies in Carrickfergus, were based in Ireland and either received these shipments or arranged to purchase of their own from local, English or Scottish contractors. Military supply

contracts were highly lucrative and there was considerable competition between the commissaries, and their circles of suppliers, to acquire the largest share of contracts.

139 BL, Add Ms 4782, ff. 243-245. The agents were William Jennings, Henry Parker, Robert Bishop, Richard Fitzgarrat, Hugh Adlington, Richard Loake, Anthony Sexbie, John Salmon, Christopher Dobson, Thomas Beale, John Traighton, William Hale, Hugh Roberts, William Franklin, Thomas Price, James Meddon, Christopher Hill, Thomas Rooke, Gilbert Whitehead, Thomas Meade, Humfrey Norton, Owen Thomas and Jenkin Price.

140 BL, Add Ms 4782, ff. 260-307. George Thomson went from door to door in London persuading people to contribute, but church wardens in London – responsible for collections in their areas – refused to hand over their collections and lists of contributors. Other collections made locally by members of the Adventurers core group, for example the Assessments, were more successful.

141 BL, Add Ms 4782, f. 332.

142 BL, Add Ms 4782, f. 298.

143 BL, Add Ms 4782, ff. 339-340.

144 BL, Add Ms 4782, ff. 347-348.

145 Foote and Kendrick had become aldermen, and Bunce was sheriff of London – a position which allowed him to instruct the trained bands to enforce payment.

146 A&O, I, pp. 192-197, 'July 1643: An Ordinance for the encouragement of Adventurers, to make new Subscriptions for Towns, Cities, and Lands in Ireland'.

147 For example, John Goodwin, Sir Robert Reynolds and Sir John Clotworthy were increasingly obliged to settle warrants from the commissaries John Davies and George Wood while Thomas Hesilrige, the London merchant brother of Sir Arthur Hesilrige MP, extended an additional £400 in credit to Wood for supplies purchased in London (TNA SP/16/539, part 2, ff. 30-33).

148 Limerick and Waterford were for sale for £30,000 each, Galway £25,000 and Wexford £7,000.

149 *Mercurius Aulicus*, 15-21 January (London, 1643), p. 6.

150 CCAM, I, p. 17.

151 By the 1640s, excise accounted for one-third of Dutch state revenue. For the Dutch case see Oscar Gelderblom (ed.), *The Political Economy of the Dutch Republic* (Farnham, 2009).

152 A&O, I, pp. 202-214, 'July 1643: An Ordinance for the speedy Rising and Levying of Moneys, set by way of Charge or new Impost, on the several Commodities mentioned in the Schedule hereunto annexed; As well for the better securing of Trade, as for the maintenance of the Forces raised for the Defence of the king and Parliament, both by Sea and Land, as for and towards the Payment of the Debts of the Common-wealth, for which the Publique Faith is, or shall be given'. In a concession to the colonial merchants' re-export trade, excise was not levied on imports that were to be exported within three months.

153 Brenner, *Merchants and Revolution*, p. 379. Langham and Edmonds had been involved in both the official Levant Company trade and the unofficial Levant trade with William Pennoyer in the 1630s. The Culmes were undertakers in

County Cavan during the Ulster Plantation, and Arthur Culme rose to Lieutenant Colonel in the parliamentary army in Ireland in 1648. See also TNA SP 16/539/4 f.181.
154 The case of soap-making provides an example. Charles became a shareholder in a soap-making monopoly, and imposed a price maintenance order in 1636 to maintain his own dividend on soap production, of £4 per ton. The monopoly supplanted the London soap-makers, along with those in other centres of production, leading to the imprisonment of soap-makers and merchants who refused to pay a levy to the monopoly. One of the imprisoned soap-makers was Richard Rogers, who became an Adventurer for Irish land and financed the contributions of several other Adventurers. See Harold Matthews, *Proceedings, Minutes and Enrolments of the Company of Soapmakers 1562–1642* (Bristol, 1940), pp. 3–8; TNA, SP 63, vol. 299, f. 211.
155 J.R. Powell and E.K. Timings (eds), *Admiralty Documents relating to the Civil War* (London, 1963), p. 40. The Navy Commission had been appointed in November 1642, and comprised Sir Henry Vane Jr and Giles Green, with the Adventurers Alexander and Squire Bence, Richard Crandley, John Morris, John Rolle and Samuel Vassall. The other members of the Navy Commission – William Batten, Phineas Pett and John Tweedy – spent most of their time at sea, so the Navy was effectively run by the Adventurers. A total of £1,200 was subscribed for Sir John Holland to the Adventure for Irish land, and paid in on his behalf by agents George Almery, Edward Alston and Joseph Alston. The disguised subscription may have been on the instructions of Holland's wife, Mary Knyvett, a Catholic. Joseph Alston was married to Elizabeth Thomson, a daughter of Maurice.
156 CCAM, I, pp. 1–8.
157 D'Maris Coffman, 'Towards a New Jerusalem: The Committee for Regulating the Excise, 1649–1653', *English Historical Review*, 128 (December, 2013), pp. 1418–1450, p. 1426.
158 For a list of London merchants, ranked by wealth or 'ability to lend' see TNA SP 16/453, ff. 116–165. Of the leading Adventurers, only Maurice Thomson and Sir David Watkins were ranked as 'first class'.
159 John Kenneth Galbraith, *Money, Whence It Came, Where It Went* (London, 1995), pp. 45–62.
160 Bottigheimer, *English Money and Irish Land*, p. 51.
161 A&O, I, pp. 220–221, 'July 1643: Ordinance appointing Commissioners to receive Subscriptions in Holland for Ireland'. Hoast was a potential lender of 'the best sort' in 1641, one of the wealthiest men in London.
162 Bulstrode Whitelocke, *Memorials of the English affairs...* (London, 1732), p. 329. For an account of the collection of these supplies see Ole Peter Grell, 'Godly Charity or Political Aid? Irish Protestants and International Calvinism, 1641–1645', *Historical Journal*, 39 (1996), pp. 743–753.
163 Allan A. MacInnes and Arthur H. Williamson, *Shaping the Stewart World 1603–1714: The Atlantic Connection* (Leiden, 2006), pp. 245–255.
164 Grell, 'Godly Charity', p. 748.

165 Cornelius Ch. Gosling, *The Dutch in the Caribbean and the Wild Coast* (Gainsville, FL, 1972), pp. 262–265.
166 Abraham Corsellis, the father of Nicholas, was a member of a consortium of merchants who loaned money to Randal Mac Donnell, marquis of Antrim in the 1630s. This debt was partly redeemed with income from the sale of the king's goods in the 1650s (Jane Ohlmeyer, *Civil War and Restoration in the Three Stuart Kingdoms* (Cambridge, 2001), p. 252).
167 Keith L. Sprunger, *Dutch Puritanism, a History of the English and Scottish Churches of the Netherlands in the Sixteenth and Seventeenth Centuries* (Leiden, 1982), pp. 6, 67.
168 K.R. Andrews, 'The English Tobacco Trade in Trinidad and Guiana 1590–1677' in K.R. Andrews, N.P. Canny and P.E.H. Hair (eds), *The Westward Enterprise: English Activities in Ireland, the Atlantic and America, 1480–1650* (Liverpool, 1978), pp. 124–150.
169 Chad van Dixhoorn (ed.), *The Minutes and Papers of the Westminster Assembly 1643–52*, 5 vols (Oxford, 2012), Vol. iv, p. 15.
170 *House of Lords Journal*, Vol. vi, p. 244.
171 TNA SP 16/539/3, f. 184. A further consignment was despatched by Watson via the Kentish Downs and assigned to John Davies for delivery to Carrickfergus (BL, Add Ms 6749A, ff. 10–11v).
172 Grell, 'Godly Charity', p. 748; TNA SP84/157, f. 180.
173 *House of Lords Journal*, Vol. 9, p. 50. The Adventurers and merchants concerned are: Thomas Andrews, Maurice Thomson, William Pennoyer, Martin Noel, Richard Bateson, Jeremy Blackman, Nicholas Butler, Richard Chambers, James and Thomas Cooke, Michael Davison, Thomas Frere, Elias Roberts, George Pasfield, Thomas Walker, John Webster and John Vincent.
174 Evidence of the cultivation of sugar in Barbados around 1643 is through the first use of sugar as a currency on the island which began in 1644, and became the sole commodity used as a currency by 1649. The doubling of Barbadian land prices between 1638 and 1642 suggest that the investors could see the potential for the island. The population of Barbados surpassed that of Virginia throughout the 1640s (Russell R. Menard, *Sweet Negotiations, Sugar, Slavery and Plantation Agriculture in Early Barbados* (Charlottsville, VA, 2006), pp. 18–27).
175 Maurice Thomson was frequently in Holland, and, apparently, enjoyed very good relations with the Dutch authorities. He travelled to Rotterdam and purchased a frigate for Warwick's fleet in February 1643 (CJ, 24 Feb 1643). During his December visit, on behalf of the Adventurers, he had a royalist ship laden with ammunition, the *George*, stopped at Rotterdam, until parliament could procure an ordinance purporting the ship to be theirs (TNA SP 16/539/2, f. 109).
176 Van Dixhoorn, *Minutes and Papers*, Vol. iv, pp. 170–175. These included leading figures: Cornelius Burgess, Jeremiah Burroughs, Richard Byfield, Calybute Downing, Thomas Hodges, Stephen Marshall, John Maynard, Obadiah Sedgwick and Thomas Young.
177 Ole Peter Grell, *Brethren in Christ, a Calvinist Network in Reformation Europe* (Cambridge, 2011), p. 221; Grell, *Dutch Calvinists in Early Stuart London: The Dutch Church at Austin Friars 1603–42* (London, 1989), pp. 260–262.

178 Grell, *Dutch Calvinists*, pp. 260–262.
179 *Mercurius civicus, Londons intelligencer, or, Truth really imparted from thence to the whole kingdome to prevent*, Number 16 (London, 7–14 September 1643), p. 122; BL, Add Ms 4771, p. 192; Bodleian Library, Carte Ms 195, f. 173. Crispe attempted to have a debt for £2,195 for the hire of his ship, the *Good Hope*, for the Additional Sea Adventure written into the Act of Explanation in 1664.
180 *Mercurius civicus*, Number 18 (London, 21–28 September 1643), p. 143.
181 Parliamentary Archives HL/PO/JO/10/1/130, 29 July 1642.
182 Maurice Bond (ed.), *Manuscripts of the House of Lords*, Vol. 11 (New Series) (London, 1962), p. 358. John Oldfield was a kinsman of Maurice Thomson as Oldfield's son, William, had married Thomson's daughter, Mary, in 1641. The parliamentary committee was very similar in composition to the various committees for Ireland, John Ash, Denis Bond, Sir John Clotworthy, Sir Gilbert Gerard, John Goodwin, Sir Arthur Hesilrige, Sir John Holland, William Spurstowe and Sir Henry Vane Jr.
183 Brenner, *Merchants and Revolution*, p. 123; David Reid, 'Alexander, William first earl of Stirling (1577–1640)', ODNB.
184 David Stevenson, *Scottish Covenanters and the Irish Confederates* (Belfast, 1981), p. 144.
185 These figures for Scottish expenditure are from Laura A.M. Stewart, 'Fiscal Evolution and State Formation in Mid Seventeenth-Century Scotland', *Historical Research*, 74:225 (August, 2011), pp. 443–469.
186 *Mercurius civicus*, Number 19 (London, 28 September–6 October 1643), pp. 147–148.
187 LJ, 6, p. 202. The sub-committee was led by Sir David Watkins and Michael Herring.
188 BL, MS Add 4771, f. 3v.
189 A&O, I, pp. 331–333, 'November 1643: Ordinance for the Government of the Plantations in the West Indies'.
190 See David Scott, *Committee for Foreign Plantations*, unpublished essay, p. 3. Courtesy of the History of Parliament Trust.
191 Scott, *Committee for Foreign Plantations*, p. 1.
192 Sarah Barber, *The Disputatious Caribbean: The West Indies in the Seventeenth Century* (Basingstoke, 2014), pp. 70–74. The Leys and James Hay, earl of Carlisle, had originally been business partners in the early development of the Caribbean colonies, although Carlisle managed to assert a sole, if disputed, proprietorship. Ley established a short-lived colony on St Croix, Virgin Islands, in the 1640s.
193 Falkiner, *Ormonde*, II, p. 340.
194 BL, Add Ms 4769A, f.4.
195 BL, Add Ms 4769A, f. 2.
196 BL, Add Ms 4769A, f. 4v. Ayers, Clement, Featherstone, Floyd, Leader and the Thomsons were all members of significant Virginia planter families in the 1620s (Martha W. MacCartney, *Virginia Immigrants and Adventurers 1607–35: A Biographical Dictionary* (Baltimore, MD, 2007), *passim*). Floyd was formerly High Sheriff of Providence Island in the 1630s and Captain Governor of Association

Island (Tortuga) where he pioneered the English use of male and female African slaves for land-clearance projects. See also Kupperman, *Providence Island*, p. 167.
197 TNA SP 16/539/2, ff. 13–20.
198 NLI, Ms 14305, ff. 234–237.
199 NLI, Ms 14305, f. 238.
200 BL, Add Ms 4769A, ff. 6–10.
201 BL, Add Ms 4769A, f. 14; TNA SP 16/539/2, f. 9 The London Companies had contributed to the defence of Derry with loans in 1642–43. They were, perhaps, somewhat aggrieved that £620 had been paid to the Adventurer – and now Customs Commissioner – Francis Allein, for a jewel sent to the earl of Ormond for his 'faithful service against the rebels'.
202 TNA SP 28/1B, ff. 358, 360.
203 TNA SP 28/139, ff. 13–14.; 1C, f. 603; 1D, f. 128. In a single month, July 1642, Davies brought in six cargoes of supplies to Carrickfergus.
204 Anon, *The State of the Irish Affairs for the Honourable members of the Houses of Parliament as they lye represented before them, from the Committee of Adventurers in London for lands in Ireland sitting at Grocer's Hall for that service* (London, 1645), p. 3.
205 TNA SP 28/139, p. 4.
206 TNA SP 16/539/2, ff. 106–110.
207 TNA SP 21/21, f. 7.
208 Allan I. MacInnes, *The British Revolution, 1629–1660* (Basingstoke, 2005), p. 140.
209 For this committee I have also relied on an unpublished essay, generously made available by the History of Parliament Trust: David Scott, *The Committee of Both Kingdoms*.
210 BL, Add Ms 4769A, f.22.
211 BL, Add Ms 4769A, f.23.
212 Scott, *The Committee of Both Kingdoms*, p. 2.
213 Scott, *The Committee of Both Kingdoms*, p. 50.
214 Scott, *The Committee of Both Kingdoms*, p. 52.
215 BL, Add Ms 4769A, f.9.
216 TNA SP 16/491, f. 274.
217 BL, Add Ms 4769A, f.19.
218 'Paul Pindar', ODNB.
219 Brenner, *Merchants and Revolution*, p. 175.
220 TNA SP 16/539/2, f. 214. Pennoyer and Thomson used this outstanding payment warrant as security to finance their contributions towards the Sea Adventure.
221 BL, Add Ms 4769A, f.20. The other investigators were Sir John Clotworthy, John Browne, Thomas Erle and Maurice Thomson's friends – John Goodwin and Sir Robert Reynolds.
222 BL, Add Ms 4769A, f.22.
223 BL, Add Ms 4769A, ff.31–39.
224 BL, Add Ms 4769A, f.33.
225 BL, Add Ms 4769A, f.44.
226 BL, Add Ms 4769A, f.46.

227 BL, Add Ms 4769A, ff.38–40, 49.
228 BL, Add Ms 4769A, f.51.
229 NLI, Ms 14305, f. 244; LJ, VI, p. 265. For an account of the establishment of the Committee for Both Kingdoms see John Adamson, 'The Triumph of Oligarchy' in Chris R. Kyle and Jason Peacy (eds), *Parliament at Work: Parliamentary Committees, Political Power and Public Access in Early Modern England* (Woodbridge, 2002), pp. 101–128. The Committee for Both Kingdoms reserved the right to summon the committee of Adventurers to discuss Irish affairs. This measure was proposed by Sir Thomas Barrington on 23 May 1644 and supported in the House of Lords by the earls of Essex, Warwick, Northumberland and Manchester.

5

Commonwealth

TRADE

Although the Adventurers had withheld funds for Ireland during 1645 as the row with Clotworthy ran its course, they had quickly intervened when asked in March 1645 to provide emergency finance for Sir Thomas Fairfax's New Model Army in England.[1] Thomas Andrews, John Dethwick, John Warner and Sir John Wollaston were among those appointed treasurers at war by parliament and urgently tasked with borrowing £80,000 from their sources in London. The money was raised quickly from the pool of merchants dominated by the leadership of Adventurers in Irish land, all of whom contributed large sums.[2] The March 1645 loan financed the preparation of parliament's forces for the battle of Naseby, the final major battle of the first English Civil War. These forces were commanded by Fairfax, alongside Oliver Cromwell, late of the Committee for Irish Affairs, and Phillip Skippon who had been supported by the Adventurers since the reform of the London militia in 1642. The financing of Naseby marked a turning point for the Adventurers. From this point on, their interests were aggressively promoted by the leaders of the New Model Army, leaving them less exposed to the shifting political sands of Westminster. In return, the Adventurers provided the New Model's leading generals with the financial means to prosecute their military campaigns. Their control of finance also enabled the Adventurers to keep a tight grip on military supplies.[3] Clothing, for example, was provided by Estwick, Gethin and Milner while Thomas Player, Laurence Bromfield and John Browne supplied swords and gunpowder. The Adventurers coordinated their military supply efforts with intense lobbying for licences to dislodge their royalist merchant adversaries.

This new alignment of commercial interest with military finance is evident in a permission given on 12 April 1645 to a consortium of Yarmouth merchants to infringe on the Muscovy Company's monopoly on whale oil.[4] The principals behind this initiative were led by Maurice Thomson, the Bateman brothers, William Cockayne Jnr and Samuel Moyer. The new commercial licence was awarded by the Adventurers' friends on the Committee of the Navy.[5] A diplomatic mission sent to London in November 1645 by Tsar Alexei to negotiate the renewal of the Muscovy Company's concession was informed that any future trade would be conducted by London merchants, meaning the merchants who had been licensed independently.[6] The resulting competition weakened the Muscovy Company to the extent that in November 1645 it was taken over by Richard Snelling, a brother of George Snelling, one of Maurice Thomson's partners in the Virginia tobacco trade in the early 1640s.[7] This strategy of lobbying for an exchange of favours – state finance for commercial concessions – became the familiar template for the next decade, breaking up the old companies and creating a mutually dependent relationship between the state and the Adventurers.

A similar combination of commercial and diplomatic pressure was brought to bear on the Levant Company, control of which was also gradually transferred to Adventurers. In 1643, Charles I had moved the base of operations of the Levant, Muscovy and East India companies to Bristol. While this move kept much needed revenue from customs on imported goods out of the hands of the parliamentarians, the relocation from London's markets was bad for trade.[8] From 1642 London merchants sent their own vessels to the Mediterranean, ignoring the Levant Company monopoly. Starved of ships and finance, by 1645 the Levant Company had fallen under the control of Isaac Pennington and William Cockayne (respectively Governor and Deputy Governor), and the active members of the General Court of the company were drawn from the usual group of senior Adventurers.[9] Thereafter, the Levant and Muscovy companies were mainly financed by these individuals, who were reinvesting their profits from state finance.[10] To prevent English royalists from adopting the Adventurers' own tactics of sending unlicensed ships to the eastern Mediterranean, parliament appointed a new ambassador to Istanbul, Sir Thomas Bendish, to serve both their own political interests and those of the reconstructed Levant Company.[11] Another chartered company had fallen into the Adventurers' hands.

The Adventurers' assault on the EEIC also began in 1642 with their squeezing out of other merchants from shares in the General Voyage of that year. The company's monopoly was already fragile, as Charles had chartered a second company, Sir William Courteen's Association, to trade with the Indies. A relatively easy target, the Association was purchased from Lady Katherine, Sir William Courteen's widow, by Maurice Thomson late in 1643 following disastrous losses.[12] Bearing in mind that Courteen's nephew, Peter Boudin of the Netherlands, was already one of Thomson's business partners, this was a friendly takeover that licensed Thomson to do whatever he liked in the Indies.

In a further blow, the EEIC was obliged to charter two ships, the *Antelope* and the *Greyhound*, from Thomson and Gregory Clement for its own voyage as the company's own vessels had been pressed into the king's navy.[13]

The emboldened Adventurers did not confine themselves solely to trade and launched their first plantation scheme in the east. Using a strategy that bore a striking resemblance to the Providence Island project a decade earlier, Maurice Thomson and his partners sent out a group of 140 planters under the command of John Smart to colonise the island of Nosy Be, north of Madagascar in the Indian Ocean.[14] The project, under the Courteen 'brand', was directed by the Adventurer John Bond and financed by Thomson with Thomas Andrews, John Dethwick, Robert Hunt and William Pennoyer. By 1645 the EEIC was losing money on its fourth joint stock and the majority of its General Court was in no position to oppose the Nosy Be colony.[15] Although this initial effort at colonisation was too limited to be succesful, the door was now open for further trading voyages organised by the Adventurers.[16] The Nosy Be colony failed, but the overall expedition returned a tenfold profit to its investors as the return trip from the Indies yielded a rich cargo of spices and saltpetre.[17] The supply of saltpetre, used for making gunpowder, reinforced the interdependence between the army and the Adventurers while denying royalist merchants access to Indian saltpetre had further strategic benefits. Maurice Thomson's next move was the accumulation of shares in the East India Company proper, beginning with those originally bequeathed by Endymion Porter in May 1645. This assault was leveraged further with a shrewd move by the Adventurers to temporarily avoid supporting the war in Ireland. In order to obtain permission to set out its own voyage in 1645, the EEIC agreed to pay a fine to support parliament's army in Ireland.[18] A new General Court of the EEIC was elected in July 1645, and a new committee appointed, that included John Cordwell, parliament's gunpowder-maker, the Bateman brothers, Rowland Wilson and Thomas Andrews.[19] Rowland Wilson was a former partner of the Sea Adventurer, John Wood, in the Guinea Company in the 1630s. The West African trade had since drawn in both William Pennoyer and Maurice Thomson as the English trade in African slaves developed.[20] In the aftermath of Naseby, the Adventurers had effectively taken over the three big chartered trading companies.

The more prosaic and economically far more important cloth trade continued to dominate England's exports. Cloth exports were monopolised by the Fellowship of Merchant Adventurers of England who elected a new governor in April 1645, the Adventurer committee-man, John Kendrick.[21] Kendrick was a familiar in the Thomson circle through his membership of the Dutch church in Austin Friars.[22] He directed collections for Calvinist refugees from the Palatinate in the 1630s and with this experience was appointed collector in Middlesex for the Relief of Poor Protestants of Ireland in 1643.[23] He shared this responsibility with Sir Paul Pindar, the treasurer of the second

Adventure for Irish land, and became an integral member of the Adventurers' inner circle.[24]

Kendrick was quickly drawn into many of parliament's early fundraising efforts. In July 1643 he was treasurer with Samuel Warner for a further collection in London of plate, money and horses. In October 1645, to help finance the continuing war effort in Ireland, Kendrick agreed to help borrow £30,000. For this effort he went into partnership with Samuel Avery, James Bunce and Thomas Foote, and Kendrick volunteered to collect a portion of the money in Middlesex. Yet again, these treasurers agreed at the last minute to re-direct their cargo assembled for Ireland to a parliamentary army based near Plymouth and Kendrick became an integral member of a select group that raised money for Ireland but used the proceeds to support parliament's military efforts in England.[25] Kendrick's presence at Grocers' Hall meant that the Adventurers were in almost complete control of all of England's foreign trade as 1645 drew to a close. Their takeover of England's trade and finance had happened with astonishing speed.

STATE FINANCE

The redirected October 1645 loan was the last organised contribution provided by an Adventurer-led group for the military conquest of Ireland until the spring of 1648. In the interim, military funds for Ireland appeared only in dribs and drabs, secured on either the excise or from various committees dealing with the sequestration of royalist assets. Much of the business of the Committee for Irish Affairs during this period was handled by Sir John Clotworthy, John Goodwin, John Reynolds, Sir Robert Reynolds, Sir John Temple and, until his departure for Ireland, Lord Lisle, who had previously tried to sign up to William Tucker's extension of the Adventure in 1642.[26] None could be considered at this time a senior figure, either in parliament or the City of London. Only two contributions were forthcoming from the Adventurers' own treasury, a loan of £10,000 in June 1646, and an even smaller sum, £2,700, in January 1648.[27] From mid-1645 until the end of 1646, only about £60,000 was earmarked from state revenue overall to support parliament's efforts in Ireland, rising to £150,000 in 1647 as the military situation worsened. It was far short of what was needed.

This lack of enthusiasm on the part of the Adventurers reflected their growing suspicions that parliament was on course to conclude a peace treaty in Ireland that would deprive them of their land. News of various secret deals between English factions and the Irish Confederates had reached London. Edward Somerset, earl of Glamorgan, conducted one such negotiation in the wake of the battle of Naseby, promising freedom of worship for members of the Catholic church in exchange for 10,000 men to bolster royalist armies in England.[28] This agreement, swiftly disowned by Charles I, was published in

London in October 1645. Ormond's direct negotiation with the Confederates rested on a promise of a general pardon for all acts of rebellion since 1641, a concession that would deprive the Adventurers of most of their land. Parliament's principal concern was that peace in Ireland would release an Irish army to serve the king in England, and a delegation was hurried to Belfast to negotiate with Ormond in February 1646.[29] The Adventure was contingent on the total conquest of Ireland and an unconditional surrender, not on a negotiated peace that included any kind of pardon. The Adventurers' interests diverged from those of parliament. Although parliament's last-minute approach was rebuffed by Ormond, who signed a treaty with the Confederates in March 1646, the unity of purpose that had existed between the Adventurers and parliament was disrupted. Charles I's surrender to the Scots in April and the emerging prospect of a Scots–Irish alliance against the English parliament underlined, for the Adventurers, the naivety of any attempt to make a political settlement with the Irish.

During 1646, the Adventurers were content to maintain a factional war of attrition in Ireland. Financially stretched at the end of the first Civil War, London's merchant community was more preoccupied with paying off and disbanding the parliamentary army in England, and expanding their hard-won business interests, than with taking decisive action in Ireland. Sir David Watkins and John Oldfield were added to the committee at Goldsmiths' Hall in March 1646 to drum up some more money but, despite the presence of these prominent individuals, only one loan of £10,000 for Ireland was raised from central state funds in 1646, secured on English sequestered estates rather than on Irish land.[30] Nathaniel Wright, one of the merchants awarded a trading licence against the Muscovy Company, agreed to advance a £5,000 loan for Ireland on 15 August 1646.[31] This loan followed the normal pattern of finance in return for some business, and was not necessarily politically motivated. Even these business opportunities were becoming harder to find, and another loan of £10,000, advanced to parliament in November, had to be personally guaranteed by Watkins, William Hawkins and Oldfield as there was nothing to trade it against.[32] There was a change in policy in October 1646, when an ordinance was published to raise £200,000 for 'the present service of the state', intended both to resolve the constant under-supply of funds for Ireland and to invigorate the Munster campaign of Philip Sidney, Viscount Lisle.[33] This loan was secured on both the excise and the sale of bishops' land, but only the payment of interest was promised, with no definite date for repayment of the capital sum. In addition, lenders who already had sums outstanding on the vaguely worded 'public faith' could transfer those loans to the supposedly better double security of both the excise and bishops' land.[34] These forms of double security became more common as parliament's creditworthiness began to be questioned due to its inability to meet the pay arrears of its army.

As was the case with the transfer of the original Adventure for Irish land to parliament in 1642, the £200,000 loan was redirected. On this occasion, the emergency was to draw the frustrated parliamentary army away from London and avoid a revolt over pay.[35] London had not paid any assessments towards the upkeep of the parliamentary army since the beginning of 1646 and the City institutions had called for disbandment in December of that year. In March 1647, the New Model Army sent its list of grievances to parliament, but was rebuffed. The Adventurers' old patron, the earl of Warwick, returned to London to fulfil his appointment by the Derby House Committee in May 1647 to a commission to disband the army.[36] The earl of Ormond travelled from Ireland, enticed to leave Dublin in June 1647 with the promise of a £3,000 cash gift, provided to parliament by James Bunce.[37] With Ormond gone and Warwick back, the Adventurers hoped to reinvigorate their own vision for an Irish campaign, involving the confiscation of Irish land. On 13 July 1646, parliament had sent proposals for peace to the king at Newcastle. The Newcastle Propositions favoured the Adventurers by annulling the treaty in Ireland brokered by Ormond, but they significantly reduced the amount of potential forfeited land by exempting those who had only assisted the Irish rebellion, as opposed to those who had actively participated in it, from confiscation.[38] The first Ormond peace was proclaimed in Dublin on 30 July, making a negotiated end to the war in Ireland seem inevitable. The sudden death, however, on 10 September of the earl of Essex, the main architect of the peace initiative, put an end to what was, from the Adventurers' perspective, a catastrophic settlement.[39] Ormond's peace settlement was voided by the Irish Confederates at Kilkenny the following week.

These proposals were revived in July 1647 in the wake of riots in London, triggered by plague and nervousness due to the New Model Army's advance on London in search of its arrears of pay. Parliament's revised proposals for a settlement with the king, *Heads of Proposals*, were agreed with the army and contained a commitment to prosecute the war in Ireland.[40] The proposals also laid out several of parliament's grievances with the Adventurers.[41] One of these, unsurprisingly, was the widely unpopular excise. An offer was made to suspend it, an attempt to appease the ill-tempered London crowds. The proposals also promised to 'curb the large powers given to Committees', recognition that the financial committees, dominated by Adventurers and with wide-ranging power to seize property arbitrarily, had become far too powerful. Parliament's more pressing concern, however, was in dealing with the army, and £200,000 for Ireland collected in May 1647 gave parliament an opportunity to settle its debts with this large supply of cash. In the course of its march to London, the army became politicised around Fairfax, Cromwell and the Adventurers' friends at Westminster. By the time the army entered London on 6 August, an army council had been created, a new political opponent to the sitting Long Parliament, that demanded both a purge and a reform of its political master.

The £200,000 loan was secured on the sale of bishops' lands in England and marks a watershed in the financing of wars in Ireland. The conquest of Ireland was no longer financed, even notionally, with forfeited Irish land, but with sequestered English property. Any person who contributed to the new loan could transfer a similar amount from any outstanding loan for Irish service, beginning with the original loan taken out in December 1641, onto the security of income from bishops' land and the excise.[42] The treasurers for the £200,000 loan were Sir John Wollaston, James Bunce, Laurence Bromfield and Richard Glyde. Unusually for treasurers, these men were responsible for borrowing the money but not for paying it back. That duty fell to the treasurers for the sequestration of bishops' lands and for the excise, who were acting as guarantors.

It was a necessarily complicated structure designed to break up the cosy arrangements made at Grocers' Hall. At Common Council, where the loan was approved, there was a push against the Adventurer committee-men and their tightly woven network controlling trade and state finance. Isaac Pennington, John Foulke, John Warner, John Kendrick, Rowland Wilson and Stephen Estwick were removed from the militia committee and James Bunce, John Langham, Sir John Wollaston and William Gibbs appointed in their place. Stephen Estwick was so angry that he had to be forcibly ejected from the Common Council meeting that voted on the loan.[43] Despite this row, parliament's financial arrangements had become so dependent on the Adventurers that it was impossible, even by removing them from representative committees, to excise them completely. Wollaston, Bunce, Glyde and Bromfield were indeed treasurers both for the £200,000 loan and for the sale of bishops' lands, but so were the core Adventurers: Francis Ash, Samuel Avery, Stephen Estwick, John Foulke, Thomas Noel and Christopher Pack.[44] The convoluted way in which the sale of bishops' lands was structured meant that the treasurers took these lands into a form of trusteeship, whereby they and their heirs became the legal owners of the properties with an obligation to forward all rents and proceeds from sales to Goldsmiths' Hall. The trustees could keep a commission of 2% for their services. The sales were handled by a separate sub-committee, this one again dominated by Adventurers who reported to their friends, the trustees, to have each sale approved.[45] Although the system was optimised to allow cut-price sales of prime land to a favoured few, such sales were rare until 1648 as the trustees had no incentive to diminish their newly acquired estates and the power that went with them. After 1648, financial pressures became sufficiently intense to encourage the trustees to begin the process of liquidating the lands for cash. Until the estates were sold, however, the trustees were responsible for collecting the rent in whatever inventively opaque way they could design. The physical money from the proceeds of bishops' lands was not handled by the trustees or the agents, but by the receivers, the Adventurers William Gibbs, Francis Ash and Thomas Noel. John Foulke was appointed comptroller to keep the trustees in check. Foulke thereby became both treasurer and auditor of the trustees. These structures demonstrate how many avenues were available to the Adventurers to profit from state finance and how difficult it was to bypass them. Even if their influence on committees was diluted, or they did not dominate a particular group of treasurers, the combination of committee-men, lenders, treasurers, auditors and various agents that surrounded each finance committee ensured that the Adventurers were able to protect their own interests.

The combination of the Adventurers' mistrust of the dominant faction in parliament and the changes at Common Council rendered the £200,000 loan for Ireland a Presbyterian undertaking, notable for the reluctance of any of the leading Adventurers to contribute to it.[46] Maurice, George and Robert Thomson contributed a token £146 each and Isaac Pennington a derisory £136. Stephen Estwick and the Noels made no contribution at all. The Adventurers who made large contributions can be assigned to the Presbyterian faction, for example George Almery subscribed £614.[47] The largest single supporter was Lady Anne Moulson, widow of leading a Merchant Adventurer and assistant for the Londonderry Plantation, Sir Thomas Moulson, who contributed £3,041, one of the largest individual contributions by an English merchant to the military conquest of Ireland.[48] The final passage of the ordinance through parliament was difficult, as the lenders sought additional security from the Committee for Compounding at Goldsmiths' Hall, but this was refused by the treasurers, Michael Herring and Richard Waring. To add to these distractions, the negotiations for the loan in parliament were also interrupted by the comings and goings of Oliver Cromwell and other army officers seeking clarity about their arrears and the reappointment of the London militia.[49]

Ultimately, the £200,000 loan for Ireland was never repaid.[50] From June 1648 any unpaid balance from the loan could be used as a credit against the purchase of bishops' lands, the purchase price for which was to be determined by the commissioners. The £200,000 loan for Ireland was, therefore, ultimately exchangeable for lands in England.[51] These loans, and an additional loan for £150,000 raised for the army in May 1647, also shunned by the Adventurers, demonstrate attempts at state finance by the Presbyterian faction in parliament, using their own circle of sympathetic merchants. From the evidence of subscribers' and creditors' lists it is clear that each faction of parliament at this time had its own group of funders. In the case of the Independents in parliament it was, to a large degree, the original leadership of the Adventurers and in the case of the Presbyterians it was a more diverse group comprising some Merchant Adventurers and the few elite merchants who had doggedly remained in London. As had happened time and again, none of the money was sent to or spent on Ireland; this time it was used by parliament to pay off the New Model Army. The Adventurers, at little cost to themselves, had achieved two goals. First, they stymied the Irish campaign of a parliament they no longer fully trusted and, second, they stood by while Fairfax and the army council paid their soldiers' arrears with the money that had been collected.

Thus, the Committee of Adventurers at Grocers' Hall came to control much of England's trade and parliament's finances by 1647, while keeping tight control over London's political institutions. Thomas Andrews, Maurice Thomson and John Warner had spread themselves across a wide range of activities. Michael Herring, who had first entered the Adventurers' circle in the 1620s as a receiver of pirated cargoes, was treasurer of the vital Committee for Compounding at Goldsmiths' Hall.[52] Samuel Moyer was a senior officer in the London militia in addition to his roles as a commissioner for compounding, a navy commissioner and collector for assessments in London. Samuel Avery was elected an alderman of London in 1645 and was a trustee for the sale of the vast church estates. Sir David Watkins, the secretary of parliament's Committee for Irish Affairs, was also a commissioner for compounding. Richard Hill was a commissioner for the navy and for customs. Thomas Foote continued as a leader of London's Common Council and was elected an alderman in 1643, latterly becoming commissioner for the excise. John Kendrick also continued on the Common Council and served as a commissioner for the excise from 1653. John Dethwick was appointed parliament's treasurer at war in 1647 and John Kendrick became governor of the Fellowship of Merchant Adventurers. William Methold was deputy governor of the English East India Company from 1643 while James Bunce served as Sherriff of London. Samuel Langham, treasurer of the Levant Company, was elected governor in 1653. The Committee of Adventurers could also rely on George Thomason to provide detailed intelligence from throughout the Three Kingdoms from his enormous library of pamphlets.[53] A further small group of Adventurers, including William Pennoyer, George Thomson and Richard Waring, who were not members but were extremely close to the committee at Grocers' Hall, further concentrated this financial and political power.

THE COLONIES

By the middle of 1647, the Adventurers were busy abroad and glad that the army could be paid off using somebody else's money. The Dutch West India Company went bankrupt in 1646, brought down by extending too much credit to Portuguese merchants in the Caribbean. The company had established a lucrative and large-scale trade in African slaves, centred on Curaçao. Unlike English colonies, the Dutch colonies had never been peopled with servants from their home provinces, as there were never an excess population available.

Although there is some evidence that the Dutch purchased Irish servants for their colonies, they preferred to avoid Catholic labourers and relied heavily on Amerindian and, later, African slaves. In addition to the slave trade, the Dutch had absorbed sugar processing techniques from the Portuguese as colonies changed hands along the northern coast of South America and this expertise had found its way to Barbados by 1646.[54] Maurice Thomson was at the head of a consortium that had built a major sugar works on Barbados by the middle of 1646, and he applied to the House of Lords for permission to transport 100 oxen from Virginia to Barbados in October of that year to drive the new equipment.[55] An ordinance of January 1646 freed merchants from customs and other duties for three years on goods destined for the Americas to develop the colonies. This ordinance also lifted any restriction on the number of servants that could be transported to the colonies, but in an effort to regulate the trade stipulated that 'neither force be used to take up any such servants, nor any apprentices enticed to desert their Masters, nor any Children under age admitted without express consent of their Parents'.[56] The inclusion of this clause suggests that even if such practices were not widespread, they were at least common. Finally, as a precursor to the Navigation Ordinance of 1651, the January 1647 ordinance stipulated that all colonial produce must be transported from the colonies in English shipping, in an attempt to make inroads into Dutch dominance of the carrying trade.

In addition to the carrying trade, the Dutch also dominated the trade in African slaves and sold 23,000 slaves for almost seven million guilders through their market at Pernambuco (now Recife, Brazil) between 1636 and 1645.[57] It suited the Dutch slave traders, therefore, following their move to Curaçao, to assist in the development of labour intensive sugar plantations in the English Caribbean, owned by fellow Calvinists who should be more reliable trading partners than the Spanish and Portuguese. African slaves had already been brought in large numbers from Curaçao to St Kitts in 1639, as the island was intensively developed following Warwick's purchase of its patent.[58] The sugar boom continued into the late 1640s, led by the Adventurers and their associates in Zeeland who had been invited into the Adventure for Irish land in 1643. Close links between the promoters of Caribbean commerce in London, Middelburg and Amsterdam could not shield this business from the problems of distance. Legal contracts were difficult to enforce in the colonies and political allegiances, in the absence of a central bureaucracy and means of enforcement, were in the hands of the local governor or dominant political figure. Until the sugar boom, the fragility of the English diaspora was not a strategic worry, but once the boom had begun in earnest the increasing importance of the vulnerable colonies to the monetary supply of the English parliament would lead to a royalist revolt and two state-financed naval expeditions.

Immediately following the January 1647 ordinance for the loan of £50,000 to parliament, the heavily indebted earl of Carlisle sold a lease for the entire English Caribbean to Lord Willoughby of Parham for the sum of five shillings.[59] Under the terms of this arrangement, all of the rents due to the patentee from the planters in various islands were to go to Carlisle's creditors. Once these debts had been paid off, any future rents were to be divided between Willoughby and Carlisle. While not the largest of Carlisle's creditors, Maurice Thomson was the most prominent.[60] With the expertise the Adventurers had developed in exploiting royalist estates it was unlikely that Willoughby and Carlisle would see a penny for quite some time. Irrespective of who was making money from the processing and sale of sugar, the commodity boom had also set off a property boom on the Caribbean islands. Following the introduction of Dutch sugar processing technology to the island, the value of Barbados land doubled every year from 1643 until the mid-1650s, a process spurred on by new speculative tenants.[61] No longer trusted by their English neighbours, many of the established Irish planters on Barbados sold up in 1643 and the land market, though active, was far from vibrant until 1647, when £27,000 was spent on Barbados land.[62] Investment poured into Barbados as confidence grew in the potential profits to be made from sugar. The Caribbean land market also demonstrates that the core Adventurers, who in 1642 owned substantial colonial estates, had, by 1647, moved away from agriculture and left plantations to others. Although they maintained their hold on the profitable business of shipping, their core commercial interests had shifted west to east, from colonial investments to the enticing profits on offer in Africa, Asia and the Mediterranean, and the opportunities that came with their newly acquired companies. A new generation of Barbados planters emerged, led by the Noel brothers, cousins of Lord Willoughby of Parham, who scooped up considerable tracts of the best land in Barbados in 1647.[63] Some army officers, who had done well financially from military contracts during the Civil War, were also prominent during this surge of investment.[64] Some key planters sold out, notably Samuel Vassall and the Crispes, although one of Vassall's brothers remained on the island as a merchant.[65]

Retaining a commercial presence on the island was as important as being a landowner. Led by Maurice Thomson and Samuel Vassall, the richest Adventurers threw themselves directly into the African slave trade to profit from unfree labour for the sugar boom. There was also a strategic motive, as Sir Nicholas Crispe's Guinea Company continued to serve as a source of both profits and bullion for the royalist cause. With this combination of strategic and commercial imperative the Adventurers had no difficulty persuading parliament to cancel the Guinea company's franchise and license their own informal association. Maurice Thomson and Samuel Vassall concentrated on the slave markets of the Bight of Benin, while William Pennoyer, Robert Thomson and

Elias Roberts preferred the Portuguese markets of Principe and Sao Tomé.[66] A further consortium, again led by Vassall, traded with the slave markets of the Bight of Biafra.[67] The slave trade drew the Adventurers into an overdue confrontation with the Dutch West India Company, who had dominated deliveries of slaves directly to Barbados as the trade expanded exponentially in the mid-1640s.[68] More than the lucrative slave trade was at stake, as slaves were typically sold for sugar that could then be re-sold for even greater profits anywhere in Europe that could pay with the silver that was essential for military finance. Key changes, therefore, had taken place in 1647 that catapulted Barbados from colonial backwater to a key component in the Adventurers' trading system. The Adventurers' shift from plantation agriculture to the slave trade and the marketing of sugar exacerbated the need for a constant supply of cash. The money was required to fuel both their expanding commercial ambitions and to make available the state finance necessary to control political developments in London.

IRELAND

A rare general meeting of all Adventurers for Irish land was convened in London on 1 December 1647 and an appeal read out in London's churches for further subscriptions.[69] To drum up support, the London news sheets published a report of Lord Inchiquin's latest victory for parliament at the battle of Knocknanaus, County Cork, and a large crowd of Adventurers converged for the meeting.[70] The aim of this meeting was to determine which of the Adventurers had not paid their subscriptions in full in 1642 or had subscribed to but not paid in their money for the doubling ordinance of 1643. It was hoped that these arrears could be collected and that new Adventurers could also be attracted, with the money intended to support Lord Inchiquin's ongoing successes.[71] The meeting took on a new dimension, however, when the general meeting of Adventurers proceeded to make some changes to the committee that represented them.[72] The effect of this election was to widen membership of the committee to include representatives of the army and rising figures in parliamentary finance who had emerged since 1642. The old stalwarts Andrews, Thomson, Pennoyer, Watkins, Hawkins and their many associates remained, but they were now joined by the goldsmith, Sir Thomas Viner, and a banker, Thomas Vincent. The army paymaster, Sir John Wollaston, had a seat at the table alongside Phillip Skippon, now a Major General and member of Cromwell's army council. A second Major General, Richard Browne, was also elected. The entire commission for the navy also decamped to Grocers' Hall. Somewhat at odds with the Committee for Both Kingdoms, the reformed Adventurers' committee was given the additional role of a sub-committee of parliament with powers to act 'in such Irish matters & things' as parliament might direct and to make 'such propositions as they think fit ... to carry on the war there'. The Adventurers had regained the position they occupied in 1643, with wide-ranging powers to influence parliament's policy towards Ireland and to determine the outcomes. There was, however, scant enthusiasm for further subscriptions and the list of recalcitrant Adventurers requested by parliament had still not been provided by Thomas Andrews by March 1648.[73] Practically no money was raised in England for parliament's forces in Ireland and, exasperated, Lord Inchiquin, who had sent numerous unanswered requests to the Derby House Committee for money and supplies during the winter of 1647–48, officially declared his allegiance to Charles I on 3 April 1648, profoundly altering the military balance.[74]

This failure of the Adventurers was not due to a shortage of money. They were more interested in the lucrative business of supplying the military effort in Ireland than they were in financing local loyalists such as Lord Inchiquin. To overcome this particular obstacle, on 27 March 1648 the Derby House Committee negotiated the largest provisioning contract of the Civil War era, placing £83,000 worth of business with ten Adventurers from Grocers' Hall.[75] Supplies moved swiftly thereafter, with goods and cash sent simultaneously to Dublin, Kinsale, Carrickfergus and Carlingford and with the Adventurers to be repaid from the proceeds of a £20,000 per month assessment for Ireland, published in advance of the contract being awarded on 16 February 1648.[76] The treasurers for the assessment were Thomas Andrews and Maurice Thomson, who, having spent the money originally collected for Ireland in 1642 on parliament's army in England, could now look forward to the conquest of Ireland being paid for with English taxes.

These were lucrative arrangements, with profits to be made from the supply of goods and the financing arrangements. Until the tax was collected, the contractors were to supply money and provisions at their own cost but at an interest rate of 8%. The earl of Warwick and Oliver Cromwell steered the rest of the details through parliament from Derby House, resolving the issue of who should be commissary for Ireland, which had been a major source of confrontation between the Adventurers and other merchant factions since 1642.[77] On 7 April 1648 William Dobbins was appointed sole commissary for Ireland, ending Sir John Clotworthy and John Davies's operation in Carrickfergus.[78] The New Model Army sustained a political campaign against the MPs who had failed to support it in 1647 and Clotworthy, accused of embezzlement and colluding with the Confederates, exiled himself in Calais with other fugitive MPs and peers.[79] Even the reliable Dobbins became more figurehead than supplier, for on 12 June 1648, William Hawkins was appointed commissary-general of victuals for Ireland.[80] This ensured that Thomson's circle of merchants could take their pick of supply contracts during any mobilisation for Ireland. Plans to raise the subsidy and repay the contractors proceeded quickly with collection instructions issued to county commissioners repeatedly during May and June 1648, but the process was interrupted and then abandoned by the outbreak of the Second Civil War in England.[81] Although the treasurers would have to wait for their money, their consolation was that Irish affairs were again being influenced from Grocers' Hall.[82]

THE SECOND CIVIL WAR

The Adventurers had regained control of army supply contracts with relative ease, but navy contracts presented a more formidable challenge. In 1648, vice-admiral William Batten was replaced by the Sea Adventurer Thomas Rainsborough, an appointment that was seen as an attempt to bring the navy under the control of the New Model Army. On 27 May 1648, Rainsborough's ship revolted, put him ashore and called for parliament to treat with the king. On 17 June the Committee for Both Kingdoms appointed a special group, reporting to the earl of Warwick and charged with devising a strategy to secure the return of the ships that had revolted to the royalist cause.[83] This special group decided that three of the four merchants sent to Holland in 1643 to propose the Dutch adventure for Ireland, Maurice Thomson, Nicholas Corsellis and Derrick Hoast along with the navy victualler, captain John Limbery, would travel to Holland and negotiate with the mutineers.[84] None of the four was a naval officer or member of the admiralty committees, although Limbery, as victualler, could hold out some promises for food and arrears of pay. Maurice Thomson's role was to negotiate directly with the revolted ships and to secure their return. In the meantime, Prince Charles, the future Charles II, had taken command of the royalist fleet and announced that he was prepared to ransom recently captured merchant ships for £20,000, to be paid by London merchants.[85] Maurice Thomson now had two objectives. Prince Charles sent his ransom demand to the Common Council, assuming, correctly, that the council had more rapid access to cash than parliament, and could make decisions more quickly.[86] Charles had assumed a special title, 'King of the Seas', and the capture of parliamentary merchant shipping and selling the ships and cargo to the Dutch to raise money was his central strategy.[87] To help bridge the gap between the two sides, on 29 June the Common Council took the bold step of calling for a negotiated treaty between king and parliament, supported by a mass petition to parliament from 'well-affected seamen, merchants and masters of ships'.[88] The merchants' mission had no effect on the navy, yet set an important precedent. Although there is no evidence that Maurice Thomson dealt directly with Prince Charles at this stage, he was the leader of a mission that dealt directly with the prince's court. Key events of the Second English Civil War enhanced the reputation of both Maurice Thomson and the Adventurers' leadership as unwavering supporters of parliament. The earl of Warwick had returned as Lord Admiral, and became ever-present at Derby House. Phillip Skippon once again commanded the army in London and was despatched to Kent to quell the rebellion in the southeast.[89] One of the Adventure's original treasurers, John Warner, was elected as Lord Mayor of London.[90] In May 1648 Maurice Thomson was instructed by Warwick to take command of all the ferryboats on the Thames from London and through Kent and Essex, to prevent the opponents of parliament from approaching the city.[91] Thomson was now more reliable and effective than parliament's navy.

The Londoners got their ships back. On the surface, the Adventurers appeared utterly central to the Independent party in parliament, and were the key financiers and equippers of the New Model Army. Despite this, they could deal with the Stuart court when their interests were threatened, and divert money collected for the state to serve their own interests. The initial proceeds of the £20,000 per month subsidy for Ireland were taken by Maurice Thomson and brought to the Netherlands to pay off the mutineers.[92] Once again, events in England had intervened to prevent the coordinated despatch of supplies to Ireland. Instead the supplies were sent piecemeal to Dublin by Maurice Thomson, Thomas Andrews and Stephen Estwick. The capital was armed at the expense of both Munster and Ulster, breaking the Adventurers' tradition of always arming the Boyles first.[93] As the conquest of Ireland became a realistic proposition, military strategy began to replace personal loyalty as the basis for supplying the forces there. The Second English Civil War interrupted any serious escalation of parliament's war in Ireland, but military resources were built up steadily in Dublin during the winter of 1648–49. An initiative was expected imminently from a parliament increasingly dominated by the Adventurers' friends, or an army dominated by their clients, to build a financial war chest for an invasion of Ireland.[94] In June 1648, the Adventurers' Irish jackpot was swollen further when parliament included Dublin, Cork, Kinsale, Youghal and Drogheda in a new Adventure for Irish land to repay £50,000 loaned to parliament in January 1647 and using the sequestered estates of Francis Lord Cottington as additional security.[95] Although the London-based receivers, William Hawkins and Gabriel Beck, were drawn from the Adventurers' inner circle, and the loan was arranged by Sir David Watkins from the usual circle of Adventurers, Protestant Ireland was also allowed to participate for the first time.[96] The effect of this urban Adventure, however, had the opposite effect to raising money for Ireland. The money collected from investors based in Ireland was used to quickly repay the Adventurers, consequently drawing money out of Ireland.[97]

In the political fallout that followed the Second Civil War in England, parliament was purged of the MPs who had tried to negotiate with the king. The army's Council of Officers was determined that the king would be tried for his life for high treason, and had him moved to Windsor in December 1648. The king had suffered his final military defeat, the first step towards the Adventurers' Irish land settlement, but at no point had the Adventurers entertained or promoted the punishment of their monarch. On 16 January 1649, with the trial of the king about to get underway, Maurice Thomson and his closest associates were appointed to a committee of enquiry into financial wrongdoings in customs, the navy, the Navy Commission and Trinity House.[98] It became a useful way to be too busy to become embroiled in an act that the Adventurers had never openly called for, the trial and execution of the king. The Adventurers had called repeatedly for a negotiated end to the Civil War throughout the revolted ships episode, even though Prince Charles was holding their assets to ransom. Trinity House published a lengthy petition to parliament on 21 June 1648, calling for a negotiated personal treaty with the king.[99] The petition was passed by a vote of ninety for to twelve against, demonstrating that the mariners, the core constituency of the Adventurers' leadership, were overwhelmingly against the trial of the king. The new committee of enquiry gave the Adventurers a pretext to keep away from the trial. The earl of Warwick left London for its duration.[100]

The following day, 17 January 1649, in order to ensure the security of the City of London, a new militia committee was constituted, once again dominated by Adventurers for Irish land but with the notable absence of the Thomsons and Pennoyer.[101] Parliament had instructed that any citizens of London who had campaigned for a treaty with the king and opposed his trial should be barred from the City's elected bodies. Maurice Thomson had negotiated for the return of the ransomed ships only a few months before the trial. Perhaps a wider negotiated settlement would have been possible, but support for the king within the Adventurers' leadership had evaporated when the news reached London on 18 December 1648 of a treaty between the States General of the Dutch Republic and the Irish Confederates for 'mutual trade and commerce'.[102] This agreement posed a direct threat to the Adventurers' Atlantic interest as it combined the growing strength of the Confederate fleet with the implicit protection of their far more powerful Dutch allies. It allowed the Confederate fleet, which had grown rapidly and was likely to be reinforced by Prince Charles, license to act with impunity. The threat quickly became a reality when reports reached London by 21 December that the Confederate fleet had captured fourteen English merchantmen in a single engagement.[103] Taken from the perspective of transatlantic trade, the Irish Confederate fleet, operating from Wexford, could operate as a proxy for Dutch naval interests, amplifying their threat to the Adventurers' merchant fleet. The reality was that the provinces of Holland and Zeeland were profiting too much from their English trade to risk a full-scale military confrontation with parliament, but from the perspective of the Adventurers, the king had betrayed their Atlantic empire to the Dutch. At the very end though, Charles had made it clear that the conquest of Ireland was necessary to ensure the survival of the English Republic. On 30 January 1649, the king was dead.

NOTES

1 A&O, I, pp. 656–660, 'March 1645: An Ordinance for securing of the Eighty Thousand pounds advanced by and under the eight Treasurers hereafter named, and for a further provision for the Raising and Maintaining of the Forces under the command of Sir Thomas Fairfax'.
2 The particulars for this loan comprise TNA SP 28/350/5. The treasurers contributed £3,000 each and prominent individuals such as Francis Ashe, James Bunce, Stephen Estwick, John Kendrick, Thomas Noel, Richard Shute, Maurice Thomson and Sir David Watkins all contributed large sums. Less politically active Adventurers, the London Aldermen Francis Allein and George Witham, also advanced £3,000 each.
3 Ian Gentles, *The New Model Army in England, Ireland and Scotland, 1645–1653* (Oxford, 1992), p. 42.
4 TNA SP 46/96, f4. Petitioners also included Henry Spurstowe and Nathaniel Wright.
5 TNA SP 46/96, f4. The entire committee comprised John Rolle, Alexander and Squire Bence, Thomas Bell, Giles Greene, William Allenson and Thomas Soame.
6 Geraldine M. Phipps, 'The Russian Embassy to London 1645–46 and the Abrogation of the Muscovy Company Charter', *The Slavonic and East European Review*, 68:2 (April, 1990), pp. 257–276, p. 268.
7 Robert Brenner, *Merchants and Revolution* (Princeton, NJ, 1993), p. 139; Phipps, 'Russian Embassy', p. 262.
8 For detail see TNA/SP 115/159, 'Levant Company Account Books, 1642–1651'.
9 In this case, Richard Bateman, Thomas Hodges, Richard Middleton, Samuel Moyer and William Vincent.
10 TNA/SP 105/150, ff. 99, 104–105, 167. Samuel Spurstowe joined the General Court in 1647.
11 Brenner, *Merchants and Revolution*, pp. 372–378; SP 105/111, ff. 133, 135, 212. Bendish had been imprisoned for royalism in 1643 but released and found his way back into favour.
12 Edward Graves, *A brief narrative and deduction of the several remarkable cases of Sir William Courten, and Sir Paul Pyndar, Knights, and William Courten late of London esquire...* (London, 1666), p. 4.
13 W. Noel Sainsbury, *Calendar of the Court Minutes of the East India Company 1644–1649* (Oxford, 1912), pp. xii, 301. The ships were owned by Gregory Clement, Maurice Thomson and John Wood.
14 Marguerite Eyer Wilbur, *The East India Company and the British Empire in the Far East* (Oxford, 1945), p. 200. Nosy Be was known in seventeenth-century England as Assada.

15 Ben Coates, *The Impact of the English Civil War on the Economy of London, 1652–1650* (unpublished PhD Thesis, University of Leicester, 1997), pp. 182–186.
16 For a more complete account of the colonisation of Nosy Be, see Alison Games, *The Web of Empire: English Cosmopolitans in an Age of Expansion* (Oxford, 2008), pp. 181–218.
17 Graves, *Brief narrative*, p. 4.
18 Sainsbury, *East India Company 1644–1649*, p. 84. After Naseby, it was sensible for royalist merchants to sell what they could to the Adventurers for the best price they could get. Their alternative was the Committee for Compounding and sale 'by the candle' of their assets.
19 Sainsbury, *East India Company 1644–1649*, p. 91.
20 Brenner, *Merchants and Revolution*, p. 165.
21 George Burton Hotchkiss (ed.), *A Treatise of Commerce by John Wheeler* (Clark, NJ, 2004), p. 104.
22 Ole Peter Grell, *Dutch Calvinists in Early Stuart London: The Dutch Church at Austin Friars 1603–42* (London, 1989), p. 179. The Corsellis family were also members of this congregation.
23 Ole Peter Grell, *Brethren in Christ, a Calvinist Network in Reformation Europe* (Cambridge, 2011), p. 148.
24 TNA SP 16/497, ff. 81–84. Kendrick collected a respectable £110 and his efforts brought him into contact with the colonial merchants he may not have known otherwise. Although Sir Thomas Barrington donated £5, the Batemans were only able to donate sixpence.
25 TNA SP 16/503, f. 24.
26 For the general proceedings of the Committee for Irish Affairs during this period see BL, Add Ms 4769A and TNA SP21/27-8, Committee for Irish Affairs, 1647-8. For the perspective from Ireland see Micheál Ó Siochrú, *Confederate Ireland: 1642–1649* (Dublin, 1999), pp. 87–176.
27 TNA SP 28/202, ff. 331–336, Account of all such monies received by Nicholas Loftus, Treasurer of Wars for Ireland for the service of that kingdom.
28 For a survey of the political situation in Ireland, see John Cunningham, 'Politics, 1641–1660' in Jane Ohlmeyer (ed.), *The Cambridge History of Ireland*, II (Cambridge, 2018), pp. 72–95.
29 Bodleian Library, Carte Ms, Vol. 16, p. 220, The Parliament's Commissioners to Ormond.
30 CCAM, I, p. 40.
31 TNA SP 63/262, f. 85.
32 John Oldfield was the father of William Oldfield who married, in turn, Mary Thomson, the daughter of Maurice and following Mary's death at a young age, Anne Hawkins, the daughter of William. See: www.historyofparliamentonline.org/volume/1660-1690/member/oldfield-%28Oldfield%29-william-1623-64 [accessed 1 November 2019].
33 Patrick Little, 'The "Irish Independents" and Viscount Lisle's Lieutenancy of Ireland', *Historical Journal*, 44 (2001), pp. 941–961.
34 A&O, I, p. 884, 'October 1646: An Ordinance for securing of all those that shall advance the Two hundred thousand pounds for the service of the State'.

35 For a full treatment of the occupation of London by the army see Ian Gentles, 'The Stuggle for London in the Second Civil War', *Historical Journal*, 26 (1983), pp. 277–305.
36 TNA SP 28/27, f. 33, Derby House to the earl of Warwick, Lord Delawarr, Sir Gilbert Gerard, etc.
37 CCAM, I, p. 69; TNA SP 28/27, ff. 44–45v, 'To the Commissioners at Dublin'. Ormond had already arranged that £10,000 in bills of exchange owed to him could be converted into cash at Goldsmiths' Hall. He was allowed to transport 5,500 men to the continent and, as a final carrot, £2,800 in cash was ready to be collected by him in Holland on his arrival.
38 John Rushworth, *Historical Collections of Private Passages of State: Vol. 6, 1645–47* (London, 1722), p. 311.
39 John Morrill, 'Robert Devereux, 3rd earl of Essex (1591–1646)', ODNB.
40 For the negotiations around the *Heads of Proposals*, see John Adamson, 'The English Nobility and the Projected Settlement of 1647', *The Historical Journal*, 30:3 (September, 1987), pp. 567–602
41 S.R. Gardiner, *The Constitutional Documents of the Puritan Revolution, 1628–1660* (Oxford, 1906), pp. 316–326.
42 A&O, I, pp. 928–935, 'May 1647: An Ordinance for securing of all those that advance 200,000l. for the service of this kingdom and of the kingdom of Ireland'. The named loans which could be transferred were the original loan of £50,000 from 1641, the £40,000 raised for the Scots army in November 1642, the £40,000 raised in the provinces by Maurice Thomson in April 1643 and the £23,000 raised from the mariners of London in May 1643. None of this money had been repaid.
43 Gentles, 'The Struggle for London', p. 283; Keith Lindley and David Scott (eds), *The Journal of Thomas Juxon, 1644–1647* (Cambridge, 1999), p. 157.
44 A&O, I, pp. 887–904, 'November 1646: An Ordinance for the setling of the Lands of all the Bishops in the kingdom of England and Dominion of Wales, for the Service of the Commonwealth, with the Instructions and Names of all the Contractors and Trustees, for the speedy execution of the same'.
45 Francis Eagle and Edward Younge, *A Collection of the Reports of Cases, the Statures and Ecclesiastical Laws relating to Tithes*, Vol. iv (London, 1826), pp. 110–114. The agents were William Roberts, Thomas Viner, Richard Turner, James Russell, William Methold, Thomas Eyres, Robert Fenwick, Timothy Middleton and Edward Cressey.
46 The complete list of contributors to the £200,000 loan for Ireland comprises TNA SP 28/350/2A.
47 TNA SP 63/283, f. 329; TNA SP28/350/2A, f. 23. Holland was excluded in Pride's Purge.
48 CCC, I, p. 780. Lady Anne Moulson is remembered by her maiden name, Anne Ratcliffe, for her donation of £100 to Harvard College in 1643 and its women's college was named Ratcliffe College (1879) in her memory. She had also loaned £600 towards the 1644 loan of £20,000 for the Scottish army and her nephew was the army treasurer, Sir Gilbert Gerard.
49 Lindley and Scott, *Journal of Thomas Juxon*, pp. 156–158.

50 CJ, 8, 29 December 1660, pp. 238–240.
51 Parliamentary Archives, HO/PO/JO/10/1/264, f. 43.
52 TNA SP 14/215, f. 34: 8 November 1627, Nicholas to Richard Wyan to expedite the case of the Dolphin, a French prize.
53 See appendix for the official appointments of all Adventurers.
54 Peter Emmer, *The Dutch in the Atlantic Economy 1580–1880: Trade, Slavery and Emancipation* (Farnham, 1998), pp. 70–96.
55 LJ, IX, pp. 491–493.
56 A&O, I, pp. 912–913, 'January 1647: An Ordinance for encouragement of Adventurers to the several Plantations of Virginia, Bermudas, Barbados, and other places of America'.
57 C. Ch. Goslinga, *The Dutch in the Caribbean and on the Wild Coast* (Assen, 1985), p. 350.
58 Goslinga, *The Dutch in the Caribbean*, p. 352.
59 TCD MS 844, f. 1. Original deed of demise from the earl of Carlisle to the Lord Willoughby of Parham C1 22 in return for settling the debts mentioned to the earl of Carlisle.
60 TCD MS 844, f. 14.
61 Hilary MacDonald Beckles, *White Labour in Black Slave Plantation Society and Economy: A Case Study of Indentured Labour in Seventeenth Century Barbados* (PhD Thesis, University of Hull, 1980), p. 19.
62 BDA, RB3/1, f. 25 (Cornelius Clancy); f. 27 (John Dermott); f. 308 (James Dillon); f. 903 (John Dyer). See also Russell R. Menard, *Sweet Negotiations, Sugar, Slavery and Plantation Agriculture in Early Barbados* (Charlottsville, VA, 2006), p. 53.
63 BDA, RB3/2, ff. 152, 167, 201, 196, 468; RB3/3, f. 628.
64 John Jones and Thomas Herbert made modest investments, dwarfed by two figures closely connected with Ireland, John and Sir Robert Reynolds, who aggregated a total of eight tracts of land on Barbados. For Jones see BDA RB3/2, ff. 174, 200; for Herbert see RB3/3, f. 699 and for the Reynolds RB3/2, ff. 57, 257, 272–274, 300 and 301.
65 BDA RB3/2, ff. 83, 291.
66 www.slavevoyages.org [accessed 1 November 2019], voyage IDs 21877, 26258.
67 www.slavevoyages.org [accessed 1 November 2019], voyage IDs 21879, 26255, 21256. Vassall's partners were Peter Andrews, Jeremy Blackman and Benjamin Cranley.
68 www.slavevoyages.org [accessed 1 November 2019], voyage IDs 11855, 21962, 21979, 21985 and 21990 for examples. It was not uncommon for Dutch ships to have English crews, and vice versa.
69 TNA SP 28/27, f. 72: Notice from Derby House to the Lord Mayor of London.
70 Anon, *Perfect occurrences of every dayes journall in Parliament*, Number 48 (London, 26 November–3 December 1647), p. 333.
71 Anon, *Mercurius Pragmaticus …*, Number 12 (London, 30 November–7 December 1647), pp. 4–5.
72 TNA SP21/26, f. 121, Meeting of Adventurers for Lands in Ireland of Citizens of London & others, Grocers' Hall.

73 TNA SP 28/27, f. 91v; Karl S. Bottigheimer, *English Money and Irish Land* (Oxford, 1971), p. 111.
74 Micheál Ó Siochrú, *Confederate Ireland, 1642–1649: A Constitutional and Political Analysis* (Dublin, 2008), p. 172.
75 Maurice Thomson, Thomas Andrews, Stephen Estwick, Maurice Gethin, Tempest Milner, Thomas Player, Thomas Smith, Richard Shute and Thomas Vincent. For more details on these consignments see Brenner, *Merchants and Revolution*, pp. 528–529; NAI MFS 42/4: John Lodge, *Records of the Rolls*, Vol. 6 Charles I to 1648, pp. 397–398. Thomas Vincent was the secretary at Goldsmiths' Hall and purchased the Monaghan estate of Lord Edward Blaney in September 1648 for £4,800, the first Adventurer from the merchant community to become a significant Irish landowner.
76 TNA SP 16/539, part 4, f. 159, Schedule of goods to be supplied.
77 TNA SP 16/539, part 4, f. 161, 'Instructions to Adam Loftus'. Warwick had stepped down from his command as Lord Admiral under the self-denying ordinance in April 1645.
78 TNA SP 16/539, part 4, f. 164, Order from the Committee for Irish Affairs. The order was signed by Gualter Frost, formerly the commissary for Munster but installed as secretary of the committee at Derby House by 1648. Clotworthy had been absent from parliament since August 1647, having fled to Holland when expelled with ten other members for opposing the army's occupation of London.
79 Robert Ashton, *Counter Revolution: The Second Civil War and its Origins, 1646–8* (London, 1994), pp. 171–174.
80 TNA SP 28/27, f. 124v: Derby House to William Hawkins.
81 TNA SP 28/27, f. 123v: From Derby House to London, Worcester, Devon, Derby, Cambridge, Warwick, Wiltshire, Berkshire, Dorset and Surrey. For an overview of the Second Civil War see Robert Ashton, *Counter Revolution: The Second Civil War and its Origins, 1646–8* (London, 1994).
82 TNA SP 28/27, f. 128: 'To the Lord Mayor and the rest of the Commissioners for the Irish Assessment'.
83 TNA SP 28/9 f. 129 (7), Rushworth, *Historical Collections*, Vol. 7, p. 757; CJ, III, p. 363; LJ, X, pp. 135–154. William Williams's house was used by Lord Fairfax as his base during the army's occupation of London in 1647 and was the reception house for ambassadors from the States General. The accounts of the Dutch contribution to the parliamentary cause in Ireland were presented to the House of Lords on 22 March 1647. This fundraising afforded Maurice Thomson and his partners an open passport to travel between England and the Netherlands, 1643–46, essential for maintaining their business with the colonies.
84 TNA SP 28/9 f. 181, 21 June 1647, report to both houses; Peter Wilson Coldham, *English Adventurers and Emigrants, 1609–1660* (Baltimore, MD, 1984), p. 99. The Limberys were involved in the St Kitts tobacco trade in 1640.
85 Sean Kelsey, 'King of the Sea: The Prince of Wales and the Stuart Monarchy, 1648–1649', *History*, 92:308 (October, 2007), pp. 428–448, p. 441.
86 Anon, *The Parliament-kite, or, The tell-tale bird. Communicating intelligence from all parts of the kingdome, touching all affaires, humours, conditions and designes,*

especially from Westminster, Scotland, Wales, Ireland, and the head-quarters, Number 12 (London, 3–10 August 1648), pp. 1–2.
87 *The Parliament-kite, or, The tell-tale bird*, p. 70.
88 LJ, X, pp. 352–353, Petitions from Trinity House and 'Masters of ships, maariners and others' for a negotiated treaty with the king.
89 Bottigheimer, *English Money and Irish Land*, pp. 106–108. Skippon was selected as field marshal for Ireland in 1647 but had not taken up the post. The supply contract negotiated with Maurice Thomson and his partners in 1648 was intended to supply Skippon's Irish campaign.
90 Ashton, *Counter-Revolution*, p. 190.
91 Brenner, *Merchants and Revolution*, p. 529.
92 TNA SP 21/28 (unfoliated), 5 September 1648, instructions to Thomson and Andrews.
93 TNA SP 21/28, 19 October 1648, instructions to Thomson and Andrews.
94 See David Underdown, *Pride's Purge, Politics in the Puritan Revolution* (Oxford, 1971), esp. pp. 'The Purge', 143–173 and Appendix A: 'Members of Parliament, December 1648-January 1649', pp. 361–398.
95 A&O, I, pp. 1147–1166, 'June 1648: An Ordinance for the explaining and enlarging of an Ordinance made the 13th January 1647 for raising 50,000l for the speedy relief of Ireland, and reducing the Rebels there'.
96 The Irish investors were Sir William Parsons, Sir Gerald Lowther, Sir Robert Meredith, Sir Robert king, Sir James Barry, Sir Paul Davies, Fenton Parsons. The London based underwriters were Thomas Andrews, William Hawkins, Richard Hill, William Pennoyer, Thomas Smith and Thomas Vincent. The rents raised from the Cottington estate were lower than expected, as parts of the estate had been given as gifts to Hugh Peter and Oliver Cromwell.
97 For these investors see National Archives of Ireland, QRO/4/3/32, Survey of Waterford City; QRO/4/3/33, Survey of Limerick City, QRO/4/3/3, Survey of Galway City; Oxford University, Rawlinson MS B 508, Survey of Dublin City.
98 A&O, I, pp. 1257–1260, 'January 1649: An Act touching the Regulating of the Officers of the Navy and Customs'; Kenneth. R. Andrews, *Ships, Money and Politics: Seafaring and Naval Enterprise in the Reign of Charles I* (Cambridge, 1991), pp. 200–202. The commissioners were Jonathan Andrews, Thomas Andrews, William Berkeley, Stephen Estwick, Richard Hill, Richard Hutchinson, John Langley, Samuel Moyer, Samuel and William Pennoyer, James Russell, Maurice and Robert Thomson and William Willoughby.
99 BL, Thomason Tracts 1251, f. 1.
100 CJ, VI, pp. 149–150; John Barratt, *Cromwell's War at Sea* (Barnsley, 2009), pp. 7–9; Andrews, *Ships, Money and Politics*, p. 201. The committee of inquiry also afforded the opportunity for these Adventurers to purge both the Commissioners of the Navy and Trinity House.
101 A&O, I, pp. 1261–1262, 'January 1649: An Act of the Commons Assembled in Parliament, For the setling of the Militia (of the City) of London, and Liberties thereof'. The militia committee was dominated by Adventurers and merchants closely associated with the supply of the English army in Ireland: Francis Allein,

Thomas Andrews, Gregory Clement, John Dethwick, Stephen Estwick, Tempest Milner, Samuel Moyer and Thomas Noel.
102 John Adamson, 'The Frighted Junto: Perceptions of Ireland, and the Last Attempts at Settlement with Charles I' in Jason Peacey (ed.), *The Regicides and the Execution of Charles I* (Basingstoke, 2001), pp. 36–70, p. 44.
103 Adamson, 'Frighted Junto', p. 58.

6

Republic

The regicide was a step too far for most of the Adventurers. Thomas Andrews was a commissioner at the king's trial and although present when the sentence was passed, he would not sign the king's death warrant. Out of the fifty-nine regicides and additional nineteen commissioners who were present at the trial but refused to sign, only nineteen were Adventurers for Irish land.[1] Of these, eleven Adventurers signed and eight refused to do so. Of the eleven who signed, none was from the Adventurers' leadership, while the majority of those who declined to sign were among the original leading subscribers in 1642. Approaching the peak of their influence, and central to events during the first and second English Civil Wars, they kept powerful company; their most influential patron in the army, Lord Fairfax, also refused to sign the king's death warrant and the earl of Warwick withdrew from politics once again.

The execution of the king presented the Adventurers with considerable challenges. Their transatlantic traffic was seriously threatened by the arrival of Prince Rupert, a nephew of Charles I, in command a fleet of royalist ships at Kinsale, County Cork at the end of January 1649. This continued the threat posed by the naval protection offered to the Confederates by the Dutch Republic. Charles II was proclaimed king by the Covenanter parliament in Scotland. When word of the regicide reached Virginia in March 1649 Governor George Berkeley also immediately recognised Charles II as monarch and invited him to travel to the relative safety of the colony and rule his dominions from there.[2] As the Caribbean colonies were now devoted almost entirely to sugar production, Virginia had become the only source of English tobacco. Royalist Virginia made its crop available to Dutch shipping for general sale in Europe, diverting profits to the royalist cause, depriving London of customs and denying the Adventurers the profitable carrying trade. With evidence that he was about to gain an income from the colonies, Charles II signalled his intention in May to borrow £20,000 in the Netherlands, travel with it to Ireland and raise an army.[3] Parliament responded by announcing that Oliver Cromwell would be given the command of an English army for a pre-emptive invasion of Ireland.[4] Despite distractions in the wider Atlantic world, the Adventurers were first committed to concentrating their considerable resources on the re-conquest of Ireland, securing the southern Irish ports.

The perennial difficulties faced by parliament in its attempts to supply its forces had taught it that the conquest of Ireland could not be attempted without adequate supplies of currency to pay for wages, weapons, gunpowder and food. On 14 April 1649, parliament advised the Council of State that a large consignment of gold bullion had been made available to the state from a ship recently arrived from West Africa belonging to the Guinea Company.[5] The Guinea Company was now run by Maurice Thomson, John Wood and Rowland Wilson, while its vessels were hired from Samuel Vassall.[6] Thomson and his partners made a gift of £10,000 in gold to the Council of State in return for free trading privileges in the Gambia, reinforcing their involvement in the slave trade. The implosion of the Dutch West India Company provided an entry route for the Adventurers both to service the English Caribbean sugar plantations and to gain access to the main slave markets in Brazil and Spanish America. The main source of income for the Dutch had been the supply of African slaves to Spanish and Portuguese colonies in South America, a trade that Thomson, Wilson and separately the Noels were eager to move into. The African gold trade was also of considerable importance and this, with the profits in American silver from the sugar and slave trades, enabled the completion of the Adventurers' Atlantic trade loop. It was this highly complex and integrated supply chain that provided Cromwell with the cash and munitions he needed for the invasion of Ireland.[7]

The EEIC was by then also controlled by the Adventurers, even if they only owned the ships and cargo of general voyages, and not the actual company shares.[8] The shares had little value if the ship-owners could charge what they liked and owned the cargoes in any case. EEIC ships exported bullion to Asia and exchanged it for several valuable commodities, including saltpetre, essential for the manufacture of gunpowder. Gunpowder was the key commodity that Cromwell needed to secure in bulk before any invasion could commence. On 17 August the entire incoming cargo of saltpetre belonging to the Second General Voyage of the East India Company, freighted in Maurice Thomson's vessel, the *Ruth*, and commanded by William Thomson, was placed at the disposal of the Commonwealth.[9] Cromwell was appointed Lord Lieutenant of Ireland on 22 June and in this capacity the Council of State wrote to him on 24 July advising him that seven EEIC ships had arrived home, containing a sufficient supply of saltpetre for at least another year.[10] To secure the supply, William Pennoyer was promised the enormous sum of £150,000 from the expected proceeds of the Irish excise.[11] Although the saltpetre comprised, by volume, only 3% of the incoming East India cargo, the profit margin obtained by Pennoyer for his consortium was a magnificent 300%.[12] With this potential profit the Adventurers now had two reasons to expedite the conquest of Ireland: their lands and the proceeds of the Irish excise. The Indian saltpetre was a critical component in Cromwell's arsenal, as it allowed him to use his muskets and siege artillery with abandon throughout the campaign. The saltpetre transaction underlined the strategic importance of the EEIC to the military supply chain, and parliament was easily convinced that the Company would be more secure if it were put into the hands of the Adventurers rather than left with the group of former royalist merchants who made up the majority of the shareholders.

The formal merger of the EEIC and the Maurice Thomson-controlled Courteen Association occurred in January 1650 and the new company was given a renewed monopoly by parliament over East Asian trade.[13] Although many royalist merchants had returned to London following the execution of Charles I, and the existing East India Company officers, William Cockayne, William Methold and John Massingberd retained their senior posts of president, deputy-president and treasurer respectively, the company was controlled by the Adventurers who were wealthy enough to underwrite the general voyages: Thomas Andrews, Samuel Moyer, Thomas Smith and Maurice Thomson.[14] Thomson arranged for the EEIC to purchase supplies of hardwood from the Guinea Company, which he also effectively controlled, for the construction of a new fleet.[15] The introduction of the Adventurers' shipping expertise had a galvanising effect on the company and it grew from one-third of the size of the Dutch East India Company in 1650 to one-half of its size by 1660.[16] The company was organised into departments that oversaw shipping, the management of the Asian factories and the sale of the imported merchandise. Thomas Andrews, Samuel Moyer and Andrew Riccard were responsible for managing the distribution of saltpetre.[17] A consequence of the rise of the East India Company under the Adventurers' leadership was that its success required an increased supply of silver, necessary for the purchase of Asian cargoes. The main elements of the leading Adventurers' global trade were therefore in place by the start of the 1650s. African slaves were traded for Spanish silver and Barbados sugar, which in turn were traded for more European silver that purchased Indian cloth which was then exchanged for more slaves. Before long, more elements would be added to this trading system, but the global flow of goods, capital and profit became firmly established and was controlled by very few hands.[18] When they took their seats around the EEIC boardroom table with Cockayne, Massingberd and Riccard, the Adventurers knew they had climbed to the top.

The Adventurers now appeared on almost every state committee and their associates had infiltrated both state finance and military and naval supply at every level. This control is evident by examining, for example, the supply of that key commodity, gunpowder. After the saltpetre was acquired from William Pennoyer, responsibility for converting it to gunpowder for the army was vested with the Committee for Powder Match and Bullet, comprised of the Adventurers Samuel Vassall, Sir Robert Pye, John Rolle, Sir Walter Erle, Alexander Bence and Thomas Pury.[19] Bence, a key business partner of the Noels, was primarily in the wine trade and maintained an office in Seville that doubled as a quasi-embassy and source of intelligence. The remaining member of the committee was Giles Greene, an old Dorchester Company member and MP with decades of experience in Atlantic commerce, beginning with an enterprise to smuggle beaver pelts from New England in the 1620s.[20] Since then, he had risen to be chair of the Adventurer-dominated Navy Committee during the 1640s, and also of the Excise Committee until that role passed to George Thomson.[21] The secretary of the committee was Joseph Hutchinson, a brother of the Adventurer Richard Hutchinson. The saltpetre was sent to three gunpowder manufacturers, Robert Cordwell, John Beresford and Daniel Judd, who briskly despatched 1,000 barrels of powder to the Irish expedition.[22]

Despite Cromwell's impressive military credentials, Ormond later described the Adventurers' war chest as the more formidable adversary.[23] The scale of the Adventurers' financial resources became apparent when the Council of State committed £535,000 to Cromwell's conquest of Ireland, in addition to money secured on Irish revenues and spoils plundered in Ireland during the course of the campaign.[24] The entire apparatus of state finance was committed to the success of the campaign and key figures from the Adventure for Irish land were at the centre of this financing effort. The principal sources of finance were the loan for £50,000 arranged by Sir David Watkins in 1648, secured against specific sequestered English estates; the £20,000 per month subsidy administered by Thomas Andrews and Maurice Thomson to be collected across England; proceeds from the sale of Dean and Chapter lands managed by Stephen Estwick, William Hobson and Thomas Noel; money loaned against the security of additional sequestered estates arranged by Richard Waring and Michael Herring; and money raised against a further £150,000 loan charged against the English excise under the chairmanship of George Thomson.[25]

These financial arrangements were not all created specifically for Cromwell's campaign but were pre-existing measures that had either not been implemented or were previously unsuccessful. The £20,000 per month subsidy for Ireland was created by a parliamentary ordinance on 16 February 1647 but the treasurers had not been appointed until 3 April 1648.[26] The collection of this money did not begin until August 1649, but the initial response was promising, with £2,500 coming in from Norfolk alone by the end of September and similar amounts from Essex, Kent and Hertfordshire.[27] Overall, the assessments came in consistently until March 1650 and a respectable £108,500 was raised from a target of £120,000, with £87,000 of that paid directly to Cromwell's campaign.[28] Of the remainder, £5,000 was paid to Sir Edward Hill for the maintenance of his forces in Ulster, £445 to Thomas Andrews and Maurice Thomson for their handling fees, and £150 to Maurice Thomson, Edward Willoughby and William Pennoyer for transporting supplies. Finally, the bills of the four agents for the Dutch Adventure of 1643 were paid out of this collection.[29] One notable debt charged on the assessment was not paid. Sir John Clotworthy had his accounts approved by parliament on 6 September 1648 and £2,000 was charged against the assessment for Ireland.[30] This left Clotworthy in the uncomfortable position of having to ask Thomas Andrews and Maurice Thomson for the money. Their exact response has not survived, but Clotworthy was back in parliament two days later looking for a specific ordinance to compel Andrews and Thomson to pay him. The result of this petition was an order postponing Clotworthy's payment and instructing that the assessment could be used for Cromwell's Irish campaign alone.[31]

The raising and disposal of the £20,000 subsidy demonstrates the level of control Cromwell asserted over his sources of finance, as this was the first major subsidy for Ireland used almost entirely for an Irish campaign. The subsidy was financed in advance by Maurice Thomson, Thomas Andrews and Stephen Estwick and their interest charge of £4,859 was approved by Sir John Wollaston in December 1649. Taking the fees and interest together the contactors took a comfortable 5%. More significantly, Cromwell travelled with an ample war chest for an extended campaign. Unusually, and perhaps to ensure the money, for once, could not be diverted, the subsidy was managed not from one of the London's livery halls or a room at Westminster, but from the home of Thomas Andrews. The contractors also made use of an extensive network of London merchants who accepted bills of exchange from the regional collectors and then paid the relevant subsidy in cash to Andrews and Thomson, obviating the time and risk of transporting cash from the provinces into London.[32] Large amounts of cash were delivered directly to Ireland, by, for example, the arrival of the *Guinea Frigate* at Cork in January 1650 with thirty barrels of freshly minted Commonwealth coin.[33]

However practical this arrangement may have been, it left the treasurers open to criticism that their methods led to unnecessary costs for the state and to profiteering. Writing in 1653, Thomas Fauntleroy accused the treasurers of the excise of long-term pilferage by advancing loans with interest but leaving the repayment of those loans until as late as possible, thereby maximising their fees.[34] If the £20,000 subsidy had been collected efficiently, an interest bill of almost £5,000 could have been avoided. Michael Braddick has identified a similar scheme among excise commissioners in Norwich in 1663 where the collector loaned the excise money to a third party, presumably with interest, and the transaction was only discovered when the borrower was unable to repay the money in time for the commissioner to make his return.[35] A £50,000 loan arranged by Sir David Watkins and secured on a portfolio of sequestered estates provides further evidence of these practices.[36] The money was advanced to David Watkins by William Hawkins, who was to be repaid from the proceeds of these sequestrations. Hawkins was paid £3,075 in interest for this loan, presumably raised in turn from his brother-in-law, Maurice Thomson.[37] The accounts reveal that the collectors would typically retain up to half of the rent for their 'charges' and that rents were routinely allowed to fall into arrears.[38] The management of the loans reveals a large cohort of merchants and managers all profiteering from the administration of sequestered estates. At the same time, it should be stated that the while the Adventurers were in charge of its finance committees the English Commonwealth never defaulted, despite the financial strains of the Wars of the Three Kingdoms. The same cannot be said of France, which defaulted on its sovereign debt three times during the same period, or Spain, which defaulted once. This was a stunning achievement that enabled parliament to turn a blind eye to corruption, if indeed anybody in power cared at all as long as the financial machinery of state continued to run smoothly.

In fact, the treasurers of the Dean and Chapter lands were so awash with cash that on 3 October 1649 parliament appointed a small committee of merchants, all Adventurers, to organise the repayment of the 1642 donation of plate, money and horses out of the money at Weavers Hall, or to swap it for double the value in church land.[39] This repayment reflected a new confidence among the treasurers that they would have little difficulty raising the full amount required to support both Cromwell's campaign in Ireland and the continued disbandment of forces in England. The treasurers for the Sale of Forfeited Lands and Estates at Goldsmiths' Hall expected receipts of £213,000 and promised both to begin transferring money to the Committee of the Navy and to take over the loans made by the treasurers at Weavers Hall to finance Cromwell's army.[40] A second body responsible for selling this property, the Committee for the Sale of Forfeited Lands and Estates, was comprised of Francis Allein, Thomas Andrews, John Dethwick and Sir John Wollaston.[41] The arrangement ensured that the most desirable properties, at the best prices, were offered to their friends. A series of ordinances was passed by parliament from 21 July 1651 to 18 November 1652 allocating the repayment of £1,000,500 from various debts to the proceeds from these sales. As treasurer for the army, Sir John Wollaston received £150,000 of this money and, as navy treasurer, Richard Hutchinson received a further £262,000.[42] John Massingberd accepted £20,000 on behalf of the East India Company for saltpetre.[43] The exchequer received £39,000 for general expenditure and there were many other small payments. Significantly, out of the £619,976 collected, £56,427 was paid out to 'surveyors, clerks and messengers' of the committee.⁴⁴ The Adventurers were practising patronage on a grand scale.

For Cromwell's Irish campaign, the Adventurers took over complete control of military supplies. William Dobbins was retained in London as a purchasing agent and William Hawkins appointed commissary for the armies in Ireland. Hawkins travelled to Ireland with the invasion force. The former commissary, Gualter Frost, was promoted to the position of Secretary to the Council of State to ensure that the Adventurers remained informed of the Council's deliberations during Hawkins's absence.⁴⁵ As commissary, Hawkins could conduct his own survey of the country and assess which areas remained relatively prosperous. The Adventurers expected to begin receiving their land shortly after a swift campaign of conquest. Maurice Thomson, Thomas Andrews and Stephen Estwick assumed the roles of primary contractors for the Irish campaign and purchased £41,000 worth of food, clothes and small weapons in London in August 1649.⁴⁶ The contractors also acted as financiers and lent £20,000 in cash, part of the £100,000 brought by Cromwell to pay his soldiers.⁴⁷ Maurice Thomson also arranged freight, billing for £1,240 for freight charges on goods to be shipped from England to Ireland.⁴⁸ All of these consignments arrived on time. Thomson's old shipping circle transported Cromwell's men to Ireland, in return for £2,500 charged on Dean and Chapter lands, and awarded to Robert Thomson, William Willoughby, Thomas Smith and John Holland.⁴⁹ The invasion fleet was commanded by George Ayscue, who would next be sent to Barbados, in 1651, to execute a similar mission.

These continuing services to the state had brought forth a stream of profitable state agencies. In April 1649, Adventurers including Maurice and Robert Thomson, Thomas Smith, John Holland, John Dethwick and John Upton were appointed Commissioners for the Sale of Prize goods.⁵⁰ The Adventurers' circle, newly bolstered with sugar money, widened and asserted ever more control over parliamentary military finance. A large proportion of the County Commissioners for Compounding, for example, was drawn from the friends and family members of the leading Adventurers, recruited in the months following the execution of Charles I. On 5 January 1649 Francis Allein and Samuel Moyer were appointed to farm all of the compositions by delinquents in the City of London, highlighting the increasing cash pile at the Adventurers' disposal.⁵¹ Farming, the purchase of the right to collect a particular tax, could be far more profitable that commission-based administration. The compositions became another windfall as the royalist cause in England deflated with the death of the king, leading many to make compounding deals with the commissioners. Once the minimum threshold of money agreed with parliament had been received, the farmers could keep the rest. By 1650 the county commissioners in charge of collecting the excise included William Watkins, another brother of Sir David, William Thomson, brother of Maurice, Thomas

Shute, son of Richard, John Peck, brother of Francis and Thomas Bateman, brother of John, to name but a few.[52]

The Adventurers had efficiently financed Cromwell's Irish campaign, and their bonanza in land was moving ever closer. First, though, the Adventurers' leadership grabbed the greatest prize in state finance, the excise. On 20 September 1650, following the death of the original treasurer for the Adventure and excise commissioner, John Towse, the old commission was dissolved and a new one formed, led by Maurice Thomson and Thomas Foote.[53] Under the original arrangement of 1643, the commissioners were paid 2% of all excise collected for their services. At that time, the Adventurers had argued that farming was inefficient and that the commissioners should only get paid a small percentage of the money actually collected. Not only did the excise commissioners of 1650 resurrect farming, they also raised their commission to 3%. Under this new arrangement, Maurice Thomson and his partners could bank huge profits at parliament's expense, with commission, interest and the surplus of any money collected over parliament's estimate of what they hoped to collect. In addition, the September ordinance allowed the commissioners to sub-farm any branch of the excise, by locality or commodity, to their friends, holding out the prospect of a tidy profit for the sub-commissioners while guaranteeing a healthy additional commission of 3% to Thomson, Foote and their partners, as the sub-farmers were required to advance the full year's agreed excise for their farms. The excise commissioners, without having to finance this office directly, could expect to earn £12,000 per year from this enterprise.[54]

Some of this windfall was spent on crown, church and royalist estates, together with fee-farm rents, a financial instrument whereby the investor purchased the future rent of an estate for a fixed upfront payment in the hope of making a profit over the term of the farm. The widespread use of farming at so many levels of the economy demonstrates the large increase in capital available to the Adventurers. Some of their money was earned from trade, but much was also extracted from defeated royalists, or cheated from parliament. Some Adventurers decided to purchase trophies with their money. In 1649 Thomas Andrews invested the enormous sum of £10,759 in a sequestered church estate in Kent and a portfolio of fee-farms. Thomas Boone, a Devon merchant who had originally invested £600 in the Irish Adventure and had more recently joined with Andrews, Pennoyer and Maurice Thomson in their 1647 East India voyage, invested £7,274 in fee-farms alone.[55] Richard Clutterbuck and Stephen Estwick both purchased church estates in Kent for £4,892 and £3,012 respectively. William Heveningham bought a church estate for £4,161 in Cumberland while Richard Hunt, another partner in the 1647 East India adventure, sank £4,576 into a church estate in Norfolk for a new family home. John Kendrick chose London, and bought a £3,300 estate, while Sir Robert Parkhurst assembled a portfolio of £7,280 worth of property in the capital. Maurice Thomson kept out of the market for English plundered land, although his brother Robert and son John both invested heavily.[56] William Pennoyer had just a single small investment of £170.[57] Thomson and Pennoyer's disinterest in plundered English estates mirrored their distaste for the regicide. Overall, the Adventurers' original leadership, the 1642 cohort, kept the late king's, and most other royalist property, at arm's length.

Financially sophisticated merchants, Maurice Thomson and Sir David Watkins in particular, profited by means of financial instruments developed around the sequestered land sales, but avoided purchasing the estates directly. Ordinances for the sale of sequestered estates were normally accompanied by a call for loans against future proceeds from these sales. For example, the ordinance to sell Dean and Chapter lands of 27 June 1649 was accompanied by a call for a loan of £300,000 at 8% interest to be repaid out of future sales, and £350,000 was ordered to be borrowed against the future proceeds of sales of crown and church lands on 25 June.[58] It was a better arrangement than farming from parliament's perspective, as once the loans were repaid the state could retain any excess. By the 1650s Sir David Watkins was also acting as a private banker to the earl of Warwick.[59] Warwick's ships, and those provided by a chartering group created by the investors in the Additional Sea Adventure, were contracted by navy commissioners George Thomson and Sir Henry Vane II for state service. Such transactions required sophisticated financing, as these contracts could run for a considerable length of time.[60] Increasingly, the primary source for this this finance was the burgeoning slave economy of the West Indies, or, more accurately, the sugar and hard bullion that were the derivatives of this trade.

The African slave population of Barbados had increased from a few hundred people in 1640 to 12,800 in 1650, while the European population on the island rose more slowly, from 14,000 to 23,000 over the same period of time.[61] Between 1650 and 1660 the European population actually fell to 19,000, while the African population increased to 27,100. The European population of St Kitts remained stable at 12,000, but that of Nevis increased from 3,000 to 12,000 between 1640 and 1650, reflecting the Cromwellian transport of Irish and Scottish prisoners of war. Consequently the African population of the smaller Leeward Islands grew more slowly than that of their southern neighbour, from 2,500 in 1650 to 6,400 in 1660.[62] This extreme concentration of people in Barbados reflected how successful and labour-intensive the early sugar industry had become since it was pioneered, in part, by Thomas Andrews, Martin Noel and Maurice Thomson in the 1640s. Just as he had secured a near monopoly on the two-way trade of British servants for Virginia tobacco in the 1630s, Thomson and his partners in this arena, Pennoyer, Samuel Vassall, the Noels and the Barbados planter, James Drax, built up a dominant position in the carrying trade for African slaves and Caribbean sugar.[63] These profits fuelled their efforts in state finance, giving the English commonwealth its fiscal stability.

Large numbers of royalist merchants resumed their normal trade in London after the execution of Charles I, prompting new alliances and creating a powerful new dynamic within the city. In addition to their capital, the former royalists had contacts and skills the Adventurers badly needed, particularly in the eastern arenas of the Levant and East India companies. The Adventurers applied relentless pressure on the Council of State to further secure their burgeoning empires, preferring to lobby this body than sparsely attended Westminster. Samuel Vassall, working with Maurice Thomson and John Wood, sought the annulment of the old, Sir Nicholas Crispe-controlled Guinea Company's charter to trade in West Africa, claiming that the existing company had never made any significant investment in Africa, but had made a gift to Charles I of £10,000 instead.[64] Vassall also proposed a new settlement at what is now Port Elizabeth in South Africa.[65] A further Assada Company fleet was despatched to India in 1650, led by the *Assada Merchant* under the command of Captain Richard Swanly, the former Sea Adventurer.[66] Leadership of the Levant Company passed into the hands of William Pennoyer and Martin Noel, with the last of the old royalist shareholders excised from the company's ranks.[67] All of this activity was happening in the east as the Adventurers picked off what was left of the old chartered trading companies. In the west, some retained their old agricultural plantations, obtained in the 1620s and 1630s, but the big money was in the carrying trade, state finance, and military and naval contracting, all of which was could be discussed in private at the committee room in Grocers' Hall. Although the English parliament was compliant with these new arrangements, opposition was brewing in the assemblies of the western colonies.

THE COLONIAL REVOLT

In 1649, while the Adventurers concentrated on Cromwell's Irish campaign, Charles II made a huge grant of land in Virginia, the Northern Neck, to a group of wealthy courtiers as a reward, or advance payment, for their support during his exile.[68] The five million acre grant was equivalent in size to the existing Virginia colony and popular with royalist sympathisers from Virginia, Maryland and New England. The new colony was intended as a tobacco plantation, so that the king's rent would be paid in a commodity that could be sold for ready cash anywhere in Europe. In the aftermath of the execution of Charles I, there was an outpouring of sympathy for the royalist cause in the American colonies. The notional owner of Barbados, Lord Willoughby of Parham, had opposed the formation of the New Model Army, defected to the royalist cause shortly after he acquired Carlisle's patent, and served with then Prince Charles during the 'revolted ships' episode. Later, when the Second Civil War ended in parliament's favour, he went to Barbados, ousted the island's parliamentarian assembly and assumed the governorship under a commission from Charles II, with little local opposition. Royalists who had 'lately slid abroad from the hand of justice' were invited to settle in Barbados, if they could pay a fine of 100 pounds of tobacco for each acre of land they wished to develop.[69] To make space for these new settlers, Willoughby's government summarily evicted the staunchest supporters of parliament from their plantations, mirroring the treatment of royalists in England. In April 1650, the Barbados Council declared that it was extending the umbrella of its government over the 'lesser islands', including the smaller sugar producing colonies in the Antilles.[70] During the summer of 1650, Barbados began to construct fortifications to protect it against parliamentary attack and on 17 October the colony recognised Charles II's 'right to the dominion of this Island and the rights of the Right Honourable earl of Carlisle'.[71]

These measures presented the Adventurers with the greatest challenge they had faced in the colonies so far. The royalist colonies would avoid using English shipping, owned to a substantial degree by Adventurers, and use Dutch shipping based at New Amsterdam to export their produce. By offering their allegiance to Charles II, the colonies were in effect transferring the colonial carrying trade to the Dutch, and the customs and profits to the Dutch Republic. The reinstatement of the Carlisle patent provided some legal cover for the new Barbados planters to occupy the plantations currently held by parliamentarian Adventurers and army officers, acquired at enormous expense during the mid-1640s.[72] Barbados was a key source of revenue for the Adventurers, providing the cash that enabled them to finance Cromwell's Irish campaign, as well as their expansions in the East. The loss of Barbados could cause their entire commercial edifice to collapse. The sugar plantation owners in London, led by William Pennoyer, launched a vigorous petitioning campaign and offered ships to mount a campaign against the islands.[73] Pennoyer's petition also made reference to the number of recently arrived 'incenderies' on Barbados. Perhaps the transportation by Cromwell of the survivors of the sack of Drogheda to the colony in 1649 had not been such a good idea, as the incoming royalist planters found loyal labourers who were also experienced soldiers. By 3 April 1650, most of the Adventurers' estates in Barbados had been sequestered by Willoughby's royalist government.[74]

These two developments, the Northern Neck grant in Virginia and the seizing of Barbados by Willoughby, forced the Council of State to intervene directly in the colonies and Benjamin Worseley was employed to prepare a list of all grants of land issued for the American mainland up to the execution of Charles I.[75] Worseley's long association with the Adventurers had begun in October 1642 when, acting as an agent for Richard Fitzgerald on behalf of the Lords Justices of Ireland, he successfully lobbied for scarce supplies of medicine to be sent to Dublin by the Adventurers' committee.[76] Worseley was awarded a license by an unpublished ordinance of parliament in 1646 to manufacture saltpetre in England, in an effort to reduce the cost of importing it from France.[77] This enterprise became unnecessary following Thomson and Pennoyer's successful mission to India in 1647, but it kept Worseley and the Adventurers moving in the same circles.[78] A committee comprising William Allen, Maurice Thomson, William Pennoyer and Worseley was established on 28 December 1650 to recommend a course of action that would secure Virginia and Maryland for parliament. This committee morphed into the Council of Trade in 1651, with the additions of navy commissioner and former governor of Massachusetts, Sir Henry Vane II, as president and Worseley as secretary.[79] The Council of Trade also included veterans from the London Trained Bands and plate money collections of 1642, John Foulke and Richard Waring. A conspicuous addition to this core group was William Methold, a former contractor with Thomas Andrews and Maurice Thomson for the sale of prize ships in 1644 who subsequently served both as an auditor for the accounts of the whole kingdom and a contractor for the sale of bishops' lands.[80] An EEIC officer of long standing and member of the Committee of Adventurers at Grocers' Hall since its inception, Methold underscored both the dominance of the Adventurers on the Council of Trade and its global scope.[81]

The task of the first meetings of the Council of Trade in 1650 was to formulate a new external trade policy for the Commonwealth, a task made more urgent as parliament was forced to ban all trade with Virginia and the Caribbean in the wake of the royalist uprising. The Common Council, the main representative body for London's merchants, preferred a policy of making London a free port to compete more effectively with Amsterdam.[82] Their idea was to open up London to vessels of all nations, and to make goods for re-export free of the usual import duties and customs. This proposal was quickly blocked by Pennoyer, who inserted himself onto the committee of the Common Council to influence its decisions in line with the Council of Trade's thinking. Pennoyer appears to have performed most of the lobbying work in London to pave the way for the Navigation Act, while Thomson concentrated on the formulation of policy. The centrepiece of the Navigation Act that emerged from the Council of Trade in 1651 was a ban on all non-English shipping from interacting with the colonies, in line with the needs of the Council's members who sought to dominate the carrying trade in colonial produce. This idea had been around for a while. In August 1633, Captain William Tucker had petitioned the king for such an arrangement and singled out the Dutch for particular criticism.[83] The Navigation Act of 1651 was more about logistics than about the management of colonial production, which was left to the local assemblies. The Navigation Act, published by parliament in October 1651, enshrined in legislation for the first time that 'no goods shall be imported from Asia, Africa or America, but in English ships', rendering the royalists' arrangements in the colonies illegal and declaring an open season on Dutch merchant shipping.[84] In addition to these export restrictions, all colonial produce destined for Ireland and Scotland also had to be carried in English shipping. The only concession was to John Dethwick and the Fellowship of Merchant Adventurers, who were to be allowed to continue importing goods carried across Europe by land into English ports in small foreign vessels. The Navigation Act, the foundation of English imperial policy for the next century, was a complete victory for the Adventurers.

In October 1651, however, the Navigation Act was merely aspirational; it would have to be imposed on the colonies. The act was intended to starve the colonies into submission, a strategy alluded to in a statement from the Bermuda Assembly, signed by Henry Tucker in January 1652, promising the island's future allegiance to parliament.[85] The re-conquest of the colonies was entrusted to parliament's navy and its navy commissioners.[86] The navy despatched two fleets: the main fleet under the command of George Ayscue and Edward Thomson targeted Barbados and the second fleet, under Robert Bemiss and Edward Courtis, sailed to Virginia.[87] Both task forces reached their destinations in December 1651 and the attacks were coordinated with two further squadrons already in place in other theatres. The third squadron was the main parliamentary navy under General Robert Blake. Blake's task was to contain Prince Rupert's resurgent royalist fleet off the coasts of West Africa and to prevent the prince from interfering with the Caribbean mission. The fourth squadron, privately owned but synchronised with the state-led naval actions, was a slaving expedition sent by the Adventurers to the Gambia.

While the preparations to subjugate the colonies were under way, Maurice Thomson had shifted his attention to West Africa. In September 1651 Maurice Thomson and John Wood, who had formerly supported the Additional Sea Adventure, despatched the *Friendship* to the Gambia to purchase fifteen slaves and bring them to London.[88] It was an unusual and expensive mission, but the slaves were to impress potential investors for a wider project. Thomson and Wood had been awarded the Guinea Company patent by the Council of State the previous April, but appear to have had trouble raising support for a substantial slaving venture until the Navigation Act was passed. By developing this partnership with Wood so soon after his teaming up with Methold in the East India Company, Thomson exhibited his unique gift for forming optimal alliances with partners in trading ventures. John Wood's deep knowledge of African trade mirrored that of Methold in the India theatre, and both complemented perfectly Thomson's logistical prowess. Politically and commercially, his was an astonishing feat of coordination as the Gambia venture was intended to populate the sugar plantations on Barbados with African slaves once the royalist estates on the island were seized by Ayscue's men.

Once it became clear that the state would foot the bill for subjugating the colonies, Thomson and Wood had little difficulty in attracting more investors to their slaving enterprise. The *Friendship* was replaced by a larger vessel, the *Supply*, and a frigate owned by Samuel Vassall and Robert Llewellin, the *John*, to purchase a full cargo of slaves and bring them to Barbados.[89] The new partners intended a regular supply run between the Gambia and Barbados, to resurrect a fortified settlement built by the Guinea Company in the river Gambia, St James Island (now Kunta Kinteh), and they contracted to deliver a further 200 slaves to Barbados by 1652.[90] The Gambia fleet was, in effect, a fourth parliamentary squadron, privately funded but an essential component of an integrated transatlantic mission.[91] Despite these careful plans, however, the fourth fleet unexpectedly ran into royalist opposition at the old company fort. In 1639, Duke James Kettler of Courland, a godson of James I of England, negotiated the rights to settle the island of Tobago in the Caribbean. After several false starts, in 1651 the duke purchased the rights to the abandoned fort from local rulers in the Gambia and built a new structure alongside it.[92] While not hostile, the Courlanders were certainly not friendly towards the small parliamentary merchant fleet when it arrived. Furthermore, the entire region was theoretically under the control of the Portuguese, also sympathetic to the cause of Charles II. With intelligence from these sources, the royalist fleet commanded by Prince Rupert intercepted the three English ships at the mouth of the Gambia River, capturing one and swiftly ending the slaving expedition. Overall, however, this was the only setback. Willoughby quickly surrendered to Ayscue's first fleet in Barbados and was deported from the island together with his followers.[93] The entire cost of the mission was met by the capture of the island's sugar stock, amounting to 158,000 pounds of sugar.[94]

Although denied his slaves in the Gambia, the arrival of the second parliamentary fleet in Virginia provided Maurice Thomson with an ideal outcome. Bemiss's fleet was supervised by three commissioners appointed by the Council of State. These commissioners were William Claiborne, Maurice Thomson's former partner in the Kent Island project, Thomas Stegge, Thomson's former Virginia factor, and Richard Bennett, with whom the Thomsons had a long association.[95] Virginia surrendered without a fight and on 12 March 1652, Bennett was appointed governor of the colony and Claiborne became secretary of state. The Virginia colonists were forced from the status of a royal colony into a government of 'a company of Merchants'.[96] In this case, articles of peace agreed between Bennett and the colonists were designed to continue business as usual and avoided the bout of retribution that had occurred in Barbados.[97] The Book of Common Prayer was tolerated, any Dutch ships that had completed their business were allowed to depart and any committed royalists who disliked the new arrangements were granted leave to travel to England with one year to dispose of their estates.[98]

By 1652, Virginia and Barbados were very different colonies. Virginia was far less dependent on unfree labour, with 6,000 servants and 2,000 African slaves in a total population of 40,000.[99] Mortality had reduced considerably, and deaths among newly arrived immigrants were rare. Given its stability, revenge forfeitures in Virginia were unnecessary and bad for business. It helped that Claiborne had a great many friends in senior positions in England, including Maurice Thomson on the Council of Trade and the navy commissioner, George Thomson. The naval expeditions to the Caribbean and Virginia, more than the Navigation Act itself or Cromwell's Western Design of 1655, marked a turning point in English colonial policy. Until 1651, the colonial planters, merchants, chartered trading companies and naval partnerships had been expected to manage their own affairs and to send out their own vessels to protect these investments, sometimes under letters of *marque* to effect reprisals when necessary. The naval expeditions of 1651, intended to secure the private business interests of merchants in the Atlantic colonies, were paid for with public funds, in this case the proceeds from sequestered estates. Parliament, initially financed by the colonial merchants, was now subsidising them. For the first time, the Atlantic colonies had become a primary responsibility of the state, in which treasure must be invested rather than merely extracted, and the colonies had reached such a level of economic and strategic importance that they could no longer be left to private interests. The colonies had, in fact, become like Ireland – with the significant difference that Ireland had its own supply of labour. The English slave trade emerged permanently from the shadows in 1651, an integral part of the colonial strategy of the Council of Trade.

By the end of 1652 the Adventurers, led by Maurice Thomson, Thomas Andrews and William Pennoyer, with a small circle of investors and partners, had achieved a virtual monopoly over England's external trade. Cromwell's capture or destruction of the southern Irish ports had removed the threat from Irish privateering that the colonial merchants had often struggled to contain.[100] Their remaining challenge was to curtail the aggression of Dutch commercial shipping, despite their close personal and commercial ties to Dutch merchants. With the precedent established for resolving their difficulties using the state's resources, the Adventurers, through their control of the navy commissioners, enlisted the English navy to fight the First Dutch War, 1652–54. The navy, which had increased dramatically both in size and efficiency since the review conducted in January 1649, was heavily reinforced with armed merchant vessels leased from the Adventurers. They were remarkably fortunate when a storm disabled the Dutch fleet, helping the English to win a series of victories that left England, or the Adventurers, as the dominant commercial naval power in the Atlantic, for the time being. The First Dutch War was a particularly profitable one for the Adventurers' leadership, as Rowland Wilson and Richard Hill were appointed commissioners for the sale of Dutch prizes in December 1652.[101] The Adventurers had their pick of, and could name their price for, the dozens of ships captured by the English navy during the war. It was a total victory, with the Dutch merchant fleet emasculated and their best surviving ships in the Adventurers' hands.

By supporting Generals Cromwell and Fairfax, and in the wake of their military successes, the Adventurers had achieved leadership in most areas of the Commonwealth's administrative structures. Thomas Noel was put in charge of the mint, adding control of coin to the Adventurers' pre-eminence in paper-based credit.[102] The committees appointed by parliament on 2 December 1652 to sit for a further twelve months were comprised primarily of Adventurers for Irish land or their close supporters.[103] George Thomson, John Goodwin, William Purefoy and Sir Arthur Hesilrige sat on the Committee for the Ordnance with overall control of military procurement. The Committee for Ireland and Scotland included George Thomson, Goodwin and Purefoy with Sir Henry Vane II, Denis Bond, Oliver Cromwell and Francis Allein. The Committees for the Admiralty, Trade and Plantations were almost entirely composed of Adventurers for Irish land. Despite these successes in the colonies and at Westminster, there was still one theatre where the Adventurers for Irish land had failed to assert their control and where their interests were disregarded or subordinated. This place was Ireland.

Oliver Cromwell left Ireland on 26 May 1650 leaving his son-in-law, Henry Ireton, in command to complete the conquest and impose the surrender. When Ireton died unexpectedly on 26 November 1651, this task fell to a 'Commission for Ireland', officially representing the English parliament but composed almost entirely of army officers under the overall charge of Edmund Ludlow, formerly Ireton's second-in-command. The war in Ireland came to an effective end with the surrender of Galway on 12 April 1652 and most of the remaining Irish forces surrendered during the next few weeks. Articles of agreement were negotiated at Kilkenny on 12 May between the parliamentary commissioners and representatives of the Irish Confederate forces of Leinster.[104] The centrepiece of this agreement was that any Irish soldiers who chose to do so were free to travel to France, or any other jurisdiction at peace with England, and continue their military careers. An additional clause to the agreement was sent to Westminster for approval, 'that they [the Irish] may enjoy such moderate part of the said estates as may make their lives comfortable who live among us or for the comfort and maintenance of the families of such of them as shall go beyond seas'.[105] This was not the unconditional surrender and free possession of lands that the Adventurers had envisioned, but an emissary, John Vernon, was nonetheless sent from Ireland to London by the commissioners to seek the approval of parliament's Committee for Irish Affairs for this concession.[106] Further disturbances in Ireland prevented the agreement of Kilkenny from taking root, but the attitude of senior army officers in London towards the Adventurers' claims had become clear. An end to the war and the welfare of their soldiers was more important than the Adventurers' old claim for dispossessed Catholic land dating back to 1642. The unconditional surrender, for so long the sole goal of the Adventurers, was now off the table.

Concerned Adventurers in London were already conferring with parliament. An earlier agreement between Colonel O'Dwyer, for his Irish regiment, and Colonel Hierome Sankey, for the English parliament, was agreed on 23 March 1652 and included a clause that O'Dwyer's father would retain the family lands as long as his army embarked for France.[107] When the agreement was presented to the House of Commons on 8 April, not only was it approved with little discussion, but Sankey was awarded land in Ireland worth £100 per year for his good deeds, before a single acre was settled on the Adventurers.[108] The following week, on 13 April, an officer MP, Colonel Thomas Wogan, was awarded land in Ireland worth £300 per year, to settle a claim for arrears and the very next day Oliver Cromwell ordered a full audit of all of the army's accounts so that all arrears could be quantified, making possible the distribution of Irish land to any soldier that wanted it.[109] The army was preparing to distribute Irish land before the Adventurers had begun the process of making their claims. Parliament received its first formal proposals from the Adventurers on 20 April, and referred these to the Council of State together with an instruction that the Council of State must also consider how the army in Ireland was to be paid off and disbanded.[110] The Council of State was made responsible for drafting an Irish land settlement and this draft was to be returned to Westminster for approval.[111] From the Adventurers' perspective this work was superfluous as the Adventurers' Act was perfectly unambiguous and made no reference to sharing or negotiating. This key report, when it appeared, also included the original proposals for transporting Irish soldiers out of the country, and for removing civilians from one part of the country to another, the Transplantation to Connacht. Both proposals carried the implication that the commissioners in Ireland were going to negotiate. Worryingly for the Adventurers, this work was not actually drafted by the Council of State, but by John Weaver, a commissioner from Dublin sent to London to represent the interests of the army in Ireland and a constant reminder of where the sympathies of the military government in Dublin lay.

As the Council of State was, at heart, representing Ludlow's forces in Ireland, the Adventurers secured the creation of a parliamentary committee, the 'Committee for Proposals from the Adventurers for Ireland', to lobby for their interests.[112] In London, on 12 May, as a treaty for the surrender of the Confederates in Leinster was being agreed at Kilkenny, the Adventurers were informed by the Council of State that they were to be offered 'as manie forfeited lands within the counties of Limerick Kerry and Tipperary or within the counties of Limerick Kerry and Corke or within the counties of Waterford Wexford Wicklowe and Kilkenny (at their election) as their present adventures amounts to'.[113] This was not a great offer. The Adventurers knew Ireland well, as their agents and factors had been stationed throughout the country to assist with the distribution of military supplies since the end of 1641. In addition, William Hawkins had remained in Ireland at the end of Cromwell's campaign and moved to Munster, where most of the land on offer was located. Of the counties mentioned, huge swathes of Cork and Waterford were already in the hands of the Boyles or other Protestant landowners who had been loyal to parliament, as was much of County Wexford. The Adventurers were also informed that they must plant their lands with non-Irish Protestants, although where these were to be obtained from was unclear. If this Protestant plantation was not completed within three years, the Adventurers would permanently forfeit their entitlement to Irish land. These proposals were unacceptable to the Adventurers in two ways. First, they had expected their pick of two and a half million acres of forfeited land, anywhere in the country. Second, although the Adventurers of 1642 included major colonial planters, the Adventurers of 1652 had shifted almost entirely from planting to shipping. Even had they retained their planting expertise, they were unlikely to raise the necessary colonists in post-Civil Wars England. The demand for English settlers was reiterated on 19 May, with a further order that linked planting and possession, clarifying the vague references to planting in the original Adventurers' Act.[114]

Heated exchanges over Ireland dominated proceedings at Westminster for the next couple of days until General George Fleetwood arrived in the chamber on 21 May and steered though a motion suspending any further debate on the issue.[115] Fleetwood knew that this was not the time for a serious row with the Adventurers. The news of the surrender of Barbados to Ayscue had not only reached London, it had also reached Amsterdam. Twice denied the Atlantic carrying trade, by the Navigation Act and by the rendition of the colonies to parliament, and stripped of their Confederate Irish proxies, Dutch naval squadrons appeared menacingly off the coast of Kent.[116] Moreover, an audit into army and navy accounts revealed that England would need to raise £650,000 in the course of the year, which would require an unpopular new subsidy as the state was already deeply in debt.[117] The Council of State was discovering how costly it was to maintain a fleet capable of sustaining an empire, and how dangerous it could be to make enemies of the group that financed it. A truce was called.

As stasis descended in London on negotiations over Irish land, the commissioners in Ireland continued to dole out estates to army officers, despite having no mandate to do so. Sir Robert Reynolds was awarded a large part of the earl of Ormond's estate in Tipperary and Colonel Daniel Axtell, captain of the parliamentary guard at the trial of Charles I, was granted the town of Ballyragget.[118] The commissioners became landlords, letting both farmland and houses in the cities to raise revenues.[119] The Adventurers changed tactics and tried to undermine the army's control over the settlement process by seeing to it that the most salacious details of the 1641 rebellion, extracted from what are now known as the 1641 Depositions, appeared again in the newspapers. With these embarrassing reminders, sentiment in parliament turned by the beginning of June and the clause in the Articles of Kilkenny concerning freedom of religion in Ireland was rejected.[120] Then, as the cost of the Dutch naval war escalated, a familiar pattern reasserted itself. Sir John Wollaston, Thomas Andrews, John Dethwick and Francis Allein, all members of the Committee of Adventurers for Irish land, agreed to become treasurers for a new £200,000 loan for the navy, arranging an advance of the money from their friends that was secured on the sale of further forfeited English estates.[121] By the end of June the Adventurers' point of view was, once again, being considered favourably by parliament.[122] The result of this lobbying and financial support for the navy was draft legislation entitled 'An Act for the speedy and effectual Satisfaction of the Adventurers for Lands in *Ireland*, and of the Arrears due to the Soldiery; and for the Encouragement of Protestants, to plant and inhabit in Ireland'. The bill received its first reading on 5 August 1652. The Adventurers were mentioned first and the army in Ireland second, and the onerous requirement to provide English settlers was now merely an encouragement.

The final text, the Act for Settling Ireland of 12 August 1652, sought to codify terms for concluding the conflict and provided for the confiscation of both Old English and Irish estates.[123] Parliament, emboldened by its progress in the Dutch war and with its finances bolstered by the success of the sale of crown, church and delinquent lands in England, resolved that all the forfeited lands in Ireland be 'reserved for the use and benefit of the ... Commonwealth', and there was no mention of the Adventurers in the text. According to one pamphlet, although the Adventurers were completely within their rights to begin the process of drawing lots for their land, their claims could not take precedence over those of soldiers already in Ireland.[124] There was little public sympathy for the Adventurers, as their army had never been sent to Ireland and the country had been conquered at public expense. Nevertheless, the pamphlet's author recognised that the state needed to deal with the Adventurers 'circumspectly'.[125] Public opinion, it seems, had checked the Adventurers' powerful lobby just as they were about to get their way. The Act for Settling Ireland was followed with supplementary legislation, on 25 August, ordering the calculation of army arrears of pay and stipulating that all such arrears for service performed in England, Ireland or Scotland could be satisfied with Irish land.[126] This was a very open-ended arrangement, as there was no way to estimate the amount of land that might be required to satisfy army claims until the process was complete nor any mention of the Adventurers in this piece of legislation. The Adventurers were expected to wait behind the army. After several protests, a new group of parliamentary commissioners for Ireland was appointed with instructions for putting the Act for Settling Ireland into effect. Under Cromwell's direct command, these commissioners were Lieutenant Generals Fleetwood and Ludlow, Colonel John Jones, Miles Corbett and John Weaver, who was to remain in London for the time being. The land settlement was to be controlled by Cromwell and the army, from Dublin and not from London as the Adventurers would have preferred.[127] The act was redrafted by John Weaver and the Council of State, not by a parliamentary committee, and parliament was effectively bullied into accepting the new draft, created by the Council of State where the Adventurers' lobby was far less effective.

Once back in Ireland, the new commissioners busied themselves with demilitarisation, which took the form of shipping as many former Irish soldiers as possible out of the country, and raising taxes locally to pay their own standing army. As it quickly became apparent that the devastated country could not support the high rates of taxation required, and fresh funds were slow in coming from the disgruntled Adventurers in England, an imperative emerged to distribute land as quickly as possible to the soldiers, both to settle their arrears and to get them off the payroll.[128] The Adventurers were presented with a simple choice: allow the soldiers to take up lands without delay, or continue to foot the bill for paying them. The Adventurers opted to do nothing until their demands were heard. The squeeze on supplies for Ireland was maintained until a new delegation of officers arrived back in Westminster in December 1652 to register claims of arrears for the army, and a new round of negotiations began.[129] Despite their dominance of parliamentary committee rooms, the Adventurers were again unable to prevent MPs agreeing to proposals, presented to parliament by the representatives of the army in Ireland, for an immediate large-scale seizure of Irish land to settle arrears of army pay.[130] Ten counties in Ireland were set aside for both soldiers and Adventurers, restricting the potential scope of the Adventurers' land grab and excluding all urban property from their settlement. Furthermore, although it was possible for the army, if their claims were too great to be met by the contents of ten counties, to be awarded land elsewhere, the Adventurers were restricted to the named counties. Maurice Thomson, William Pennoyer, Robert Thomson, Thomas Smith and Gregory Clement promptly petitioned parliament, objecting to these proposals. They were supported by no less a figure than the earl of Warwick, but they were rebuffed. Not only was the army to be preferred in any land settlement, but the town of Gloucester and county of Cheshire were both added to a compensation list for losses suffered during

39　CJ, VI, pp. 301–302. The Adventurers were George Cooper, Maurice Gethin, William Hiccocks and Sylvanus Taylor.
40　CJ, VI, pp. 311–312.
41　TNA E164/60, f. 1.
42　TNA E164/60, f. 3.
43　TNA E164/60, f. 4.
44　TNA E164/60, f. 85.
45　TNA SP 21/26, f. 142. This was also paid by the treasurers for the sale of Forfeited Lands and Estates (TNA E164/60, f. 85).
46　TNA SP 46/95, f. 164. The Adventurers Elias Palmer and Thomas Sprigg were subcontracted to manage the warehousing and despatch of this material.
47　TNA SP 46/95, f. 228. The interest charged was £1,082.
48　TNA SP 46/95, f. 224.
49　TNA SP 21/29, f. 43.
50　A&O, II, pp. 75–78, 'April 1649: An Act for appointing Commissioners for Sale of Prize goods'. Upton invested the enormous sum of £7,500 in fee-farms in 1650 (SP 26, Vol. 1, ff. 62–63). John Upton's daughter, Ursula, married George Clarke who became the second largest aggregator of Adventures after Sir David Watkins.
51　CCC, I, p. 136.
52　CCC, I, p. 172. John Bateman was also invited onto the central committee of the East India Company in 1652.
53　A&O, II, pp. 422–423, 'September 1650: An Act for appointing Commissioners for the Excise'. The other commissioners were George Snelling, Thomas Bulstrode, William Parker and Richard Downes. William Parker's brother, John, was a minister and key figure in the local government of Barbados during the 1640s and 1650s. See Larry Gragg, *Englishmen Transplanted: The English Colonization of Barbados 1627–1660* (Oxford, 2003), p. 25.
54　To put this amount into contemporary perspective, the earl of Ormond valued his estate in 1660 at £8,000 pa and the earl of Cork £12,000 pa.
55　TNA SP 26/1, f. 62.
56　TNA SP 28/288, f. 113; TNA SP 26/1, f. 7.
57　TNA SP 26/1, f. 87. The fee-farm was purchased by an agent, Jeffry White, on Pennoyer's behalf.
58　A&O, II, pp. 155–156a, 'June 1649: An Act for Encouragement of Purchasers of Deans and Chapters Lands'.
59　BL, Add Ms 46190, f. 40.
60　A&O, II, pp. 140–142. 'June 1649: An Act for Instructions for the Trustees Treasurer and Register-Accountant for the Sale of the Deans and Chapter Lands, for the admitting such as have moneys owing them by the Parliament, to double the same upon the Credit of the Lands of the Deans and Chapters'. Two of the original loans advanced for the suppression of the Irish rebellion in 1642, the £100,000 borrowed from the City of London and the £100,000 borrowed from the Adventurers, were still outstanding in 1649.
61　Barry Higman, *Slave Populations of the British Caribbean* (Baltimore, MD, 1984), pp. 417–421; Henry A. Gemery, 'Emigration from the British Isles to the New

World: 1630–1700: References from Colonial Populations', *Research in Economic History*, 5 (1980), pp. 179–231, p. 211.

62 The Leeward Islands comprise St Kitts, Nevis, Antigua, Montserrat and the Virgin Islands.
63 John C. Appleby, 'English Settlement During War and Peace' in Robert L. Paquette and Sidney L. Engerman (eds), *The Lesser Antilles in the Age of European Expansion* (Gainesville, 1996), pp. 86–104.
64 TNA CO 1/11, f. 29.
65 TNA CO 1/11, f. 29v.
66 William Foster, *The English Factories in India 1646–1650* (Oxford, 1914), p. 329.
67 TNA SP 71/25, f. 9.
68 Anon, 'The Northern Neck of Virginia', *William and Mary Quarterly*, 6:4 (April, 1898), pp. 222–226. The territory was inherited by Thomas Fairfax, 6th Lord Fairfax, following a marriage between Fairfax and a Culpepper.
69 TNA CO 1/11, f. 40.
70 TNA CO 1/11, ff. 26–27.
71 TNA CO 1/11, ff. 32, 60–61.
72 These sales were subsequently voided. See BDA RB2/68, index to the recopied deed books, *passim*.
73 TNA CO 1/11, f. 62.
74 TNA CO 1/11, f. 84.
75 W. Noel Sainsbury (ed.), *Calendar of State Papers Colonial, America and West Indies*, 1, 1574–1660 (London, 1860), p. 331.
76 BL, Add Ms 4771, f. 25. Worseley reported the supplier, Richard Clay, to the committee for over-charging and had Clay's accounts audited and his payments suspended. FitzGerald owned a plantation in Barbados from before the rebellion in Ireland until 1648. See BDA 2/3, p. 507. Sale of plantation by FitzGerald to Robert Dowden.
77 Michael Hunter, Antonio Clericuzio and Laurence M. Principe (eds), *The Correspondence of Robert Boyle*, 6 vols (London, 2001), Vol. 1, pp. 42–44.
78 W. Noel Sainsbury (ed.), *Calendar of the Court Minutes of the East India Company 1644–1649* (Oxford, 1912), p. 81.
79 James E. Farnell, 'The Navigation Act of 1651, the First Dutch War, and the London Merchant Community', *Economic History Review*, New Series, 16:3 (1964), pp. 439–454, p. 441.
80 A&O, II, pp. 387, 392, 890.
81 K.N. Chaudhuri, *The English East India Company: The Study of an Early Joint-Stock Company 1600–1640* (London, 1965), pp. 40, 81, 224, Methold, who subscribed £700 to the Adventure for Irish land, and £400 to the Sea Adventure, was the East India Company's representative in Surat, 1633–38, and before that an escheator for inquisitions post mortem in Ireland.
82 Farnell, 'The Navigation Act', p. 448.
83 Norma Tucker, *Colonial Virginians and Their Maryland Relatives* (Baltimore, MD, 1994), p. 14.
84 A&O, II, pp. 559–562, 'October 1651: An Act for increase of Shipping, and Encouragement of the Navigation of this Nation'.

of the earl of Ormond's estate in Tipperary and Colonel Daniel Axtell, captain of the parliamentary guard at the trial of Charles I, was granted the town of Ballyragget.[118] The commissioners became landlords, letting both farmland and houses in the cities to raise revenues.[119] The Adventurers changed tactics and tried to undermine the army's control over the settlement process by seeing to it that the most salacious details of the 1641 rebellion, extracted from what are now known as the 1641 Depositions, appeared again in the newspapers. With these embarrassing reminders, sentiment in parliament turned by the beginning of June and the clause in the Articles of Kilkenny concerning freedom of religion in Ireland was rejected.[120] Then, as the cost of the Dutch naval war escalated, a familiar pattern reasserted itself. Sir John Wollaston, Thomas Andrews, John Dethwick and Francis Allein, all members of the Committee of Adventurers for Irish land, agreed to become treasurers for a new £200,000 loan for the navy, arranging an advance of the money from their friends that was secured on the sale of further forfeited English estates.[121] By the end of June the Adventurers' point of view was, once again, being considered favourably by parliament.[122] The result of this lobbying and financial support for the navy was draft legislation entitled 'An Act for the speedy and effectual Satisfaction of the Adventurers for Lands in *Ireland*, and of the Arrears due to the Soldiery; and for the Encouragement of Protestants, to plant and inhabit in Ireland'. The bill received its first reading on 5 August 1652. The Adventurers were mentioned first and the army in Ireland second, and the onerous requirement to provide English settlers was now merely an encouragement.

The final text, the Act for Settling Ireland of 12 August 1652, sought to codify terms for concluding the conflict and provided for the confiscation of both Old English and Irish estates.[123] Parliament, emboldened by its progress in the Dutch war and with its finances bolstered by the success of the sale of crown, church and delinquent lands in England, resolved that all the forfeited lands in Ireland be 'reserved for the use and benefit of the ... Commonwealth', and there was no mention of the Adventurers in the text. According to one pamphlet, although the Adventurers were completely within their rights to begin the process of drawing lots for their land, their claims could not take precedence over those of soldiers already in Ireland.[124] There was little public sympathy for the Adventurers, as their army had never been sent to Ireland and the country had been conquered at public expense. Nevertheless, the pamphlet's author recognised that the state needed to deal with the Adventurers 'circumspectly'.[125] Public opinion, it seems, had checked the Adventurers' powerful lobby just as they were about to get their way. The Act for Settling Ireland was followed with supplementary legislation, on 25 August, ordering the calculation of army arrears of pay and stipulating that all such arrears for service performed in England, Ireland or Scotland could be satisfied with Irish land.[126] This was a very open-ended arrangement, as there was no way to estimate the amount of land that might be required to satisfy army claims until the process was complete nor any mention of the Adventurers in this piece of legislation. The Adventurers were expected to wait behind the army. After several protests, a new group of parliamentary commissioners for Ireland was appointed with instructions for putting the Act for Settling Ireland into effect. Under Cromwell's direct command, these commissioners were Lieutenant Generals Fleetwood and Ludlow, Colonel John Jones, Miles Corbett and John Weaver, who was to remain in London for the time being. The land settlement was to be controlled by Cromwell and the army, from Dublin and not from London as the Adventurers would have preferred.[127] The act was redrafted by John Weaver and the Council of State, not by a parliamentary committee, and parliament was effectively bullied into accepting the new draft, created by the Council of State where the Adventurers' lobby was far less effective.

Once back in Ireland, the new commissioners busied themselves with demilitarisation, which took the form of shipping as many former Irish soldiers as possible out of the country, and raising taxes locally to pay their own standing army. As it quickly became apparent that the devastated country could not support the high rates of taxation required, and fresh funds were slow in coming from the disgruntled Adventurers in England, an imperative emerged to distribute land as quickly as possible to the soldiers, both to settle their arrears and to get them off the payroll.[128] The Adventurers were presented with a simple choice: allow the soldiers to take up lands without delay, or continue to foot the bill for paying them. The Adventurers opted to do nothing until their demands were heard. The squeeze on supplies for Ireland was maintained until a new delegation of officers arrived back in Westminster in December 1652 to register claims of arrears for the army, and a new round of negotiations began.[129] Despite their dominance of parliamentary committee rooms, the Adventurers were again unable to prevent MPs agreeing to proposals, presented to parliament by the representatives of the army in Ireland, for an immediate large-scale seizure of Irish land to settle arrears of army pay.[130] Ten counties in Ireland were set aside for both soldiers and Adventurers, restricting the potential scope of the Adventurers' land grab and excluding all urban property from their settlement. Furthermore, although it was possible for the army, if their claims were too great to be met by the contents of ten counties, to be awarded land elsewhere, the Adventurers were restricted to the named counties. Maurice Thomson, William Pennoyer, Robert Thomson, Thomas Smith and Gregory Clement promptly petitioned parliament, objecting to these proposals. They were supported by no less a figure than the earl of Warwick, but they were rebuffed. Not only was the army to be preferred in any land settlement, but the town of Gloucester and county of Cheshire were both added to a compensation list for losses suffered during the civil wars. On 7 January 1653, the Adventurers learned that even the earl of Clanricarde was to get a hearing. A key army officer now chaired parliament's Committee for Irish Affairs: Algernon Sidney, son of the earl of Leicester and brother of Lord Lisle, parliament's former Lord Lieutenant. Control of parliamentary committees and the effective lobbying of MPs ceased to be effective when the army, or the Council of State, required a different outcome.

NOTES

1 The Adventurers who signed the death warrant were John Allured, John Barkstead, John Blackiston, Gregory Clement, Miles Corbett, Oliver Cromwell, Henry Marten, Gilbert Millington, Henry Smith, Robert Tichborne and Edward Whalley. The Adventurers present at the trial but who did not sign the death warrant were Thomas Andrews, James Harrington, Edward Harvey, Wiliam Heveningham, John Lisle, William Mounson, Isaac Pennington and Gilbert Pickering.
2 Percy Scott Flippin, *The Royal Government in Virginia 1624–1775* (London, 1919), p. 105.
3 Micheál Ó Siochrú, *God's Executioner, Oliver Cromwell and the Conquest of Ireland* (London, 2008), p. 67.
4 Eamon Darcy, *The Irish Rebellion and the Wars of the Three Kingdoms* (Woodbridge, 2013), p. 136.
5 TNA CO/ 1/ 10, f. 23.
6 R. Porter, 'The Crispe Family and the African Trade in the Seventeenth Century', *The Journal of African History*, 9:1 (1968), p. 68; TNA CO1/10, f. 29
7 Ernst van den Oogart, 'The Trade between Western Africa and the Atlantic World, 1600–1690: Estimates of Trends in Composition and Value', *The Journal of African History*, 33:3 (1992), pp. 369–385. For comparisons between the gold and slave trade see p. 370. For a background to European trade with West Africa see Toby Green, *A Fistful of Shells: West Africa from the Rise of the Slave Trade to the Age of Revolution* (London, 2019).
8 W. Noel Sainsbury, *Calendar of the Court Minutes of the East India Company 1644–1649* (Oxford, 1912), p. 342. The owners of the second general voyage were William Barkley, Samuel Moyer, Maurice Thomson, Roger Vivian, Nathan Wright, William Vincent, Captain William Ryder, Captain Jeremy Black-man and Aaron Baker; the Joint Stock by William Cockayne, William Methold, William Ashwell, Rowland Wilson, Gilbert Morewood, Thomas Jennings, Gilbert Keate, James Mann and Thomas Andrews.
9 Sainsbury, *East India Company*, p. 343. The owners of the cargo were John Robinson, Nicholas Corsellis, William Pennoyer, Thomas Hall, Robert Thomson, Samuel Pennoyer, William Harris, Richard Batson, Michael Davison, William Thomson, John Woods, Martin Noel, Cornelius Mounteney, James Houbolon, John Casier, Adam Laurence, Hugh Norris, William Boone, Thomas Harris and Ahasuerus Regemont.
10 Sainsbury, *East India Company*, p. 335.
11 Sainsbury, *East India Company*, p. 350.

12 Ronald Findlay and Kevin H. O'Rourke, 'Commodity Market Integration, 1500–2000' in Michael D. Burdo (ed.), *Globalisation in Historical Perspective* (Chicago, 2003), p. 21.
13 William Robert Scott, *The Constitution and Finance of English, Scottish and Irish Joint Stock Companies to 1720*, 3 vols (Cambridge, 1910), Vol. 2, p. 245.
14 BL IOR/B/25, Court Minutes of the East India Company, f. 33.
15 BL IOR/B/25, Court Minutes of the East India Company, f. 33.
16 Niels Steensgard, 'The Growth and Composition of the Long-Distance Trade of England and the Dutch Republic before 1750' in James D. Tracey (ed.), *The Rise of Merchant Empires* (Cambridge, 1990), pp. 102–152, p. 110.
17 BL IOR/B/25, Court Minutes of the East India Company, f. 33v.
18 For more on the nascent circular trade see Margaret Makepeace, 'English Traders on the Guinea Coast, 1657–168: An Analysis of the East India Company Archive', *History in Africa*, 16 (1989), pp. 237–284.
19 TNA SP 28/350/3, f. 3.
20 www.historyofparliamentonline.org/volume/1604-1629/member/greene-giles-1596-1656.
21 I am grateful to Professor John Adamson for the background to Greene's career.
22 TNA SP 26/29, ff. 115–116.
23 Micheál Ó Siochrú, *God's Executioner, Oliver Cromwell and the Conquest of Ireland* (London, 2008), p. 77.
24 LJ, VI, p. 15. To place this figure in context, parliament's entire naval expenditure from January 1643 to May 1645 was £641,000 and £450,000 of this money came from customs. The Irish campaign was a huge undertaking, particularly as it was compressed into a relatively short time-span.
25 TNA SP 21/29, ff. 34, 81; D'Maris Coffman, *Excise Taxation and the Origins of Public Debt* (Basingstoke, 2013), p. 1435. The most active members of the English excise in 1649 were George Thomson, Richard Aldworth, Gregory Clement, Edmund Harvey, Robert Brewster and Luke Hodges.
26 TNA SP 28/ 350/7, f. 1.
27 TNA SP 28/350/7, f. 2–6. For a complete list of county collectors see LJ, 10, pp. 49–55.
28 TNA SP 28/350/7, f. 30.
29 TNA SP 28/350/7, f. 31. The four agents were Maurice Thomson, Nicholas Corsellis, Derek Hoast and Adam Laurence.
30 CJ, VI, pp. 8–9.
31 CJ, VI, pp. 10–16.
32 TNA SP 28/350/7, *passim*.
33 Gregory Moule, *The Irish Mercury* (London, February 1649), p. 2.
34 Thomas Fauntleroy, *Lux in Tenebris or, A Clavis to the Treasury on Broad Street* (London, 1653), p. 11.
35 Michael Braddick, *Parliamentary Taxation in Seventeenth Century England: Local Administration and Response* (Woodbridge, 1994), p. 207.
36 The full particulars of this loan are in TNA SP 25/125.
37 TNA SP 25/125, f. 192, 'memorandum'.
38 TNA SP 25/125, f. 87 provides an example. This volume of State Papers is a detailed record of the management of these sequestered estates.

85 TNA CO 1/11, f. 100.
86 Samuel Rawson Gardiner (ed.), *Letters and papers relating to the First Dutch War 1652–54*, 6 vols (London, 1899–1930), Vol. I, p. 54. The Navy Commissioners were Robert Thomson, John Holland, Thomas Smith, who joined the EEIC, Peter Pett, parliament's principal ship-builder, Richard Hutchinson and Robert Mounson.
87 Gardiner, *First Dutch War*, Vol. I, p. 61; TNA CO 1/10, f. 107.
88 Elizabeth Donnan, 'Documents Illustrative of the Slave Trade to America', I (Washington, DC, 1930), p. 126: The Guinea Company to James Pope 17 September 1651.
89 Donnan, 'Documents Illustrative', p. 129: The Guinea Company to Bartholomew Howard. The corresponding merchant in Barbados was Francis Soane, a kinsman of John Wood.
90 Donnan, 'Documents Illustrative', p. 131: The Guinea Company to James Pope 9 December 1651.
91 Donnan, 'Documents Illustrative', p. 133.
92 Harry Merritt, 'The Colony of the Colonized: the Duchy of Courland's Tobago Colony and Contemporary Latvian National Identity', *Nationalities Papers*, 38:4 (July, 2010), pp. 491–508, p. 492.
93 Donnan, 'Documents Illustrative', p. 134
94 TNA CO 1/10, f. 158.
95 Lois Green Carr, *Colonial Chesapeake Society* (Williamsburg, 1988), p. 82.
96 Lothrop Withington, 'Surrender of Virginia to the Parliamentary Commissioners', *Virginia Magazine of History and Biography*, 11:1 (July, 1903), pp. 32–41, p. 33.
97 The Articles of Surrender of Virginia to parliament were first published in William Waller Hening, *The Statutes at Large; being a Collection of all the Laws of Virginia*, Vol. 1 (Richmond, VA, 1888), pp. 363–365.
98 Berkeley also insisted on being allowed to visit Charles II in Europe to apologise in person for surrendering the colony.
99 Albert Bushnell Hart (ed.), *American History told by Contemporaries*, Vol. I (London, 1897), p. 239.
100 Jane Ohlmeyer, 'Irish Privateers during the Civil War 1642–50', *The Sea Mirror*, 76 (1990), pp. 119–134.
101 CSPD, 1652–3, p. 21.
102 CSPD, 1652–3, p. 45.
103 CSPD, 1652–3, p. 2.
104 Bodleian Library, Firth Ms C (5), p. 64.
105 Bodleian Library, Firth Ms C (5), p. 69.
106 Bodleian Library, Firth Ms C (5), p. 72.
107 Royal Irish Academy, Ms H2424, p. 81.
108 CJ, 7, p. 117, Grant to Sankey.
109 CJ, 7, pp. 119–121.
110 CJ, 7, p. 123.
111 Royal Irish Academy, Ms H2424, p. 82.
112 CJ, 7, p. 131.
113 CJ, 7, p. 83.

114 Samuel Peck, A Perfect Diurnall of Some Passages of Parliament (London, 1652), p. 1895, Wednesday 19 May.
115 CJ, 7, p. 134.
116 Peck, *Perfect Diurnall*, p. 1898.
117 CJ, 7, p. 127.
118 Robert Dunlop, *Ireland under the Commonwealth: Being a Selection of Documents Relating to the Government of Ireland from 1651-9, Vol. II* (Dublin, 1912), p. 205; Prendergast Ms, 2, p. 68.
119 BL, Egerton 1761, p. 214: Dwelling Houses; NLI, Ms. 11959, p. 73: 'Waste Lands'.
120 CJ, 7, p. 138.
121 A&O, II, pp. 591–597, 'August 1652: An Act for several Lands and Estates forfeited to the Commonwealth for Treason, appointed to be sold for the use of the Navy'.
122 CJ, 7, p. 144.
123 A&O, II, pp. 598–603, 'August 1652: An Act for the Setling of Ireland'.
124 Anon, *The Present Posture and Condition of Ireland* (London, 1652), p. 17.
125 *The Present Posture…*, p. 16.
126 A&O, II, pp. 603–612, 'August 1652: An Act for stating and determining the Accompts of such Officers and Soldiers as are or have been imployed in the Service of this Commonwealth in Ireland'.
127 CJ, 7, p. 144, p. 169.
128 NLI, MS. 11959, pp. 98–100, 'Some proposals humbly offered by a General councell of officers to the Genl. & Comrs. of Parliament which they humbly pray may be presented to the Parliament of the Comm. wealth of England'.
129 John Cunningham, *Conquest and Land in Ireland: The Transplantation to Connaught, 1649–1680* (Woodbridge, 2011), p. 33.
130 CJ, 7, pp. 242–243: *Irish Army and Adventurers*.

7

Restoration

THE ADVENTURERS AND THE CROMWELLIAN PROTECTORATE

The last sitting of the Long Parliament before it was ejected by Cromwell was held on 19 April 1653. The final debate concerned amendments to the draft bill for the 'effectual Satisfaction of the Adventurers for Lands in Ireland, and of the Arrears due to the Soldiery'.[1] The amendments to the bill proposed by the Adventurers either failed to pass or were referred to a council of army officers for an opinion. The final discussion concerned the transfer of a debt for £5,000 to Colonel Owen Rowe from lands in Scotland to lands in Ireland. The result of the vote for this amendment, a precedent to enshrine individual army claims for land, has been inked out in the official journal, expunged by an ordinance in 1659. All army claims for arrears could be inserted into the bill for Adventurers and soldiers, moving army claims to the front of the payment queue. An officer named in the bill would have received his parcel of land while the process for allocating lands to the Adventurers had yet to begin. Parliament, under the sustained influence of its Adventurer friends, baulked at handing over the entire Irish land settlement to the army, and the Long Parliament was dismissed by Cromwell the next morning.

By 20 April 1653, the Adventurers for Irish land dominated the financial machinery of the state, both in London and at many of the county committees of England and Wales through a dense web of committees, collectors, treasurers and procurers. When parliament was dismissed, its financial committees went with it and choked off the primary route for the Adventurers to influence or direct policy. Parliament's financial machinery had become increasingly corrupt and was failing to supply Cromwell with sufficient revenue. In particular, the formerly crucial Committee for Compounding that collected fines, rentals and settlements from former royalists and recusants was now receiving only a trickle of money through its collection agents in the provinces.[2] The best estates had been sold, normally for a fraction of what they were worth, and the income that remained was being siphoned off on its way from the provinces to Goldsmiths' Hall. In response to this new crisis, the Council of State formed two committees on 7 May, mainly comprised of army officers, to examine the accounts of the nation and particularly those of the Derby House Committee for Scottish and Irish Affairs.[3] Lieutenant Colonel Thomas Kelsey, the examiner for the excise, reported back to the Council of State on 14 May that the 'Excise Commissioners have likewise considered selling and disposing of the lands in Ireland'.[4] The excise had been farmed to a consortium of merchants led by Maurice Thomson. The consortium guaranteed to pay the state an agreed sum, collected the tax and pocketed the excess. To make up the disappointing shortfall in collections, the excise farmers now proposed selling forfeited Irish land. The effect of this move would be to transfer debts secured against the excise onto Irish land otherwise claimed by the army, strengthening the Adventurers' negotiating position. The Adventurers also personally held unpaid bills for military supplies sent to Ireland that could be offset against Irish land sales. An Irish land settlement performed on this basis would displace the army as the state's principal creditor in Ireland. The most pleasing part of this scheme for Maurice Thomson and the rest of the excise commissioners, however, was that once all of the debts secured on the Excise were transferred to Irish land, they were still free to pocket the entire proceeds of the excise. Both army and Adventurers, therefore, were attempting to seize control of the Irish land settlement. Cromwell's forced closing of Westminster put an abrupt end to both plans, and to the passage of a land settlement favourable to the Adventurers and endorsed by MPs.

Cromwell had deposed the Council of State on the same day as the dissolution of parliament, and the Irish land settlement was taken up by an interim council chosen by the army.[5] A committee, chaired by John Lambert, was set up by an interim Council of State on 17 May 1653 to draw up 'instructions' for 'disposing of the forfeited lands in Ireland' and to 'frame them so as may be for the best advantage of the service'.[6] The following day, and to avoid interruptions from the Adventurers, the interim Council of State appointed John Thurloe as its gatekeeper in Westminster, to receive and reply to petitions and to report back to the councillors.[7] The Adventurers were informed that they would eventually get a meeting with Lambert, but only after he had assessed the claims of both the army and the army's commissaries.[8] Now furious, the Adventurers decided to bypass the interim Council of State and to confront the council of army officers directly. Thomas Andrews and Stephen Estwick delivered a petition to the army officers on 20 May.[9] Estwick delivered a short speech demanding the restoration of parliament and new elections according to 'the ancient fundamental laws of the nation'.[10] The Adventurers made it clear that they would not offer any financial support to a military government and that they regarded

Cromwell as a usurper. The petition was signed by five aldermen: Sir John Wollaston, Thomas Andrews, Thomas Foot, John Kendrick and Stephen Estwick, and thirty-one common councillors, including Maurice Thomson, William Pennoyer, Richard Waring, Michael Herring, Thomas Allen, Thomas Stone and Tempest Milner. Acting alone and without instructions from the peerage, an English merchants' revolt had finally occurred, directed not against the king but against Oliver Cromwell and his council of army officers. It was clear to the Adventurers that Cromwell was determined to loosen their grip over both parliamentary committees and the fiscal state. With their control over England's foreign trade, and the supply of new bullion that went with it, the Adventurers thought they were in a very strong position. They had, however, completely misread Cromwell's determination to ensure proper redress for his soldiers and to preside over an orderly disbandment of much of his army. He had selected John Thurloe as secretary to the Council of State with good reason, as Thurloe was the nephew of Martin Noel, the Master of the Mint. Just as Charles I had locked away the merchants' gold, Cromwell could now do the same. Foreign bullion could only be converted into coin of the realm with the cooperation of the mint.

Cromwell acted decisively. Everyone associated with the petition was summarily dismissed from public office, or else resigned.[11] George Thomson, who had not signed the petition but was associated with it, was expelled as both navy commissioner and commissioner of customs. As one of the few sitting MPs in 1653, it is possible that it was George Thomson who organised the vote in parliament against Colonel Owen Rowe's arrears. Francis Allein and Denis Bond were removed from the Committee for Inspection of the Treasuries. Maurice Thomson and Thomas Foote resigned as excise commissioners, and the money they had advanced to the excise was withheld from repayment.[12] Michael Herring and Richard Waring ceased to be commissioners for compounding and Stephen Estwick and Thomas Noel were dismissed from their posts as treasurers for the sale of Dean and Chapter lands.[13] Richard Waring and Thomas Vincent lost their posts at Goldsmiths' Hall and Thomas Andrews, John Sir Wollaston, John Dethwick and Francis Allein were all dismissed as contractors for the sale of ecclesiastical land.[14] Another commissioner of the navy, Sir Henry Vane II, who was not an Adventurer in Irish land but was a key supporter of the leading Adventurers dating back to his time as governor of Massachusetts Bay, escaped from London into the countryside. Colonel Owen Rowe was given the job of inspecting the accounts of the customs commissioners.

On 21 May, as the news that the Adventurers had been dismissed from all of their government posts was circulated, the Council of State moved against the Adventurers' colonial interests. First, they demanded the papers of the Bermuda Company with the intention of dismissing the sitting patentees. To break the Adventurers' effective monopoly over the sugar trade, a new group of merchants, unconnected to the Adventurers, was licensed to establish a sugar works in Barbados. Although parliament was in the middle of debating the Irish land settlement when it was interrupted by Cromwell, the Council of State abruptly declared that the soldiers in Ireland would receive five counties. Most damaging of all to the Adventurers, and a sign that the Council of State would go to any lengths to protect the interests of the army, the key provision in the Navigation Act that all colonial exports be restricted to English shipping was abrogated.[15] By this last action the Council of State accepted the reality that while they intended to wrest control of colonial production from the Adventurers, they would not be able to do so without resorting to using foreign ships. For their part, the Adventurers continued to circulate their petition in London, seeking further signatures to increase pressure on the Council of State.[16] The appointment of Samuel Moyer to the Council of State on 24 May helped to defuse the situation and the petition evaporated.[17] Although Moyer was close to the Adventurers' leadership, he had not signed their petition and could act as a point of contact between the two groups. Thomas Smith, dismissed as a commissioner of the navy on 21 May, was reinstated on 27 May, another sign that tempers were cooling, and Moyer had brokered a deal with the Adventurers by the end of the day.[18] Moyer explained that the mint, far from being full of bullion, had fallen idle and that there was no money available to pay warrants presented by army officers at Goldsmiths' Hall. He arranged for an immediate loan of sufficient cash – the army's representatives were demanding an initial payment of £30,000 for arrears – to ensure that the bills could be met, and officers were invited to present their warrants for payment.[19]

The Adventurers had bought their way out of their deep disagreement with Cromwell, and on 1 June the Council of State announced that, with regard to Ireland, 'every Adventurer may receive satisfaction by lot where his dividend of land shall be'.[20] The Adventurers would still have to deal with the army on equal terms and would not get to choose where their lands would be located, but by 23 June the lobbying by the Adventurers for commercial concessions resumed. On that day, a petition arrived at the Council of State, signed by William Pennoyer and Andrew Riccard, respectively the senior men in the Levant and East India companies, demanding that they and their associates become responsible for civil appointments on Barbados.[21] Regardless of the importance of sugar as a means to raise cash, the slave trade had increased in importance within the Adventurers' trading system after setbacks in 1651. A further signatory, Nathaniel Goodyer, was a shareholder in the Guinea Company and the petitioners had taken care to exclude Maurice Thomson, together with the other merchants who had staged the confrontation with Cromwell, from the petition. The global ambition of the Adventurers began to manifest itself with this petition, and with it a new-found alliance between parliamentarian William Pennoyer and royalist Andrew Riccard.

THE IRISH LAND SETTLEMENT

The Council of State appointed a committee headed by William Webster and Elias Roberts, both London merchants, to design the Adventurers' land settlement.[22] Neither man was a major investor in Irish land, although Roberts had invested in Irish fee farm rents in the late 1640s. Elias Roberts, in his new post, bought a bundle of smaller adventures between 1653 and 1658 in and around Waterford City, including a £50 debenture owned by Maurice Thomson, which he then resold at a 50% discount, sparing his friend this small loss.[23] Webster was an old business partner of Maurice Thomson: they jointly owned an armed merchantman, the *Merchant's Hope*, in the late 1630s.[24] As theirs was a private committee, not a public post from which they could be dismissed, Maurice Thomson, Robert Thomson, William Pennoyer and other leading Adventurers continued meetings of their own representative committee at Grocers' Hall.[25] It was still a valuable forum in which to discuss other business. Webster and Roberts announced that the lottery for Irish land would take place at Grocers' Hall on 20 July 1653 and the Adventurers were invited to consolidate their investments into larger holdings, if they wished, in advance of this. A simple formula was proposed, with land to the value of £110,000 to be drawn in Munster, £205,000 in Leinster and £45,000 in Ulster.[26] No land was reserved for the Adventurers in Connacht, as the entire province was reserved for the transplantation of Catholic Irish landowners. The value of land allocated, £360,000, was considerably higher than the original amount invested in 1642, and the probable explanation is that the loan brokered by Samuel Moyer in April was added to the total. Although it appeared initially that Cromwell had surrendered to the Adventurers' demands, the price the Adventurers would pay for their land settlement was revealed later in the afternoon when the Council of State confirmed the suspension of the Navigation Act.[27] The Irish land settlement was thus a creation of the army's interim Council of State that met in the weeks between Cromwell's dissolution of the Rump and the first meeting of the Nominated Parliament, on 4 July 1653.

The military authorities in Dublin had acted very quickly to assume control over state finance in Ireland. As early as 11 November 1651, district commissioners for assessment were drawn from under-officers to collect local taxes, pre-empting any offers from merchants to act as farmers.[28] A Commission for Revenue in Ireland was established and, as the assessments failed to bring in any meaningful contributions, this commission decided to issue leases for a term of seven years to any soldier or English migrant who wished to take up a parcel of forfeited or abandoned farmland. These instructions, issued on 3 February 1652, laid out an ambitious programme for the colonisation of Ireland with the state as landlord.[29] To encourage settlers, the new tenants were freed from their obligation to pay assessments for the first two years, leaving the commissioners entirely dependent on the rents for revenue. This initiative, taken well in advance of the Act for Settling Ireland or any other deal reached in London, created yet another obstacle to the early land settlement that the Adventurers hoped for. The government in Ireland, as landlord, had no incentive to proceed quickly to process the Adventurers' claims, as they would continue to receive the rents from any tenants they recruited until 1659 at the earliest, seven years from the date of issue of the leases. It was fortunate for the Adventurers, therefore, that Benjamin Worseley, formerly the secretary to the Council of Trade, arrived in Dublin in January 1652 to try his hand at saltpetre manufacturing.[30] A skilled administrator, within a year Worseley had risen to the position of keeper of all official records, giving him access to all of the Dublin commissioners' financial minutes and agreements with tenants.[31] The Adventurers now had someone at the heart of the Dublin government they could trust. This useful state of affairs culminated with the appointment of Benjamin Worseley as Surveyor General of Ireland later in 1653, placing the Adventurers' former secretary for trade at the heart of any future Irish land settlement.[32] In addition, another of their long-term associates, the former commissary Gualter Frost, became treasurer in London of the Trustees for Ireland, the committee responsible for managing the assorted outstanding loans for Ireland secured on the public faith.[33]

There was still a great deal of financial housekeeping to do before the Adventurers' lottery could take place. Leading Adventurers had to untangle the complicated financial instruments and shared ownership arrangements created to finance the original purchase of Adventures by MPs in 1642. Since then, the Adventures, individual entitlements to land, had become tradable bonds in their own right, used to settle private debts between merchants, albeit for far less than the original sums subscribed. By 1652, small Adventures for Irish land were changing hands for less than 50% of their face value and larger Adventures were traded for very little more.[34] The trade in Adventures culminated early in 1653 when the secretary at Goldsmiths' Hall, Thomas Vincent, gambled on an early land settlement and purchased a large number of Adventures of all size, becoming the leading Adventurer. There were even better bargains to be had outside of London, demonstrated when Nicholas Poynter of Norwich purchased an Adventure with a face value of £600, owned by a consortium of four Norwich merchants, for a mere £100.[35] Thomas Vincent also purchased the Blayney estate in County Monaghan from the financially distressed Lord Blayney, before giving the land back to Blayney, together with the hand of his daughter, as a means to elevate his family into the peerage.[36] He was well versed in Irish affairs and had more confidence that an Adventurers' settlement would eventually take place than did the gloomier investors he relieved of their future entitlements.

The market for Irish land was similar to the disorderly trade in British Crown Lands, formerly owned by Charles I and his family and distributed mainly to army officers in lieu of their arrears of pay. Parliament had established a committee in 1643 to collect rents from the king's estates, which included the Adventurers Denis Bond, Cornelius Holland and John Pym. The amounts at the disposal of this committee were modest compared with the more powerful committees such as the Committee for Compounding, but it did become a useful source of patronage.[37] Throughout the Civil Wars, most Adventurers chose not to buy the king's properties. The same was not true of the army. At an equivalent scale to the Irish land settlement, soldiers had recently exchanged £497,000 worth of debentures for these properties.[38] Allocations were made of debentures, the vouchers for repayment, on a non-competitive basis, meaning that there was normally only one officer competing for an estate. The nominal value of the land was disregarded and it was simply divided up among the officers with little attention paid to the value of individual parcels. The task of identifying crown lands was left to former officers in exchange for a bounty and no effort was made to create a market with standard values for the crown lands.[39] In Ireland, by contrast, all attempts to oblige soldiers to accept their pay in land or to exchange their arrears for land used the Irish Adventure rates to establish a value. The two groups, soldiers and Adventurers, pressed their claims in parallel and the Adventurers were left to organise their own settlement out of the lands allocated to them with a new Adventurers' committee appointed in September 1653.[40]

The reformed committee reflected the power the Adventurers retained, despite the events of May 1653. Thomas Andrews, William Pennoyer and Maurice Thomson were members, as was Sir David Watkins, the former secretary to both the Adventurers' and parliament's Committees for Irish Affairs. They were joined by Michael Herring, former treasurer of the Committee for Compounding, Thomas Vincent, former secretary of Goldsmiths' Hall, Samuel Avery, governor of the Merchant Adventurers of England, Richard Waring, the former treasurer at Goldsmiths' Hall, Thomas Foote, the former excise commissioner and the irrepressible Sir John Clotworthy, returned from an exile suffered in 1648 and anxious to protect his investments in Ulster. The merchants who stepped down from the old committee were the trio of Stephen Estwick, Thomas Noel and William Hobson, formerly the treasurers for the sale of Dean and Chapter lands, a market most of the leading Adventurers had kept away from. A struggle was underway for control over the Atlantic sugar trade, for which Estwick, Noel and Hobson had begun to compete with the group centred on Maurice Thomson.

On 4 July, Cromwell replaced the Rump with a Nominated Parliament, and this body finally passed, on 26 September 1653, 'An Act for the Speedy and Effectual Satisfaction of the Adventurers for Lands in Ireland … and of the Arrears of the Soldiery There', reflecting the wishes of Cromwell and the army-dominated committee.[41] This new act called for a committee of trustees to be established in Dublin, headed by Sir Hardresse Waller, a major-general in Cromwell's invasion force, and comprising Colonel Daniel Abbott, Colonel Thomas Sadlier, Major Anthony Morgan, Vincent Gookin, a Munster landowner, William Petty, the army's chief medical officer, and Myles Symner, a mathematician from Trinity College Dublin.[42] Most of the work of the trustees was undertaken initially by Gookin, Petty and Symner, until Gookin's election to the parliament of 1654 and his departure for London.[43] The Committee for Settling Claims was thus taken away from Benjamin Worseley's survey office and placed in the hands of a separate body controlled by the army. He was reduced to the unenviable position of being responsible for the survey of confiscated land, but not for its distribution.

The Commissioners for Settling Claims moved quickly to complete their initial surveying work on behalf of the army, leaving the Adventurers, in some disarray, to appoint agents in Ireland to determine the extent of the territories they had been allocated.[44] Before any surveying work could take place, it was first necessary to determine which lands were subject to forfeiture under the terms of the Act for Settling Ireland of November 1652. A working group was established on 16 November 1653, comprised of Richard Laurence, Dr Henry Jones, William Ivory, Thomas Hook, Isaac Dobson, Henry Markham and Robert Dayley, all based in Ireland and with knowledge of the country, to review the work of an ongoing 'Dublin Survey' into Irish guilt as defined by this act. The 'Dublin Survey' was to remain a secret, only reported to the commissioners who would then make recommendations to the trustees.[45] On 21 November, the parliamentary commissioners in Dublin issued orders to survey the largest prize, the estates of the earl of Ormond.[46] This survey was ordered independently of the elaborate bureaucracy then being established to administer an overall land settlement. By surveying Ormond's estates first, the parliamentary commissioners were making an important symbolic gesture. Landowners in Ireland were forced to understand that all supporters of the royalist cause, irrespective of their religion, were to suffer the forfeiture of their estates, beginning with the king's former Lord Lieutenant. The Adventurers in London were quickly forced to realise that as they were only entitled to Catholic owned land, forfeited under the terms of the Adventurers' Act, the Dublin authorities could do whatever they liked with the estates of Protestant royalists. Not only would they begin forthwith the process of distributing land to soldiers, they were in no particular hurry to measure the Catholic estates as they would continue to collect rent from the remaining tenants. Further instructions were issued the same day to determine the value of the lands and to create a list of all tenants and employees of the estate. Taken together, these orders anticipate the later Civil Survey, conducted across most of the country.[47]

Two further orders were issued the same day, 21 November 1653. The first was to Roger Lord Broghill, Colonel Richard Laurence, Colonel Arthur Hill, Dr Henry Jones, Benjamin Worseley and Jenkin Lloyd to design the instructions for the transplantation of the Catholic Irish to Connaught.[48] For the Cromwellian authorities, these preparations were essential in order to clear the land in time for their envisaged plantation of English soldiers and settlers throughout the country. The inclusion of Worseley on this committee ensured that the Surveyor General could inform the rest of the committee how much land in Connaught could be awarded to the transplanted. The final preparatory commission was to examine titles and certify that the forfeiting landowner had legal title to their estate, ensuring that it could be seized and reallocated without a challenge.[49] Once these preliminary committees of investigation were all in place, the commission to undertake the first major Cromwellian survey of Irish land, the Gross Survey, was issued on 26 November 1653. This was in advance of the Adventurers' lottery on 24 January 1654, to determine in which Irish baronies they would ultimately draw their parcels of land.[50] This well-coordinated set of instructions indicates that the aim of the Cromwellian authorities was to clear the land of its inhabitants. The owner of the land was to be identified and their guilt established. The land was then to be cleared of its inhabitants, measured and redistributed proportionally to its new owners.

Far from being a unifying effort, the Gross Survey was derived from an ordinance of 26 September 1653, specifically to determine whether or not the Adventurers, who had conducted their own survey, had been allocated more land than they were entitled to.[51] Despite the careful planning, the Cromwellian land settlement had already become a fierce competition for spoils between the military government in Dublin and the Adventurers. The first team to work specifically on the Gross Survey was comprised of army officers working under the direction of a surveyor, Nicholas Holland, in County Cork. Once again, the army was pre-empting the Adventurers' settlement as Cork was not part of the ten county scheme. Instructions immediately followed to survey additional areas, each surveyor leading a team of military officers and prominent local landowners, who also doubled as commissioners for determining the delinquency of the Irish for transplantation.[52]

The additional surveying work should not have been unexpected, as by July 1653 it had already become evident that the selected counties would be insufficient to meet all of the claims emerging for Irish land, and instructions were issued from London to set out additional lands for allocation.[53] What came as a surprise to the Adventurers, however, was that these additional lands, measured separately and entirely outside of the remit of the ten county scheme proposed in the existing acts, were to be mapped. On 30 November, instructions were issued, the first to Nathan Pickles, surveyor, to receive the gross surveys of the baronies of Duhallo, Kilmore and Orrery in County Cork, and to convert the surveys into maps. Each parcel of forfeited land was numbered and carefully measured using instruments and chains.[54] It was expensive and detailed work, a sign that the Dublin commissioners meant to keep control of their part of the land settlement, and far superior in detail to the Gross Survey being produced to allocate lands within the ten counties to soldiers and Adventurers. On 10 January 1654, the Dublin Commission for Setting out Lands issued instructions for the allocation of lands in County Cork to favoured officers, in advance both of the completion of the other surveys and of the Adventurers' first lottery.[55]

The Gross Survey made its preliminary report on 19 December 1653, returning the total areas of the baronies contained in the ten counties originally allocated for soldiers' and Adventurers' claims: Antrim, Armagh, Down, Laois, Limerick, Offaly, Meath, Tipperary, Waterford and Westmeath.[56] It was a remarkable feat of surveying, performed over a period of four weeks. There was no mention of the mapped survey of Cork that was then ongoing. The surveyors reported that the country was generally laid waste and that the true owners of each parcel of land could not possibly be determined in such a short space of time. As the counties contained only slightly over two million acres of land, the minority of which was Catholic owned, it was also impossible that all of the claims could be met from these counties alone. Additional instructions to survey further counties were issued the following day, 20 December, to encompass the baronies of Monaghan, Trough, Dartree and Cremorne in Monaghan, together with County Fermanagh. A more realistic completion date of 20 June 1654 was allowed for this part of the Gross Survey. These additional areas, again, were not part of the ten county scheme and no plans were announced to begin the process of making a detailed survey of the land to be shared between Adventurers and soldiers.

The only forfeited lands initially allocated by the Dublin Commission to claimants were from the estates identified in the mapped survey of additional counties. Furthermore, a vague catch-all in an ordinance of June 1654 that 'all Counties, Baronies and Places returned or certified in or by miswritten, mistaken or wrong names, shall be enjoyed by those whose Lots are or shall be on such Counties, Baronies or Places, as if they had been certified by their true and proper names'.[57] From this it is clear that a free-for-all had taken place, nobody really knew who was entitled to what lands or even in what county some of the lands were supposed to be located. As the soldiers' lottery ran its course, soldiers objected and claimed different estates. In other cases, the amounts of land allocated were wrong, there were cases of fraud and forgery and a habit by the Council of Officers of pulling rank on the Committee for Setting out Lands, awarding grants to favoured applicants.[58] The result of these preliminary surveys and allocations was that before any formal assignment of lands had taken place, the Council of Officers had already distributed some of the choicest parcels to their friends and favoured creditors. Two lists of the best land within the ten counties were in circulation, one derived from the inquisitors sent down by the Committee for Setting out Lands and another prepared by the Adventurers' surveyors.[59] With no clear way of determining what each parcel was even called, let alone its area, the land settlement was at risk of descending into chaos.

In September 1654, the Adventurers in London decided to press their claims for land by conducting their own lottery to identify individual parcels. Just as they might when financing a voyage, the Adventurers organised themselves into consortia and nominated an agent to draw lots for the respective groups.[60] A preparatory lottery of January 1654 had allocated specific baronies to Adventures and these lots had already been exchanged and traded between the Adventurers in considerable numbers. The purpose of the second lottery in September 1654 was to determine where in each barony the Adventurers' allocations would translate into land. The wealthier Adventurers, who had conducted their own surveys, knew precisely where the most valuable land was located within each barony. After a wait of twelve years, this lottery would determine the profitability of each speculation, and the leading Adventurers were not about to submit to the vagaries of drawing names out of a hat. The most powerful Adventurers manipulated the process to ensure that it was not random at all. Agents appointed by the Adventurers aggregated the debentures for their clients and arranged for each collection to be drawn from the same barony. This ensured that all the lots drawn for each consortium were adjacent to one another, or to the estate of a potential purchaser, facilitating the aggregation of larger estates.

Consequently, Sir John Clotworthy's adventure was conveniently drawn in Massareene barony, County Antrim, adjacent to his existing land. Maurice Thomson also drew in Massareene, and by a somewhat implausible coincidence he drew the land of the earl of Antrim, against whom a Thomson/Corsellis financial consortium still held a large outstanding mortgage. Adventurers with an active interest in Irish land tended to draw on behalf of those who saw their Adventures as investments. Thomas Vincent, who had already purchased an Irish peerage for his daughter, also drew for Maurice Thomson and other merchants. William Jessop, the earl of Warwick's long-standing business manager in London, drew for the old Providence Island group or their descendants, including Alexander Pym and the Barringtons.[61] The Adventurers had figured out how to game the lottery. The lots were drawn in Grocers' Hall, but the registration for each allocation was recorded by

George Almery, one of the original Adventurers, at his office in Old Jewry. It was a short walk from one to the other, but long enough to do a deal over a slip of paper. The surviving record is of the registrations and not the results of the lottery, and it provides valuable evidence for the composition of merchant groups during the Cromwellian Protectorate.[62] Ireland's fate was determined by these associations, and not by chance.

With the registration of individual land parcels in September 1654, the Adventurers had a reasonably good idea where their new land would be located. By December, however, William Petty of the Committee for Setting out Lands had convinced the General Council of Officers in Dublin that a new survey of forfeited lands was required and would take several years to complete. This was a major setback for the Adventurers. They continued to employ two surveyors of their own, Captain Robert Newcomen and William Perkinson, to survey the Adventurer allotments, but Petty was awarded a lucrative contract to conduct the official survey, known as the Down Survey.[63] Benjamin Worseley, the Surveyor General who had previously worked with the Adventurers on the Council of Trade, had also completed a major survey, now known as the Civil Survey. Worseley had taken a pragmatic approach, using existing deeds and local juries to obtain reasonable estimates of the owner, area and value of each parcel of forfeited land. Parts of Petty's Down Survey were simply copied from either Worseley's Civil Survey or from the earlier Strafford Survey, 1636–38, taken to assist the work of Wentworth's Commission for Defective Titles.[64] Despite the quality of Worseley's work, however, it was essential for the Council of Officers to undermine the Adventurers' surveyors and have an army surveyor, Petty, in control of the process of allocating land and adjudicating on claims. Worseley had his defenders: on 3 June 1657 Lady Ranelagh lobbied Lord Broghill to ensure that Worseley remain in his post, but the bickering and delays continued.[65] An ordinance of 9 June gave Petty the right to re-survey the Adventurers' allotments and to verify that the Adventurers' figures agreed with his own.[66] The suspicion was that the Adventurers had under-declared the land they had measured. As a compromise, both Worseley's and Petty's surveys were ordered to be housed in the High Court of Exchequer, ensuring that neither man had custody of all of the survey material. Almost three years had passed since the Adventurers had drawn their final lots, but hardly any land had been awarded.

NEW ALLIANCES

As the slow surveying work and opportunistic granting of lands was taking place in Ireland, the rift that had opened up between the Adventurers and Cromwell following the quarrel of 20 May 1653 continued to widen, and new alliances began to form. The most significant of these was the deepening relationship between the Adventurers and their former rivals among the royalists. The Adventurers had continued their takeover of the East India Company and by November 1652 Maurice Thomson, Thomas Andrews, Samuel Moyer and Thomas Smith were managing the company. Moyer's main task was to present petitions to the Council of State on the Company's behalf including one, signed by Smith, Moyer and William Cockayne, seeking to prohibit any private voyages by independent English merchants to the Indies.[67] On 18 May 1653, the eve of the Adventurers' confrontation with Cromwell, the royalist Sir Jacob Garrard was added to the Court of the Company. There was little to distinguish how the Company ran from how it had operated prior to the Civil War, apart from the addition of Adventurers to its governing councils. It still maintained its monopoly, and lobbied aggressively to preserve it. After May 1653, imports of saltpetre were managed by Samuel Moyer, but the Adventurers with their new royalist friends managed the remainder of the business.[68] A similar process had taken place within the Levant Company, and it had fallen under the control of William Pennoyer, John Foulke and Richard Chambers by 1656, alongside such royalist luminaries as Sir John Wylde, Nicholas Sandys and George Smith, the son of Sir Thomas Smith.[69]

By a somewhat tortuous route, royalist English merchants became involved in both the Caribbean sugar business and the slave trade in the aftermath of the execution of Charles I. Helpless in the face of continuous losses to Dutch privateers, in 1649 the Portuguese government established the Portuguese Brazil Company in Lisbon to organise a convoy system between Portugal and the Americas.[70] Portuguese naval power was limited to protecting its East India trade and a convoy system was urgently needed to protect Portuguese Atlantic interests. Lacking sufficiently well-armed merchant shipping of its own, the new Portuguese company chartered larger ships from the royalist English, who were anxious to be seen to support their Portuguese allies and also to disrupt the parliamentarian merchants' dominance of the English colonies. This strategy had been successful and the Dutch naval threat in Brazil was removed, but the English ships were seized by a parliamentarian squadron in March 1650, sparking a diplomatic row. These English merchants were led by the governor of the English East India Company, William Cockayne, and Oliver St John, a parliamentarian with extensive Irish landed interests.[71] One threat, taken seriously by the Cromwellian authorities, was that the powerful English fleet aiding the Portuguese would simply take over the enormously valuable Brazilian slave trade, transforming the finances of the royalist cause.[72] This worry encouraged a diplomatic agreement between the Protectorate and the king of Portugal, removing the imposition of unfriendly tariffs on English parliamentarians in Portuguese ports. The convoying arrangement came to an end in 1654, its work completed when the Portuguese retook their colony from the Dutch. From their shared experience in the slave trade, the global trade of the Adventurers and their former royalist adversaries now overlapped to a considerable degree.

While the Adventurers who had protested against the dissolution of parliament became closer to their old royalist adversaries, a smaller group stepped into English state finance. Led by the Noel brothers, Thomas and Martin, and Thomas Povey, this group attempted to seize control of the Barbados sugar trade and, with it, the money supply. The main problem for Noels and Povey was that as Maurice Thomson's circle effectively controlled much of the English transatlantic merchant fleet, their only realistic alternative was to revert to Dutch merchant shipping. From the perspective of the new English merchant group, this arrangement was less than satisfactory as the Dutch shipping network that serviced the English colonial trade operated through the port of New Amsterdam. The Dutch merchants involved in this carrying trade circulated around Zeagar Corsellis, who became a kinsman of Maurice Thomson when Corsellis's nephew married Thomson's daughter.[73] There was really no way to keep England's colonial trade away from Thomson's increasingly long reach.

All of the leading English merchants, the Protectorate merchants led by the Noels and Povey, and the Adventurers led by Maurice Thomson, had competing interests on Barbados. Both groups had family and an extensive network of planter clients on the island. Opening the sugar business to Dutch as well as to English merchants had a galvanising effect on the island's economy and in 1654 the Barbados land market, which had been moribund following the disturbances of 1651, suddenly sprang back into life.[74] 1654 is also when the first reports began to appear of integrated plantations with their own sugar mills and hundreds of African slaves.[75] The sugar boom exacerbated a labour shortage, caused partly by the old ban on Dutch traders, but also by the failure of the Gambian slaving expedition of 1651. While Dutch slave traders began immediately to fill this gap, a further solution was found in Ireland where an established practice of shipping convicts to the colonies as unfree labour was extended to all Irish Catholics who had yet to transplant.[76] These efforts were led by no less a figure than Lord Broghill, who, acting as a factor for the earl of Suffolk, organised the transport of 300 men to Antigua in August 1655.[77] The Irish transportations brought the first profits the Adventurers' leadership had made from Cromwell's victory in Ireland. William Hawkins decided to remain in Ireland after Cromwell's departure and was appointed High Sherriff for Cork with the power to commit captives to the transportations ships.[78] Irish servants were typically sold on the island for £10–£13, half of the cost of African slaves at the Dutch slave market at Pernambuco, the largest nearby source of unfree labour.[79] Thousands of people were captured and shipped from Ireland until the trade was reduced, if not entirely banned, in March 1657 to prevent the accidental capture and consignment of English settlers in Ireland as well.[80]

To solve this problem of a shortage of unfree labour, Maurice Thomson turned again to his new royalist allies and sold his shares in the Guinea Company to the East India Company.[81] This merger, through William Cockayne and his contacts in the Portuguese Brazil Company, gave the Adventurers access to the slave markets of southern Africa and the Irish captive trade ceased to be of interest.

The Adventurers continued to ship large quantities of sugar from the Caribbean region, but due to the suspension of the Navigation Act the Dutch returned quickly to dominate the carrying trade once again. The Dutch West India Company was re-capitalised by the Dutch East India Company in 1649 and reasserted its control over the African slave trade to Spanish America and the Caribbean.[82] In Dutch hands, most Barbadian sugar then made its way to the sugar refineries of Amsterdam, not London. Although the Council of State intended that Dutch shipping would be a simple replacement for Adventurer-owned vessels, instead of shipping Virginia tobacco to London, the Dutch simply shipped it to their port of New Amsterdam and from there to a European port of their choice.[83] The free trade approach greatly benefited the colonies, increasing sugar volumes substantially and, through competition, maintaining prices.[84] For the Adventurers and their new royalist allies, the policy had the opposite effect. They had long since reduced or abandoned their interests in plantations. They relied on the carrying trade in sugar and their monopoly of the English slave trade to take profits from the region. The suspension of the Navigation Act had two further consequences for England: reducing customs and currency receipts from colonial production, and reinvigorating the Dutch merchant navy in spite of England's victory in the first Anglo-Dutch war.

The Atlantic trade had begun to have an impact on other areas of the English economy, which was still orientated towards manufacturing cloth. English cloth quickly became central to the slave trade, replacing iron that was in great demand for the Protectorate's naval cannons. One African person on the Gold Coast could be purchased for approximately two bales of perpetuanos, a type of hard woollen cloth.[85] The cost of manufacturing this quantity of cloth in England was less than ten pounds in 1659.[86] Demand for English cloth provided the means to purchase the 31,364 Africans imported as slaves into Barbados in the 1650s, in response to the labour demands of the sugar boom.[87] This formed a circular trade of English cloth for African slaves who made Barbadian sugar for the European markets. The quantity of sugar produced in Barbados doubled from 3,750 tons in 1651 to 7,787 tons in 1655.[88] The 'farm gate' price for sugar in Barbados in the mid-1650s was approximately twenty shillings per hundredweight, or £20 per ton, making a total of £155,740 paid to the Barbadian planters annually in manufactured goods, slaves or money. This trade, which the Adventurers would have dominated had the Navigation Act been enforced, was given away instead to Dutch merchants.[89]

Due to casualties, the final battle of the first Anglo-Dutch war in 1653 at Texel was commanded by a former army commander, George Monck, promoted to General at Sea. At the outbreak of the Irish rebellion in October 1641, Monck was a royalist colonel under James Butler, earl of Ormond, and commanded a contingent of Irish soldiers brought over to fight in England by Charles I. After a period of imprisonment, Monck fought in both Ireland and Scotland for Cromwell, who, after Texel, appointed him commander-in-chief in Scotland. Monck's main contact with the Adventurers was as first cousin of Thomas Smith, himself both an Adventurer and long-standing business partner of Maurice Thomson. This connection explains how Monck had no difficulty getting paid throughout both his army and later navy career, when many of his payments were approved by George Thomson. Monck's naval role came to an end when the Anglo-Dutch war was formally ended with the Treaty of Westminster on 5 April 1654, and the Adventurers' close partner took up his position of considerable power in Edinburgh.

The Treaty of Westminster was negotiated by William Thomson, brother to Maurice and George, with three others at Skinners' Hall in London. England's main concession was formally admitting the Dutch to free trade with the colonies, not really a concession at all as the Council of State had previously set the Navigation Act aside. In return, the Dutch agreed to exclude Charles II from their territories, making it more difficult for the exiled king to raise finances. William Thomson's additional goal in these negotiations was to secure massive reparations for damages caused by the Dutch East India Company to English shipping since 1621. Having acquired both the Courteen franchise in the 1640s and the residual rights to the early EEIC voyages in 1653, Maurice Thomson and his partners became entitled to any possible Dutch reparations for earlier damages. On their behalf, William Thomson claimed fl48,900 for damage to EEIC ships, fl50,000 for the loss of their Jakarta factory, fl20,000 for stock, and sundry other items making a total of fl195,000. A further fl10,000 was added for the Courteen Association losses. After protracted negotiations, the Dutch agreed to compound for these losses on 7 August 1654 and compensation was paid through trustees: Thomas Andrews, Thomas Kerridge, John Oldfield, Thomas Burnell, Anthony Bateman and John Dyke. Therefore, and with some irony, the Dutch East India Company provided much of the finance for the expansion of its English counterparts. Also to the English Company's advantage was that the reparations could be kept in Amsterdam until required, away from possible arbitrary taxes or a forced loan to the Protectorate. With fl205,000 in the Bank of Amsterdam and no obligation to tie up their winnings in state finance, the Adventurers were free, while the arguments over their Irish land entitlements were ongoing, to concentrate on trade.

Although they controlled much of the English state's financial machinery in April 1653, by 1654 the Adventurers had surprisingly little money tied up in state debt. As a direct consequence of the argument between the Adventurers and Cromwell, and their dismissal from state positions, the Council of State had ordered a survey to be made of all outstanding loans secured on the public faith.[90] This accounting exercise tabulated 1,225 individual debts outstanding since before the Council of State was appointed in February 1649, and a further 300 loans made since its foundation.[91] Parliament's sales of royal, church and delinquent assets had enabled the repayment of much debt and as the Adventurers were the treasurers for these transactions their friends had been at the front of the queue for repayment. With the exception of the excise, farmed on the Dutch model, most of the amounts outstanding to the Adventurers were very small, £100 or less. All of the larger amounts were owed to royalists who had made loans to parliament in preference to compounding.[92] There is no evidence of any large sums outstanding to the Adventurers from Cromwell's Irish campaigns or the Anglo-Dutch war, with the exception of the land promised under the Adventurers' Act.

The Cromwellian Protectorate, between the dissolution of the Barebones Parliament in December 1653 and the sitting of the First Protectorate Parliament in September 1654, made some efforts to bring the Adventurers back into their fold, although not to the extent of appointing them to senior positions with financial responsibility. The Adventurers' advocate was probably Philip Skippon, appointed major-general for London and Middlesex by Cromwell in 1655 and close to the Protector. In June 1654, a remodelled English High Court of Justice was established to hear trials for treason and a core of Adventurers for Irish land was reappointed as Justices of the High Court.[93] The appointment of, among others, Thomas Allen, Thomas Andrews, Stephen Estwick, George Langham, Maurice Thomson, Richard Shute and John Stone to the bench gave the Adventurers a working majority of the thirteen-member court, with which to dispense justice on the Protector's behalf. One of the Justices' powers was to commute death sentences to transportation to the colonies, opening up a new source of free labour for their sugar plantations.

In August 1654, the Adventurers were also given a prominent role in reforming the church. 'An Ordinance for ejecting Scandalous, Ignorant and Insufficient Ministers and Schoolmasters' sought to further embed the Puritan project.[94] The leadership of the Adventurers in London was entrusted with the task of remodelling the religious life of the capital, and the commissioners included Thomas Andrews, Stephen Estwick, Phillip Skippon and both Maurice and William Thomson. Most of the provincial commissions to reform the church included a strong cohort of Adventurers. This new, civic-minded role was a departure for the almost exclusively trade-orientated merchants and reflects the elevation of the Adventurers into the upper level of civic society. Sir Thomas Viner, a relative newcomer to Grocers' Hall who had become a significant supplier of bullion both to the state and to the EEIC, was elected Lord Mayor of London in 1654. Viner was also invited to join the committee reforming the church in London, a further sign of the growing ties between senior merchants.

These attempts at bridge-building were capped by a major financial concession in favour of the Adventurers' Irish land settlement, 'An Ordinance for the Further Encouragement of the Adventurers for Lands in Ireland …' of June 1654.[95] Total taxation in Ireland was capped at £10,000 per month for two years with small increases over the following two years. The Adventurers could take up possession of lands free from Quit Rent for five years and were to enjoy a free trade zone with England for seven years to promote the economic development of their estates. The valuable land of County Kildare, so far excluded from the land settlement, was made available to settle any outstanding claims with a provision that 23 October 1654 was the last day on which new claims would be accepted. These were extraordinarily generous concessions. The Adventurers were allocated 710,000 acres of land, and at an average quit rent of three pence per acre. As ever, concessions made to the Adventurers meant that the state was desperate for money, and in this case it required finance for the Western Design, the Council of State's grand strategy for conquering Spain's Caribbean colonies and intercepting the treasure fleets travelling from Spanish Central America.[96] There was nothing new in this policy and Spain had worried about English intentions towards their Caribbean possessions since the 1630s.[97] The attraction for the Adventurers was that colonial Spain, with its vast territories, was one of the few colonial markets that remained closed to them. Jamaica was larger than all of the English sugar islands combined, and sugar was the most profitable of all of the Adventurers' business concerns.

From the Adventurers' perspective, as it turned out, the Western Design was a disaster. Two thousand servants taken by Colonel Robert Venables from Barbados to Hispaniola for military service were killed, further exacerbating the labour shortage on the sugar plantations.[98] The fleet was provisioned in the summer of 1654 by Maurice Thomson, whose partners on this occasion were Andrew Riccard, John Limbery, William Williams, Martin Noel, Thomas Aldersey and William Vincent. It was a rare joining of forces by Thomson, a parliamentarian, Riccard, a former royalist, and Noel, the Protectorate's favourite contractor. Already in Barbados, Thomas Noel, Edward Thomson, Thomas Hawkins and John Roberts were put forward as commissioners for the project and the London contractors also proposed names for future governors of Barbados, Nevis, St Kitts, Monserrat and Antigua.[99] The commander of the naval expedition was Sir William Penn, who was paid for his labours with Irish land, while Venables, a veteran of Cromwell's campaign in Ireland, commanded the land forces. Relying on a poorly trained Barbados militia, Venables was unable to wrest Hispaniola, the main goal of the expedition, from Spanish control, leaving thinly populated Jamaica as the sole return from an enormous expense of men and materiel. Penn and Venables were both were imprisoned on their return to England and Jamaica, with its reinforced naval base of Port Royal but little by way of developed plantations, became a new Providence Island, a pirates' refuge used to harass Spanish shipping. Compounding the disaster was a renewed official war with Spain, that included a significant success in the capture of the port of Dunkirk for the Protectorate in June 1658, but resulted in huge maritime losses elsewhere.[100]

THE NEW COMMERCIAL ORDER

Early modern merchants left few memoirs, but a detailed description of their ambitions and the structure of their commercial empires is contained in a petition written by Richard Baker, and presented to parliament in 1659.[101] In an echo of the merchants' petition to parliament in December 1641 in which merchants claimed that they had £1 million at risk in Ireland, the merchants of 1659 claimed that they had lost £800,000 in 1655, impounded in Spain as soon as news of the attack on Jamaica reached Philip IV. Although colonial Spain remained beyond their reach, Spain proper was a key component of their highly complex global trading network. English merchants both exported home-produced cloth and re-exported Newfoundland fish to Spain and were paid in Spanish silver.[102] This silver was the key to purchasing valuable commodities in India and the East Indies, imported from there to England and to the rest of Europe, resulting in the final profits that accrued from this lengthy series of transactions.[103] To a considerable degree, this global trade was a precursor to the triangular slave trade that matured in England after the restoration of Charles II, and a substitute for the Adventurers' lack of access to Spain's colonies. English goods were also exchanged for Spanish tobacco, as England was no longer self-sufficient in that commodity following the switch to sugar production in the Caribbean.[104] The destruction of English merchant shipping by Spanish forces was so catastrophic that in June 1657, in order to prevent the economic collapse of Newfoundland and New England, parliament was again forced to permit the transport of fish in foreign vessels in contravention of the Navigation Act. There were not enough English ships left to maintain the trade and French merchants became the leading suppliers of Atlantic cod to Spain.[105] The vitally important English cloth trade was hit next when Spain embargoed English cloth. Raw English wool of far lower value than woven cloth or finished garments was shipped to Holland for manufacture and re-exported to Spain, presenting Dutch merchants and industry with the windfall profits of England's largest export industry.[106] By the late 1650s, despite losses in the first Anglo-Dutch war, Dutch merchant shipping had risen again to dominate the Atlantic slave and sugar trade, and the English cloth trade. This carrying trade was valued by merchants in England at £500,000 per year and provided employment for thousands of men, it was now at risk of permanent destruction. In addition to costing the merchants their business, the war with Spain and free trade with the Dutch and other European nations was also costing the English state its revenue from customs.[107] In this context, the Adventure for Irish land would appear to be small change if it were treated as a traditional landed proposition in which the new owners acted solely as landlords.

The Adventurers, however, had big plans for Ireland within their vision of an imperial trading network. Ireland had many advantages in terms of a temperate climate, a large population and the comparatively low price of land, which the Adventurers intended to acquire for a mere one-tenth of the cost of land in England. According to their lengthy petition, the Adventurers wanted to convert Ireland into a great centre for raw materials, to supply cheap wool and flax into England, where artisans would convert it into the cloth that was the foundation of early modern England's international trade. Cheap Irish wool would give England a huge competitive advantage in the international market. Large numbers of English tradesmen, desperate for work, had moved to Holland during the Anglo-Spanish war to circumvent the Spanish ban on English cloth. The merchants could see the negative effects of mass skilled emigration from home and their petition demanded the recall of the tradesmen. Skilled manufacturing would stay in England while Ireland would produce the raw commodities, the classic imperial economic structure. Recalling how their last period of extended prosperity coincided with peace between England and Spain in the early seventeenth century, the merchants challenged the Protectorate to bring its war to an end.[108]

THE END OF THE PROTECTORATE

Thanks to Dutch reparations and the successful development of its business since 1654, the EEIC was one of the few English organisations that was replete with cash in 1659. Maurice Thomson had kept a relatively low profile since the rift of May 1653, quietly acquiring Adventures in Irish land and building up both his African slave business and the EEIC. He had not neglected his Irish interests and, on 18 August 1659, moved into banking by underwriting the expansion of Sir William Balfour's estates in County Down.[109] Balfour had served with George Thomson at Edgehill in 1643. Maurice Thomson also sold part of his allocation of land in County Antrim to Hugh Lord Hamilton.[110] Thomson's contacts in Scotland also were on the rise: his old client, Roger Boyle, Lord Broghill, was appointed president of the Council of State in Edinburgh in 1655 and Thomson petitioned Cromwell to ensure that money that he had personally loaned to Broghill would be repaid instead in Irish land. Broghill and Monck worked together to engineer the return of a number of reliable MPs to represent Scotland at Westminster in 1656. First among these was George Downing, the son of Emmanuel Downing, Maurice Thomson's partner in the Cape Ann fishery in Massachusetts.[111] The second New Englander elected was Stephen Winthrop, the son of John Winthrop II, also a partner in the Cape Ann fishery.[112] Monck's most trusted subordinate, and a kinsman, was John Cloberry, a nephew of Oliver Cloberry, Maurice Thomson's partner in the Kent Island project. John Cloberry was engaged to the daughter of Nathaniel Wyche, Thomson's business partner at the Court of Committee of the EEIC.[113]

By 1659, Maurice Thomson was governor of the EEIC and was joined on the company's Court of Committee by his closest partner, William Pennoyer.[114] Other members of that Court included Thomas Smith, Monck's cousin, Samuel Moyer, their interface with the Council of State, William Cockayne, William Vincent and Edward Wood, the son of John Wood, Thomson's long-standing partner in the Guinea Company. The company treasurer was Andrew Riccard. In July 1659, Riccard deposited £16,000 into a scriveners bank operated by Robert Clayton, much of which found its way into accounts opened in the names of Monck and Lord Fairfax.[115] Money continued to flow into Monck's account, and this was loaned to Fairfax to meet his military obligations. After Monck arrived in London in January 1660, his account in Clayton's bank was used to receive payments from the Chamber of London, also used to pay his officers. In 1659, Robert Clayton married Martha Trott, the daughter of a Bermuda Company member, Perient Trott, from whom he received shares in the Bermuda Company as a wedding gift, becoming yet another business partner of Maurice Thomson.[116] In this murky world of early modern banking, the Adventurers were finding ways to make clients once again of their friends in the army, away from the interference of the Council of State or MPs. The Clayton transactions bear a startling resemblance to the early stages of the Adventure for Irish land, during which the Adventurers had used, in 1642, their own private treasury to finance the army used against Charles I.

The Adventurers made no secret of their distaste for the policies of the Cromwellian Protectorate. In February 1659, when parliament was debating an 'act for recognising his highness the Lord Protector and disclaiming the title of Charles Stuart', Samuel Moyer presented a petition on the Adventurers' behalf, protesting against tyranny and calling for free elections.[117] State finances, in stark contrast to the successful expansion of the exchequer during the Adventurers' period of management, were in a disastrous state. The large standing army in Ireland and the enormous cost of maintaining the naval war with Spain, set against no further revenue from the sale of royalist estates, left the Protectorate with an accumulated debt of £2.5 million in April 1659. This debt was expected to grow further at a rate of £383,000 per year.[118] With little hope of collecting their arrears of pay under the Protectorate, the army's Council of

Officers restored the Rump Parliament on 5 May and Richard Cromwell, who had succeeded Oliver in September 1658, abdicated on 25 May 1659.

With the restoration of the Rump came the restoration of its committees and the influence of the Adventurers in the machinery of state. The Adventurers acted quickly to take revenge on their enemies and bring some order to the state's finances. George Thomson returned to a reformed Council of State, along with Sir Henry Vane II, who took over executive responsibility for trade, colonies and taxation.[119] Vane II and George Thomson also took up their old posts as navy commissioners, with instructions to set the navy to the task of convoying English merchant ships on the model of the Portuguese West India Company, in an effort to reduce losses to Spain.[120] Samuel Moyer was assigned the task of sequestering the property of Sir Martin Noel and his partners, who had failed to provide the up-front money promised under the terms of their excise farm.[121] Hoodwinked by the Dutch, ostracised by the Adventurers and broken by the war with Spain, the Noel-led consortium never had the financial resources to operate the excise farm successfully.

In Ireland, the Down Survey and an inquiry to settle the Adventurers' claims were incomplete when the Protectorate was overthrown, putting the stuttering land settlement into disarray once again. A reconstituted parliamentary Committee for Irish Affairs, led by Sir Arthur Hesilrige, Sir Henry Vane II and General George Fleetwood, summoned Sir Hardresse Waller to London and promoted Colonel John Hewson in his place as commander-in-chief of the army in Ireland. Benjamin Worseley was appointed commissary general in charge of all Irish military supplies, wresting control from the Noel-led consortium and returning this business to the Adventurers.[122] The Adventurers' claims for Irish land, however, were far from secure as the original allocations had been made, and the ten county scheme constructed, according to instructions made by the interim Council of State in 1653 and not by king or parliament. The receipts from 1642 were under an authority 'according to certain Propositions made for the speedy reducing of the Rebells of Ireland, and confirmed by the assent of his Majesty, and of the Lords and Commons in Ireland'.[123] Lands allocated according to subscriptions received under the Doubling Ordinance of July 1643 were also guaranteed by the state, albeit only 'according to the tenor and effect' of the relevant ordinances. Subscriptions made to the Additional Sea Adventure, lacking both a royal commission and a parliamentary ordinance appointing a treasurer, had no secure legal foundation. The important pieces of legislation determining the Adventurers' claims to Irish land were all passed by the successors to the Long Parliament, or by the Council of State. In abjuring the Protectorate, the Adventurers had placed their own land settlement in doubt. A possible solution was to present all of the legislation – English ordinances, declarations of the Council of State, regulations and decisions of the various commissions in Dublin and sundry awards – to parliament for debate and, hopefully, an overarching Irish land settlement act could be passed against which letters patent could be awarded. This was a strategy not without risk. A possible alternative, as the Adventurers Act was signed both by parliament and Charles I, was a royal proclamation. Such a solution would require the restoration of Charles II.

RESTORATION

In an almost exact reprise of the events of the first weeks of January 1642, on 14 July 1659 the Adventurers took advantage of local elections to seize control of all of London's militias. Maurice Thomson, Thomas Chamberlain, William Hobson, Francis Reynolds, Benjamin Andrews and John Brookhaven formed the core of the militia committee for Tower Hamlets.[124] The Southwark Militia, on the south side of the Thames, fell under the control of George Thomson, Nathaniel Rich, Maurice Craddock, James Child and William Hickock. The leadership of the Middlesex Militia comprised Robert Thomson, Francis Allein, William Baker, Chaloner Shute and Charles Fleetwood.[125] William Thomson sat on the militia committee for Westminster alongside some of the Adventurer MPs. The command for London's militias, the Committee of Safety, comprised William Pennoyer, Thomas Andrews, Thomas Foote, Stephen Dethwick, Francis Allein, William Thomson, Thomas Vincent, Richard Bateman and William Harrington.[126] Thomas Andrews was elected Lord Mayor. The Adventurers for Irish land, therefore, took control of the defence of London and of access to MPs. On 3 November, General John Lambert began his march north to intercept the forces of George Monck, on their way to London. The Adventurers, acting under the authority of Thomas Allen, who had replaced Thomas Andrews as Lord Mayor after Andrews's untimely death, quashed any dissent from the Court of Aldermen or the Common Council. Political leadership on London's representative councils was provided by William Pennoyer, John Dethwick, Robert Bateman and Richard Waring.[127] A letter was sent to Monck on 29 December 1659, in the name of the Lord Mayor, Aldermen and Common Council, formally renouncing the Protectorate and inviting the general to approach the city.[128] Monck's initial invitation to London was, therefore, the work of the Adventurers, as parliament's formal invitation was not approved and despatched to the general until 6 January 1660 and was merely falling into line with the Adventurers' initiative.[129]

The war with Spain had gone from bad to worse and English merchants claimed to have lost 1,800 ships during the war with Spain, although this was not entirely one-way traffic as England also recorded the capture of 550 prize ships.[130] The Adventurers' gloom was compounded by several deaths at the apex of their leadership pyramid, particularly the earl of Warwick in March 1658 and Thomas Andrews in August 1659. By then, however, the Adventurers no longer required noble patrons and they placed their own men at the heart of government. William Jessop, the former Providence Island Company's secretary, became clerk for the Council of State in March 1660 and John Thomson, Maurice's son, was appointed joint secretary of state in March 1660, alongside John Thurloe.[131] George Thomson was also in frequent attendance as a prominent member of the Council of State. Sir Arthur Annesley, John Thomson's future father-in-law, was president. The attention of the Council of State was turned to Monck's finances, supposedly maintained by Martin Noel as farmer of the excise for inland commodities, but now abandoned by Noel and supported instead with secret payments from the Clayton accounts.[132] Repayment agreements with creditors stretched out to several months as the Council of State found funds increasingly difficult to come by. The largest of these debts was for £20,000, payable to George Monck by 21 March 1660, and late.[133] The collection of the Scottish assessment had become impossible due to a shortage of currency as the war with Spain cut off new supplies of currency.[134]

The declaration of Breda, issued from exile by Charles II on 4 April 1660, contained no specific mention of Ireland in the text, but did include a willingness to look favourably on soldiers who had accepted payment in forfeited land.[135] This at least opened the door to negotiating with the exiled king for the settlement of the Adventurers' claims. The Adventurers were in an advantageous position regarding sequestered private estates, church and crown properties in England. For reasons either of strategy or distaste, most of the Adventurers had kept out of these sales and the largest purchaser among their leadership, Thomas Andrews, who invested £10,000, was dead. The Adventurers' land purchases had been in the form of fee-farms, a financial instrument that involved buying future rent at a discount and making a profit, over time, on the difference. Almost all of the fee-farm purchases were of ten years in duration and were at the point of expiration. The profit had been made. The Adventurers were not at risk of losing their gains in the event of the king's return, as long as their entitlements in Ireland were not thrown into question. General Monck was in a similar position to the Adventurers as he was also not a purchaser of crown or church land, but had been granted lands in Ireland worth £4,000 per annum.[136] In this area, the interests the Adventurers and Monck coincided. The Common Council elected for London in December 1659 included no purchasers of crown or church lands, despite nineteen of the twenty-four alderman in London having such holdings.[137] Maurice, William and Robert Thomson had kept out of the delinquent land market in England, while George Thomson had a mere £1,100 invested in Southwark. Stephen Estwick and John Foulke had each invested £3,000 but could probably afford to lose the residual value once the rents had been offset. Although a £3,000 loss was a fortune to a common councillor, it was a manageable sum for the giants of international trade. The Adventurers could afford to be generous with their English land.

The Adventurers were in a similarly advantageous position with state finance. They had disengaged from providing money to the Protectorate and 'openly refused' a request by Cromwell for a loan in March 1658.[138] Samuel Vassall, owed £20,000 by the state, was made bankrupt in 1656 and sent to prison, where he was joined by Samuel Avery.[139] Sir Thomas Viner, Thomas Foote, John Dethwick and Christopher Pack had made small loans, but these were quickly repaid once the Rump was restored. The Adventurers could not expect the restored king to honour the debts of the Protectorate, but some were still owed significant sums by the Long Parliament, outstanding since 1647.[140] Samuel Langham, John Dethwick, Sir David Watkins, Michael Herring and Benjamin Whetcomb were each owed up to £4,000. In addition, £76,000 was outstanding to suppliers of the navy. These are small sums given that the overall debt of the Protectorate was £2.5 million, but hardly pocket change.[141] As was the case with English sequestered land, the Adventurers, should they have to negotiate with the restored king, could afford to be forgiving concerning the debts of the Cromwellian Protectorate. Whomever the £2.5 million was owed to, very little of it was owed to them.

In any case, the Adventurers had to make a deal, and quickly, as international trade, already in a perilous state, was about to take a turn for the worse. To maintain their supply of silver, essential for what remained of the East India trade, the Adventurers were now dependent on Dutch shipping. This arrangement was convenient for Dutch merchants, but the outcome of the first Dutch War had not left the two nations as friends. Although it could count Portugal as a minor ally, England's sole major ally in Europe was France, whose ruler, Louis XIV, was about to enter into a marriage with Infanta Maria Theresa of Spain. France and Spain made peace with the Treaty of the Pyrenees, on 7 November 1659.[142] The loss of their French ally, and with it French naval protection, would mean the end of the Adventurers' global trading ambitions. Their Atlantic colonies would come under attack from all sides: from Spain and the Netherlands in the Caribbean and from France and the Netherlands in New England. For the Adventurers, this was a nightmare scenario over which they had no influence at all. There was no possibility that a small fleet could make the long journey to India and back without encountering the ships of one of the three strong maritime nations. State diplomacy, however, was not a skill that the Adventurers had developed. England had been a virtual pariah state for almost two decades and the Adventurers had managed international relations either through privateering or by using local factors in ports where there was mutually beneficial business to be conducted. The Bourbon and Habsburg courts were far removed from Grocers' Hall and the meeting rooms at Trinity House.

For the Adventurers, only one person had any chance of resolving their two most pressing problems, the security of their Irish land settlement and the survival of their trading empires. This person was the exiled king, Charles II, whom they had so far refused to recognise.

Urgent as the Adventurers' need was to approach Charles II, devising a strategy to make contact with him would not be easy. From the perspective of Charles II, the Adventurers had been instrumental in ejecting his father from London and had stood aside while he was executed. Maurice Thomson may have met Charles II, and had certainly met his advisers, when Thomson negotiated the ransom of English merchant shipping from then Prince Charles in 1648. William Thomson also had diplomatic contacts in the Dutch Republic, a legacy of his involvement in negotiating the Treaty of London in 1654. The key English diplomatic figure in The Hague in 1660, however, and the best placed to make an approach to Charles, was one of Monck's MPs from Scotland, George Downing, the Council of State's envoy to Holland. Downing reported to John Thurloe, but as his budget was managed by William Jessop and John Thomson, he had a classic Adventurer pedigree. George Downing's many duties in The Hague included the maintenance of the ban on Charles II visiting Holland, enshrined in the Treaty of Westminster. Downing, however, raised no objection when Charles II moved from Brussels to Breda in March 1660, and by April was referring to Charles in correspondence as 'the King'.[143] Prior to the move to Breda, James Butler, marquis of Ormond, arranged for Downing to be received by Charles, where the diplomat was knighted.[144] Close to Ormond, Downing would provide the necessary link between the Adventurers and Ormond, who could advise the king on the most advantageous position to take with regards to an Irish land settlement.

On 1 May 1660 the Common Council of London received Charles II's Declaration from Breda, and ordered the City's guilds to procure a gift of £10,000 for the king.[145] On the same day, the House of Commons resolved that £50,000 should be raised and presented to Charles on his return a with further £50,000 to be provided to satisfy the army.[146] There was no opposition to the gifts, and no delay in raising the money. On 3 May, the Common Council proposed a delegation comprising of Thomas Adams, William Wilde, Sir John Robinson, William Bateman, Theophilus Biddolph, Thomas Vincent and William Bludworth to present the £10,000 gift to Charles.[147] The planned delegation was swooped upon by the Adventurers and by 5 May had swollen to twenty-two members.[148] Charles was also moving quickly and on 9 May *The Parliamentary Intelligencer* reported that a truce had been negotiated between English and Spanish forces at Dunkirk.[149] At risk of being upstaged by the Common Council, parliament decided that delegations from both the Lords and the Commons would also travel to The Hague with the money. With continued echoes of 1642, the five Lords included Robert Greville, fourth Lord

Brooke and Charles Rich, fourth earl of Warwick, as well as Denzell Holles with twelve additional MPs.[150] Accompanied by these delegates from parliament, the twenty-two-man strong delegation from the City of London arrived in The Hague on 14 May. Ten of its members were Adventurers for Irish land.[151] A second group had been excluded from their aldermanry during the Second Civil War.[152] The remaining five members were royalist or Presbyterian leaders from the City of London.[153] Several ties had been created between Presbyterian and royalist merchants, and the Adventurers. John Lewis was married to Sarah Foote, daughter of Maurice Thomson's business partner, Thomas Foote. John Robinson's association with Maurice Thomson and the Adventurers began in August 1649 when he sponsored the failed colony at Assada.[154] This partnership was eventually merged by Oliver Cromwell with the 'official' EEIC, bringing the established royalist traders, including Sir Nicholas Crispe, into Thomson's fold.[155] Alderman Anthony Bateman was a brother of William Bateman and William Thomson, the Batemans, Biddolph, Chamberlin and Robinson all sat on London's Committee of Safety, alongside Thomas Foote.[156]

Knighthoods were conferred on all members of the City delegation not already in possession of an honour and Charles II duly arrived in Dover on 25 May 1660. Parliament had begun the process of drafting an act of general pardon, in accordance with the principles set out by Charles's Breda declaration, on 9 May.[157] The Council of State, meanwhile, was winding up its affairs. The final piece of correspondence of the Council of State, the last act of the Interregnum, was signed by Annesley and George Thomson on 26 May 1660, promising money advanced by John Frederick and Thomas Rich to pay for the table and household of Charles II upon his arrival in London.[158] George Thomson and his friends evidently knew what was transpiring at The Hague and what conditions would be imposed by Charles II. As his final move as an MP, George Thomson ordered that Hugh Peter be brought in chains to London.[159] The king required a sacrifice from the Adventurers, and their pastor was chosen for the role. Charles II's declaration concerning Ireland was issued on 1 June and provided for 'the effectual Settling and Confirming of all and every the Estates of Adventurers'.[160] It had taken just days for Charles II to deliver to the Adventurers what the Protectorate had dithered over for seven years.

On 9 June, Charles II signed Maurice Thomson's personal pardon 'for anything done between 10 November 1640 to date' and guaranteed him the 'restitution of all lands, tenements, goods and chattels'.[161] Thomson's pardon, despite his key role in the English Commonwealth, places him at the heart of the efforts to bring about the restoration. Almost everybody else had to wait for their pardons until 29 August, when parliament passed 'An act of Free and General Pardon, Indemnity, and Oblivion' on the same day as it passed 'An Act for the speedy Provision of Money, for disbanding and paying off the

Forces of this kingdom, both by Land and Sea'.[162] There was an unmistakable continuity in how the Adventurers went about their business. The subsequent Act of Oblivion could not have been more tailor-made to the Adventurers' demands, and might as well have been drafted by Thomson himself.[163] Article XLVIII restored all lands to the king and church but left any sequestered or confiscated private lands in the hands of their purchasers. This provision left most of the Adventurers, who had acquired such lands cheaply during the war years, in legal possession of their new estates, but stripped the purchasers of crown and church lands of their spoils. Crucially for the Adventurers, Article XXV excluded from pardon anybody included within the scope of the Adventurers Act of 1642. This comprised almost every Catholic landowner in Ireland.

On 29 December 1660, parliament agreed to honour all of the public debts outstanding from the Long Parliament until 1647 and all of the debts outstanding for supplies made to the navy, but to exclude £95,000 of outstanding public debt incurred between 1652 and February 1660.[164] None of this excluded debt was owed to the Adventurers. In September 1660, while the unmolested EEIC returned from the Indies fully laden with cargo, Charles II ended the war with Spain and confirmed the Navigation Act of 1651. The Adventurers were duly awarded their Irish lands in full by of the Acts of Settlement (1662) and Explanation (1665).[165] Maurice Thomson acquired 1,000 acres around Cong, County Mayo. In addition, he was awarded the County Galway estate of Sir Roger O'Shaughnessy, the Catholic knight whose castle had been destroyed by Thomson's Sea Adventurers in 1642, the Adventurers' first assault on royalist forces. With this transaction, the award of the estate of its first victim into the hands of the leading Adventurer, the Adventure for Irish land was complete.

NOTES

1 CJ, 7, p. 280.
2 CCAM, I, p. 312.
3 C.H. Firth, *The Clarke Papers*, 4 vols (London, 1891–1901), Vol. iii, 4.
4 Firth, *The Clarke Papers*, Vol. iii, p. 5.
5 Peter Gaunt, *The Councils of the Protectorate: From December 1653 to September 1658* (PhD Thesis, University of Exeter, 1983), p. 28. Lambert was appointed lord deputy of Ireland in January 1652, but did not take up the post in opposition to the Rump Parliament's Irish policies. He accompanied Cromwell to the Council of State for its dissolution.
6 TNA SP25/69, f. 86. The other members of the committee were Colonel Robert Bennett, Colonel Philip Jones, Henry Scobell and John Thurloe 'or any three of them'.
7 TNA SP25/69, f. 96.
8 TNA SP25/69, f. 115.

9 British Library, Thomason Tracts, E697/18, f. 107. 'Anon, To his Excellency Oliver Cromwell'.
10 Firth, *The Clarke Papers*, Vol. iii, p. 6.
11 Firth, *The Clarke Papers*, Vol. iii, p. 6; Bernard Alsop, *'A Perfect Account of Intelligence…22–29 June'* (London, 1653).
12 CSPD, 1652–53, pp. 437, 392; D'Maris Coffman, *Excise Taxation and the Origins of Public Debt* (Basingstoke, 2013), p. 138.
13 TNA SP 25/87, f. 51. The appointment for the sale of Dean and Chapter lands was made on 12 May 1649 and the lands valued at £300,000.
14 A&O, ii, 176.
15 TNA SP25/69, ff. 122, 124, 126.
16 TNA SP25/69, f. 135.
17 TNA SP25/69, f. 148.
18 TNA SP25/69, f. 155.
19 TNA SP25/69, f. 158, 159.
20 TNA SP25/69, f. 178.
21 TNA CO 1/12, f. 42. 'The Humble Petition of Merchants in London interested in, and trading to, the Island of Barbados'.
22 TNA SP 63/301, f. 153.
23 TNA SP 63/292, f. 177.
24 TNA SP16/264, f. 30.
25 Robert Dunlop, *Ireland under the Commonwealth: Being a Selection of Documents Relating to the Government of Ireland from 1651–9, Vol. II* (Dublin, 1912), p. 465: Lord Deputy and Council to Mr Maurice Thomson, Mr Pennoyer, Mr Robert Thomson and others.
26 TNA SP25/69, ff. 179–180.
27 TNA SP25/69, f. 190.
28 Ferns Diocesan Archive, FDA/1/52, p. 11.
29 BL Egerton Ms 1762, ff. 92–96.
30 Ferns Diocesan Archive, FDA/1/53, p. 124.
31 NLI, MS. 11959, p. 146.
32 James E. Farnell, 'The Navigation Act of 1651, the First Dutch War, and the London Merchant Community', *Economic History Review*, New Series, 16:3 (1964), pp. 439–454, p. 441.
33 CCAM, I, p. 187.
34 For example, Richard Shute sold his £500 Adventure to the merchant John Mossyer who was aggregating similar mid-size Adventures for presumably similar sums. See Robert Pentland Mahaffy (ed.), *Calendar of State Papers Relating to Ireland Preserved in the Public Record Office: Adventurers for Land, 1642–59* (London, 1903), p. 59.
35 CCAM, pp. 135–137.
36 For Vincent's involvement in Irish estates see Micheál Ó Siochriú and David Brown, 'Survival Strategies in a Time of War: The Blayneys of Monaghan, 1640–1670' in William Nolan and Éamonn Ó Ciardha (eds), *Monaghan History & Society: Interdisciplinary Essays on the History of an Irish County* (Dublin, 2017).

37 See John Adamson, *The Committee for the Revenue*, unpublished essay, courtesy of the History of Parliament Trust.
38 Sidney Madge, *Domesday of Crown Lands: A Study of the Legislation, Surveys, and Sales of Royal Estates Under the Commonwealth* (London, 1938), p. 223. Cromwell, Fleetwood, Fairfax, Ireton and Whalley, among others, dominated this group.
39 Madge, *Domesday of Crown Lands*, p. 224.
40 TNA SP 66/B, f. 26: *Copy of Award of certain Commissioners who are empowered to make Regulations in regard to allotments in different Baronies in Ireland*.
41 BL, Add Ms 35102, 'The Day Book of the Proceedings of the Trustees Appointed for Satisfying of the Armyes Arrears, due for Service in Ireland since ye 6th Day of June 1649: as also English Arrears satisfyable in Ireland, by Act of Parliament', f. 8.
42 BL, Add Ms 35102, f. 9. Miles Symner served as a major in Daniel Abbott's dragoon regiment in Ireland and also clearly belonged to the army faction. See Peter Gaunt (ed.), *The Correspondence of Henry Cromwell* (London, 2007), p. 362n.
43 The work of this committee can be traced through minutes preserved in BL, Add Ms 35102 and correspondence preserved in the Library of the Oireachtas, MS 11D. This committee was responsible for the claims of soldiers in Ireland. The Adventurers' claims were dealt with in London.
44 TNA SP 63/300, f. 222, Letter from William Petty to the Committee of Adventurers sitting at Grocers' Hall [London].
45 NLI, Ms 11959, pp. 321–326.
46 NLI, Ms 11959, p. 288. The surveyors were Jeremy Green, John Brockas and Thomas Hunter.
47 NLI, Ms 11959, pp. 330–332. This work was contracted to Tobiah Wickham, Mr Rawlins, Mr Cornock and William Whalley.
48 NLI, Ms 11959, p. 333.
49 Sir Gerald Lowther, William Basil, Sir John Temple, William Allen and Walter Carwarde.
50 NLI, Ms 11959, p. 335; Karl S. Bottigheimer, *English Money and Irish Land* (Oxford, 1971), p. 143.
51 A&O, II, p. 731.
52 NLI, Ms 11959, p. 349.
53 A&O, II, p. 733.
54 NLI, Ms 11959, pp. 341–344.
55 Library of Kings Inns, Prendergast Ms, II, pp. 572–573.
56 Prendergast Ms, II, p. 358.
57 Prendergast Ms, II, p. 928.
58 BL, Add Ms 72877, ff. 94r–96v.
59 TNA SP 63/301, f. 170: Committee of Adventurers to the Parliament of England. The Adventurers in London were also given the responsibility for approving claims for English debts to be paid with Irish land, expanding further the amounts of land required.
60 This account of the 1654 lottery is given in BL, Add Ms 2648, Barrington Papers, Vol. VIII, ff. 229–235.
61 BL, Add Ms 2648, f. 229.

62 TNA SP 46/130, State Papers Domestic: Supplementary, ff. 64–66, 'List of receipts from adventurers'.
63 John P. Prendergast, *The Cromwellian Settlement of Ireland* (Dublin, 1890), p. 240.
64 Since the destruction of the Public Record Office of Ireland in 1922, the sole surviving complete parish map from the Strafford Survey from which to compare is for Ballingarry Parish, Tipperary, preserved in the Library of the Honorable Society of King's Inns, Dublin.
65 Michael Hunter, Antonio Clericuzio and Laurence M. Principe (eds), *The Correspondence of Robert Boyle*, 6 vols (London, 2001), Vol. 1, p. 216.
66 A&O, II, pp. 1100–1110, 'June 1657: An Act for the assuring, confirming, and settling of Lands and Estates in Ireland'.
67 BL IOR B/25, f. 175.
68 BL IOR B/25, f. 261–262.
69 TNA SP 71/125, f. 9.
70 David Grant Smith, 'Old Christian Merchants and the Foundation of the Brazil Company, 1649', *The Hispanic American Historical Review*, 54 (May, 1974), pp. 233–259.
71 TNA SP 89/4, ff. 120, 108, 110. The English ships were mainly laden with Indian silks and English iron guns, indicating that a slave purchase was to be made on the west coast of Africa before the Atlantic crossing.
72 Leonor Friere Costa, 'Merchant Groups in the 17th Century Brazilian Sugar Trade: Reappraising Old Topics with New Research Insights', *Journal of Portuguese History*, 2 (Summer, 2004), pp. 1–11.
73 Stadsarchief Amsterdam 5026/54DE3, f. 7, Petition of Dutch merchants trading to Virginia and the West Indies detailing their trade with the English colonies during their period of revolt from Parliament, 1649–51.
74 BDA RB3/78–79, *passim*.
75 Russell R. Menard, *Sweet Negotiations, Sugar, Slavery and Plantation Agriculture in Early Barbados* (Charlottsville, VA, 2006), p. 94.
76 IMA, Jennings Notebooks 2, p. 14.
77 IMA, Jennings Notebooks 3, p. 4.
78 IMA, Jennings Notebooks 3, p. 44; TNA PRO 31/17/43, 'Minutes of the Council of Barbados 1654–1658', f. 43.
79 Hilary MacDonald Beckles, *White Labour in Black Slave Plantation Society and Economy: A Case Study of Indentured Labour in Seventeenth Century Barbados* (PhD Thesis, University of Hull, 1980), pp. 147–148.
80 IMA, Jennings Notebooks 4, p. 14.
81 R. Porter, 'The Crispe Family and the African Trade in the Seventeenth Century', *The Journal of African History*, 9:1 (1968), p. 66.
82 Richard S. Dunn, *Sugar and Slaves* (Williamsburg, 1972), pp. 77–108.
83 For a more detailed account of these Dutch trade activities see Jan de Vries, 'The Netherlands in the New World, the Legacy of European Fiscal, Monetary and Trading Institutions for New World Development from the Seventeenth to the Nineteenth Centuries', in Michael D. Bordo and Roberto Cortés-Conde (eds),

Transferring Wealth and Power from the Old to New World (Cambridge, 2001), pp. 100–139.
84 Menard, *Sweet Negotiations*, p. 22.
85 Stephanie Smallwood, *Saltwater Slavery: A Middle Passage from Africa to America Diaspora* (London, 2007), pp. 64–67.
86 Richard Baker, *The marchants humble petition and remonstrance to his late Highnesse, with an accompt of the losses of their shipping, and estates, since the war with Spain. And how as well themselves as strangers have strengthned and enriched both the enemy, and the Hollanders, by the secret trade for the dominions of Spain. And how the national English stock suffers thereby, and by many other trades: as is made out by several demonstrations. ... Of the inquisition; and of the death of the English agent, Mr. Askham: and the prosecution of the murtherers. A general remedy proposed for the restauration of the trade. All most humbly submitted to his Highness, and the most honorable Houses of Parliments consideration* (London, 1659), p. 5.
87 Menard, *Sweet Negotiations*, p. 47.
88 Menard, *Sweet Negotiations*, p. 47.
89 LJ, IX, pp. 49–54. Thomas Andrewes, Elias Roberts, Maurice Thomson, Jeremy Blackman, Thomas Frere, Richard Bateson, William Pennoyer, Lawrence Chambers, Martin Noel, Nicholas Butler, Thomas Cooke and John Vincent.
90 TNA SP25/69, f. 102.
91 For the Council of State see Sean Kelsey, 'The Foundation of the Council of State' in Chris R. Kyle and Jason Peacy (eds), *Parliament at Work: Parliamentary Committees, Political Power and Public Access in Early Modern England* (Woodbridge, 2002), pp. 129–148. The survey of outstanding loans is preserved as TNA SP 19/59 (unfoliated), 'An account of such persons to whom the publicke faith is committed...'.
92 For example, Sir Edward Hales was owed £1,300, John Egerton, 1st earl of Bridgewater, was owed £1,000 and John Bennett £740. The largest amount owed, £2,662, was to Sir George Whitmore, Lord Mayor of London in 1631 and a strong supporter of Charles I who died, unpaid, in December 1654.
93 A&O, II, pp. 917–918, 'June 1654: An Ordinance for Establishing a High Court of Justice'. The appointments were originally made in 1650, but had lapsed after May 1653.
94 A&O, II, pp. 968–990, 'August 1654: An Ordinance for ejecting Scandalous, Ignorant and insufficient Ministers and Schoolmasters'.
95 A&O, II, pp. 924–929, 'June 1654: An Ordinance for the Further Encouragement of the Adventurers for Lands in Ireland, and of the Soldiers and other Planters there'.
96 For the Western Design see Carla Gardina Pestana, 'English Character and the Fiasco of the Western Design', *Early American Studies: An Interdisciplinary Journal*, 3:1 (Spring, 2005), pp. 1–31; Pestana, *The English Conquest of Jamaica: Oliver Cromwell's Bid for Empire* (Cambridge, MA, 2017).
97 ADD MS 36326, Venezuela Papers, f. 204 31 December 1633.
98 CSPD, 1652–1653, pp. 205–208.
99 Thomas Birch (ed.), *A Collection of the State Papers of John Thurloe*, 7 vols (London, 1742), Vol. ii, 542. Riccard was, in 1654, treasurer of the East India Company while Limbery had been a major supplier to the navy prior to 1653.

100 For a further account see John Barratt, *Cromwell's War at Sea* (Barnsley, 2009).
101 Baker, *The marchants humble petition*, passim; Mahaffy, *Adventurers*, p. 124. The Baker family financed the Adventure of £600 paid in by John Crewe, an MP for Northamptonshire.
102 A&O, II, pp. 1099–1100, 'An Act for giving Licence for Transporting of Fish in Forein bottoms'.
103 Baker, *The marchants humble petition*, p. 2.
104 Baker, *The marchants humble petition*, p. 3.
105 A&O, II, p. 1100.
106 Baker, *The marchants humble petition*, p. 4.
107 Baker, *The marchants humble petition*, p. 5.
108 Baker, *The marchants humble petition*, p. 16.
109 PRONI, D1939/15/8/11.
110 PRONI, D1939/15/4/1.
111 Paul J. Pinckney, 'The Scottish Representation in the Cromwellian Parliament of 1656', *Scottish Historical Review*, 46:2 (October, 1967), pp. 95–114 at p. 102.
112 Pinckney, 'Scottish Representation', p. 104. The final partner in St Ann, John Limbery, was actively engaged in a campaign to have the Irish Society's patent for Londonderry renewed by the protectorate. Limbery had helped negotiate the return of the hostage ships from Prince Charles and partially finance the Western Design.
113 www.historyofparliamentonline.org/volume/1660-1690/member/cloberry-john-1625-88 [accessed 1 November 2019].
114 BL IOR B/25, f. 334.
115 Frank T. Melton, *Sir Robert Clayton and the Origins of English Deposit Banking: 1658–1685* (Cambridge, 1986), pp. 58–59. A scriverers' bank was a simple form of deposit banking, used for making deposits and withdrawals, but also for tranfers of money between members of the bank. Clayton's commercial interest in Ireland concerned an iron mine that he operated in Enniscorthy, County Wexford. His partners included Sir Thomas Abdy and John Barrington (NLI, Ms. 325).
116 Melton, *Sir Robert Clayton*, p. 69n. Trott had purchased his Bermuda shares from the estate of the earl of Warwick.
117 Patrick Little and David L. Smith, *Parliaments and Politics during the Cromwellian Protectorate* (Cambridge, 2007), p. 159; Firth, *The Clarke Papers*, Vol. iii, p. 181.
118 CJ, VII, 627–631.
119 A&O, II, pp. 1272–1276, 'May 1659: An Act for Constituting a Councell of State'.
120 A&O, II, pp. 1277–1282, 'May 1659: An Act for Constituting Commissioners for Ordering and Managing the Affairs of the Admiralty and Navy'.
121 A&O, II, pp. 1342–1343, 'August, 1659: An Act appointing Commissioners for Sequestrations'.
122 TNA SP 25/129, f. 5.
123 For a convenient sequence of these different forms of receipts see TNA SP 63/290, ff. 64–69.
124 A&O, II, p. 312, 'December 1649: An Act for an Assessment for six Moneths, from the Five and twentieth of December, 1649, for maintenance of the Forces raised

by Authority of Parliament for the Service of England and Ireland, at the rate of Ninety thousand pounds per mensem for the first three Moneths, and at the rate of Three score thousand pounds for the last three Moneths'.
125 A&O, II, p. 1328, 'July, 1659: An Act for settling The Militia in England and Wales'.
126 A&O, II, pp. 1293-1298, 'July 1659: An Act for Setling the Militia for the City of London, and Liberties thereof'.
127 Anon, *A Narrative of the Proceedings of the Committee of the Militia of London, concerning a letter, in part resolved to be sent to General Monck, and the Officers under his command in Scotland* (London, 1659).
128 Thomas Sadler, *A True Copy of the Letter sent from the Lord Mayor, Aldermen and Common-Council...* (London, 1659).
129 CJ, VII, p. 804.
130 Maurice Ashley, *Financial and Commercial Policy under the Cromwellian Protectorate* (London, 1792), pp. 145, 172.
131 TNA SP 25/108 Letter Books 3 March to 26 May 1660, f. 11, 45. Working under Jessop and John Rushworth until 28 March 1660, when there was a change of personnel, was Samuel Hartlib, the intellectual patron of William Petty and Benjamin Worseley.
132 TNA SP 25/108, f. 53.
133 TNA SP 25/108, f. 15.
134 Pinckney, 'Scottish Representation', p. 98.
135 LJ, XI, pp. 6-9.
136 John Habbakuk, 'Presidential Address: The Land Settlement and the Restoration of Charles II', *Transactions of the Royal Historical Society*, 28 (1978), pp. 201-222 at pp. 201-202.
137 Habbakuk, 'Presidential Address', p. 205.
138 Ashley, *Commercial Policy*, p. 99.
139 Ashley, *Commercial Policy*, p. 101.
140 A tabulation of the Long Parliament's outstanding debts to merchants at the Restoration is presented in CJ, XIII, pp. 234-244.
141 Ashley, *Commercial Policy*, p. 107.
142 For this outline, I have relied upon Keith Feiling, *British Foreign Policy 1660-1672* (London, 1968), pp. 28-34. The Franco-Spanish treaty of 1659 negated a treaty of 23 March 1657 between England and France against Spain, their common enemy.
143 Roger Downing and Gijs Rommelse, *A Fearful Gentleman: Sir George Downing in The Hague, 1658-1672* (Hilversum, 2011), p. 72.
144 Downing and Rommelse, *A Fearful Gentleman*, p. 73.
145 Carolyn A. Edie, '"For The Honour and Welfare of the City": London's Gift to Charles II on His Coming Into The Kingdom, May 1660', *Huntington Library Quarterly*, 50:2 (Spring, 1987), pp. 119-131.
146 Giles Dury (ed.), *The Parliamentary Intelligencer* (London, 1659-60), p. 292.
147 Dury, *The Parliamentary Intelligencer*, p. 299.
148 Dury, *The Parliamentary Intelligencer*, p. 304.
149 Dury, *The Parliamentary Intelligencer*, p. 318.
150 Dury, *The Parliamentary Intelligencer*, p. 306.

151 Richard Bateman, Theophilus Biddolph, Richard Ford, William Bateman, Thomas Chamberlin, Samuel Langham, Richard Brown, William Thomson, Sir Nicholas Crispe and Thomas Vincent.
152 Thomas Adams, Abraham Reynardson, Thomas Bludworth, Sir James Bunce and Samuel Langham.
153 William Wilde, Sir John Robinson, Alderman John Frederick, Alderman William Wade, John Lewis and Colonel Bromfield. Bromfield was a former Recorder of London who was imprisoned in 1649. See John Rushworth, *Historical Collections of Private Passages of State: Volume 7, 1647–48* (London, 1721), p. 1125.
154 W. Noel Sainsbury (ed.), *Calendar of the Court Minutes of the East India Company 1644–1649* (Oxford, 1912), p. 97.
155 Ashley, *Commercial Policy*, p. 87.
156 Firth, *Clarke Papers*, Vol. iv, p. 118.
157 CJ, VIII, pp. 18–20.
158 TNA SP 25/108 Letter Books 3 March to 26 May 1660, f. 91; Thomas Rich was a Gloucester merchant and unrelated to the earl of Warwick. He was involved in both the Levant and East India companies, and was married to the daughter of William Cockayne.
159 TNA SP 25/116 Passes and Warrants 25 February 1660 to 26 May 1660, f. 20. The Council of State began issuing arrest warrants for Regicides, for those whom Charles II might find most objectionable, on 16 April when the arrest was ordered of Charles Whalley and Edward Goffe, who later turned up in New England. Sir Arthur Annesley signed the final warrant, for the arrest of Gregory Clement, on 25 May (ff. 4, 22).
160 Aidan Clarke, *Prelude to Restoration in Ireland: The End of Commonwealth* (Cambridge, 1999), p. 306.
161 TNA SP 29/83, f. 103.
162 LJ, XI, pp. 146–148.
163 John Raithby (ed.), *Statutes of the Realm: Volume 5, 1628–80* (London, 1819), pp. 226–234, 'An Act of Free and Generall Pardon Indemnity and Oblivion'.
164 CJ, VIII, pp. 234–244.
165 NAI QRO 2A-12-51, An Abstract of Forfeited Lands; NAI QRO 1/1/3/1–20, Books of Survey and Distribution. These will be published shortly by the Irish Manuscripts Commission as David Brown and Micheál Ó Siochrú, *The Books of Survey and Distribution*, 5 vols (Dublin, forthcoming 2020).

Conclusion

Between 1663 and 1669, England exported £2 million worth of manufactured goods through the Port of London.[1] Sixty-three per cent of this total was exported to West Africa, the Atlantic colonies and the East Indies. At the same time, London re-exported almost £1 million worth of commodities that originated in these markets. From 1640 to 1660, in the midst of the upheavals of the Wars of the Three Kingdoms, a revolution in international trade took place, and this revolution was brought about by the group of merchants who originally coalesced in March 1642 as the Adventurers for Irish land. This tightly woven alliance of parliamentary peers and merchants, identified here for the first time, dominated England's external trade and state finance throughout the 1640s and early 1650s. England's commercial policy developed thereafter along the imperial lines first put in place by the Adventurers.

Control of the domains of trade and finance enabled the Adventurers to influence England's policy towards Ireland, either by formulating policies directly or through persuading parliament that they had common cause. By far the most belligerent of all factions in England aiming to punish Catholic Ireland for the rebellion of 1641, the Adventurers frustrated all attempts to bring the conflicts in Ireland to an early conclusion, including King Charles I's cessation in 1643 and the efforts of Cromwell's under-officers to bring the war to a close almost a decade later. Their relentless campaign to take the estates of the defeated Catholic Irish was pursued over a period of some twenty-five years. Few Adventurers, however, attempted any kind of plantation scheme in Ireland and fewer still brought in any new investment. In these intervening years, from 1642 to 1665, the businesses of the leading Adventurers had changed considerably in emphasis, most notably from a predilection towards privateering towards more capital-intensive, but more certain, imperial trade. Ireland was their last and greatest plunder before a new generation, financed to some degree through the sale of their Irish estates, specialised in the burgeoning African slave trade and commodity trade in the Indies. In the history of Ireland, the Adventurers closed the chapter of plantation Ireland and began a new one. Ireland became part of the British imperial system, an important provider of labour and agricultural produce to England and to other countries, but with limited self-government and eventually none at all.

In English history, this study of the Adventurers contributes towards the debates around several of the most perplexing aspects of the English Civil Wars: how parliament was able to challenge the king militarily in 1642, what finally caused Oliver Cromwell to eject the Rump Parliament in 1653 and the impetus behind the elected parliament's invitation to Charles II to be restored to his kingdoms in 1660. This is not to say that the Adventurers for Irish land were the sole cause of any of these events, but every political and social system has a tipping point and the Adventurers made forceful interventions on all three occasions.

The financial system created by the Adventurers also endures to a considerable degree. The circulation of silver provided the fiscal framework for the development of the Atlantic world and much of the Adventurers' trade was built upon this foundation. The Adventurers' control over the silver supply was the underlying source of their influence and the tiny island of Barbados became a focal point that gave their financial system its liquidity. In fact, Caribbean silver was so necessary to fund the English state that the Protectorate fought its disastrous last war for it. Colonial silver in the Adventurers' hands enabled their innovations in state finance. Recruiting from their own trusted commercial networks, the Adventurers established a broad-based apparatus for taxation and sequestration. Their principal method was to introduce Dutch financial innovations and apply them to state finance. These innovations included the excise, which accounted for one-third of Dutch state revenue by 1640 but was new to England in 1643, and the integration of the parliamentary financial committees under their control into an informal form of exchange bank on the Amsterdam model. Their regular meetings in Grocers' Hall enabled this process. As the owners of incoming bullion, the holders of payment warrants and the treasurers of parliament's taxation committees were drawn from one small group, their system proved easy to maintain. The genesis of a proto-fiscal state is to be found here, as the purchasing power of the initial plate or bullion deposits was multiplied by circulating instruments of credit, enabling parliament to raise armies without resorting to punitive taxation.

As the war economy expanded beyond the means of the core group of Adventurers to underwrite it, further developments increased parliament's money supply and fuelled the expansion of further credit. The sequestration of opponents' assets, and their sale at bargain rates, encouraged further flows of hoarded plate into the central treasury committees. The excise increased the rate of circulation of minted coin and brought it back into state coffers, to settle outstanding warrants and to circulate it once again. A further Dutch innovation, the integrated sugar mill introduced into Barbados in 1643, greatly increased the money supply in the hands of the Adventurers by making possible the sale of refined sugar of far higher value than the raw crop at the markets of Amsterdam. The sale of royalist, church and, finally, the king's own lands repeated the initial success of the Adventure for Irish land by monetising the landed assets of parliament's enemies. The success of the Adventurers' financial system can be judged by the fact that the Protectorate was £2 million in debt at its fall in 1660, indicating a high level of public confidence in the 'public faith'.

Although there were 1,300 Adventurers and a core committee of twenty leaders who changed over time, the narrative of this book has brought one, Maurice Thomson, to the fore. A highly skilled financier and logistician, he may well have been a genius. Unfortunately, Maurice Thomson has left no diaries, opinions or recollections, so it is difficult to establish the theoretical foundations of a career that progressed from the farming of tobacco to the development of an integrated global supply chain. Underpinning his commercial success was a particular instinct for political opportunism and he charted his own course from royal government, through parliament, Commonwealth, Protectorate and back to royal government again. Aided by his close and extended family, his relations with the earl of Warwick, with Oliver Cromwell and finally with Charles II appear to have been based on mutual dependence. All trusted and rewarded him, even if this trust was not always reciprocated. Thomson embraced the availability of English and Irish unfree labour, and then African slavery, with unparalleled enthusiasm for his time and these contributed significantly to his wealth. His many roles in state finance yielded him enormous riches, often at the expense of the state or its enemies. Maurice Thomson, despite his Dutch connections, had no difficulty in promoting a war with Protestant Holland in 1652. Prizes and reparations took priority over religion or friendships. Despite this, the execution of Charles I was a step too far and Thomson, in common with the vast majority of Adventurers, distanced himself from it. A dispute over their Irish land entitlements accruing from the Adventure precipitated the Adventurers' departure from state finance in 1653 and their stance thereafter was one of quiet opposition to the Protectorate, finally manifested in their support for the restoration of the monarchy. Self-interest resulted in the Adventurers facilitating the invasion of London by Monck's army in January 1660 and London's subsequent mission to The Hague to entice Charles II to return. Charles II demonstrated his personal gratitude towards Maurice Thomson for his Restoration and accomplished what the Protectorate could not, re-establishing a peace at sea modelled on the principles established by Thomson in the Navigation Act of 1651. For Charles II, Catholic Ireland was the price to be paid for the support of the Adventurers and England's future wealth.

This study originally set out to identify the Adventurers for Irish land and to reconcile their unwavering support for the parliamentary cause with the settlement of their claims by the restored monarch, Charles II. It has revealed how the actions of a remarkable group of skilled and innovative individuals, fewer than twenty in number, developed and maintained a stable system of state finance in highly challenging times. They profited enormously from their efforts and left behind them both an early form of a centralised English fiscal state and the framework upon which England's overseas empire was built. In the turbulent twentieth century, the British Prime Minister, Neville Chamberlain, stated that were no winners in war, and all were losers.[2] Maurice Thomson and the Adventurers would have accepted the challenge.

NOTES

1 Ralph Davis, 'English Foreign Trade, 1660–1700', *Economic History Review*, Second Series, 7:2 (1954), pp. 150–166, pp. 154–160.
2 Anon, '"Avoidance of War": Mr Chamberlain on his "Prime Duty"', *The Times* (London, 4 July 1938).

Appendix

The original Adventurers for Irish land

This composite list of the original Adventurers for Irish land is drawn from four sources: TNA SP 63/302, a list of all Adventures paid in full; TNA SP 63/301, ff. 197–200, a list of all Adventures not paid in full; *Calendar of State Papers, Adventurers for Land* and the remainder from Bottigheimer, *English Money and Irish Land*, Appendix A. The names in Bottigheimer's list, not drawn from the first three sources, were derived from list drawn up by John Prendergast, compiled from the Record Office in Dublin Castle and the Carte Manuscripts at the Bodleian Library in Oxford. This list does not include those whose first subscription was for one of the subsequent Adventures, or the Sea Adventure. The term 'cert' indicates adventures not recorded in the original compilation of paid up Adventures, and those who could not produce receipts. These claims relied on a 'certificate' from Thomas Andrews, the only surviving treasurer in 1653, to verify their entitlements. There are clearly issues surrounding the authenticity of these certificates as many were awarded to leading figures, such as Oliver Cromwell, whose adventures might reasonably be expected to have been recorded in a more formal manner. Some of these certificates are debts transferred from other securities, the creditors preferring Irish land to nebulous offers of repayment. Others may just have been gifts to persons of influence, an attempt to encourage the rapid plantation of Ireland intended in 1653.

The following list gives the name of each Adventurer in bold type, followed by their place of residence in 1642 (where known), and the amount speculated. The information that follows includes each Adventurers' membership of parliamentary or local financial committees, together with any involvement in the key commercial enterprises promoted by the Adventurers' leadership. These details have been principally collated from State Papers, the lists of collectors of the subsidies and taxes in *Acts and Ordinance of the Interregnum*, the lists of parliamentary committees and biographies of MPs produced by the History of Parliament Trust and other lists that appear as footnotes in the main text. Family connections between the leading Adventurers are also stated.

Alcock, Thomas	London, haberdasher, £300; Artillery Company 1635.
Alcock, William Jnr	London, Canon Street, merchant tailor, £25.
Aldersey, Margaret	Kent, merchant, £60; widow of Samuel Aldersey, investor in the Massachusetts Bay Company 1628.
Alderton, John	£25.
Alford, John	London, £50; Artillery Company 1630; subsidy for Fairfax and Ireland 1647.
Allanson, William	London, chaplain, £150; brother of Richard Allanson of Devon; Chaplain to lord Digby in London 1638–?, later a Puritan minister in Bristol.
Allanson, William	York, draper, MP, £300; knighted by Charles I 1633; Lord Mayor of York 1640, Collector of £400,000 subsidy; died 1656.
Allein, Francis	Surrey, Lambeth, goldsmith, £700; Commissioner Customs 1643–45; Alderman, Farringdon Without, 1649–52; Councillor of State 1651, 1652–53; MP Cockermouth 1645–53; Collector Plate Money July 1642; Commissioner Customs 1643–45; Treasurer £80,000 loan for Fairfax 1645; Commissioner for Compounding 1647; Treasurer at War 1647; Collector £90,000 per month subsidy 1649; Treasurer, Forfeited Estates 1651; Prime Warden Goldsmiths 1650–51; Treasurer for Delinquent lands 1652; Derby House Committee 1652–53; Commissioner for Trade and Plantations 1652–53; EEIC Shareholder 1657; died 6 September 1658. Advanced £700 to Adventure in July 1642 in partnership with John Barkstead, John Coltman, Nicholas Bond, Christopher Towse and John Witham. The other partners assigned their shares to Allein in 1653.
Allein, Tobias	Devizes, Wiltshire, gentleman, £80; father of Joseph Allein, a Puritan divine and cousin of Francis Allein.
Allen, John	£100.
Allen, Richard	Devon, Ditchet, clerk, later Puritan divine, £200; Dorchester Company 1624; Commissioner for Somerset for Ejecting scandalous ignorant and insufficient Ministers and schoolmaster 1654–?

Allen, Thomas	London, grocer, £300; Assessments, London 1648; High Court Justice 1650, 1653; Commissioner for Excise 1653.
Allen, William	London, grocer, £550; Bermuda Company; Advance Money Collector 1642; EEIC General Voyage 1643; Alderman, Langbourne Ward, 1650–51, died 1651.
Allott, Richard	London, haberdasher, £50.
Allwood, John	Dorset, £25.
Almery, George	London, gentleman, £800; Adventure paid in for Sir John Holland; Committee of Adventurers 1654.
Almond, William	London, pewterer, £25.
Alston, Edward	London, physician, £200; Adventure paid in for Sir John Holland.
Alston, Joseph	London, merchant, £200; Adventure paid in for Sir John Holland; married Elizabeth Thomson, daughter of Maurice Thomson; collector £90,000 per month subsidy 1649.
Alston, Pennyus	London, grocer, £50.
Amys, John	London, £200; Artillery Company 1636.
Anderson, Nathaniel	Middlesex, clothier, £125.
Andrews, Matthew	London, grocer, £50.
Andrews, Nathaniel	London, £200; investor Massachusetts Bay Company 1628; Artillery Company 1628.
Andrews, Richard	London, Cripplegate, girdler, £40; Collector Plate Money July 1642.
Andrews, Thomas	London, leatherseller, £3,537; investor Massachusetts Bay Company 1628; Plymouth Company 1628–38; Artillery Company 1630; Master Leathersellers 1638–39; Alderman, Tower, 1642–49, Aldgate, 1649–59; loaned £100 Brotherly Assistance 1641; Treasurer Adventure for Irish land 1642; Commissioner for Assessments 1642; Treasurer Advance of Money 1643–; EEIC General Voyage 1643; Commissioner for Prize Goods 1643; Commissioner Customs 1643–45; Accounts for the Whole kingdom 1644; Treasurer £80,000 loan for Fairfax 1645; Treasurer for Arrears 1645; Treasurer Assessment for Ireland 1645; Lender, Subsidy for Fairfax and Ireland 1647;

APPENDIX

	Treasurer at War 1647; Treasurers £20,000 per month for Ireland 1648; Assessments, London 1648; Forfeited Estates 1651; Commissioner for Navy and Customs 1649; Collector £90,000 per month subsidy 1649; High Court Justice 1650, 1653; Treasurer for Delinquent lands 1652; Committee of Adventurers 1654; Knighted (by the Protector) 14 November 1657; President St. Thomas' Hospital 1650–59; Committee EEIC 1643–59 (Deputy Governor 1657–59, Governor 1659); Mayor of London 1659; died (buried 20 August) 1659.
Annesley, Edward	London, Portsoken, armourer, £1,400; Collector Plate Money July 1642.
Anthony, Edmond	£200.
Anthony, Hannah	£110.
Archbold, Stephen	£50.
Archer, Francis	London, haberdasher, £25; EEIC Shareholder 1657.
Arnold, George	London, Farringdon, girdler, £200; Collector Plate Money July 1642.
Arnold, William and John	London, £100; Artillery Company 1635.
Arundel, Henry	Middlesex, £150.
Arundel, John and William	Middlesex, £100.
Ash, Edward	London, draper, £400; Drapers Company 1624; Artillery Company 1626; Commissioner for Compounding 1647; Subsidy for Fairfax and Ireland 1647; Militia Committee (Kent), 1648; Collector £90,000 per month subsidy 1649.
Ash, Francis	London, goldsmith, £250; Trustee for Bishops' Lands 1646; Alderman Bridge, 1648; Auditor 1644–46; Assessments, London 1648; Prime Warden Goldsmiths 1649–50; EEIC Shareholder 1657; died 1660.
Ash, John	Somerset, Taunton, gentleman, £50; Collector, Somerset 1643; Commissioner for Plantations 1646; Commissioner for Compounding 1647; Commissioner for Trade 1650.
Ashley, John	London, Portsoken, fishmonger, £100; Virginia Company, Collector Plate Money July 1642.
Ashley-Cooper, Anthony	Shaftsbury, gentleman, MP, £600; Council of State 1653.

Ashton, Michael	Dorset, £15.
Ashurst, Richard	London, draper, £100.
Ashwell, William	London, grocer, £400; EEIC General Voyage 1643; Alderman, Aldersgate, 1643–44; Treasurer St. Bartholomew's Hospital 1643; Committee EEIC 1638–47, 1648–51, 1652–53, 1654–55; died November 1675.
Aston, Raphe	London, yeoman, £50; Artillery Company 1625.
Athuis, Benjamin	£50.
Atkins, Peter	Devon, £25.
Atkins, William	Southampton, £50.
Austen, Edward	London, fishmonger, £500.
Austin, Henry	London, fishmonger, £600; Artillery Company 1620.
Avery, Samuel	London, merchant tailor, £4,800; Treasurer, Doubling Ordinance (Irish land) 1643; Commissioner for Prize Goods 1643; Commissioner Customs 1645–49; Ransom of Algiers Captives 1645; Trustee for Bishops' Lands 1646; Subsidy for Fairfax and Ireland 1647; London Militia 1647; Alderman, Cripplegate, 1645–47, Relief of the Poor, London 1647; Collector £90,000 per month subsidy 1649; Alderman Bassishaw, 1647–53; MP London 1654–55; Committee of Adventurers 1654; Master Merchant Tailors 1645–46.
Aynell, John	Devon, £20.
Ayres, Thomas	London, £200; patentee Piscataqua, New Hampshire, 1631; Fee-farm Trustee 1647; High Court Justice 1650, 1653; Committee of Adventurers 1654.
Ayscough, Edward	Lincoln, gentleman, MP, £150; Customs Inspector for Tobacco 1635; Compounder for those caught smuggling or growing tobacco; Investigator of alum farmers 1640.
Babb, William	London, fishmonger, £50.
Babington, Abraham	London, draper, £500; Common Council 1641.
Babington, Michael	London, £200.
Babington, Thomas	Leicestershire, £100; County Association 1642; Subsidy for Fairfax and Ireland 1647.
Bailey, Thomas	Wiltshire, £150; Militia Committee Wiltshire, 1648.
Baker, John	London, weaver, £100; Artillery Company 1628.

Baker, Katherine	Buckinghamshire, £80.
Baker, William	London, merchant tailor, £150; Alderman, Farringdon Without, 1649.
Balam, William	London, Lincolns Inn, lawyer, £50; partner of Valentine Figg.
Ball, Elizabeth	£100.
Ball, George	London, merchant, £200.
Ball, William	London, £200; Assessments, London 1648.
Ballard, John	London, silkweaver, £200; Artillery Company 1640.
Ballard, William	London, yeoman, £200; Providence Island Company 1632.
Banford, Patrick	London, merchant tailor, £100; Artillery Company 1635; Assessments, London 1648.
Bankes, John	London, grocer, £100; EEIC Shareholder 1657.
Barber, Gabriel	Hertfordshire, gentleman, £200; Treasurer, Somers Island Company, Providence Island Company 1631, Feoffee for Impropriations.
Barber Surgeons Company	London, £50.
Bard, Maximilliam	Southwark, £200; Artillery Company 1642; Collector Plate Money July 1642; £5,000 loan relief of Munster 1645; Paymaster of soldiers 1647; High Court Justice 1650, 1653.
Bardolf, Symon	Surrey, merchant, £300.
Barfoote, Robert	London, leatherseller, £50; Artillery Company 1641.
Barker, George	Surrey, £200.
Barker, Humphry	Bristol, £1,000; Massachusetts Bay Company 1630.
Barker, John	Warwickshire, gentleman, £1,200; Alderman of Warwick.
Barker, William	London, merchant, £200; EEIC Shareholder 1657.
Barkham, Edward	London, gentleman, £600; Trustee for sale of king's goods 1649.
Barkstead, John	London, goldsmith, £100; EEIC Shareholder 1657.
Barlow, Francis and James	£20.
Barnard, Richard	Sussex, draper, £200; Artillery Company 1623.
Barnardiston, Nathaniel	Suffolk, gentleman, £700; Assessments Suffolk 1643; Commissioner for Compounding 1647;

Barnardiston, Thomas	Subsidy for Fairfax and Ireland 1647; EEIC Shareholder 1657. London, gentleman, £322; Artillery Company 1622; Collector Plate Money July 1642; Assessments Essex 1643; Subsidy for Fairfax and Ireland 1647; Assessments, London 1648; Africa Company 1649; Levant Company 1654; Committee of Adventurers 1654.
Barnes, Josias	Middlesex St James Clerkenwell, lawyer, £400; Collector Plate Money July 1642.
Barrett, Robert	London, haberdasher, £50; Artillery Company 1637.
Barrett, Thomas	£100; Artillery Company 1627.
Barrington, Sir Thomas	Colchester, gentleman, MP, £1,200; Providence Island Company 1631; Committee of Safety 1642.
Bartlett, Bernard	merchant, £80.
Bartlett, John	clothworker, £30.
Bartlett, William	London, £10; Assessments, London 1648.
Barton, William	London, stationer, £300.
Barwick, Thomas	London, grocer, £100.
Bassett, William	Kent, mariner, £1,030; Plymouth, New England colonist 1621.
Bate, John	London, Bridge Within, merchant tailor, £200; Collector Plate Money July 1642.
Bateman, John	London, gentleman, £100; EEIC Shareholder 1657.
Bateson, Richard	Middlesex Sepulchres without the Bares, £100; Collector Plate Money July 1642; Assessments, London 1648.
Bayliff, John	Somerset, £10.
Beadle, Thomas	London, tallow chandler, £100.
Beale, Richard	Kent, captain, £337; Sequestrations, Kent 1643; Subsidy for Fairfax and Ireland 1647.
Beale, Stephen	London, Bridge Within, leatherseller, £1,300; Artillery Company 1642; Collector Plate Money July 1642.
Beale, Thomas	London, mariner, £100; Captain of the *Great Lewis* 1644. Land was assigned in lieu of debt owed for a shipment of coal to Duncannon.
Beard, Robert	Exeter, £200; EEIC Shareholder 1657.
Beaumont, Richard	London, apothecary, £58.

APPENDIX

Beck, Gabriel	London, lawyer, £300; Parliamentary Committee for Gloucester 1646; City Planning Officer in London, 1656–57; Commissioner £50,000 for Ireland 1648.
Bedingfield, Anthony	London, mercer, MP, £180; Alderman Langbourn, 1650; Master Mercers 1651; died 1652.
Bedingfield, Henry	London, grocer, £200; royalist, adventure forfeited in 1651.
Beeke, William	London, Gracechurch Street, merchant tailor, £625; Artillery Company 1642; Common Council 1643; Commissioner for arrears 1645; Court of the Company of Merchant Tailors 1657; EEIC Shareholder 1657.
Beighton, Richard	London, sadler, £50.
Belfield, Anthony	Hertfordshire, £180.
Bell, Angelo	£50.
Bellers, Foulke	Warwickshire, £25.
Bence, Alexander	London, grocer, £600; Navy Commissioner 1642; £120,000 per month 1645; Subsidy for Fairfax and Ireland 1647; Alderman Walbrook 1653; Master, Trinity House 1659.
Bendish, Thomas	Essex, gentleman, £400; royalist; imprisoned 1642–43; confined to London until 1646; later ambassador to Istanbul 1647; Levant Company.
Bengoe, James	London, merchant, £25.
Benion, Gabriell	London, tallow chandler, £100.
Bennett, John	London, Deptford, mariner, £60; Master Trinity House, 1636; Assessments, London 1648.
Benning, Richard	£200.
Bentley, William	London, mariner, £200.
Bernard, Richard	London, gentleman, £200.
Berry, John	London, carpenter, £50; Artillery Company 1641.
Best, Sarah	Surrey, Kingston, £35.
Betsworth, William	Sussex, blacksmith, £50.
Bewley, Thomas	London, draper, £100; EEIC Shareholder 1657.
Bewley, William	London, draper, £100; Artillery Company 1635.
Biddle, Christopher	London, shoemaker, £25.
Biddolph, Theophilus	London, grocer, £100; EEIC Shareholder 1657; Committee of Safety 1659.

Bifield, Adoniram	London, clothworker, £50.
Bigge, Anna	London, £200.
Bigge, Samuel	Stratford, mariner, £7.
Bigges, Thomas	London, clothworker, £200.
Biggs, Joseph	clothworker, £50.
Birch, Thomas	Manchester, gentleman, MP, £200; Colonel in parliamentary army; Of Birch Hall, Manchester and Governor of Liverpool, 1645–48; Subsidy for Fairfax and Ireland 1647; Militia committee Lincolnshire, 1648.
Bird, John	London, £10, Artillery Company 1633.
Birkenhead, Theophilus	London, actor, £100.
Biscoe, John	Westminster, St Margaret, apothecary, £125; Collector for Plate Money 1642; Vestryman for St Margarets Church Westminster.
Bishop, Ephriam	Surrey, merchant, £20.
Bixby, William	London, salter, £100; Artillery Company 1634; Church Elder, St Laurence Jewry 1645.
Blackburrow, William	London, leatherseller, £62.
Blackstone, John	Durham, gentleman, £750; son of William Blackston, the first settler of Rhode Island; MP; Sequestrations Durham 1643; County committee for Assessments, 1643; Northern Association, 1645; County committee, Assessment for transporting forces to Ireland, 1647; Subsidy for Fairfax and Ireland 1647; Commissioner for Compounding 1647.
Blackwell, John	Durham, Newcastle-upon-Tyne, gentleman, £500; Artillery Company 1642; £200,000 loan for Ireland 1647; Deputy Treasurer of War for Ireland 1653; Committee of Adventurers 1654; Lands set out for supposed Adventure of £2,350, Blackwell allowed to choose between Dublin, Kildare and Cork, none of which was included in the Adventurers' land settlement.
Blackwell, Joseph and Jonathan	London, £468; Artillery Company 1645.
Blague, Nicholas	London, merchant, £50.
Blake, Emmanuel	London, mercer, £30; EEIC Shareholder 1657.
Blake, George	London, £12; EEIC Shareholder 1657.
Bland, Joanne	£200.
Blatt, Emmanuel	London, £66.

Blatt, James	London, merchant tailor, £200; Artillery Company 1642.
Blinhorne, John	£50.
Bluikerne, Joshua	£150.
Blunden, Overington	London, soldier, £70.
Boate, Gerrard	London, physician, £410.
Boggest, Thomas	London, Billingsgate, currier, £50; Artillery Company 1635; Collector Plate Money July 1642.
Boggis, William	Suffolk, gentleman, £50.
Bond, Denis	Dorset, Dorchester, gentleman, MP, £2,000; Dorchester Company 1624; did not subscribe his own money but arranged a subscription in trust for the 'well affected' of Devon, many of whom were also prominent in the Dorchester Company; Assesments Devon 1643; Committee for the Revenue 1643; Government of the West Indies 1643; Committee for Foreign Plantations 1643; Commissioner for Compounding 1647; Committee of the Admiralty 1648; Derby House Committee 1652–53; Committee of the Admiralty 1652–53; Commissioner for Trade and Plantations 1652–53.
Bond, Nicholas	London, gentleman, £100; Fee-farm Trustee 1647; Auditor of army accounts 1648.
Bonner, Margaret	London, Bridge Within, £50; Nicholas Bonner was Collector Plate Money, 1642.
Boone, Thomas	Devon, gentleman, MP, £600; Commissioner for Trade 1650; Committees for West Indies and Bahamas in 1652.
Borlase, Sir John	Buckinghamshire, gentleman, MP, £200; royalist; Lord Justice of Ireland 1643–44.
Bossevile, William	London, lawyer, £400; Artillery Company 1642; Fee-farm Trustee 1647.
Boulton, Everard	London, barber surgeon, £25; Artillery Company 1642.
Boulton, William	London, merchant tailor, £100.
Bourchier, Nathaniel	Sussex, singleton, £4.
Box, Henry	London, grocer, £400; Alderman, Bridge, 1650.
Boyce, Henry	London, tallow chandler, £100.
Boyce, John	Kent, £100.
Boynton, Edward	£450.

Boynton, James	£150.
Boynton, Matthew	Buckinghamshire, Uxbridge, Hedgeley House, gentleman, MP, £1,000; recruited in 1645; like Cromwell, planned to emigrate to the Saybrook colony in Massachusetts in 1635, a project of viscount Saye-and-Sele and Lord Brooke, but was prevented from doing so by the commissioners for plantations; Commissioner for assessment (E. Riding 1643–d.), levying and sequestration money, N. Riding 1643, Northern Assoc. Yorks. 1645–46; his son Matthew inherited the Adventure, declared for the royalists and was killed in 1651.
Bradley, George	London, stationer, £100; Artillery Company 1635; Collector for Plate Money 1642.
Bradley, Mark	London, scrivener, £100.
Bradshaw, Elizabeth	£50.
Brand, Joseph	London, sadler, £200.
Brand, Matthew	Surrey, gentleman, £600; Collector for Plate Money 1642; Assessments Surrey 1643; Subsidy for Fairfax and Ireland 1647.
Brereton, William	Cheshire, Handforth, gentleman, MP, £900; author of *Travels of Sir William Brereton in Ireland* (1635); New England land patentee 1630s, responsible for shipping troops to Ireland from Chester 1642; Parliamentarian commander Cheshire.
Bretland, Thomas	Dorset, £100.
Brett, John	London, St Benet Gracechurch, merchant tailor, £1,000; Artillery Company 1635; son-in-law of Randall Mainwaring; entered colonial trade in 1640s and patented land in New England after the Restoration; Commissioner for Sale of goods by the candle, 1643.
Brewer, Christopher	Somerset, £3.
Brewster, Edward	London, stationer, £133.
Brickdell, James	London, £10.
Bridges, John	London, gentleman, £300; Artillery Company 1635; brother of William Bridges, Divine.
Bridgoe, John	Edson, £175.
Briggs, Miles	London, merchant tailor, £125; Artillery Company 1628.

Briggs, Thomas	London, mercer, £200.
Bright, John	Yorkshire, £600; Assessments Yorkshire 1643.
Bright, Thomas	Suffolk, gentleman, £200.
Brightwell, Thomas	London, bowyer, £791; Collector for Plate Money 1642; Common Council 1643; Church Elder, St Giles Cripplegate 1645; Commissioner for arrears 1645; Committee of Adventurers 1654; Associate of Thomson; Committee of Citizens to seize Gunpowder appointed by parliament, 1642: Richard Waring, Thomas Foote, Thomas Brightwell, Samuel Langham, Samuel Hartnett, George Foxcroft, Thomas Stock, Richard Hunt, William Thomson, John Lane, Thomas Browne, John Greensmith, Edward Bolton.
Brimblecombe, John	Devon, mariner, £50.
Brinley, Laurence	London, merchant, £250; Church Elder, Mary Magdalene Milk Street, 1645.
Brinley, Nicholas	London, merchant, £262.
Bringley, Laurence	London, gentleman, £100; Collector for Plate Money 1642; Accounts for the Whole kingdom 1644; Commissioner for Compounding 1647.
Briscoe, Thomas	London, upholder, £50.
Bristoe, Henry	Retford, £50; Subsidy for Fairfax and Ireland 1647.
Brocket, John	London, clothworker, £100.
Broking, Nicholas	London, mercer, £200.
Bromfield, Laurence	London, leatherseller, £125; Master Leathersellers Company 1625–26; Artillery Company 1632; son of Aldeman Edward Bromfield, Walbrook, 1637–42, Governor Irish Society 1637–38; Colonel Trained Bands 1638–42; Collector for Plate Money 1642; Trustee for Bishops' Lands 1646; London Militia 1647; £200,000 loan for Ireland 1647; Committee of Adventurers 1654; Master Leathersellers 1625–26; Prime Warden Fishmongers 1636.
Bromwich, William	London, £125; Relief of the Poor, London 1647.
Brooking, Nicholas	Exeter, gentleman, £200; Militia 1659.
Broomer, Richard	London, £25.
Browker, Thomas	Kent, Sundridge, gentleman, £200.
Browne, George	Dorset, Frampton, barrister, £25.

Browne, Humphrey	London, girdler, £305; Collector for Plate Money 1642.
Browne, John	Dorset, Frampton, barrister, £100; Dorchester Company 1624; appointed Justice of the Peace for Dorset 1638; Subsidy for Fairfax and Ireland 1647.
Browne, John	London, gunfounder, £150; Collector for Plate Money 1642; Artillery Company 1640; gunfounder and inventor of the Drake Cannon; appointed the king's gunfounder in 1640; imprisoned by parliament 1645; died 1652. He was owed £1,842 by parliament in 1642.
Browne, John	London, lawyer, MP, £450; Clerk of parliament 1643; Commissioner for Compounding 1647; Subsidy for Fairfax and Ireland 1647.
Browne, Richard	London, woodmonger, £600; Subsidy for Fairfax and Ireland 1647; Alderman, Langbourn, 1648–49, EEIC Shareholder 1657; 1660–69; Cromwell's ambassador to Paris, 1658, knighted May 29, 1660; created Baronet July, 1660; MP Wycombe 1645–48, 1660; London 1656–57, 1659, 1660–61, Ludgershall 1661–69; Colonel Orange Regiment 1660–69; President Bethlem and Bridewell 1660–69; Commissioner Appeals 1662–69; died 24 September 1669.
Browne, Samuel	Bedford, cutler, £50; Sequestrations, Bedford 1643.
Browne, Thomas	London, lawyer, £50; Collector for Plate Money 1642; £5,000 loan relief of Munster 1645; Assessments, London 1648; son of John Browne of Frampton.
Brustoe, Samuel and Daniel	Sussex, yeoman, £133.
Bull, Thomas	£200.
Buller, George	Cornwall, gentleman, £600; Assessments 1643; Loan for Fairfax and Ireland 1647; Assessment £20,000 per month for Ireland 1648; Militia 1659.
Bunce, James	London, leatherseller, £1,000; Artillery Company 1627; Alderman, Bread Street, 1642–49, 1660; Commissioner London Militia 1642; Treasurer, Doubling Ordinance (Irish

land) 1643; Trustee for Bishops' Lands 1646; £200,000 loan for Ireland 1647; led campaign in London to force parliament to negotiate with Charles I and convicted of high treason 1648; financed Charles II from 1651; knighted May, 1660; created baronet 1660 but never passed his patent; President Honourable Artillery Company 1645; London Militia 1647; Subsidy for Fairfax and Ireland 1647; Master Leathersellers 1643–44; died 13 December 1670. Certificate from Thomas Andrews 1654 for £1,000 doubled to £2,000. Adventure acquired by William Hawkins in July 1654 in Laois and Offaly, who then assigned it to Thomas Vincent. Brother-in-law of Alderman John Langham.

Burges, Cornelius	London, divine, £700.
Burgis, James	Somerset, £5.
Burkit, Thomas	London, £100; Collector for Plate Money 1642.
Burlace, John	Buckinghamshire, £25.
Burton, Symon	London, stationer, £50.
Bushell, Edward	London, merchant, £400; Navy Commissioner 1659.
Byde, Thomas	London, tallow chandler, £25; Artillery Company 1660, father John Byde 1627; EIC Shareholder 1657.
Cambell, James	London, ironmonger, MP, £300.
Cammock, Ann	Surrey, Kingston, £25.
Campfield, Nathaniel	London, Farringdon Without, mariner, £100; Artillery Company 1628; Collector for Plate Money 1642; Common Council 1643; London Militia 1647; Assessments, London 1648; Collector in London for £120,000 per month ordinance of November 1650; son Thomas Campfield settled in New Haven, Conneticut, 1648.
Carlton, John	London, brewer, £50.
Carter, Edward	London, grocer, £200; Collector for Plate Money 1642; Collector £90,000 per month subsidy 1649.
Carter, John	London, leatherseller, £50.
Carter, Ralph	London, £25.

Carwithin, Nicholas	Essex, £150.
Caryll, Joseph	London, clothworker, £100; EEIC Shareholder 1657.
Caryll, Thomas	London, gentleman, £600.
Case, William	London, mariner, £300; Elder of Trinity House, 1636.
Casteel, Richard	London, merchant, £120; military supplier to Ireland during the 1640s.
Catlin, John	Hertfordshire, yeoman, £25.
Caulier, James	London, merchant, £200.
Cave, Richard	Somerset, £3.
Chamberlain, Abraham	London, merchant, £300; Collector for Plate Money 1642; Treasurer £80,000 loan for Fairfax 1645; Relief of the Poor, London 1647; Assessments, London 1648.
Chamberlain, Thomas	London, merchant, £300; Artillery Company 1623; Commissioner Sea Adventure 1642; Commissioner for Assessments 1642; EEIC Shareholder 1657; Committee of Safety 1659.
Chambers, Humphrey	Somerset, £3.
Chandler, Richard	London, haberdasher, £100.
Chaveney, Humphrey	Leicestershire, £100.
Cheny, Francis	Buckinghamshire, £600.
Cheswick, James	York, £250.
Chewning, Thomas	London, silkweaver, £120.
Child, John	Surrey, Kingston, £5; Artillery Company 1642; EEIC Shareholder 1657.
Child, Raphe	London, £50; Collector for Plate Money 1642.
Chillingworth, Roger	London, fishmonger, £50.
Clapp, Richard	Devon, yeoman, £200.
Clark, James	Middlesex, Staines, mercer, £50.
Clarke, George	London, grocer, £250; Artillery Company 1622; Alderman, Bridge, 1641–48; Collector for Plate Money 1642; EEIC General Voyage 1643; Auditor 1635–37; Subsidy for Fairfax and Ireland 1647; Relief of the Poor, London 1647; President St. Bartholomew's Hospital 1646–49; Committee EEIC 1640–44; Trustee for Bishops' Lands 1646; Assessments, London 1648; died January 1649.
Clarke, James	£100.

Clarke, James	London, Bishopsgate, £200; Artillery Company 1638.
Clarke, John	London, £400; New England Company, husband of Ursula Upton and aggregator of Adventures; EEIC Shareholder 1657.
Clarke, Ralph	Dorset, £275.
Clarke, Samuel	Warwickshire, £25.
Clay, Roger	London, factor, £100; Collector for Plate Money 1642.
Claydon, John	London, Sheep Lane, gentleman, £350.
Cleare, George	London, tallow chandler, £10; EEIC Shareholder 1657.
Clement, Gregory	London, gentleman, MP, £2,600; regicide; dismissed from the East India Company 1630 for illegal trading practices but successful trader to New England in 1630s; Commissioner Sea Adventure 1642; EEIC General Voyage 1643; Collector £90,000 per month subsidy 1649.
Clotworthy, Sir John	Antrim, gentleman, MP, £1000; Committee for Irish Affairs 1642; Commissioner for Plantations 1646; Commissioner for Compounding 1647; Committee of Adventurers 1654.
Clutterbuck, Richard	London, mercer, £900; Assessments, London 1648; Alderman, Vintry, 1650; merchant adventurer; Committee EEIC 1655–57; Master Mercers 1650; died 1670.
Cock, John	London, £100; Collector for Plate Money 1642; Assessments, London 1648.
Cock, Thomas	London, £100; Committee of Safety 1659.
Cocks, James	London, £50.
Cocks, Richard	London, £50; Collector for Plate Money 1642.
Cogan, Humphrey	Devon, merchant, £100.
Coish, Elisha and Mary	London, silkweavers, £300.
Colborne, Henry	London, £275; Assessments, London 1648; Committee of Adventurers 1654.
Colchester, Osmond	London, merchant, £31; purchased 600 acres of land in Norfolk County, Virginia, in 1640.
Coles, Henry	London, £50; Assessments, London 1648.
Coles, Peter	London, £12; Artillery Company 1641.

Coles, Thomas	London, merchant tailor, £375; Artillery Company 1627; Subsidy for Fairfax and Ireland 1647; Assessments, London 1648.
Collett, Richard	London, haberdasher, £100.
Collins, Francis	London, £215; Collector of Assessments 1643; Assessments for London 1648.
Collyer, Joseph	London, grocer, £50; Collector Subsidy Southwark 1643; EEIC Shareholder 1657.
Coltman, John	London, haberdasher, £100.
Connock, Anna	Surrey, £50.
Cooke, Cornelius	London, vintner, £100; Assessments Surrey 1643; £120,000 per month 1645.
Cooke, Edward	London, Langbourne, apothecary, £675; Common Council 1643; EEIC general voyage 1643.
Cooke, John	£100; Artillery Company 1644; EEIC Shareholder 1657.
Cooke, Thomas	London, grocer, £300.
Coomb, John	Devon, Broadwick, £37.
Coomb, Thomas	Devon, merchant, £100.
Cooper, Samuel	London, fishmonger, £50.
Cooper, William	London, haberdasher, £100.
Cope, James	£100.
Corbett, Thomas	London, £125; Artillery Company 1641; Collector for Plate Money 1642.
Corne, Thomas	London, £200; Artillery Company 1624.
Cornish, John	Dunkirton, £12.
Corporation of Bath	Bath, £25.
Corporation of Gloucester	Gloucester, £1350.
Coulson, John	York, merchant, £200.
Coxon, Clement	London, tallow chandler, £50.
Cressey, Simon	London, girdler, £5.
Creswick, Mary	York, £20.
Crew, Arthur	London, £100.
Crewe, John	Northampton, £600; Assessments Northampton 1643; Derby House Committee 1648.
Crewe, Randall	Northampton, £80.
Crispe, Sir Nicholas	London, salter, MP, £900; member, Salters' Company 1619, Master 1640–41; Artillery Company 1621; Merchant Adventurer; Barbary Company 1628; Guinea Company 1631;

	Captain of militia in London 1632–41, Farmer of Customs 1638–40; Common Councillor 1640–41; JP. Middlesex 1641–42, Commissioner of Array, London 1642; Sea Adventurer 1642; EEIC General Voyage 1643; July 1660–, Colonel of Horse (royalist) Cornwall 1644–46; Commissioner for customs Sept. 1660–62, Trade Nov. 1660–d., Plantations Dec. 1660–d.; Gentleman of Privy Chamber 1664–d.; died 1666.
Crispe, Richard	London, merchant, £600; Guinea Company.
Croame, Henry	London, £50.
Cromwell, Oliver	Huntington, gentleman, MP, £300; County Association 1642; Committee for Irish Affairs 1642; Sequestrations Cambridgeshire 1643; Malignants 1643; Government of the West Indies 1643; Committee for Foreign Plantations 1643; Collector, Fairfax's Army 1645; Subsidy for Fairfax and Ireland 1647; Council of State 1649; Committee of Both kingdoms 1644; Derby House Committee 1648–49; Commissioner for Trade and Plantations 1652–53; Lord Protector 1653–58.
Crooke, Charles	Buckinghamshire, clothworker, £225.
Crossing, Richard	Exeter, gentleman, £200; Subsidy for Fairfax and Ireland 1647; Mayor of Exeter 1647.
Crossing, Thomas	Exeter, gentleman, £100.
Crowley, Robert	London, Whitechapel, haberdasher, £200; Militia, Tower Hamlets 1648.
Crowther, Samuel	London, merchant tailor, £100.
Cullen, Richard	London, £25.
Culmer, Richard	Kent, Sundridge, clothworker, £200.
Culpepper, John	Leeds, gentleman, MP, £150; royalist; granted five million acres in Virginia by Charles II in 1649.
Curl, John	£50.
Custom House	London, corporate, £2,000.
Dabbs, Samuel	London, grocer, £85.
Dacres, Thomas	Hertfordshire, gentleman, MP, £600; loaned two sums, £500 and £100, to Nichlas Loftus in March 1642 that appears to have been placed onto the Adventurers' books. Had loaned

	the money in interim to Arthur Capel, a delinquent; Committee of Adventurers 1654; surrendered his Adventure and instead had £250 charged on the excise in 1660.
Daniel, William	London, St Saviours, goldsmith, £100; Collector Advance of Money, 1643.
Darmolly, Richard	£350.
Dartmouth Burgesses	Devon, Dartmouth, corporate, £2,397.
Dashwood, Francis	London, Bishopsgate, sadler, £150; son of Edmund Dashwood, Dorchester Company 1624; Collector for Plate Money 1642; Alderman of London 1658, Levant Company and merchant adventurer.
Davenport, Henry	Westminster, £25; Massachusetts Bay Company 1630.
Davey, William	£150.
Davis, John	London, Billingsgate, chandler, £6; Collector of Plate Money 1642; Common Council 1643.
Davis, Thomas	£75; EEIC Shareholder 1657.
Dawes, Richard	London, pewterer, £300.
Dawes, Robert	Exeter, merchant, £300; EEIC Shareholder 1657.
Day, Henry	London, mercer, £200; Artillery Company 1642; EEIC Shareholder 1657.
Deards, Nathaniel	London, merchant tailor, £50.
Delanoy, Charles	London, tallow chandler, £100; Collector of Plate Money 1642; EEIC 1643; ransom of Algiers Captives 1645; EEIC Shareholder 1657.
Delanoy, Peter	London, dyer, £100; Collector of Plate Money 1642; EEIC Shareholder 1657.
Deline, Phillip	Kent, Sundridge, clothworker, £200.
Dennis, Sylvester	London, dyer, £160.
Dent, Giles	London, salter, £200; Assessments, London 1648.
Dethwick, John	London, Lime Street, mercer, £200; Artillery Company 1645; Collector of Plate Money 1642; Committee for Advance of Money 1642; Treasurer £80,000 loan for Fairfax 1645; Treasurer at War 1647; Assessments, London 1648; Alderman, Queenhithe, 1648; Collector £90,000 per month subsidy 1649; Treasurer, Forfeited Estates 1651; Commissioner for Prize Goods 1649; Treasurer for Delinquent

APPENDIX

	lands 1652; EEIC Shareholder 1657; knighted by Cromwell 15 September 1656; knighted by Charles II 13 April 1661; died 31 March 1671.
Diflin, Henry	London, merchant tailor, £37.
Dike, William	London, ironmonger, £100.
Dingley, Ezekial	London, salter, £60; Subsidy for Fairfax and Ireland 1647; EEIC Shareholder 1657.
Ditton, Miles	London, £100.
Dodd, John	London, Dowgate, salter, £200; Advance Money Collector 1643.
Dover, Daniel	Norfolk, £200.
Dover, George	London, apothecary, £125.
Downinge, Calibute	London, clothworker, £100; rector of Ickford in Buckinghamshire; pastor of Lord Robartes, 1642; Assembly of Divines 1643; died 1644.
Drake, Francis	Amersham, gentleman, MP, £600; Colonel of foot 1642–44; Assessments, Surrey 1643; £120,000 per month 1645; Commissioner for Assessment, Devon 1643–49, 1657, Aug. 1660–d., Sequestrations 1643; Subsidy for Fairfax and Ireland 1647; Sheriff 1645–46; JP. 1647–57, Mar. 1660–d.; Commissioner for Militia 1648; married the daughter of John Pym in 1641 with £2,500 dowry.
Drake, Roger	London, doctor, £250; Customs Commissioner, 1643–47.
Drake, William	Amersham, gentleman, MP, £100; Artillery Company 1641; travelled during Civil Wars.
Draper, Matthew	London, merchant, £50.
Dring, Anthony	London, merchant tailor, £25; Collector Advance of Money, Lime Street 1642; Assessments 1643.
Dring, Robert	London, ironmonger, £100.
Dring, Symon	London, ironmonger, £100; £60,000 loan for army 1643.
Dryden, John	Northamptonshire, Canons Ashby, gentleman, £600, MP.
Ducane, John	London, merchant, £100; EEIC Shareholder 1657.
Duke, Francis	£200.
Dupree, David	London, merchant, £300.
Duquesne, Peter	London, merchant, £200.

Dyke, John	Southampton, gentleman, £10; Bermuda Company; Providence Island Company; Warwick patent; claimed to have invested £5,200 in Sea Adventure although ships supplied were only used in English waters.
Eames, Samuel	London, factor, £100.
East, Edward	London, watchmaker, £100.
Eaton, John	London, merchant tailor, £50.
Echlin, Samuel	Middlesex, Staines, gentleman, £100.
Edward, John	London, tailor, £40; EEIC 1643; Committee of Safety 1659.
Elie, Robert	London, mercer, £100
Elliott, Samuel	London, merchant, £200; Auditor of Accounts for the Whole Kingdom 1644.
Elliston, Widow	Exeter, £600.
Emes, John	Warwickshire, Alcester, £25.
Enderby, Daniell	Middlesex, Staines, tanner, £100.
Erle, Sir Walter	Dorset, Poole, MP, £300; JP; Virginia Company shareholder 1620; Member of the Council for New England 1621; Dorchester Company 1624; underwrote the borrowing of £15,000 with Denis Bond and John Browne to fortify Dorchester against the king 1642; fled royalist forces 1643; Lt. of Ordnance 1644–45, 1647–48; Commissioner for Admiralty 1645–48, Propositions for Relief of Ireland 1645; Subsidy for Fairfax and Ireland 1647.
Errleston, Henry	£150.
Estwick, Stephen	London, Bridge Within, girdler, £100; Artillery Company 1642; Collector of Plate Money 1642; Common Council 1643; Trustee for Bishops' Lands 1646; Assessments, London 1648; Collector £90,000 per month subsidy 1649; Commissioner for Navy and Customs 1649; High Court Justice 1650, 1653; Alderman, Dowgate, 1650–52, Bridge, 1652–57; Commissioner Customs 1643–45, 1649–(?)57; died 15 December 1657.
Evans, John	Surrey, physician, £50.
Evans, Richard	Exeter, gentleman, £400; Subsidy for Fairfax and Ireland 1647.

Evelyn, Elizabeth	Surrey, Kingston, £100; sold to Luke Fawne in 1649 for £25.
Evelyn, Sir John	Surrey, Deptford, gentleman, £600; heir to the royal gunpowder monopoly; secret royalist; Committee of Safety 1642; Assessments Surrey 1643; Subsidy for Fairfax and Ireland 1647; travelled in Europe during the Civil Wars and returned to England 1652; EEIC Shareholder 1657.
Ewer, George	London, fishmonger, £50.
Exeter, Mayor and Bailiffs	Exeter, £20.
Eyres, Thomas	London, £200; patentee Piscataqua, New Hampshire, 1631.
Faldo, Henry	London, haberdasher, £100.
Farmer, George	London, lawyer, £600; Virginia Company 1609.
Farmer, Richard	London, £100; Virginia Company 1609.
Farringdon, Caldwell	London, merchant, £200; Artillery Company 1629; East India Company 1643.
Farringdon, William	London, Portsoken, £250; Collector of Plate Money 1642; Committee for Advance of Money 1642.
Farthing, John	London, cordwainer, £62.
Farwell, John	Buckinghamshire, Hoxton, gentleman, £100.
Fawne, Luke	London, £100; bookseller in St Pauls Churchyard at the sign of the Parrot, stationer, £150; sold adventure to William Shippey, London, weaver, in 1653.
Featherstone, Henry	London, stationer, £1,200; major plantations in Virginia and Ireland; Ellis Featherstone contributed to the £60,000 loan for the army, 1643.
Fenton, John	London, Lt. Col., £100; Artillery Company 1635; Assessments, London 1648; EEIC Shareholder 1657.
Fewster, William	Surrey, £150.
Fielder, John	Exeter, gentleman, £50; Committee of the Admiralty 1652–53.
Fielder, William	Exeter, gentleman, £200.
Fiennes, Nathaniel	Lincoln, gentleman, £300; Committee of Safety 1642; Subsidy for Fairfax and Ireland 1647; Derby House Committee 1648.

Figg, Valentine	London, clothworker, £100.
Fiske, John	Suffolk, gentleman, £100.
Fiske, William	Suffolk, gentleman, £200.
Fletcher, Edward	London, £100.
Fletcher, John	London, upholsterer, £110; Artillery Company 1641.
Fletcher, William	London, clothworker, £100; Collector of Plate Money 1642.
Floyd, Charles	London, gentleman, £600.
Floyd, Richard	London, girdler, £575; Assessments, London 1648; Greenland Company, 1652.
Foote, Thomas	London, Bridge, grocer, £700; Collector of Plate Money 1642; Committee for Advance of Money 1642; Common Council 1643; Alderman, Broad Street, 1643–48, Coleman Street, 1648–60; Treasurer, Doubling Ordinance (Irish land) 1643; Commissioner for Excise 1650–63; Subsidy for Fairfax and Ireland 1647; knighted (by the Protector) 5 December 1657; Collector £90,000 per month subsidy 1649; Committee of Adventurers 1654; EEIC Shareholder 1657; Committee of Safety 1659; created Baronet November, 1660; Councillor of State 1660; MP London 1654–55, 1656–58; Commissioner Excise 1643–(?)55; President St. Bartholomew's Hospital 1649–61; Committee EEIC 1657–59; Governor Irish Society 1657–60; died 12 October 1687.
Ford, Francis	Somerset, £6.
Ford, Richard	London, mercer, £100; EEIC Shareholder 1657.
Foster, Christopher	London, £200; EEIC Shareholder 1657.
Foster, Isaac	London, grocer, £62.
Foulke, John	London, £600; Commissioner London Militia 1642; Commissioner Customs 1643–45; Artillery Company 1645; Trustee for Bishops' Lands 1646; Alderman, Committed to the Fleet prison by the committee for taking the accounts of the kingdom, 1645; £200,000 loan for Ireland 1647; Subsidy for Fairfax and Ireland 1647; Relief of the Poor, London 1647; MP (1647) and opposed East India Company monopoly in parliament; Collector £90,000

APPENDIX

	per month subsidy 1649; Commissioner for Trade 1650; Committee of Adventurers 1654; Committee of Safety 1659.
Fountain, John	Devonshire, gentleman, £300; Subsidy for Fairfax and Ireland 1647.
Fountain, Thomas	Buckinghamshire, £200; County committee 1644.
Fowler, John	London, clothworker, £200; Collector of Plate Money 1642.
Fowler, Robert	Devon, Axminster, £60.
Fox, Charles	London, leatherseller, £50.
Foxwell, Phillip	£100.
Francis, John	Somerset, Combe Florey, gentleman, £25.
Franklin, John	London, Dollis Hill, gentleman, MP, £300; JP Middlesex 1625–42; London 1644; Collector, Coat and Conduct Money, Middlesex, 1640–47; Assessments, 1641–48; Sequestration of Delinquents, 1643.
Freemans, Thomas	£300.
French, John	£200, Artillery Company 1622.
Frere, Tobias	Norfolk, gentleman, £1,000; Commissioner for Assessments 1644; High Court of Justice 1650.
Frith, Francis	£200.
Gallilee, Thomas	London, £60.
Gardiner, Robert	London, £200; EEIC 1643.
Gardiner, Samuel	Worcestershire, £250.
Garland, Robert	London, merchant, £500; Company for Promoting the Gospel in New England, 1649.
Garnall, Richard	Warwickshire, Alcester, £25.
Garner, Robert	London, merchant, £200.
Garth, John	£100.
Gastrell, John	£12.
Gastrell, Joseph	minister, £7.
Gearing, George	grocer, £75.
Gerard, Sir Gilbert	London, gentleman, MP, £600; Providence Island Company 1630; Treasurer of the Army 1642; Committee of Safety 1642; Commission to Regulate Colonies 1643; Committee for Foreign Plantations 1643; Assessments Middlesex 1643; Committee of Both kingdoms 1644; Commissioner for Compounding 1647; Derby House Committee 1648.

Gerard, Jacob	London, salter, £600; Alderman Bishpsgate, 1637–40, Candlewick, 1640–48; Subsidy for Fairfax and Ireland 1647; knighted 3 December 1641; created Baronet, August 1662; Committee EEIC 1641–42, 1643–44, 1647–56; died 1666.
Gibbes, Christopher	£100.
Gibbes, Richard	Buckinghamshire, £200; Assessments, London 1648; Collector £90,000 per month subsidy 1649.
Gibbs, Thomas	Somerset, Bath, £25; Artillery Company 1635; payment on behalf of the Corporation of Bath.
Gibbs, William	London, goldsmith, £250; Artillery Company 1636; Alderman, Farringdon Without, 1642–49, Commissioner London Militia 1642; Trustee for Bishops' Lands 1646; London Militia 1647; £200,000 loan for Ireland 1647; Subsidy for Fairfax and Ireland 1647; Relief of the Poor, London 1647; Collector £90,000 per month subsidy 1649; MP Suffolk 1654–55, 1656–58; Prime Warden Goldsmiths 1643–44, Stockholder of Dorchester Company 1629; died c. May, 1689.
Giles, Samuel	Sussex, clothworker, £50.
Giles, Thomas	London/Salem, £1,000; planter in Salem, Massachusetts.
Gill, Alexander	Lurgan, Armagh, gentleman, £6.
Gippes, George	£100.
Gippes, Richard	Aldeburgh, gentleman, £200; Subsidy for Fairfax and Ireland 1647.
Gitting, Michael	London, merchant tailor, £100.
Gittings, Edward	London, plasterer, £100.
Glanville, John	Plymouth, barrister, MP, £600; royalist.
Goade, Christopher	London, clothworker, £100.
Goddard, Jonathan	London, shipwright, £100.
Goddard, William	London, shipwright, £100; Assessments, London 1648.
Godfrey, Joseph	London, £25.
Godsen, Henry	Surrey, merchant, £100.
Good, Ellis	London, horner, £100.
Goodman, John	Leicestershire, £50; County Association 1642; Assessments Leicester 1643; Subsidy for Fairfax and Ireland 1647.

Goodwin, Arthur	Buckinghamshire, gentleman, MP, £400; Sequestrations Buckinghamshire 1643.
Goodwin, Benjamin	London, gentleman, £300; Bermuda Company investor; Treasurer Loan and Contribution for Ireland, January 1643.
Goodwin, John	London, clothworker, £100; Artillery Company 1642; Coellector of Plate Money 1642; Assessments Surrey 1643; Subsidy for Fairfax and Ireland 1647; Alderman, Dowgate, 1650–52, Bridge, 1652–57; Commissioner Customs 1643–55, 1649–(?)57; Commissioner for the Ordnance 1652–53; Derby House Committee 1652–53; died 15 December 1657.
Goodwin, Robert	London, gentleman, £150; Bermuda Company investor; £120,000 per month 1645; Commissioner for Compounding 1647; Subsidy for Fairfax and Ireland 1647.
Goswell, James	London, barber surgeon, £50; Assessments 1643.
Gouch, William	£100.
Gould, Isaac	London, draper, £150.
Gould, James	Exeter, gentleman, £200; Subsidy for Fairfax and Ireland 1647.
Gower, Thomas	London, lawyer, £600; Collector of Plate Money 1642; Artillery Company 1642; London Militia 1647; Committee of Adventurers 1654; EEIC Shareholder 1657; Colonel Orange Regiment 1658.
Grannow, Nathaniel	London, merchant tailor, £25.
Grantham, Henry	London, draper, £60; Collector of Plate Money 1642.
Grantham, Sarah	London, £62.
Graunt, Samuel	London, draper, £750; Collector of Plate Money 1642.
Graves, Richard	London, gentleman, £200; High Court Justice 1650.
Graves, William	London, blacksmith, £100.
Greenhill, William	London, Farringdon Within, clothworker, £100; Artillery Company 1620; Collector of Plate Money 1642; Common Council 1643; Treasurer, Wounded Soldiers 1643; Searcher for Excise 1647; Collection for Distressed Protestants of Ireland 1647; Assessments, London 1648.

Greensmith, John	merchant tailor, £300; Artillery Company 1641; £60,000 loan for army 1643; Commissioner for Sequestrations 1659.
Greenwell, Robert	London, grocer, £50.
Gregson, George	London, clothworker, £50; Collector Advance of Money, Dowgate 1642.
Gregson, William	London, merchant tailor, £100.
Grocer, John	London, butcher, £100; Artillery Company 1640.
Grove, Hugh	Suffolk, £100; Collector of Plate Money 1642.
Gulson, Henry	London, painter stainer, £100.
Gunning, John	Bristol, gentleman, £1,000; Alderman of Bristol; Subsidy for Fairfax and Ireland 1647.
Gunston, William	London, factor, £100.
Gurdon, John	Ipswich, gentleman, MP, £1,000; Providence Island Company 1630.
Guy, Nicholas	£200.
Hales, Sir Edward	Kent, gentleman, MP, £1,200; married to Deborah Harlekenden; local committees of Sequestration and Assessment 1643; EEIC 1643.
Hales, Robert	Kent, gentleman, £1,200; Subsidy for Fairfax and Ireland 1647.
Hall, George	£250.
Hall, Godfrey	£50.
Halstead, Laurence	London, draper, £150; merchant adventurer; Treasurer of Adventure for Irish land, 1642.
Hammond, Thomas	£300.
Hampden, John	Buckinghamshire, gentleman, MP, £1,000; Committee of Safety 1642.
Hampden, Richard	£31.
Hampson, Henry	London, merchant tailor, £200.
Hampson, Thomas	London, gentleman, £600; Artillery Company 1645.
Hanna, Anthony	Surrey, Kingston, £25.
Harding, Alice and William	London, gentleman, £1,000.
Hardnett, Robert	London, Limehouse, apothecary, £200.
Harford, Heneage	£25.
Harlakenden, Martin	Essex, £200; Subsidy for Fairfax and Ireland 1647.
Harold, Nathaniel	£50.

Harpur, John	London, fishmonger, £250; Assessments, London 1648; Alderman, Vintry, 1650; Prime Warden fishmongers 1654; died March 1667.
Harrington, James	Upton, Northamptonshire, £25; Council of State 1649; Derby House Committee 1652–53.
Harrington, Lady Jane	Upton, Northamptonshire, £50.
Harrington, John	London, £200; Colonel Trained Bands Westminster, 1643.
Harrington, Sir William	Upton, Northamptonshire, £25; EEIC Shareholder 1657.
Harris, John	London, £100; Assessments, London 1648; EEIC Shareholder 1657.
Harris, Thomas	London, St Saviors, merchant, £100; £60,000 loan for army 1643; Common Council 1643; Assessments, London 1648.
Harrison, Edmund	London, £250; Committee of Adventurers 1654; EEIC Shareholder 1657.
Harrison, John	Lancaster, MP, £300; EEIC Shareholder 1657.
Harrison, William	Lancaster, £100; EEIC Shareholder 1657.
Harrison, William	Nottingham, financier, MP, £150; royalist, accompanied Charles I to Nottingham for raising of the standard August 1642; died 1643.
Harsnett, Samuel	London, £25; Artillery Company 1629; Collector of Plate Money 1642.
Harte, John	£100; Artillery Company 1622.
Harvey, Edmund	London, draper, £200; Artillery Company 1641; Collector of Plate Money 1642; Alderman, Dowgate, 1650, Farringdon Without, 1653; MP Great Bodwin 1646–53, Middlesex 1654–55; Commissioner Customs 1649–55; died 25 June 1673.
Hastings, Henry	London, £100; Committee for Speedy Raising of Money, 1643.
Hatt, John	London, gentleman, £600.
Hatton, Thomas	London, Sixth Clerks Office, £10; EEIC Shareholder 1657.
Hawes, William	London, £525; Artillery Company 1620; Common Council 1643.
Hawkins, William	London, clerk, £3,675; married to Anna Thomson, sister of Maurice, George and Robert; Secretary, Committee of Adventurers

	for Land 1642–48; Collector of Plate Money 1642; Collector, Fairfax's Army 1645; Commissioner, £50,000 for Ireland 1648; Collector £90,000 per month subsidy 1649; Commisary General Ireland 1649–51; Committee of Adventurers 1654; High Sherriff of Cork 1653–1660.
Hawks, Henry	London, tallow chandler, £62.
Heathcot, Grave	Culthorp, £32.
Henley, George	London, Castle Baynard, tobacco merchant, £300; Collector, Supplies for Ireland 1642; Common Council 1643.
Henman, William	London, merchant tailor, £150.
Herbert, Phillip, earl of Pembroke and Montgomery	London, Westminster, Peer, £600; Virginia Company, 1612; East India Company 1614; North-West Passage Company, 1612; Guiana Company, 1626. On 2 February 1627–8 he received a grant of 'certain islands between 8 and 13 degrees of north latitude, called Trinidado, Tobago, Barbadoes, and Fonseca, with all the islets within ten leagues of their shores, on condition that a rent of a wedge of gold weighing a pound should be paid to the king or his heirs when he or they came into those parts'. Challenged by James Hay, earl of Carlisle, who sent out ships to take possession of Barbados in 1629; Committee of Safety 1642; Committee for Foreign Plantations 1643; Committee for the Revenue 1645; Derby House Committee 1648.
Heveningham, William	£600; Assessments Suffolk 1643; Subsidy for Fairfax and Ireland 1647; Council of State 1649.
Heyden, Francis	£87.
Hiccocks, William	London, St Johns, brewer, £500; £60,000 loan for army 1643; Assessments, London 1648; Committee of Adventurers 1654.
Hickman, Henry	£450, Artillery Company 1627.
Higate, Edmund	£25.
Higgins, Richard	£62.
Hildesley, Mark	London, Coleman Street, vintner, £100; Artillery Company 1626; Committee for Advance of Money 1642; Alderman, Bread

APPENDIX

	Street, 1649–51, Commissioner Customs 1649(?); Collector £90,000 per month subsidy 1649; Commissioner for Prize Goods 1649; Master Vintners 1650; High Court Justice 1650, 1653; Tower Hamlets militia 1659; died 1660.
Hill, Richard	London, merchant, £450; Artillery Company 1639; Commissioner Sea Adventure 1642; Commissioner for Navy and Customs 1649; Commissioner Sale of Dutch Prizes 1652–53.
Hill, Roger	Somerset, Taunton, gentleman, £200; Collector, Somerset 1643; Commissioner for Compounding 1647.
Hill, Rowland	London, cordwainer, £100.
Hill, Rowland	Salop, gentleman, £1,000; Subsidy for Fairfax and Ireland 1645.
Hill, William	London, draper, £50.
Hind, John	£25; Artillery Company 1645.
Hippisley, Edward	Somerset, Ston Easton, gentleman, £6.
Hippisley, John	Somerset, Ston Easton, gentleman, £25; Assessments, Somerset 1643; Collector (London) £90,000 per month subsidy 1649.
Hippisley, Richard	Somerset, Ston Easton, gentleman, £6.
Hippisley, Thomas	Somerset, Ston Easton, gentleman, £25; Treasurer, Somerset 1643.
Hoare, David	Westminster, £31.
Hobland, James	Southwark, St Olaves, dyer, £250; Captain, Trained Bands Southwark, 1643.
Hobson, William	Southwark, grocer, £125; Captain, Trained Bands Southwark, 1643; Common Council 1643; Trustee for Bishops' Lands 1646.
Hodges, Thomas	London, St Saviors, merchant, £600; £60,000 loan for army 1643; Accounts for the Whole kingdom 1644; Ransom of Algiers Captives 1645; Subsidy for Fairfax and Ireland 1647.
Hodylow, Richard	London, barber surgeon, £50.
Holland, Cornelius	London, gentleman, MP, £600; Government of the West Indies 1643; Committee for Foreign Plantations 1643; Committee for the Revenue 1643; Council of State 1649.
Holland, John	Southwark, gentleman, £450; Navy Commissioner 1642; Commissioner for Prize Goods 1643; Subsidy for Fairfax and Ireland

	1647; Commissioner for Navy and Customs 1649; Commissioner for Prize Goods 1649; Navy Commissioner 1652–53.
Honnor, John	London, gentleman, £750; Collector, Westminster Subsidy 1643.
Honywood, Edward	London, Farringdon, ironmonger, £125; Common Council 1643; Assessments, London 1648.
Houghton, John	London, fishmonger, £10.
Houghton, Robert	Southwark, brewer, £25; £120,000 per month 1645; Subsidy for Fairfax and Ireland 1647.
Hovell, Hoogan	London, Broad Street, grocer, £200; Artillery Company 1635; Committee for Advance of Money 1642; Commissioner for arrears 1645; Assessments, London 1648; Collector £90,000 per month subsidy 1649.
How, Thomas	Exeter, £600.
Howard, Nicholas	£50.
Hoxton, John	London, shipwright, £100.
Hoyle, Thomas	York, gentleman, MP, £450; Committee for the Revenue 1643.
Hubland, James	Southwark, distiller, £650; Colonel Trained Bands, Southwark 1643; EEIC shareholder 1657.
Hudson, George	London, haberdasher, £100.
Hudson, Thomas	Southwark, skinner, £100; Artillery Company 1622; Lieutenant Colonel Trained Bands, Southwark 1643; £120,000 per month 1645; Subsidy for Fairfax and Ireland 1647.
Hughes, George	London, grocer, £100.
Hull, Richard	London, £200.
Humphrey, John	London, embroiderer, £50; Trustee of King's Goods 1649.
Humphreys, Nathaniel	London, ironmonger, £100; Artillery Company 1642.
Hunt, Richard	London, merchant, £600; Common Council 1643; Assada Company 1646; EEIC 1643.
Hurst, John	London, £225; Artillery Company 1638; Trustee Fee-Farms 1650.
Hussey, Thomas	London, grocer, £433; Alderman Vintry, 1645, Collector £90,000 per month subsidy 1649; MP Whitchurch 1645–53, Andover 1656–57; died 1657.

APPENDIX

Hutchins, Thomas	London, Bishopsgate, mercer, £100; Massachusetts Bay Company; Committee for Advance of Money 1642; EEIC 1643; Accounts for the Whole kingdom 1644.
Hutchinson, Richard	London, ironmonger, £150; Artillery Company 1622; Treasurer, Wounded Soldiers 1643; Searcher for Excise 1647; Collection for Distressed Protestants of Ireland 1647; Assessments, London 1648; Commissioner for Navy and Customs 1649; Navy Commissioner 1652–53; Committee of Adventurers 1654; EEIC Shareholder 1657.
Hylands, Samuel	London, distiller, £12.
Irons, Richard	London, £250; Assessments, London 1648.
Irons, Thomas	London, £60.
Isaack, Nicholas	London, £100.
Ivatt, Thomas	Devon, Combe Martin, £337.
Jackson, Abraham	London, goldsmith, £300.
Jackson, Alexander	London, £100.
Jackson, Thomas	London, pewterer, £100.
Jeffryes, John	London, haberdasher, £100; Artillery Company 1642.
Jenkins, Moses	London, gentleman, £200.
Jenner, Christopher	London, merchant, £200; Artillery Company 1629; £60,000 loan for army 1643.
Jenner, William	London, draper, £200.
Jephson, William	Mallow, gentleman, £75; son-in-law of Sir Thomas Norreys and landowner in Mallow, County Cork; MP for Stockbridge; Commissioner for Hampshire 1644, Lt. Gov. Portsmouth 1645; joined Cromwell's Irish campaign and elected for Cork in Protectorate parliament of 1654.
Jesson, William	Leicestershire, merchant tailor, £137; Subsidy for Fairfax and Ireland 1647.
Johnson, John	Warwickshire, Alcester, £25; Subsidy for Fairfax and Ireland 1647.
Johnson, Thomas	London, merchant, £150; Artillery Company 1620.
Jones, Owen	London, pewterer, £100.
Jonnor, Thomas	£50.

Juryn, Abraham	London, merchant, £200; Artillery Company 1642.
Juryn, John	London, merchant, £500; Assessments, London 1648.
Juxon, Arthur	London, Walbrook, salter, £200; Common Council 1643.
Juxon, Thomas	London, merchant tailor, £100; Artillery Company 1637; £60,000 loan for army 1643; EEIC Shareholder 1657.
Kendall, James	London, merchant, £50.
Kendall, Thomas	London, merchant, £12.
Kendall, William	London, Breadstreet, merchant tailor, £300; Common Council 1643; London Militia 1647; Relief of the Poor, London 1647.
Kendrick, John	London, grocer, £700; Committee for Advance of Money 1642; Common Council 1643; Treasurer Loan and Contribution for Ireland Jan. 1643; Treasurer, Doubling Ordinance (Irish land) 1643; Subsidy for Fairfax and Ireland 1647; Alderman, Langbourn, 1643–48, Broad Street, 1648–61; Commissioner Excise 1643–50; Collector £90,000 per month subsidy 1649; Commissioner for Excise 1650–53; died February 1661.
Kidderminster, Edmund	London, gentleman, £100.
Kilby, John	Hertfordshire, yeoman, £50.
King, Benjamin	Hertfordshire, clothworker, £25.
King, John	London, £275; Artillery Company 1640; Assessments, London 1648; Militia, Tower Hamlets 1648.
King, Nathaniel	Hertfordshire, clothworker, £25.
King, Thomas	Hertfordshire, clothworker, £100.
Kingston, Philip	London, stationer, £108; Artillery Company 1621.
Knight, John	London, scrivener, £312.
Knight, Thomas	Oxford, gentleman, £200; Artillery Company 1620; Subsidy for Fairfax and Ireland 1647.
Knightley, William	Surrey, Kingston, £12.
Knowle, James	Surrey, Kingston, £15.
Lamb, Thomas	London, woodmonger, £50.
Lambell, Robert	London, grocer, £300; Artillery Company 1641.
Lambert, Roger	London, grocer, £100.

Lambert, William	London, woodmonger, £100.
Lane, John	London, grocer, £633; Artillery Company 1635.
Lane, William	Sussex, gentleman, £600.
Langham, Samuel	London, Portsoken, grocer, £700; brother of Alderman John Langham; Common Council 1643; MP London 1654–55; Southwark 1660–61; Committee EEIC 1626–27, 1628–42; Treasurer Levant Company 1632–34 (Court Assistants 1621–32, 1634–38, elected Governor 1654); died 13 May 1671.
Langley, John	London, fishmonger, £700; Artillery Company 1639; Accounts for the Whole kingdom 1644; Assessments, London 1648; Commissioner for Navy and Customs 1649; Collector £90,000 per month subsidy 1649; Alderman, Langbourn, 1649–50; Commissioner for Prize Goods 1649; MP London 1653; High Court Justice 1650, 1653 Commissioner Admiralty and Navy 1652; Deputy-Governor Levant Company 1671–72 (Court Assistants 1643–48, 1649–50, 1664–71, 1672–73); Committee EEIC 1650–52, 1653–55, 1656–57; Prime Warden fishmongers 1652.
Lasingby, Richard	London, haberdasher, £100; Artillery Company 1627.
Later, Thomas	London; Southwark, £100; Collector, Advance of Money 1643.
Lee, John	London, salter, £175.
Lenthall, Thomas	London, Billingsgate, gentleman, £200; Committee for Advance of Money 1642; Common Councillor 1642–51; Committee for Church Government 1644; Commissioner for arrears 1645; Committee for borrowed arms 1645; Subsidy for Fairfax and Ireland 1647; Assessments, London 1648; EEIC Shareholder 1657.
Leverett, John	Surrey, mercer, £100; EEIC Shareholder 1657.
Levitt, James	Surrey, Kingston, £5.
Levitt, William	London, woodmonger, £25; Artillery Company 1641.
Lewellin, Robert	London, salter, £25.
Lewin, Edmund	London, merchant tailor, £1,200.
Lincoln, Thomas	Norfolk, £100.

Ling, John	London, gentleman, £600; East India Company agent at Surat 1633–35.
Ling, Joseph	London, stationer, £100; Henry and John Ling lived at Flowerdew Hundred, Virginia in 1623. Nicholas Ling joined the Artillery Company in 1628.
Lippiatt, Christopher	Wiltshire, £50.
Litler, Richard	London, apothecary, £100.
Littleton, Edward	Staffordshire, gentleman, MP, £450; Lord Keeper of the Great Seal.
Loader, David	London, merchant, £200.
Loader, Richard	London, merchant, £16.
Lobb, Richard	£250.
Lockyer, Nicholas	London, clothworker, £125.
Long, Walter	Whaddon, Wiltshire, gentleman, £300; Committee for Advance of Money 1642; Sequestrations Essex 1643; wounded at Edgehill; removed from parliament 1647 and exiled in France with Sir John Clotworthy.
Long, William	Cornwall, Stratton, £25; Treasurer, Somerset 1643.
Lordell, James	London, mercer, £100; Artillery Company 1642.
Loton, Richard	London, brewer, £100; Militia, Tower Hamlets 1648.
Love, Christopher	London, clothworker, £100.
Lovering, John	Exeter, gentleman, £600.
Lowe, William	Herefordshire, cleric, £100; EEIC Shareholder 1657.
Lucas, Edward	Norfolk, £50.
Lucas, John	London, pewterer, £150; Artillery Company 1621.
Lynne, Samuel	London, carpenter, £100.
Lyon, Thomas	Hertfordshire, £50.
Maberly, Thomas	London, weaver, £150.
Magott, George	London, pewterer, £50.
Mann, Elizabeth	London, £30.
Mann, James	London, Dowgate, £10; Common Council 1643; EEIC 1643.
Mann, Thomas	London, £300; Artillery Company 1620; EEIC 1643.
Mansell, John	£100.

Marriot, John	London, merchant tailor, £150; Artillery Company 1629.
Marriott, Thomas	Wapping, mariner, £150.
Marshall, William	London, mariner, £50; Artillery Company 1624.
Marten, Henry	Berkshire, gentleman, MP, £300; Regicide; creditor of earl of Warwick for £2,400 in August 1641; Committee of Safety 1642; Sequestrations, Bedford 1643; Council of State 1649.
Marten, James	London, Cornhill, fishmonger, £100; Common Council 1643; Assessments, London 1648.
Martin, John	Nottingham, gentleman, £200; Subsidy for Fairfax and Ireland 1647.
Masham, Sir William	Essex, gentleman, £600; Assessments, Essex 1643; Subsidy for Fairfax and Ireland 1647; Derby House Committee 1648; Council of State 1649.
Massey, Robert	Surrey, Kingston, £20.
Master, Richard	London, blacksmith, £300.
Master, Thomas	London, blacksmith, £23; Artillery Company 1635.
Maulthus, Robert	Berkshire, draper, £100.
May, Thomas	London, Walbrook, cordwainer, £50; Common Council 1643.
Maynard, John	London, draper, £300; cousin of George Henly, assistant to Nicholas Loftus.
Mayne, John	Exeter, merchant, £100.
Mead, Thomas	London, merchant, £600; EEIC 1643.
Meade, Robert	London, Walbrook, mercer, £475; Artillery Company 1624; Committee for Advance of Money 1642; Common Council 1643; Trustee for Bishops' Lands 1646; Subsidy for Fairfax and Ireland 1647; Assessments, London 1648.
Meredith, Christopher	London, Walbrook, stationer, £200; Artillery Company 1635; Common Council 1643.
Methold, William	London, skinner, £1700; Artillery Company 1628; Alderman, Cripplegate, 1647; Treasurer Excise 1643–(?); Committee EEIC 1640–53 (Deputy-Governor 1643–53); Commissioner for Prize Goods 1643; Accounts for the Whole kingdom 1644; Ransom of Algiers Captives 1645; Collector £90,000 per month subsidy

	1649; Commissioner for Trade 1650; nephew of William Methold, chief baron of the Irish Exchequer; joined East India Company 1615 and rose to become factor at Surat; negotiated merger of EEIC with Thomson's Assada Company; resident at Surat 1652–53; died 5 March 1653.
Miles, Abraham	£133.
Miles, Gabriell	London, mercer, £800; moved to Amsterdam in 1651 and sold Adventure to Samuel Avery.
Mills, Thomas	London, skinner, £50; Artillery Company 1620.
Molins, William	London, innkeeper, £350; Assessments, London 1648.
Moncke, Priscilla	Exeter, widow, £100.
Monsey, Mithnell	£50.
Montague, William	London, whitebaker, £31.
Moody, Samuel	Suffolk, Bury St Edmunds, £400.
Moore, Dorothy	Dublin, £150.
Moore, L.	Devon, yeoman, £25.
Morgan, Anthony	London, linen draper, £200.
Morley, Harbert	£600, Sussex, gentleman.
Morley, William	Sussex, gentleman, MP, £300; Derby House Committee 1652–53; Committee of the Admiralty 1652–53.
Morrall, Richard	London, Aldgate, goldsmith, £100, Common Council 1643; Relief of the Poor, London 1647; Assessments, London 1648.
Moundeford, Edmond	Norfolk, gentleman, MP, £300; Providence Island Company 1630.
Mountney, Cornelius	London, haberdasher, £100; Artillery Company 1642.
Mountney, Richard	London, merchant, £312; EEIC Shareholder 1657.
Moyer, Samuel	London, merchant, £375; Artillery Company 1638; Commissioner Sea Adventure 1642; Commissioner for Compounding 1647; Militia, Tower Hamlets 1648; Assessments, London 1648; Commissioner for Navy and Customs 1649; Collector £90,000 per month subsidy 1649; High Court Justice 1650, 1653; Commissioner for Compounding 1653;

	EEIC Shareholder 1657; Probate Judge 1659; Commissioner for sequestrations 1659.
Munday, William	London, merchant, £25.
Murdock, Joseph	London, silkweaver, £100.
Musgrave, Phillip	Devon, tanner, £20.
Musgrave, William	Devon, tanner, £20.
Nettle, William	Devon, £100.
Nettleship, Hugh	London, salter, £200; EEIC Shareholder 1657.
Newman, Francis	London, haberdasher, £150.
Nicholas, Christopher	London, Castle Baynard, dyer, £25; Committee for Advance of Money 1642.
Nicholas, Isaack	London, Castle Baynard, dyer, £200.
Nicholson, Christopher	London, £25.
Nobbes, John	London, bowyer, £62.
Norman, Robert	Hackney, gentleman, £100.
Norris, Hugh	London, merchant, £200; Assessments, London 1648; EEIC Shareholder 1657.
North, Richard	Cornwall, Stratton, £5.
Northcott, John	Devonshire, gentleman, MP, £225; Subsidy for Fairfax and Ireland 1647.
Official, William	Great Yarmouth, merchant, £600.
Offley, Stephen	London, merchant, £50.
Oldfield, John	London, fishmonger, £200; Common Council 1643; EEIC 1643; Commissioner for Compounding 1647; Relief of the Poor, London 1647; Alderman, Farringdon Without, 1649, Committee EEIC 1652–7; died 1657; son married to daughter of Maurice Thomson.
Oldfield, Samuel	Surrey, Kingston, gentleman, MP, £250; Artillery Company 1617; EEIC 1618; Assessments Lincoln 1643; killed 1643.
Onslow, Sir Richard	Surrey, gentleman, MP, £400; owner of the Queen's Arms Tavern, Holborn, convenient to Warwick House; commanded a Surrey regiment for parliament and dominated the Surrey county committees; Derby House Committee 1648.
Orchard, Thomas	London, pewterer, £100.
Orton, Nicholas	London, clothworker, £375.
Otgar, Abraham	London, merchant, £750.
Overing, Edward	London, salter, £200; EEIC 1643.
Overton, Nathaniel	London, stationer, £25.

Owen, John	London, grocer, £500; EEIC Shareholder 1657.
Owen, Thomas	Exeter, £50.
Ower, Mathew	London, grocer, £100.
Owner, Edward	Great Yarmouth, gentleman, £600; Adventure on behalf of town of Great Yarmouth.
Packer, John	London, gentleman, £600; Clerk of the Privy seal and a colleague of David Watkins and William Hawkins. Acquired great wealth but mainly in royalist areas, lost during the Civil War. In his will, 1645, he stipulated that his Adventure was to be invested in raising Irish children as Protestants; Collector, Fairfax's Army 1645.
Page, Edmund	London, haberdasher, £500; EEIC 1643.
Page, Thomas	Dartmouth, merchant, £100.
Painter, Nicholas	Bristol, merchant, £50.
Pargiter, Thomas	London, grocer, £100; EEIC Shareholder 1657.
Parker, John	London, St Mary, haberdasher, £700; contributed to £5,000 loan for the relief of Munster in 1645.
Parker, John	London, haberdasher, £50.
Parker, John and Charles	London, drapers, £200.
Parker, Phillip	London, skinner, £600; Adventured for John Dethwick.
Parkes, Edward	London, Farringdon, merchant tailor, £100; Advance Money Collector, Farringdon 1643; Assessments, London 1648; Collector £90,000 per month subsidy 1649.
Parkett, William	London, gentleman, £500; Artillery Company 1642.
Parkhurst, John	Kent, Margate, £7.
Parkhurst, Sir Robert	Surrey, gentleman, MP, £500; Committee for Irish Affairs 1641; Commissioner for speeding and Despatching the Business for Ireland, 1642; Assessments and sequestrations (Surrey) 1643; brother-in-law of William Spurstowe, a New England planter, and the Craddocks.
Parr, Christopher	London, merchant, £100.
Parrott, John	London, silkweaver, £200.
Parsons, Fenton	London, merchant tailor, £90; Artillery Company 1640; Commissioner £50,000 for Ireland 1648.

Parsons, Henry	Devon, merchant, £300.
Parsons, Robert	London, weaver, £50.
Partridge, Edward	Kent, gentleman, £300.
Partridge, John	London, haberdasher, £200.
Pattison, Edward	Devon, £30.
Payne, Roger	Somerset, £3.
Peacock, William	London, painter stainer, £100.
Peake, William	London, cordwainer, £100; Artillery Company 1635; EEIC Shareholder 1657.
Peasley, William	London, sadler, £30.
Peck, Francis	London, clothworker, £75; Commissioner London Militia 1642.
Peckett, William	Kent, Margate, gentleman, £200.
Pedder, Mathew	Kent, Margate, £100.
Pendleton, Michael	London, grocer, £100.
Pennington, Isaac	London, fishmonger, £1,000; Treasurer Advance of Money 1643–; Alderman, Bridge Without, 1639–57, Councillor of State 1649–51, 1651–52; MP London 1640–53, 1659–60; Colonel White Regiment 1642; Commissioner for Assessments 1642; £120,000 per month 1645; Subsidy for Fairfax and Ireland 1647; Lieutenant Tower 1642–45; Governor Levant Company 1644–54; Commissioner for Compounding 1647; Council of State 1649; Prime Warden Fishmongers 1640; died 17 December 1661.
Pennoyer, Samuel	London, clothworker, £450; Commissioner for Navy and Customs 1649; Levant Company 1654; emigrated to New England.
Pennoyer, William	London, clothworker, £150; Commissioner Sea Adventure 1642; Treasurer Loan and Contribution for Ireland Jan. 1643; Militia, Tower Hamlets 1648; Commissioner for Navy and Customs 1649; High Court Justice 1650, 1653; Committee of Adventurers 1654.
Perry, John	London, silkweaver, £750.
Pettit, Henry	London, merchant tailor, £200.
Peyton, Thomas	Kent, gentleman, MP, £400; royalist.
Pheasant, Jasper	Dublin, clergyman, £100; ordained Deacon at Dublin, 1 March 1640; appointed Dean of Killaloe, 1661.

APPENDIX

Pheasant, Stephen	London, lawyer, £200.
Phillips, Thomas	London, clothworker, £40.
Pickering, Gilbert	Northampton, gentleman, £600; present at trial of Charles I but did not sign warrant and was pardoned; Assessments Northampton 1643; Derby House Committee 1652–53; Council of State 1657–60.
Pindar, Thomas	Exeter, £100.
Pinn, Samuel	London, carpenter, £100.
Pither, William	London, draper, £100.
Player, Thomas	London, haberdasher, £200; Assessments, London 1648.
Plucknett, George	London, scrivener, £100.
Poares, Edmund	Bedford, £100.
Polen, John	London, baker, £300.
Poole, John	Dorset, Poole, gentleman, £103; served as trustee of Lismore Castle.
Popham, Francis	Somerset, gentleman, MP, £750; member Virginia Company, New England Company; Treasurer, Somerset 1643.
Pordage, John	London, physician, £100.
Porter, Richard	Hertfordshire, gentleman, £600.
Potter, Benjamin	London, sadler, £50.
Potter, Benjamin	London, Farringdon Without, soapmaker, £50; Common Council 1643.
Potts, John	London, gentleman, MP, £800; Commissioner for Excise 1645–48.
Poulstead, Henry	London, gentleman, £450; EEIC 1643.
Poulstead, Henry Jr	London, gentleman, £120.
Poulstead, John	London, gentleman, £600.
Poulter, John	London, yeoman, £70.
Prestley, William	Hertfordshire, £146; Artillery Company 1641; Assessments 1643.
Priaulx, William	Sussex, clothworker, £50.
Price, George	Esher, Surrey, £225.
Prior, Robert	London, gentleman, £675.
Proctor, Henry	London, weaver, £100.
Pritty, Peregrine	London, £200; Assessments, London 1648.
Puller, Amherst	Hertfordshire, cleric, £200.
Pury, Thomas	Gloucester, gentleman, £1323; Subsidy for Fairfax and Ireland 1647.
Pydrock, Thomas	Westminster, gentleman, £100.

APPENDIX

Pye, Sir Robert	Westminster, gentleman, MP, £1,000; capt. of horse 1642, col. 1644–47; Subsidy for Fairfax and Ireland 1647; Commissioner for militia, Berks. 1648–60; JP 1651–83, 1689–d.; capt. of militia horse April 1660.
Pyle, Edmond	Dartmouth, merchant, £100.
Pym, John	Westminster, gentleman, MP, £600; Providence Island Company 1634; Committee for Irish Affairs 1642; Committee of Safety 1642; Treasurer, Somerset 1643; Government of the West Indies 1643; Committee for Foreign Plantations 1643; Committee for the Revenue 1643; died 1643.
Pytt, Henry	Bristol, soapmaker, £300.
Quiny, Richard	London, grocer, £100; tobacco importer. Turgis was a partner in the Kent Island project; £60,000 loan for army 1643.
Rainborrow, Thomas	London, merchant, £100; Commissioner Sea Adventure 1642.
Rainborrow, William	London, mariner, £100; Master Trinity House, 1636.
Ralph, John	London, £207.
Rand, William	London, gentleman, £200.
Randolph, Tobias	Radcliff, gentleman, £75; Master of Radcliff School.
Ratcliffe, Anthony	Buckinghamshire, gentleman, £300; EEIC Shareholder 1657.
Ratcliffe, Hugh	London, haberdasher, £62; Artillery Company 1635; Assessments, London 1648.
Ratcliffe, Peter	Devon, yeoman, £20.
Rathband, William	London, clothworker, £100.
Raymant, John	London, baker, £300; Assessments, Essex 1643.
Read, John	London, carpenter, £50; Advance Money collector, Southwark 1642.
Read, Samuel	Exeter, doctor, £12.
Redferne, John	Surrey, Kingston, £7.
Reeve, Godfry	London, baker, £100.
Regemorter, Ahasuerus	London, doctor, £400; Artillery Company 1638; personal physician to Oliver Cromwell.
Rendall, William	London, merchant, £300.
Reinolds, John	Sussex, £25.

Reynolds, Sir John	Wiltshire, gentleman, MP, £1,800; Commissary General 1642; Committee for Irish Affairs 1642–48.
Reynolds, William	London, merchant, £200; Artillery Company 1635; Common Council 1643.
Rich, Thomas	London, vintner, MP, £100; married Elizabeth Cockayne; Artillery Company 1642; Levant Company merchant; EEIC 1643; Ransom of Algiers Captives 1645; Alderman, Bridge, 1650; Created Baronet March 1661; MP, Reading 1660; Sheriff Berks 1657; Committee E.I.C. 1642–43, 1648–54; died 15 October 1667.
Richardson, Richard	London, haberdasher, £31; Artillery Company 1641.
Richardson, Samuel	Westminster, gentleman, £125; Artillery Company 1641; EEIC Shareholder 1657.
Richardson, Thomas	London, scrivener, £100; Auditor of army accounts 1648.
Ridges, William	London, silkweaver, £120.
Risbey, William	London, draper, £100; Artillery Company 1641.
Roach, Henry	Cornwall, £25.
Roberts, Elias	London, Cornhill, haberdasher, £325; brother-in-law of Captain William Tucker.
Roberts, John	London, Cornhill, haberdasher, £300; Common Council 1643.
Robins, Edward	London, £100; Artillery Company 1635.
Robins, Robert	Somerset, £300.
Rodbeard, Thomas	London, fishmonger, £100.
Roe, Thomas	London, girdler, £50.
Rogers, Francis	Surrey, £100.
Rogers, Humphrey	Warwickshire, Birmingham, £25.
Rogers, Richard	London, grocer, £275; Artillery Company 1641; £60,000 loan for army 1643.
Rogers, Thomas	Exeter, £25.
Rogers, William	London, £50.
Rolfe, John	London, goldsmith, £68; father formerly governor of Virginia and husband of Pocahontas.
Rolins, Robert	London, merchant, £300; Virginia tobacco merchant.
Rolle, John	London, goldsmith, £500; goods seized by Charles I in 1628 over refusal to pay tonnage

	and poundage; Navy Commissioner 1642; Government of the West Indies 1643.
Rolle, Samuel	Devon, gentleman, £1,000; Rolle used Plymouth as a privateering base in the 1620s and 1630s. The family supplied the first group of settlers (Richard Rolle) to settle the Berkeley Hundred, Virginia. Family was slain during the Indian uprising of 1622. Subsidy for Fairfax and Ireland 1647; died in 1647.
Rose, Thomas	London, tallow chandler, £50; Artillery Company 1635.
Rothwell, John	London, stationer, £50.
Rothwell, Michael	London, stationer, £50.
Rouleston, Robert	London, merchant tailor, £100.
Russell, Francis	London, butcher, £64.
Russell, James	London, draper, £50; Commissioner Customs 1643–45; Relief of the Poor, London 1647; Commissioner for Navy and Customs 1649; Collector £90,000 per month subsidy 1649.
Russell, John	Sussex, yeoman, £250.
Rutton, Matthias	London, cleric, £200.
Sadler, John	London, merchant, £450; £60,000 loan for army 1643; Probate Judge 1659.
Sainthill, Peter	Devon, Dartwick, £225.
Salloway, Richard	London, grocer, £1,000; Artillery Company 1642; Commissioner for Compounding 1647; Commissioner for Trade 1650; brother of Humphrey Salloway, MP; brother-in-law of Richard Waring, treasurer for compounding.
Salmon, Henry	Cornwall, Stratton, £5.
Sanders, Laurence	London, factor, £100.
Samford, Christopher	Somerset, £100; County Treasurer, Somerset 1643.
Sanderson, Edward	Yorkshire, tanner, £250.
Sandon, John	London, cordwainer, £50.
Sargent, Jasper	Dublin, merchant, £25.
Savell, John	Exeter, merchant, £75.
Saville, Richard	Exeter, £100.
Scarlet, Nathaniel, John and Elizabeth	London, basketmakers, £200.
Scarlett, Israel	London, biscuitmaker, £100.
Scobell, Henry	London, lawyer, £200; Clerk of Parliament.

Scot, Edward	Kent, gentleman, MP, £400; married Mary Aldersey in 1639. Commissioner for Sequestrations and Assessments, Kent, 1643; associated with Edwin Sandys of the Virginia Company; organiser of Kentish petition of 1642.
Seagor, John	Exeter, £150.
Seagor, William	Exeter, £50.
Seale, William	Exeter, £25.
Seares, Roger	London, £100.
Searle, Christopher	Dorchester, £180.
Sedgwick, Stephen	London, brewer, £100.
Seignour, George	London, Tower, Lord of the Tower, £37.
Sewdon, John	Exeter, £25.
Shakespeare, Mary	London, £100.
Sheaf, Sampson	London, mercer, £100.
Shepherd, William	London, grocer, £50; Assessments, London 1648.
Sheppard, William and John	London, grocers, £150.
Sherbrooke, Richard	London, merchant tailor, £375; EEIC Shareholder 1657.
Sherlock, William	£200.
Shingler, Richard	London, draper, £100; Artillery Company 1641.
Shippey, William	London, Cheap, weaver, £275; Common Council 1643.
Short, John	London, grocer, £150; EEIC Shareholder 1657.
Shute, Richard	London, merchant, £200; Commissioner Sea Adventure 1642; Commissioner for Compounding 1647; Commissioner for Navy and Customs 1649; Collector £90,000 per month subsidy 1649; High Court Justice 1650,1653; EEIC Shareholder 1657.
Shute, Thomas	Somerset, Kilmersdon, gentleman, £5.
Shuttleworth, Richard	Lancashire, gentleman, £450, MP; Assessments Lancaster 1643; Subsidy for Fairfax and Ireland 1647.
Skinner, Augustin	Kent, gentleman, MP, £100.
Skippon, Philip	London, soldier, £50, Captain General Artillery Company 1641; Captain General London Trained Bands 1642; Commissioner London Militia 1642; Governor of Bristol 1645; London Militia 1647; Lt. of York 1647; Lt-Gen. Horse

	(Ireland) 1647; Subsidy for Fairfax and Ireland (Devonshire)1647; Derby House Committee 1648; Council of State 1649.
Smart, Ithiell	London, clerk, £100.
Smith, Edward	London, sadler, £125.
Smith, Francis	Greenwich, £50.
Smith, Henry	Leicester, grocer, £200; Collector, Fairfax's Army 1645; Subsidy for Fairfax and Ireland 1647.
Smith, Katherin	£100.
Smith, Richard	Leicester, grocer, £100.
Smith, Richard and **John**	London, Queenhithe, plasterer, £20; Artillery Company 1639; Committee for Advance of Money 1642.
Smith, Robert	London, draper, £675; Artillery Company 1641; Alderman, Bridge, 1650–51, knighted 25 August 1660; created Baronet, 1665; Committee EEIC 1652–53; Master Drapers 1651–52; died 12 June 1669.
Smith, Robert	Essex, gentleman, £600; EEIC 1643; Sequestrations Essex 1643; Collector, Fairfax's Army 1645; Subsidy for Fairfax and Ireland 1647.
Smith, Roger	Leicester, draper, £375; Council of Virginia Company 1621; merchant adventurer; father of Erasmus Smith; Collector, Fairfax's Army 1645; Subsidy for Fairfax and Ireland 1647.
Smith, Thomas	Southwark, gentleman, £100; major tobacco merchant; Artillery Company 1637; Secretary of the Admiralty 1642; Collector of Prize Ships 1643–44; Common Council 1643; Subsidy for Fairfax and Ireland 1647; Commissioner for Prize Goods 1649; Navy Commissioner 1652–53; EEIC Shareholder 1657.
Smyth, James	London, salter, £200.
Smyth, Joseph	London, haberdasher, £100; Artillery Company 1641.
Smyth, Simon	London, Dowgate, tallow chandler, £100; Advance Money collector 1643; EEIC Shareholder 1657.
Snell, Gregory	London, goldsmith, £325; Artillery Company 1642; EEIC Shareholder 1657.

Snelling, George	Southwark, St Olaves, distiller, £100; Captain Southwark Trained Band 1643; £120,000 per month 1645; Commissioner for Plantations 1646; Subsidy for Fairfax and Ireland 1647; Commissioner for Excise 1650–63.
Snelling, John	London, pewterer, £100.
Snow, John	London, Cannon Street, haberdasher, £100; Artillery Company 1641.
Soame, Thomas	London, grocer, MP, £1,000; Alderman, Farringdon Without, 1635–39, Vintry, 1639–41, Cheap, 1641–49, 1660–67; knighted 3 December 1641; Colonel Trained Bands 1638–42; President Honourable Artillery Company 1639–45; Commissioner for Assessments 1642; Treasurer Advance of Money 1643–48; Subsidy for £120,000 per month 1645; Commissioner for Compounding 1647; Subsidy for Fairfax and Ireland 1647; Court Assistant Levant Company 1616–17; Committee EEIC 1640–43, EEIC 1643; 1649–50; Master Grocers 1644–45; died 1 January 1671.
Sparrow, John	Suffolk, Rede, merchant, £50; Fee-farm Trustee 1647; High Court Justice 1650, 1653; Probate Judge 1659.
Sparrow, Phillip	Suffolk, Rede, merchant, £50.
Speller, John	Exeter, £50.
Spenser, Michael	York, £150.
Springal, Edmund	Sussex, £20.
Springal, William	Sussex, £300; Subsidy for Fairfax and Ireland 1647.
Squibb, Arthur	Southwark, £100; Subsidy for Fairfax and Ireland 1647; Sequestrations Surrey 1648; Collector £90,000 per month subsidy 1649; Commissioner for sequestrations 1659.
St John, Oliver	Bedfordshire, gentleman, MP, £300; Providence Island Company 1630, Solicitor General 1641; Committee of Safety 1642; Committee of Both kingdoms 1644; Derby House Committee 1648; Envoy to the Hague 1651.
Stackhouse, Roger	London, merchant tailor, £40.
Stanton, Edmond	London, clothworker, £200.

Stanton, John	London, clothworker, £100; Artillery Company 1641.
Stanton, Robert	London, clothworker, £375; Artillery Company 1642.
Starkey, Richard	Gravesend, gentleman, £75.
Steane, Thomas	London, wax chandler, £100; Assessments, London 1648.
Steedman, George	Cornwall, Stratton, £12.
Stevenfort, John	London, £50; Artillery Company 1641.
Stint, Thomas	Surrey, Kingston, £20.
Stock, Thomas	London, grocer, £200; Sale of goods by the candle, 1643; Assessments, London 1648; EEIC shareholder 1657.
Stocker, John	Somerset, £12.
Stone, Christopher	London, brewer, £100.
Stone, Samuel	London, brewer, £50.
Storey, Edward	London, ironmonger, £50; Artillery Company 1635; EEIC Shareholder 1657.
Storey, James	London, Cripplegate, merchant, £25; Common Council 1643.
Stoughton, Nicholas	Woking, gentleman, £50.
Stratton, Thomas	Bolton, £100.
Strickland, Sir William	Boynton, gentleman, MP, £600; grandson of Sebastian Cabot's lieutenant of the same name who introduced the turkey to England. John and Edward Strickland settled in New England in the 1630s. Committee for the Revenue 1643; Subsidy for Fairfax and Ireland 1647.
Stringer, Anthony	London, St Clement Dane, gentleman, £150.
Stubbins, Thomas	London, merchant, £200.
Sturmy, Joshua	Surrey, £40.
Sturning, Christopher	£20.
Swann, John	Kent, clothworker, £50.
Tallow Chandlers Company	London, corporate, £68.
Taylor, Edward	Oxford, William Street, merchant, £100.
Taylor, John	London, merchant, £75; Artillery Company 1635; EEIC shareholder 1657.
Taylor, Thomas	London, merchant, £75; Artillery Company 1640.
Temple, Thomas	Buckinghamshire, gentleman, £450; brother-in-law of William Fiennes.

Terry, Robert	London, draper, £50.
Thewar, John	Hertfordshire, £25.
Thomas, Edward	London, merchant, £100.
Thomas, Robert	Surrey, Kingston, merchant, £25.
Thomson, George	Southwark, merchant, MP, £1,150; Militia Commader Virginia 1636; earl of Essex life guard 1642; Colonel, parliamentary army; Navy Commissioner 1645–53; 1659–60; MP 1645–53; Council of State 1652–53, 1659–60; Parliamentary committees for trade, plantations and foreign affairs 1652–53; Admiralty Commissioner 1659–60; committee for intelligence 1659–60.
Thomson, Maurice	London, Worcester House, Bishopsgate Street, merchant, £1,300; Commissioner for Barbados 1640; Treasurer, Additional Sea Adventure 1642; Collector for Plate, Money and Horses 1642; Committee of Citizen Adventurers of London 1642; Commissioner for Assessments 1642; Treasurer Loan and Contribution for Ireland Jan. 1643; Bermuda Company 1643; Customs Commissioner 1643–45; Commissioner for Prize Goods 1643; Commissioner for Contributions from Holland 1643; Guinea Company 1648; Militia, Tower Hamlets 1648; Treasurers, £20,000 per month for Ireland 1648; Commissioner for Prize Goods 1649; Commissioner for Navy and Customs 1649; Assada Company 1649; Commissioner for Trade 1650; EEIC 1650; Commissioner for Excise 1650–53; Greenland Company 1653; High Court Justice 1650,1653; Committee of Adventurers 1654; Governor EEIC 1657–59; Tower Hamlets militia 1659.
Thomson, William	London, Aldgate, merchant, £50; Artillery Company 1642; Commissioner Sea Adventure 1642; Common Council 1643; £60,000 loan for army 1643; Alderman 1654; EEIC Shareholder 1657.
Thornbery, William	London, gentleman, £150; Artillery Company 1635; Commissioner for Compounding 1647.

Thoroughgood, George	London, Brownchurch, gentleman, £150; EEIC Shareholder 1657.
Thrale, Richard	London, stationer, £133.
Thrale, Thomas	London, stationer, £75.
Throgmorton, Trottman	London, merchant, £250.
Tichborne, Robert	London, skinner, £200; Artillery Company 1635; Subsidy for Fairfax and Ireland 1647; Collector £90,000 per month subsidy 1649; Commissioner for Prize Goods 1649; Alderman, Farringdon Within, 1649–60; knighted (by the Protector) December 15, 1656; styled 'Lord Tichborne' (as a member of the 'Other House') 1657–60; Councillor of State 1653; Committee of Safety 1659; MP London 1653; Lieutenant Tower 1647; Commissioner Customs 1649–(?); EEIC Shareholder 1657; Committee EEIC 1657–59; Colonel Yellow Regiment 1658; President Honourable Artillery Company 1658–60.
Tiffen, Grace	Surrey, Kingston, £75.
Tillett, John	London, salter, £100.
Tooley, Thomas	London, merchant, £450.
Towse, John	London, grocer, £700; Alderman, Cripplegate, 1640–45; Treasurer Adventure for Irish land; Commissioner London Militia 1642; Commissioner for Assessments 1642; Treasurer Advance of Money 1643–; Commissioner Excise 1643–50; Colonel Orange Regiment 1642–45; died 28 May 1645.
Trenchard, John	Dorset, gentleman, £450; Subsidy for Fairfax and Ireland 1647.
Tripplett, Ralph	London, stationer, £320.
Tuffnell, Abraham	London, gentleman, £200.
Tunbridge, Josias	Exeter, £100.
Turbridge, Robert	Middlesex, £300.
Turgis, Thomas	London, grocer, £200; Alderman, Vintry, 1650; died 1651.
Turlington, John	£120.
Turlington, William	London, Bishopsgate, merchant, £50; Common Council 1643.
Turner, Edward	London, £200; Artillery Company 1642.

Turner, Richard	London, Cordwainers, merchant, £200; Artillery Company 1639; Common Council, 1643; London Militia 1647; Assessments, London 1648; Newfoundland Company 1653; EEIC Shareholder 1657.
Turtle, Ralph	London, fishmonger, £75.
Tyler, Richard	London, salter, £200.
Tymmo, John	Cornwall, £200.
Underwood, Edward	London, £100; Artillery Company 1635.
Vassall, Samuel	London, gentleman, MP, £300; Navy Commissioner 1642; Commissioner for Assessments 1642; Committee of Safety 1642; Government of the West Indies 1643; Committee for Foreign Plantations 1643; £120,000 per month 1645; Subsidy for Fairfax and Ireland 1647.
Vaughan, Edward	London, Farringdon, £300; Committee for Advance of Money 1642; Assessments, London 1648.
Vaughan, Joseph	London, goldsmith, £100; Artillery Company 1631.
Vaughan, William and **George**	London, goldsmiths, £400.
Vernon, Richard	London, pewterer, £100.
Vincent, Thomas	London, leatherseller, £1375; Artillery Company 1635; Commissioner Sea Adventure 1642; Sale of goods by the candle, 1643; Committee of Adventurers 1654; EEIC Shareholder 1657.
Viner, Richard	London, goldsmith, £500; Trustee for Bishops' Lands 1646; Commissioner for Compounding 1647; London Militia 1647.
Viner, Thomas	London, goldsmith, £200; Alderman, Billingsgate, 1646–51; Subsidy for Fairfax and Ireland 1647; Relief of the Poor, London 1647; Langbourn, 1651–60; EEIC Shareholder 1657; knighted by Cromwell 8 February 1654, by Charles II August 1660; created Baronet June 1661; President Christ's Hospital 1658–60; Prime Warden Goldsmiths 1645–46; died 11 May 1665.
Viner, William	London, goldsmith, £100.
Wade, Richard	London, merchant, £100.

Wagstaff, Anthony and **John**	Harland, £25.
Wagstaff, Edmond	Cullow, £32.
Wagstaff, Ellin	Swathwick, £32.
Wagstaff, Joseph	Warwickshire, Harbury, soldier, £50; mercenary soldier, selected as a major for Wharton's army in 1642 but never sent to Ireland and served in Essex's army instead. Taken prisoner, switched sides and knighted by the king in 1644.
Waldoe, Daniel	London, Cheap, clothworker, £600; Common Council 1643; Assessments, London 1648.
Waller, Moses	London, merchant, £200.
Waller, Patience	London, £112.
Waller, Sir William	London, soldier, £1000; Committee of Safety 1642; Sergeant Major General Gloucester 1643; Committee of Both kingdoms 1644.
Walmesley, Thomas	Buckinghamshire, gentleman, £100.
Walter, Thomas	London, merchant, £100; Spanish trade 1630s; Artillery Company 1639; Guinea Company 1640.
Walwin, William	London, Vintry, butcher, £100; Committee for Advance of Money 1642.
Wardell, John	London, grocer, £150.
Waring, Richard	London, grocer, £1,150; Commissioner for Assessments 1642; Common Council 1643; Treasurer for Compounding 1643–53; Assessments, London 1648; Alderman, Cheap, 1649; Committee of Adventurers 1654; Assistant Levant Company 1653–54; EEIC Shareholder 1657.
Warner, John	London, St Stephen's Walbrook, grocer, £380; Alderman, Queenhithe, 1640–48, Treasurer Adventure for Irish land 1642; Commissioner London Militia 1642; Commissioner for Assessments 1642; Treasurer Advance of Money 1643–; £60,000 loan for army 1643; £120,000 per month 1645; Treasurer £80,000 loan for Fairfax 1645; Treasurer for Arrears 1645; Subsidy for Fairfax and Ireland 1647; Relief of the Poor, London 1647; Treasurer at War 1647; Colonel Green Regiment 1642–c. 1645; died 27 October 1648.

Warner, Samuel	London, grocer, £1,500; Commissioner London Militia 1642; £60,000 loan for army 1643; Alderman, Coleman Street, 1643–45.
Waterhouse, Francis	London, fishmonger, £15; Relief of the Poor, London 1647; Assessments, London 1648.
Waterhouse, Thomas	London, fishmonger, £125.
Watkins, Sir David	London, gentleman, £6,000; Cashier of the Virginia Company and resposible for issuing land patents, 1621–24; Secretary to the Committee for Irish Affairs 1642–48; Commissioner for Compounding 1647; Postmaster 1653; Committee of Adventurers 1654; married to Honora Fleetwood and uncle of Charles Fleetwood, apponted lord deputy of Ireland 1654, who was in turn the son-in-law of Oliver Cromwell; executor with Sir Nicholas Crispe of the will of Sir Thomas Smith.
Wattson, Samuel	London, apothecary, £20.
Waxley, George	£50.
Webb, Francis	London, dyer, £12; Artillery Company 1629; Assessments, London 1648.
Webster, James	Dorset, £100,
Webster, Thomas	Middlesex, innkeeper, £62.
Webster, William	London, merchant, £100; Artillery Company 1642.
Weekes, Obediah	Surrey, gentleman, £100.
Wenman, Thomas	Oxford, gentleman, MP, £600; second Lord Wenman. Attempted to negotiate peace with Charles I at Oxford in 1643.
Weston, Edward	London, merchant, £100; Artillery Company 1639.
Weston, Henry	London, merchant, £200; Subsidy for Fairfax and Ireland 1647; Militia, Tower Hamlets 1648; Commissioner for Prize Goods 1649.
Weston, John	London, merchant, £200.
Whalley, Henry	Chester, merchant, £450.
Whalley, Thomas	Chester, merchant, £100.
Wharton, Sir Thomas	York, gentleman, £200.
Wheatly, John	London, soapmaker, £25; Artillery Company 1641; Collector Advance of Money 1642.
Whetcomb, Benjamin	London, merchant, £500; related to Tristram Whetcomb, Kinsale merchant and contractor

for parliamentary navy in Ireland, and Simon Whetcomb, Dorchester merchant and investor in the Massachusetts Bay Company.

Whichcott, Richard	Lincoln, merchant, £100; Subsidy for Fairfax and Ireland 1647.
Whichcott, William	London, merchant, £150.
White, Bartholomew	London, merchant, £300.
White, Edward	London, mercer, £50.
White, Elinor and Sarah	London, £50.
White, John	London, merchant, £600; fee-farm trustee 1647; Militia, Tower Hamlets 1648; EEIC Shareholder 1657.
White, Stephen	London, Langbourne, grocer, £600; Common Council 1643; EEIC Shareholder 1657.
White, William	London, merchant, £50.
Whitehall, Robert	Buckinghamshire, clothier, £100.
Whitelocke, Bulstrode	Buckinghamshire, gentleman, MP, £100; Sequestrations Buckingham 1643; Subsidy for Fairfax and Ireland 1647; Council of State 1649; Derby House Committee 1652–53; Commissioner for Trade and Plantations 1652–53.
Whitston, Francis	London, £75.
Whittaker, Henry	London, merchant, £200.
Whittingham, Henry	London, merchant, £250; EEIC shareholder 1657;
Wicks, Thomas	London, clothworker, £50.
Wilcox, Richard	London, haberdasher, £50; Auditor army accounts 1648.
Wilcox, Robert	Warwickshire, £25.
Wilde, John	London, lawyer, £200; Sergeant of Law, Commissioner of the Common Seal, 1642, to replace the king's Great Seal.
Willett, Richard	London, Cordwainers, merchant tailor, £200; Committee for Advance of Money 1642; Common Council 1643; Sale of goods by the candle, 1643.
Williams, Nicholas	London, haberdasher, £100.
Williams, Samuel	London, haberdasher, £62.
Willoughby, Francis	London, Ratcliffe, mariner, £200; Captain Tower Hamlets Trained Band 1643; Navy Commissioner 1652–53.

Willoughby, William	London, gentleman, £37; Commissioner Sea Adventure 1642; Militia, Tower Hamlets 1648; Commissioner for Navy and Customs 1649.
Wilson, Richard	London, grocer, £200; Artillery Company 1639; £60,000 loan for army 1643.
Wilson, Rowland	London, vintner, £100; Guinea Company 1640; Ransom of Algiers Captives 1645; Alderman, Bridge, 1648–50, Councillor of State 1649–50; MP Calne 1646–50; Colonel Orange Regiment 1645–50; Assessments, London 1648; Council of State 1649; Collector £90,000 per month subsidy 1649; Commissioner Sale of Dutch Prizes 1652–53.
Winwood, Richard	Buckinghamshire, gentleman, MP, £300.
Witham, Edward	London, leatherseller, £220.
Witham, George	London, leatherseller, £400; Accounts for the Whole kingdom 1644; Treasurer £80,000 loan for Fairfax 1645; Subsidy for Fairfax and Ireland 1647; Alderman Coleman Street, 1645–48, Master Leathersellers 1646–47; Treasurer at War 1647; Trustee of king's goods 1649; EEIC Shareholder 1657.
Withers, William	London, linen draper, £200; provisioning agent, New England and Virginia.
Wollaston, Sir John	London, goldsmith, £1,150; granted the Province of New Hampshire, 1635 (sold); Alderman, Farringdon Without, 1639–42, Dowgate, 1642–44, Aldersgate, 1644–47, Bridge Without, 1657–58; knighted 3 December 1641; Deputy-Governor Irish Society 1633–34, 1636–37; Colonel Trained Bands 1641, Yellow Regiment 1642–c. 1645; Commissioner London Militia 1642; Commissioner for Assessments 1642; £120,000 per month 1645; Treasurer £80,000 loan for Fairfax 1645; Trustee for Bishops' Lands 1646; London Militia 1647; Subsidy for Fairfax and Ireland 1647; Treasurer at War 1647; Assessments, London 1648; President Bethlem and Bridewell 1642–49; President Christ's Hospital 1649–58; Treasurer, Forfeited Estates 1651; Treasurer for Delinquent

	lands 1652; Prime Warden Goldsmiths 1639–40; died 26 April 1658.
Wolley, Francis	London, haberdasher, £200.
Wolnory, Joshua	£125.
Wood, Edward	London, grocer, £675.
Wood, John	London, merchant, £850; Independent Africa trade 1630s; Artillery Company 1640; Collector Advance of Money 1642; Assessments 1643; Gambia Company 1651; Committee of Adventurers 1654; EEIC Shareholder 1657.
Wood, Thomas	London, Langbourne, merchant tailor, £25; Artillery Company 1641; £60,000 loan for army 1643.
Woodhead, William	York, £230.
Woodhouse, William	Hertfordshire, £100.
Woodruff, Abraham	London, Wapping, £50; Artillery Company 1635; Captain Tower Hamlets Trained Band 1643.
Woodward, Emanuel	London, gentleman, £600.
Wormelayton, Fulke	London, Whitechapel, distiller and baker, £50; Militia, Tower Hamlets 1648.
Worth, Zachariah	London, haberdasher, £100.
Wynn, George	London, mercer, £160; Alderman, Vintry 1650; Master Mercers 1652; created Baronet December 1660; died 18 July 1667.
Yates, James	Herfordshire, clothier, £200.
Yates, John	Sussex, £100; Subsidy for Fairfax and Ireland 1647.
Young, John	London, draper, £100; Commissioner for Compounding 1647; EEIC Shareholder 1657.

Index

1641 depositions 185
1641 rebellion 2, 9, 10, 49–54, 57, 64–73, 79, 81, 102–107, 110–112, 118, 185, 208

Abbells, Jonas 123
Abbott, Daniel 200
Abdy, Robert 114
Abdy, Sir Thomas 114
Act for Settling Ireland (1652) 185–186, 198, 200
Act for the Speedy and Effectual Satisfaction of the Adventurers (1653) 200
Act of Explanation (1665) 2, 220
Act of Oblivion (1660) 219–220
Act of Settlement (1662) 2, 220
Acton, William 113
Adams, Thomas 218
Adamson, John 10, 11, 15
Additional Sea Adventure 8, 88, 99–108, 113, 146, 175, 214, 220
Adventurers Act (1642) 2, 7, 8–9, 35, 64–73, 84, 183, 184, 215, 220
Adventurers for Lewis 122
Alcock, Thomas 81
Aldersey, Samuel 33
Aldersey, Thomas 210
Alexander, Jerome 120
Alexander, Sir William 31, 35, 125
Alexei, Tsar of Russia 145
Alford, Thomas 45–46

Algiers 102
Allein, Francis 34, 172, 173, 182, 185, 195, 215
Allen, Thomas 52, 195, 209, 215
Allen, William 119, 178
Almery, George 151, 204
Amsterdam 65, 79, 83, 122, 123–124, 153, 178, 184, 207, 208
Andrews, Benjamin 215
Andrews, Richard 32–33, 76, 78, 79
Andrews, Thomas 4, 32–33, 47, 51, 73–74, 83, 85–86, 113, 115, 118–119, 127, 144, 146, 152, 155–156, 158, 167, 169–175, 178, 181, 185, 194–195, 199, 205, 208–209, 215–216
Anglo-Spanish War 16, 211–212, 215
Annesley, Sir Arthur 216, 219
Annesley, Sir Francis, Lord Mountnorris 104
Antigua 206, 210
arms 45, 53–57, 64, 68–69, 71, 81, 83–86, 88, 100, 108, 115, 123–124, 144, 169
Armstrong, Robert 12
Armyne, Sir William 82
Artillery Company 55, 56, 84, 86, 88, 107
Ashe, John 120
Asheman, Jeronimo 122
Ash, Francis 150–151
Ashley, Maurice 13
Ashley, Thomas 100–101, 105
Assada Company 176, 219
Athlone, Co. Westmeath 115

INDEX

Atkins, Thomas 55
Avery, Samuel 115, 118, 147, 150, 152, 199, 217
Axtell, Daniel 185
Ayers, Thomas 127
Ayscue, George 173, 179, 180, 184

Baker, Richard 211
Baker, William 214
Balfour, Sir William 212
Ballyragget, Co. Kilkenny 185
Baltimore, Co. Cork 105
Baltimore, Lord *see* Calvert, Cecil, Lord Baltimore
Bandon, Co. Cork 28, 88, 104, 105, 115
banking 65, 122, 175, 212, 213
Barbados 12, 28–29, 32, 52, 87, 124–127, 153–155, 169, 173, 175–177, 179–180, 184, 196, 206–207, 210
Barbary Company 101–103
Barbary pirates 102, 105
Barebones Parliament 209
Barrington, Sir Thomas 46, 49, 67, 68, 73, 76, 129, 130
Bateman, Anthony 208, 219
Bateman, John 125, 145–146
Bateman, Richard 215
Bateman, Sir Robert 50, 51, 74, 215
Bateman, Thomas 86, 174
Bateman, William 218, 219
Batten, William 109, 157
Beale, Stephen 102
Beck, Gabriel 158
Bedford, earl of *see* Russell, William, earl of Bedford
Beecher, Henry 28
Beecher, Phane, Jr 28, 104
Bell, Philip 127
Bemiss, Robert 179, 180
Bence, Alexander 170
Bendish, Sir Thomas 145
Bennett, Edward 23, 25
Bennett, Richard 180
Beresford, John 170
Berkeley, George 167
Berkeley Hundred, Virginia 31
Berkeley, Richard 119
Berkeley, Sir William 32

Bermuda 3, 22, 25, 29–30, 179
Bermuda Company 29–30, 52, 81, 195, 213
Biddolph, Theophilus 218, 219
Bigg, John 102
Bight of Benin 27, 154
bills of exchange 110, 116, 121–122, 171
Bishops' Wars 44–45, 48, 82, 125
Blake, Robert 179
Blayney, Sir Edward 24, 198–199
Bludworth, William 218
Blunt Point, Virginia 25
Bolingbrooke, earl of *see* St John, Oliver, earl of Bolingbrooke
Bond, Denis 74–75, 120, 126, 182, 195, 199
Bond, John 146
Boone, Thomas 174
Boston 34, 46
Bottigheimer, Karl S. 7–8, 9, 74, 75–76, 77, 99
Boudin, Peter 145
Boyle, Francis, Viscount Shannon 28
Boyle, Lewis, Lord Kilnalmeaky 46, 104, 105
Boyle, Mary 64
Boyle, Richard, earl of Cork 7, 15, 24–25, 28–29, 31, 33, 37, 46, 64–65, 67, 69–70, 78, 81, 104–105, 114
Boyle, Richard, Lord Dungarvan 72, 74, 88
Boyle, Roger, Lord Broghill 46, 201, 204, 206, 212
Braddick, Michael 11, 171–172
Brazil 124, 127, 153, 168, 205
Brenner, Robert 4, 6, 8, 10, 48, 103
Briskett, Anthony 28
Bristol 24, 145
Broghill, Lord *see* Boyle, Roger, Lord Broghill
Bromfield, Laurence 144, 150
Brooke, Lord *see* Greville, Robert, Lord Brooke
Brookhaven, John 215
Brotherly Assistance fund 50, 70–71, 82, 88
Browne, John 81, 86, 120, 144
Browne, Richard 155
Buckinghamshire 80
Bunce, James 52, 115, 118, 147, 149, 150, 152

289

290 INDEX

Burke, Ulick, earl Clanricarde 100–101, 105, 106, 107, 112, 187
Burnell, Thomas 208
Burroughs, Samuel 75
Butler, James, earl of Ormond 110, 111–112, 148, 149, 170, 185, 200, 208, 218
Byron, Sir John 68

Calvert, Cecil, Lord Baltimore 31, 126
Calvinism 3, 6, 11, 124, 146, 153
Canada 31, 37, 124, 125
Cape Ann, Massachusetts 34, 57, 213
Carleton, Sir Dudley 75
Carlingford, Co. Louth 156
Carlisle, earl of *see* Hay, James, earl of Carlisle
Carrickfergus, Co. Antrim 34, 50, 70, 81, 115, 128–129
Casteel, Michael 116–117
Castleforbes, Co. Longford 103
Castlehaven, Co. Cork 105
Castlehaven, earl of *see* Tuchet, James, earl of Castlehaven
Cave, Sir Richard 56
Chamberlain, Abraham 102
Chamberlain, Thomas 215, 219
Chamber of London 114, 213
Chambers, John 119
Chambers, Richard 205
Charles I
    and the Bishops' Wars 44–45, 48
    and the Civil Wars 16, 106, 110, 158–159
    Council of Peers at York 45–46
    dissolves Virginia Company 24, 32
    execution 14, 16, 57, 160, 167, 176
    finances 32, 36–37, 44–45, 49, 83, 116, 176
    and the Irish rebellion 10, 49, 57–58, 71, 72, 83–84, 99–100, 110–112, 125, 127–128, 130, 131, 147–148
    issues arrest warrant for five MPs 53, 68
    land and properties *see* crown lands
    and monopolies 36–37, 45–46, 114, 145
    ousted from London 9, 57, 67, 73
    parliamentary confrontation with 2, 9, 10, 44–46, 48–49, 53, 57–58, 64–65, 67–69, 71–73, 88–89, 110–112, 117–118
    passes Adventurers Act 72–73, 215
    patents granted by 28, 31, 45–46
    peace proposals from parliament 149
    religious reforms 44, 46
    trial 57, 75, 159, 167
Charles II 2, 12, 16, 80, 157, 159, 167, 176–177, 208, 211, 215, 216, 218–219
Chichester, Sir Arthur 22, 27
Child, James 215
church lands 12, 128, 148, 150–152, 170, 172, 174–175, 185, 195, 209, 216, 220
City of London 10, 47–49, 52, 68, 80, 147, 149, 159, 173, 218–219
Civil Survey 201, 204
Claiborne, William 25, 31, 32, 180–181
Clanricarde, earl *see* Burke, Ulick, earl Clanricarde
Clarke, George 48
Clarke, Robert 100
Claxton, Edward 119
Clayton, Robert 213, 216
Clement, Gregory 102, 118, 127, 146, 186
Cloberry, John 213
Cloberry, Oliver 213
Cloberry, William 31, 33, 47, 78
Clonakilty, Co. Cork 104
cloth trade 3, 51, 81, 88, 146–147, 169, 207, 211–212
Clotworthy, Sir John 34, 49–50, 54, 69–70, 76, 120, 127–128, 130–131, 144, 147, 156, 171, 199, 203
Clutterbuck, Richard 174
Cockayne, William, Jr 145, 169, 205, 207, 213
Coish, John 108
Coish, William 108
Combes, Thomas 27–28
Commissioners and Council for the Government and Defence of Ireland 79–80
Commissioners for Customs 119, 121, 152, 195
Commissioners for the Sale of Prize Goods 173
Commissioners for the Speeding and Dispatching of the Businesses for Ireland 56–57, 71, 80
Commission for Defective Titles 31–32, 204
Commission for Ireland 182–186

Commission for Managing the Affairs of Ireland 69
Commission for Revenue in Ireland 197–198
Commission for the Colonies 126
Committee for Compounding 120–121, 129, 148, 151, 152, 193–194
Committee for Foreign Plantations 126–127, 131
Committee for Inspection of the Treasuries 195
Committee for Ireland and Scotland 182
Committee for Irish Affairs 7, 14–16, 49, 53–58, 69, 71–76, 79–85, 88–89, 101, 108–109, 115–116, 118, 125–127, 129–131, 144, 147, 152, 183, 187, 214
Committee for Powder Match and Bullet 170
Committee for Proposals from the Adventurers to Ireland 183–184
Committee for Scottish Affairs 120, 128
Committee for Sequestrations 128
Committee for Setting out Lands 202, 203, 204
Committee for Settling Claims 200
Committee for the Admiralty 182
Committee for the Advance of Money 113–114, 118–121
Committee for the Ordnance 182
Committee for the Sale of Forfeited Lands and Estates 172
Committee for Trade and Plantations 182
Committee of Accounts 12
Committee of Adventurers 9, 73–76, 80–81, 85–87, 89, 101, 109, 111, 113, 115, 117, 120–121, 124–127, 131, 152, 155–156, 178, 185, 197
Committee of Both Kingdoms 129–130, 149, 155–156, 157, 194
Committee of Safety 52–54, 67–68, 72, 73, 79, 83, 84–87, 89, 110, 215, 219
Common Council 46–48, 52–57, 67–69, 72–73, 76, 111, 114, 150–152, 157, 178, 215–216, 218
confiscated lands (Ireland) 2, 16, 32, 64–71, 73, 101, 118, 128, 149, 183–187, 193–194, 197–204, 214–215
see also sequestered estates

Cong, Co. Mayo 220
Connacht 35, 99, 183, 197, 201
Conway, Edward, Viscount 54, 70, 124
Cooke, Sir Robert 56, 57
Coote, Sir Charles 106
Corbett, Miles 126, 186
Cordwell, John 114, 146
Cordwell, Robert 170
Cork 28–29, 115, 158, 171, 206
Cork, earl of *see* Boyle, Richard, earl of Cork
Corporation of Dartmouth 74, 78
Corporation of London 74
Corsellis, Abraham 114
Corsellis, Nicholas 25–26, 122, 123, 124, 157, 203
Corsellis, Pieter van 123, 124
Corsellis, Zeagar 206
Cottington, Francis, Lord 158
cotton 10, 29, 126, 127
Council of Officers 158–159, 203, 204, 213–14
Council of State 16, 168, 170, 173, 176–177, 179–180, 183–187, 194–197, 205, 207–210, 212–216, 218–219
Council of Trade 178, 181, 198, 204
Courland, duke of *see* Kettler, James, duke of Courland
Courteen Association 145, 146, 169, 208
Courteen, Bouden 122–123
Courteen, Lady Katherine 145
Courteen, Sir William 28, 114, 116–117, 123, 145
Courtis, Edward 179
Court of Aldermen 45, 46, 47–48, 67, 215
Court of Common Hall 47, 50, 74, 74
Craddock, Matthew 47
Craddock, Maurice 215
Cressy, David 9–10
Crewe, John 129
Crispe, Sir Nicholas 78, 102, 114, 154, 219
Cromwellian land settlement 2, 8, 13–14, 16, 183–187, 193–194, 197–204, 214–215
Cromwell, Oliver 13–14, 16, 56, 57, 80, 87, 101, 108, 126, 129, 144, 149, 151, 156, 168–173, 177, 181–183, 186, 193–197, 200, 208–209, 212, 217, 219

Cromwell, Richard 214
Crown Jewels 83, 116
crown lands 12, 174–175, 185, 199, 209, 216, 220
Culme, Thomas 119
Cunningham, Thomas 102
Curaçao 152
Custom House of London 55, 74
customs 28–29, 48, 80, 116, 119, 121, 127, 145, 152–153, 159, 177–178, 207, 212

Darcy, Eamon 12
Dartmouth 74, 78, 127
Davenport, William 52
Davies, John 128–129, 130–131, 156
Davis, Ralph 36
Dayley, Robert 200
Dean and Chapter lands 86, 170, 172, 173, 175, 195, 199
  see also church lands
Declaration of Breda 216, 218, 219
Derby House 129, 149, 156, 158, 194
Derry see Londonderry plantation
Desmond, earl of see Preston, Richard, earl of Desmond
Dethwick, John 115, 129, 144, 146, 152, 172, 173, 179, 185, 195, 215, 217
Devereux, Robert, earl of Essex 45, 80, 85, 87, 101, 102, 108, 110, 113, 129, 149
Dillon, Hubert 25
diplomacy 109–113, 115, 116, 145, 218
diversion of funds 8, 15–16, 72, 75, 79, 84, 87–89, 113, 116–118, 129–130, 147, 149, 152, 158
Dobbins, William 84, 156, 173
Dobson, Isaac 200
Donohue, John 11
Dorchester Company 3, 53, 57, 74, 75, 78, 170
Doubling Ordinance 155, 214
Downing, Emmanuel 33, 213
Downing, George 33, 212–213, 218
Downs, battle of the 45
Down Survey 204, 214
Drax, James 175
Drimoleague, Co. Cork 104–105
Drogheda, Co. Louth 158, 177

Dublin 13, 33, 70, 84, 88, 100–101, 106, 109–113, 115–116, 149, 156, 158, 178, 183, 186, 197–198, 200
Dublin Survey 200–201
Duncannon, Co. Wexford 105, 123
Dungarvan, Co. Waterford 81, 88
Dungarvan, Lord see Boyle, Richard, Lord Dungarvan
Dunkirk 69, 122, 211, 218
Dutch Church, Austin Friars 146
Dutch East India Company 116–117, 169, 207, 208
Dutch reformed church 26, 124, 146
Dutch Republic see Netherlands
Dutch West India Company 3, 30, 35, 123, 124, 152–153, 155, 168, 207
Dyke, John 102, 208

East India Company see Dutch East India Company; English East India Company
Edgehill, battle of 88, 89, 110, 116, 212
Edinburgh 44, 208, 212
Edmonds, Symon 119
Ellis, William 120
Elsinge, Henry 108
English Civil Wars 9, 10, 12, 16, 75, 88–89, 106, 110, 120, 127, 129, 144, 148, 157–160, 177, 199, 219
English East India Company (EEIC) 3–5, 26, 35, 102, 109, 113–115, 123, 145–146, 152, 168–169, 172, 176, 178, 196, 205, 207–208, 212–213, 219, 220
English Reformed Church, Amsterdam 123
Erle, Sir Walter 56–57, 108, 170
Essex, earl of see Devereux, Robert, earl of Essex
Estwick, Stephen 52, 87, 119, 129–130, 144, 150, 158, 170–171, 173–174, 194–195, 199, 209, 216
Evelyn, Sir John 56, 57
Exchange Bank of Amsterdam 122, 208
excise 119–120, 121, 127, 147–150, 152, 169, 170, 171–174, 194, 195, 209, 214
Excise Commissioners 119–120, 121, 152, 170, 173–174, 194, 195

Fairfax, Sir Thomas 144, 149, 152, 167, 182, 213
Fairfax, William 87
Fauntleroy, Thomas 171
Featherstone, Henry 127
fee-farm rents 174, 197, 216
Fellowship of Merchant Adventurers 3, 6, 11, 32, 51, 68, 70, 81–82, 113, 115, 146, 151–152, 179
Fetherstone, William 129
Fiennes, Nathaniel 67, 82
Fiennes, William, Viscount Saye-and-Sele 30, 45, 80, 85, 101, 126
'fiery spirits' group 48–49
financial instruments 7, 122, 174, 175, 198, 216
First Anglo-Dutch War 181–182, 185, 207, 208, 211, 217
First Protectorate Parliament 209
fishing 34, 35, 66, 76, 122, 211, 213
Fitzgerald, Richard 177
Fleetwood, Charles 215
Fleetwood, George 184, 186, 214
Floyd, Richard 127
Foote, Sarah 219
Foote, Thomas 115, 118, 119, 147, 152, 174, 195, 199, 215, 217, 219
Forbes, Alexander, 10th Lord 103, 104–107, 114
Foulke, John 55, 113, 150–151, 178, 205, 216
France 37, 68, 75, 107, 125, 172, 178, 182, 183, 211, 217
Franklin, Sir John 112
Frederick, John 219
Frekes Castle, Co. Cork 115
Frost, Gualter 84, 173, 198

Galway 84, 100–101, 105–107, 118, 182
Gambia 168, 179–180, 206
Games, Alison 6
Garrard, Sir Jacob 205
Garraway, Sir Henry 113
Garrett, John 74
Garway, William 114
Gayre, Sir John 55
General Voyage (East India Company) 114, 145, 168

Gerard, Sir Gilbert 108, 126, 129–130
Gerard, William 120
Gethin, Maurice 88, 115, 128, 144
Gibbs, William 150–151
Giustinian, Giorgio 79
Glamorgan, earl of *see* Somerset, Edward, earl of Glamorgan
Gloucester 31, 75, 186
Glyde, Richard 150
gold 27, 65, 168
Gold Coast 207
Goldsmiths' Hall 120, 148, 150, 151, 152, 172, 194, 195, 196, 198
Goodwin, Arthur 87
Goodwin, Benjamin 116, 117, 130
Goodwin, John 80, 109, 111, 112, 127, 130, 147, 182
Goodwin, Robert 116, 120
Goodyer, Nathaniel 196
Gookin, Daniel 24, 29, 64
Gookin, Sir Vincent 104, 200
Gorges, Sir Fernandino 37
Greene, Giles 170
Greville, Robert, Lord Brooke 30, 45–46, 54, 57, 86, 101, 103, 218–219
Grocers' Hall 9, 12, 16, 53, 56–57, 73–76, 79–82, 84–86, 89, 100, 108–112, 115, 120–122, 125–127, 129, 131, 147, 150, 152, 155–157, 176, 178, 197, 203–204
Gross Survey 201–202
Guildhall 53, 56, 73–74
Guinea 27, 121
Guinea Company 102, 146, 154, 168, 169, 176, 179–180, 196, 207, 213
gunpowder 81, 88, 104, 115, 144, 146, 168, 170
Gurdon, John 120
Gurney, Richard 47–48, 49–50, 72

Hague, The 218–219
Halstead, Laurence 51, 73–74, 79, 115
Hamilton, Hugh, Lord 212
Hamilton, James, Viscount Clandeboye 32
Hampden, John 53, 67, 80, 82, 85
Harley, Sir Robert 56, 57
Harvey, James 101
Harrington, Willliam 215

Hawkins, John 75
Hawkins, Thomas 210
Hawkins, William 75–76, 80, 101, 114, 127, 148, 155–156, 158, 172–173, 184, 206
Hawkridge, John 108
Hawkridge, William 50
Hay, James, earl of Carlisle 27–28, 29, 32, 37, 104, 123, 126–127, 154
Hazlett, Hugh 8
Heads of Proposals 149
Henley, George 50, 108, 115
Herbert, Philip, earl of Pembroke 32, 49, 80, 101, 126
Herring, Michael 120, 125, 151, 152, 170, 195, 199, 217
Hesilrige, Sir Arthur 53, 108, 120, 126, 182, 214
Heveningham, William 75, 129, 174
Hewson, John 214
Heyn, Piet 30
Hickock, William 215
High Court of Justice 209
Hill, Arthur 71, 201
Hill, Richard 115, 152, 182
Hill, Sir Edward 171
Hispaniola 210
Hoast, Derrick 122, 123, 157
Hobson, William 170, 199, 215
Holland, Cornelius 126, 199
Holland, earl of *see* Rich, Henry, earl of Holland
Holland, Nicholas 201
Holland, Sir John 120, 173
Holles, Denzil 49, 53, 56, 57, 69–70, 85, 219
Honourable Artillery Company *see* Artillery Company
Honourable Irish Society *see* Irish Society
Hook, Thomas 200
Hull 68, 83
Hull, Sir William 104–105
Hull, William, Jr 104
Humphrey, John 34
Hunt, Richard 174
Hunt, Robert 146
Hutchinson, Joseph 170
Hutchinson, Richard 170, 172

Inchiquin, Lord *see* O'Brien, Murrough, Lord Inchiquin
indentured servants 15, 24–28, 31, 34, 78, 109, 121, 152–153, 181, 206, 210
India 5, 114, 116–117, 130, 176, 178, 211, 217
Ingram, Sir Arthur 104
Irby, Sir Anthony 72
Ireton, Henry 182
Irish armies 44, 45, 46, 124, 148
Irish Confederates 15, 100, 104, 110–112, 122, 131, 147–149, 159, 167, 182–184
Irish parliament 108–113
Irish Society 3, 67, 83, 128
Istanbul 145
Ivory, William 200

Jamaica 210–111
James I 27, 32, 35
Jessop, William 126–127, 203, 216, 218
Johnson, Isaac 33
Jones, Henry 200, 201
Jones, John 186
Jones, Katherine, Lady Ranelagh 204
Judd, Daniel 170

Kelsey, Thomas 194
Kemp, Richard 32
Kendrick, John 115, 116, 118, 119, 146–147, 150, 152, 174, 195
Kent Island 31, 33, 125, 180, 213
Kerridge, Thomas 208
Kettler, James, duke of Courland 180
Kilcolman, Co. Cork 33
Kilkenny 110, 112, 131, 149, 182–183
Kilnalmeaky, Lord *see* Boyle, Lewis, Lord Kilnalmeaky
Kinsale, Co. Cork 104, 105, 156, 158, 167
Kirle, Anthony 117
Knocknanaus, battle of 155

labour 22–23, 26–28, 65, 152–155, 177, 179–181, 206–207, 209, 210
see also indentured servants; slave trade
Lambert, John 194, 215
Lamott, John 119
land allocation lotteries 118, 197, 198, 202–204

land market 24, 154, 198–199, 206
land surveys 13, 32, 66, 128, 200–202, 204, 214
land valuation 66, 70, 71, 199, 201
Langham, John 113, 119, 150, 209
Langham, Samuel 119, 152, 217
Laurence, Adam 122, 123
Laurence, Richard 200, 201
Leader, Richard 127
Leeward Islands 28, 73, 75, 123, 175
Leicester, earl of *see* Sidney, Robert, earl of Leicester
letters of marque 103, 181
Levant Company 3, 4, 6, 35, 47, 102–103, 113, 116, 145, 152, 176, 196, 205
Lewis, Isle of 122
Lewis, John 219
Ley, James, earl of Marlborough 127
Limbery, John 157, 210
Limerick 81, 107, 118
Lindley, Keith 8
Lisle, Lord *see* Sidney, Philip, Lord Lisle
Livery Companies *see* London Companies
Llewellin, Robert 180
Lloyd, Jenkin 201
Loftus, Sir Adam 88, 109
Loftus, Sir Nicholas 49, 85, 108, 109, 128
London Companies 3, 4, 36, 50, 67, 82–83, 88, 102, 128
Londonderry plantation 3, 50, 67, 70, 83, 88, 128, 151
London militias 52, 53–57, 67, 68, 83, 88, 151, 152, 178, 215
Long Parliament 48, 150, 193, 214, 217, 220
Lord Lieutenancy of Ireland 37, 70, 75, 83, 85, 108, 111, 112, 168, 200
Lords Justices of Ireland 101, 105, 106, 110–112, 177–178
Louis XIV of France 217
Ludlow, Edmund 182, 183, 186

MacCormack, J.R. 7
MacDonnell, Randal 44, 50
Mackworth, Humphrey 75
Macmillan, Ken 10–11
Mahaffy, Robert 7, 76
Mainwaring, Robert 47

Manchester, earl of *see* Montagu, Edward
Mandeville, Lord *see* Montagu, Edward
manufactured goods 26, 27, 36, 73
mapping 202
  see also land surveys
Markham, Henry 200
Marlborough, earl of *see* Ley, James, earl of Marlborough
Marston Moor, battle of 129
Martin, Nicholas 56, 57
Maryland 31, 176, 178
Massachusetts Bay 10, 29, 32–35, 47, 86, 213
Massachusetts Bay Company 4, 33, 34–35, 47, 73, 81, 86
Massingberd, John 169, 172
mayoralty of London 9, 47–48, 54, 72, 74, 102, 113, 158, 209, 215
Methold, William 152, 178, 169, 179
Meyrick, Sir John 56, 57
Middelburg 65, 122–123, 153
Middleton, Sir William 113
Mildmay, Sir Henry 50, 109
military contracting 3–4, 14, 81–82, 154, 176
military supplies 11, 15, 36, 81–84, 86–88, 102–104, 108, 115–117, 127–130, 144, 156–158, 168–170, 173, 182, 194, 214, 220
militia committees 55, 150, 159, 215
Militia Ordinance 72
Millington, Gilbert 75
Millington, Roland 75
Milner, Tempest 88, 144, 195
Mitchell, Richard 87
Monck, George 16, 208, 212–213, 215–216, 218
monopolies 3, 32, 36–37, 45, 47, 51, 58, 104, 114, 120, 144–145, 169, 205
Montagu, Edward, Lord Mandeville, later earl of Manchester 45, 53, 80, 87, 126, 129, 130
Montserrat 28–29, 127, 210
Morgan, Anthony 200
Mortimer, Sarah 11
Moulson, Lady Anne 151
Moulson, Sir Thomas 151
Mountnorris, Lord *see* Annesley, Sir Francis, Lord Mountnorris
Mountrath, Co. Laois 33

Moyer, Samuel 115, 120, 129, 145, 152, 169, 173, 196, 197, 205, 213
Munster 15, 24, 28, 33, 70, 78, 81, 83–84, 88–89, 104–106, 115–116, 148, 158, 184, 197
Muscovy Company 3, 144–145, 148

Naseby, battle of 144
Navigation Act (1651) 178–179, 181, 184, 196, 197, 207–208, 211, 220
Navigation Ordinance 153
Navy Commission 109, 155, 159, 170, 172, 179, 181, 195, 196, 214
Netherlands 3, 4, 6, 7, 11, 27, 33, 45, 65, 83, 122–124, 127, 129, 130, 152–153, 155, 157–159, 167–168, 177–182, 184, 205–208, 211–212, 214, 217–219
Nevis 27, 28, 175, 210
New Amsterdam 177, 206, 207
Newcastle 45, 46, 149
Newcastle Propositions 149
Newcomen, Robert 204
New England 3, 5, 6, 10–12, 32–35, 37, 48, 52–53, 55, 57, 66, 70, 78, 81, 102, 170, 176, 211, 213, 217
New England Company 33, 34
Newfoundland 211
New Model Army 144, 149–150, 152, 156, 157, 158, 176
newspapers *see* popular press
Noel, Martin 127, 154, 168, 175–176, 195, 206, 210, 214, 216
Noel, Thomas 150–151, 154, 168, 170, 182, 195, 199, 206, 210
Nominated Parliament 197, 200
Norris, Tobias 112
Northern Neck, Virginia 176
Northumberland, earl of *see* Percy, Algernon, earl of Northumberland
Norwich 171–172, 198
Nosy Be 146, 219
Nova Scotia 31, 35, 66

O'Brien, Barnaby, earl of Thomond 107
O'Brien, Murrough, Lord Inchiquin 155, 156
O'Dwyer, Colonel Edmond 183
Ohlmeyer, Jane 6, 12

Oldfield, John 125, 148, 208
O'Neill, Sir Phelim 57
Ormond, earl of *see* Butler, James, earl of Ormond
O'Shaughnessy, Sir Roger 105, 220
Oxford 117, 130

Pack, Christopher 125, 150, 217
Pankhurst, Sir Robert 56, 57
paper credit 121–122, 182
pardons 219–220
Parkhurst, Sir Robert 174
Parrott, David 99
patents 27–28, 29, 31–32, 33, 45, 47, 66, 103, 127, 176–177, 179
Payne, Thomas 104
Peacy, Jason 11
Peck, John 174
Pembroke, earl of *see* Herbert, Philip, earl of Pembroke
Penn, Sir William 210–211
Pennington, Isaac 47, 48, 113, 145, 150, 151
Pennoyer, William 4, 28, 47, 58, 81, 87–88, 102–104, 108, 114–118, 127–128, 130, 146, 152, 154–155, 168–171, 174–178, 181, 186, 195–197, 199, 205, 213, 215
Percy, Algernon, earl of Northumberland 80, 129
Perkinson, William 204
Pernambuco 124, 153, 206
Peter, Benjamin 103
Peter, Hugh 33, 81, 103, 105, 107, 111, 123, 219
Petty, William 200, 204
Philip IV of Spain 211
Pickles, Nathan 202
Pierce, William 34
Pindar, Sir Paul 116–117, 123, 130, 146–147
piracy 22, 100, 102–103, 105, 211
'plate, money and horses' collections 83, 87–88, 89, 113, 119, 147, 172
Player, Thomas 144
Plymouth colony 32, 34, 66
popular press 15, 66, 72, 155, 185
Porter, Endymion 146
Portugal 124, 152–153, 168, 180, 205, 217
Portuguese Brazil Company 205, 207, 214
Potosí 1, 30

Povey, Thomas 28, 206
Powhatan uprising 23
Poynter, Nicholas 198
Prendergast, John P. 7
Presbyterian faction 115, 131, 151–152, 219
Preston, Richard, earl of Desmond 26
privateering 30–31, 32, 75, 102, 103, 122, 123, 181, 205, 217
Privy Council 10, 24–25, 32, 37, 45, 112, 124
Protectorate 13–14, 16, 204–211, 212–215, 217
Protestant reformation 44, 58
Protestation Oath 110
Providence Island 30–31, 32, 37, 102, 127, 146
Providence Island Company 30, 33–35, 44–46, 48–50, 53–58, 86–89, 101–103, 108, 124, 126–127, 216
provisioning 15, 24, 30, 31, 78, 103, 115–117, 156, 210
  see also military supplies
Purefoy, William 182
Puritanism 3, 4, 6, 11, 26, 30, 33, 35, 37, 48, 52–53, 57, 78, 124, 209
Pury, Thomas 170
Pye, Sir Robert 108, 170
Pym, Alexander 203
Pym, John 30, 35, 45–46, 49–50, 53, 56, 67–70, 72, 74, 79, 101–102, 126, 199

Rainsborough, Thomas 102, 107, 109, 157
Rainsborough, William 102
Rainton, Sir Nicholas 55
Raleigh, Sir Walter 22, 33
Ranelagh, Lady *see* Jones, Katherine, Lady Ranelagh
religious freedom 22, 35, 147, 185
religious reforms 44, 46, 209
rents 29, 32, 65, 71, 198, 199, 200
restoration 16, 80, 211, 215–220
'revolted ships' episode 157–159, 177, 218
Reynolds, Francis 215
Reynolds, John 127, 147
Reynolds, Sir Robert 56, 109, 111, 112, 120, 125, 130, 147, 184–185
Riccard, Andrew 169, 196–197, 210, 213
Rich, Charles 64, 219
Rich, Henry, earl of Holland 75, 80, 87, 101

Rich, Robert, earl of Warwick 6, 25, 27–35, 37, 45–46, 48–51, 54–55, 57–58, 64–65, 69–71, 75, 78, 82, 88, 101–102, 108–109, 113, 126–127, 129, 149, 153, 156–159, 167, 175, 186, 215
Rich, Sir Nathaniel 23, 25, 33, 215
Rich, Thomas 219
Robartes, John, Lord 80, 126
Roberts, Elias 155, 197
Roberts, John 210
Robinson, Sir John 218, 219
Rolle, John 126, 170
Rowe, Owen 193, 195
royalist lands 12, 112–113, 128, 147, 154, 174–175, 185, 193–194, 209, 216, 220
Royal Mint 65, 182, 195, 196
Rudyard, Sir Benjamin 30, 126
Rumney, Dame Rebecca 50
Rump Parliament 6, 197, 200, 214, 217
Rupert, Prince 167, 179, 180
Russell, John 119
Russell, William, earl of Bedford 85

Sadlier, Thomas 200
St Augustine's church, London 26, 124
St Eustatius 123
St John, Oliver, earl of Bolingbrooke 45, 87, 120, 129, 205
St Kitts 27–28, 75, 127, 153, 175, 210
Saltonstall, Richard 33
saltpetre 146, 168–170, 172, 178, 198, 205
Sandys, Edwin 108
Sandys, Nicholas 205
Sankey, Hierome 183
Saye-and-Sele, Viscount *see* Fiennes, William, Viscount Saye-and-Sele
Scotland 11, 31, 44–46, 49, 51, 66, 84, 122, 124–126, 128, 148, 179, 208, 212–213, 216
Scott, William 7
Scottish armies 44–45, 50, 70–71, 82–84, 88, 106, 116, 120, 124–126, 128–129, 167
Scottish Covenanters 44–45, 46, 103, 125, 129, 167
Sea Adventurers' Committee 102, 120
sequestered estates (England) 128, 147–148, 150, 158, 170, 172, 174–175, 181, 185, 193–194, 209, 216, 220
  see also confiscated lands

Shannon, Viscount *see* Boyle, Francis, Viscount Shannon
Sheppard, Samuel 13
sheriffs of London 48, 49–50, 113, 119, 152
ship money 36, 44, 47, 52, 58
shipping 5, 15, 24, 26–27, 29–30, 36, 50, 76–77, 81, 108, 115, 118, 122–123, 130, 145–146, 153–154, 157–158, 168–169, 173, 175, 177–182, 184, 196, 205–208, 211–212, 215, 217, 218
Short Parliament 44–45, 46
Shute, Chaloner 215
Shute, Nathaniel 124
Shute, Richard 45–46, 86, 111, 120, 125, 209
Shute, Thomas 173–174
Shuttleworth, John 87
Shuttleworth, Richard 87
Sidney, Algernon 187
Sidney, Philip, Lord Lisle 112, 147, 148
Sidney, Robert, earl of Leicester 75, 83–84, 85, 108, 112
silver 1, 30, 65, 129, 155, 168, 169, 211, 217
Simpson, Sidrach 4
Skippon, Philip 54–55, 56, 68, 144, 155, 158, 209
Slany, Humphrey 102
slave trade 12, 27, 28, 146, 152–155, 168–169, 175–176, 179–181, 196, 205–207, 211, 212
Smart, John 146
Smith, George 205
Smith, Thomas 169, 173, 186, 196, 205, 208, 213
Snelling, George 145
Snelling, Richard 145
Soame, Sir Thomas 47, 113
Solemn League and Covenant 125, 127
Somerset, Edward, earl of Glamorgan 147
South Africa 176
Spain 1, 16, 30–31, 45, 68, 102, 123, 168, 170, 172, 210–212, 214, 215, 217, 218, 220
Spurstowe, William 120, 126
Stapilton, Sir Philip 82, 85
Stegge, Thomas 180
Stone, John 209
Stone, Thomas 27, 114, 195
Stradling, Sir Henry 101

Strafford, earl of *see* Wentworth, Thomas, earl of Strafford
Strafford Survey 204
Strode, William 53, 67
subsidies 13, 14, 51, 52, 58, 80, 158, 170–171, 184
sugar 12, 123–124, 126–127, 153–155, 167–169, 173, 175–177, 180, 196, 199, 205–207, 209–211
Swanly, Richard 109, 176
Sweden 1, 45
Symner, Myles 200

taxation 12, 15, 44, 50–52, 58, 64, 80, 113, 118–120, 156, 186, 197, 208, 210, 214
  see also excise; ship money; subsidies
Temple, Sir John 147
Texel, battle of 208
Thirty Years War 4, 99, 102, 104
Thomason, George 115, 152
Thomond, earl of *see* O'Brien, Barnaby, earl of Thomond
Thomson, Edward 28, 87, 179, 210
Thomson, Francis 87
Thomson, George 25, 27, 29, 64, 87, 102, 108, 118, 127, 151–152, 170, 175, 181–182, 195, 208, 212, 214–216, 219
Thomson, John 175, 216, 218
Thomson, Maurice
  and the Additional Sea Adventure 88, 100, 102–104, 108, 109
  and the Adventurers' grants of land in Ireland 186, 194–195, 197, 199, 203, 220
  and the Artillery Company 56
  and Barbados 124, 127, 153, 154–155, 175–176, 179–181, 206–207
  brings merchants' petition to Charles at York 45–47, 86
  Cape Ann plantation, Massachusetts 34, 57
  collection of Cromwellian subsidy 170, 171
  and the Committee for the Advance of Money 113, 114
  and the Committee of Adventurers 80, 115, 125, 127, 130, 152, 155, 197, 199
  and the Council of Trade 178, 181

and the Courteen Association 114, 123, 146, 169, 208
as customs commissioner 119
and the diplomatic mission to Dublin 109, 111
and the English East India Company 4, 145–146, 168, 169, 205, 207, 208, 212–213
as excise commissioner 174, 194, 195
fundraising for the Dutch Adventure 122, 123
and the Guinea Company 168, 169, 176, 179, 207
imprisonment 37, 125
investigation into diversion of funds 130
investment in Adventure for Irish Land 76, 85
and the Irish rebellion 50, 58, 81, 102–103
as Justice of the High Court 209
Kent Island project 31, 125
loans and financing 28, 31, 50, 115, 125, 154, 212
and military supplies 50, 81, 87, 100, 102–103, 115, 116, 128–129, 156, 158, 171, 173
and the Muscovy Company 145
Nosy Be project 146
pardoned by Charles II 219
privateering 30–31, 102
and the Providence Island Company 30, 45–46, 88–89
and the 'revolted ships' incident 157–158, 218
and St Kitts 27–28, 75
and sequestered land financial instruments 175
and the servant trade 26–27, 31, 34
and shipping 24, 26–27, 30, 50, 81, 100, 109, 116, 118, 146, 168, 173, 206, 208
and the slave trade 27–28, 146, 154–155, 168, 175–176, 179–181, 206–207, 212
and the sugar trade 124, 127, 153, 175–176, 199, 206–207
and the tobacco trade 4, 27, 28–29, 31, 102, 104, 114
treasurer for new Irish Land Adventure 116–118

and the trial of Charles I 159
and Virginia 4, 23–27, 31
and the Western Design 210
Thomson, Robert 55, 151, 154–155, 173, 174, 186, 197, 215, 216
Thomson, William 25, 55, 73, 102, 118, 120, 168, 173, 208, 209, 215, 216, 218, 219
Thurloe, John 194, 195, 216, 218
Timoleague, Co. Cork 104–105
tobacco 1, 4, 10, 22–23, 26–32, 36–37, 73, 76–78, 80–81, 102, 104, 107, 114, 119, 123, 127, 167, 176–177, 207, 211
Tobago 123, 180
Tower of London 53–54, 55, 68, 83, 84
Towse, John 51, 52, 73, 78, 79, 83, 86, 113, 115, 118, 119, 174
trade concessions 5, 16, 36–37, 120, 145–146
Trained Bands 52, 53–57, 67, 68, 83, 88, 151, 152, 178, 215
Transplantation to Connacht 183, 197, 201
transportation 175, 177, 183, 186, 206–207, 209
Treaty of Ripon 46
Treaty of the Pyrenees 217
Treaty of Westminster 208, 218
Trevor, Sir Thomas 131
Trinidad 123
Trinity College Dublin 33, 200
Trinity House 76–77, 109, 159
Trott, Martha 213
Trott, Perient 213
Trustees for Ireland 198
Tuchet, James, earl of Castlehaven 105
Tucker, Daniel 25
Tucker, William 23–25, 27, 29, 31, 55, 57, 109–112, 114, 147, 178
Turner, Richard 81

Ulster 22, 34, 35, 50, 57, 70, 71, 81, 84, 88, 106, 115, 125, 127–129, 158, 171, 197, 199
Upton, John 173

Vane, Sir Henry, II 33, 34, 56, 87, 108, 120, 126, 175, 178, 182, 195, 214
Vassall, Samuel 47, 55, 81, 113, 126, 154–155, 168, 170, 175–176, 180, 217
Vaughan, Charles 75

Vaughan, John 127
Venables, Robert 210–211
Venn, John 33, 47, 113
Vernon, John 182–183
Vincent, Thomas 155, 195, 198–199, 203, 215, 218
Vincent, William 210, 213
Viner, Sir Thomas 155, 209–110, 217
Virginia 1, 5, 10–12, 22–29, 31–32, 37, 47–48, 55, 57, 73, 102, 109, 114, 119, 145, 153, 167, 176, 178–181, 207
Virginia Commission 24–25, 32
Virginia Company 4–5, 23, 24–25, 32, 35, 54, 57, 74, 78, 102

Waller, Sir Hardresse 200, 214
Waller, Sir William 75, 85, 129
Wallop, Robert 56, 57
Wandesford, Christopher 104
Waring, Richard 113, 120, 125, 151, 152, 170, 178, 195, 199, 215
Warner, John 51, 52, 73–74, 78, 79, 83, 86, 113, 115, 118, 144, 150, 152, 158
Warner, Samuel 51, 73, 80, 110, 147
Warner, Sir Thomas 28, 73
Warwick, earl of *see* Rich, Robert, earl of Warwick
Warwick House 46, 50, 54, 55, 58, 64, 65–67, 69, 71, 76, 82, 87, 89, 101, 103
'Warwick patent' 33–34, 53, 57
Waterford 118, 197
Watkins, Edward 119
Watkins, Sir David 74–76, 88, 108, 111, 114–115, 120, 125, 130, 148, 152, 155, 158, 170, 172, 175, 199, 217
Watkins, William 174
Watson, William 123
Weaver, John 183, 186
Webster, William 197
Wentworth, Thomas, earl of Strafford 31–32, 37, 45, 64, 103–104, 204

Western Design 16, 181, 210–211
Westminster Assembly 123, 124, 128
Wexford 104, 110, 111, 118, 159
Wharton, Philip, Lord 83, 87, 108, 110, 124, 126
Whetcomb, Benjamin 81, 217
Whitelocke, Bulstrode 116, 117
Whitmore, Sir George 113
Wilde, William 218
Williams, William 210
Willoughby, Anthony 100–101, 106
Willoughby, Edward 171
Willoughby of Parham, Francis, Lord 72, 154, 176–177, 180
Willoughby, William 173
Wilson, Rowland 146, 150, 168, 182
Windsor 72, 159
wine trade 36, 77, 170
Winthrop, John, I 33
Winthrop, John, II 33–34, 57, 213
Winthrop, John (uncle of John Winthrop I) 33
Winthrop, Stephen 213
Withers, William 69–70
Wogan, Thomas 183
Wollaston, Sir John 81, 83, 113, 144, 150, 155, 171, 172, 185, 195
Wolverstone, Charles 28
Wolverstone, Sir John 28
Wood, Edward 213
Wood, John 102, 146, 168, 176, 179–180, 213
wool 211–212
Worsley, Benjamin 177–178, 198, 200, 201, 204, 214
Wright, Nathaniel 148
Wyche, Nathaniel 213
Wylde, Sir John 205

York 45–46, 83, 86
Youghal, Co. Cork 70, 115, 158

EU authorised representative for GPSR:
Easy Access System Europe, Mustamäe tee 50,
10621 Tallinn, Estonia
gpsr.requests@easproject.com

www.ingramcontent.com/pod-product-compliance
Lightning Source LLC
Chambersburg PA
CBHW071402300426
44114CB00016B/2154